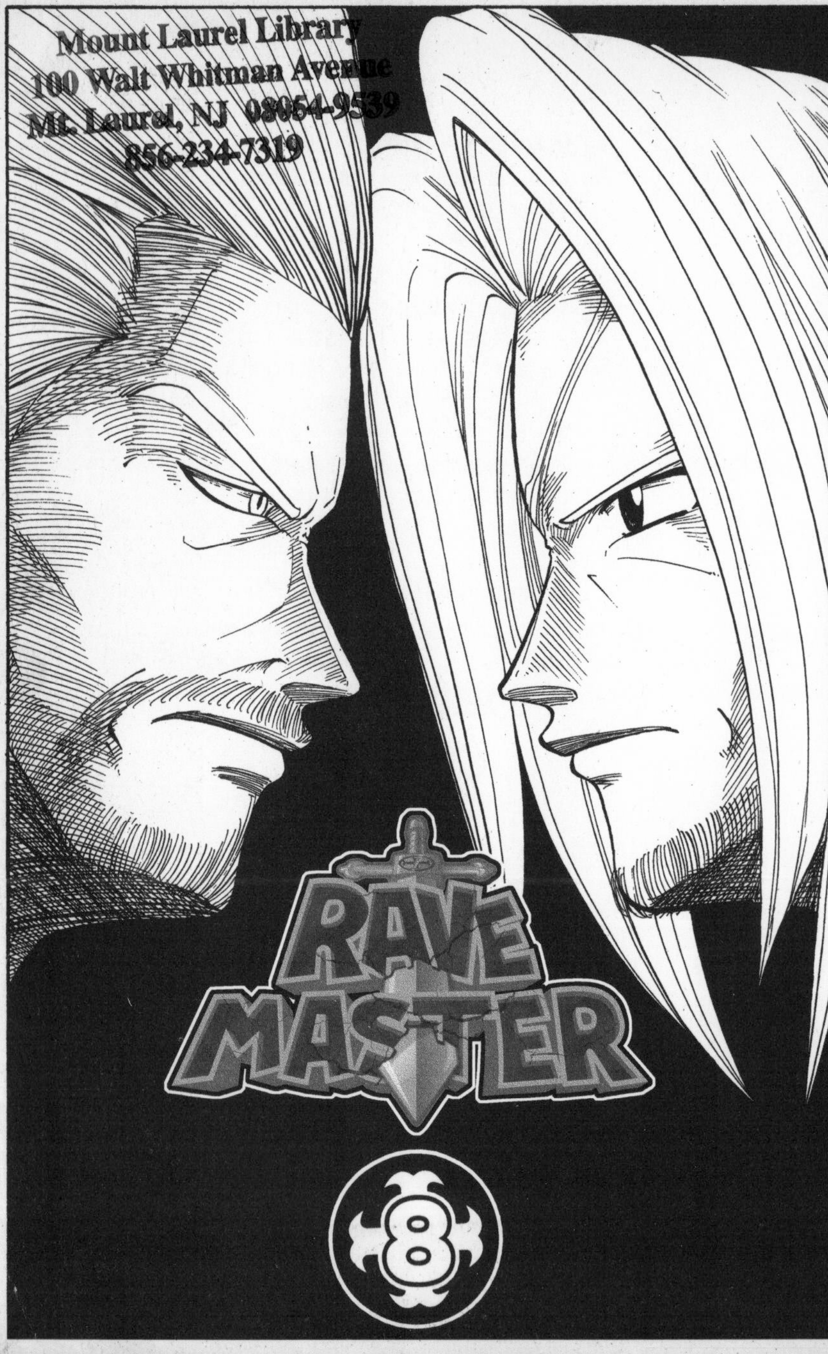

Mount Laurel Library
100 Walt Whitman Avenue
Mt. Laurel, NJ 08054-9539
856-234-7319
RAVE MASTER
8

Translator - Brian Dunn
English Adaptation - James Lucas-Jones
Retouch and Lettering - Marnie Echols
Cover Layout - Ray Makowski

Editor - Jake Forbes
Digital Imaging Manager - Chris Buford
Pre-Press Manager - Antonio DePietro
Production Managers - Jennifer Miller, Mutsumi Miyazaki
Art Director - Matt Alford
Managing Editor - Jill Freshney
VP of Production - Ron Klamert
President & C.O.O. - John Parker
Publisher & C.E.O. - Stuart Levy

E-mail: info@TOKYOPOP.com
Come visit us online at www.TOKYOPOP.com

A  Manga

TOKYOPOP Inc.
5900 Wilshire Blvd. Suite 2000
Los Angeles, CA 90036

Rave Master Vol. 8

ISBN: 1-59182-518-0

First TOKYOPOP printing: April 2004

10 9 8 7 6 5 4 3 2 1
Printed in the USA or Canada

VOLUME 8

Story and Art by
HIRO MASHIMA

TOKYOPOP®

Los Angeles · Tokyo · London

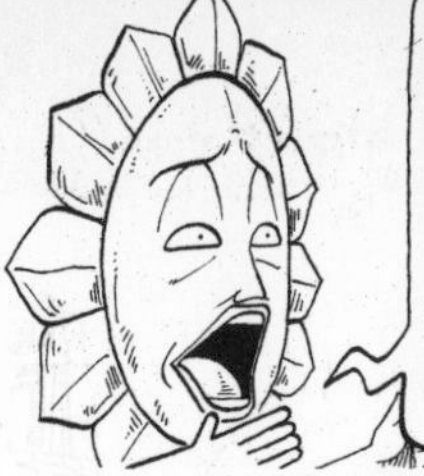

After traveling to the Luka Continent in search of the Rave of Combat, Haru found something he never expected-his father! Haru learns that a man named "Gale" is behind the recent attacks on Rabarrier City, home of the Rave of Combat. Against his friends' wishes, Haru sets out alone for the Tower of Din to find out if his dad could really be the one behind the attacks. It turns out that the "Gale" in question isn't his father-it's Gale Raregroove, also known as King, the Demon Card leader! His father, Gale Glory, came here to stop King. Haru and his father race into the tower to stop the Demon Card leader before he can complete The Enclaim, a process for creating the most destructive Dark Bring ever!

HARU GLORY: The Rave Master. Haru is the heir to Rave, the only one capable of wielding it and destroying Dark Bring. Impulsive and headstrong, he's not afraid to put himself in danger to do what is right. His father disappeared in search of Rave when he was very young.

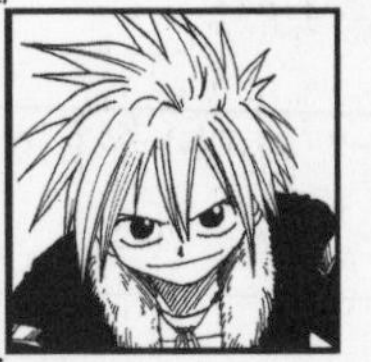

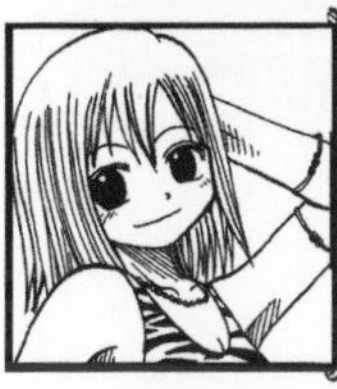

ELIE: A Girl with no past. Elie travels the world in search of the key to her forgotten memories. Outwardly cheerful, she hides a great sadness from her past. She's hot-headed, so when she pulls out her explosive Tonfa Blasters, bad guys watch out!

MUSICA: Leader of the Silver Rhythm Gang. An orphan whose family was slaughtered when he was a baby, Musica became a street-fighting petty thief, but he has a good heart.

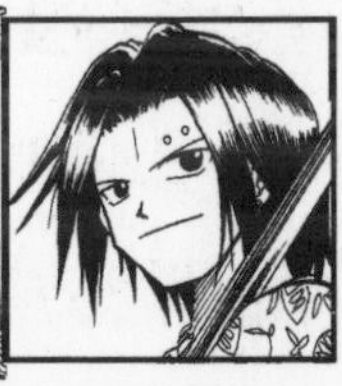

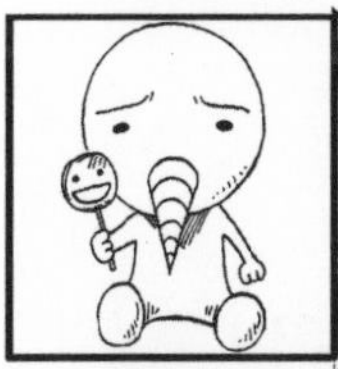

PLUE: The Rave Bearer. Plue is supposed to be Haru's guide in finding the Rave Stones, but so far he's just gotten him in and out of trouble. No one knows exactly what Plue is, but he seems to have healing abilities and is smarter than your average...whatever he is.

GRIFF: Don't even ask what this thing is. His full name is Griffon Kato, but he just goes by Griff. He works as a cart driver and is hired to transport Haru and friends across the Continent of Song. His body can stretch like rubber and he's got a crush on Elie.

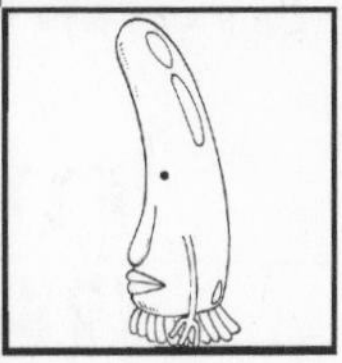

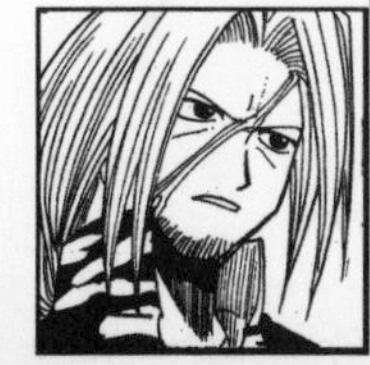

GALE GLORY: Haru's father, he left home in search of the Raves fifteen years ago and hasn't seen his family since. Gale Glory and Gale Raregroove (aka King) seem to have known each other for a long time, but how?!

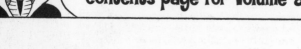

Doncha think, mon capitan?

That is correct! This is the contents page for Volume 8.

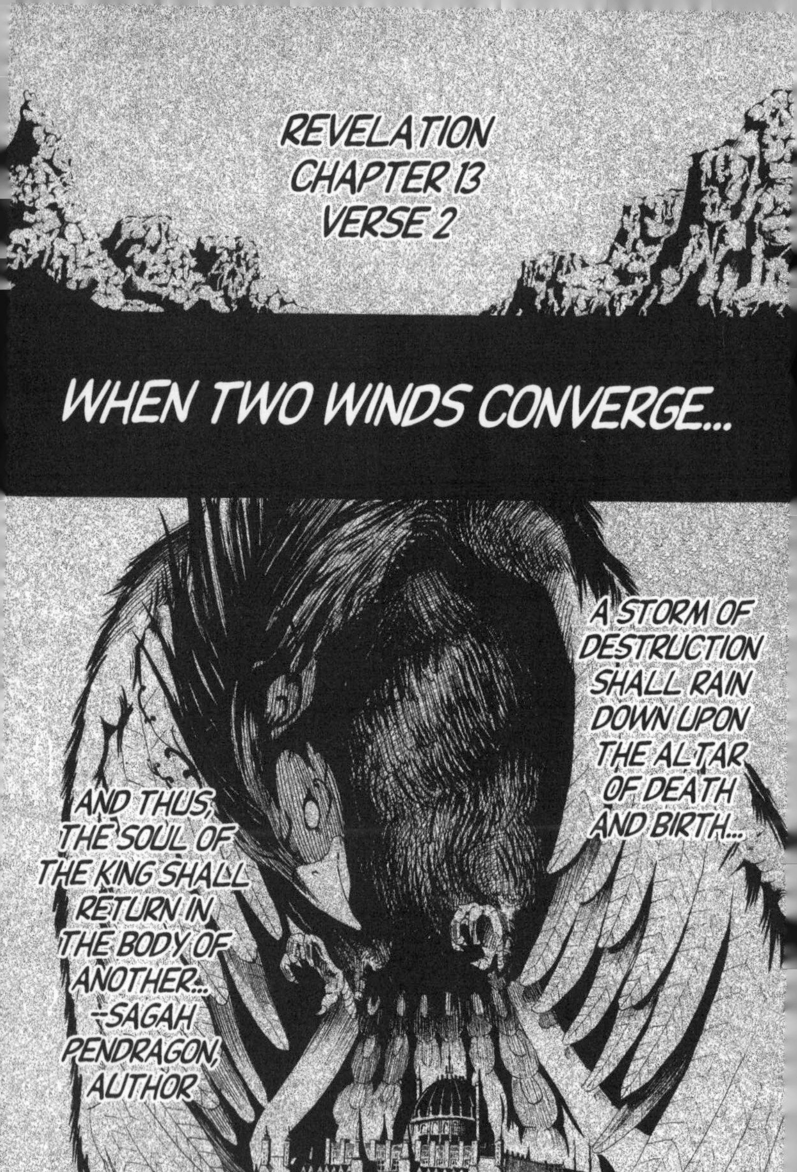
REVELATION CHAPTER 13 VERSE 2
WHEN TWO WINDS CONVERGE...
A STORM OF DESTRUCTION SHALL RAIN DOWN UPON THE ALTAR OF DEATH AND BIRTH...
AND THUS, THE SOUL OF THE KING SHALL RETURN IN THE BODY OF ANOTHER...
--SAGAH PENDRAGON, AUTHOR

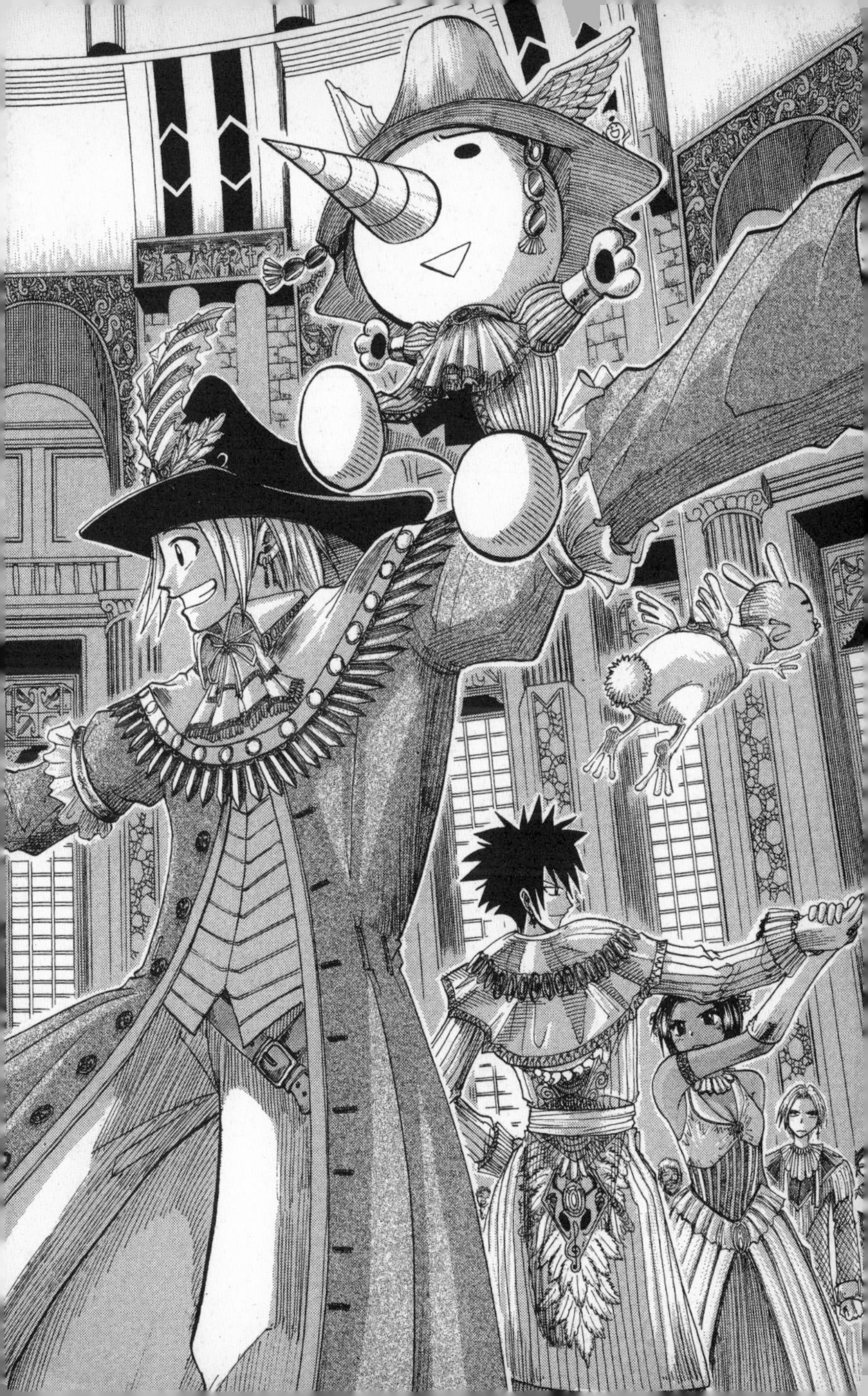

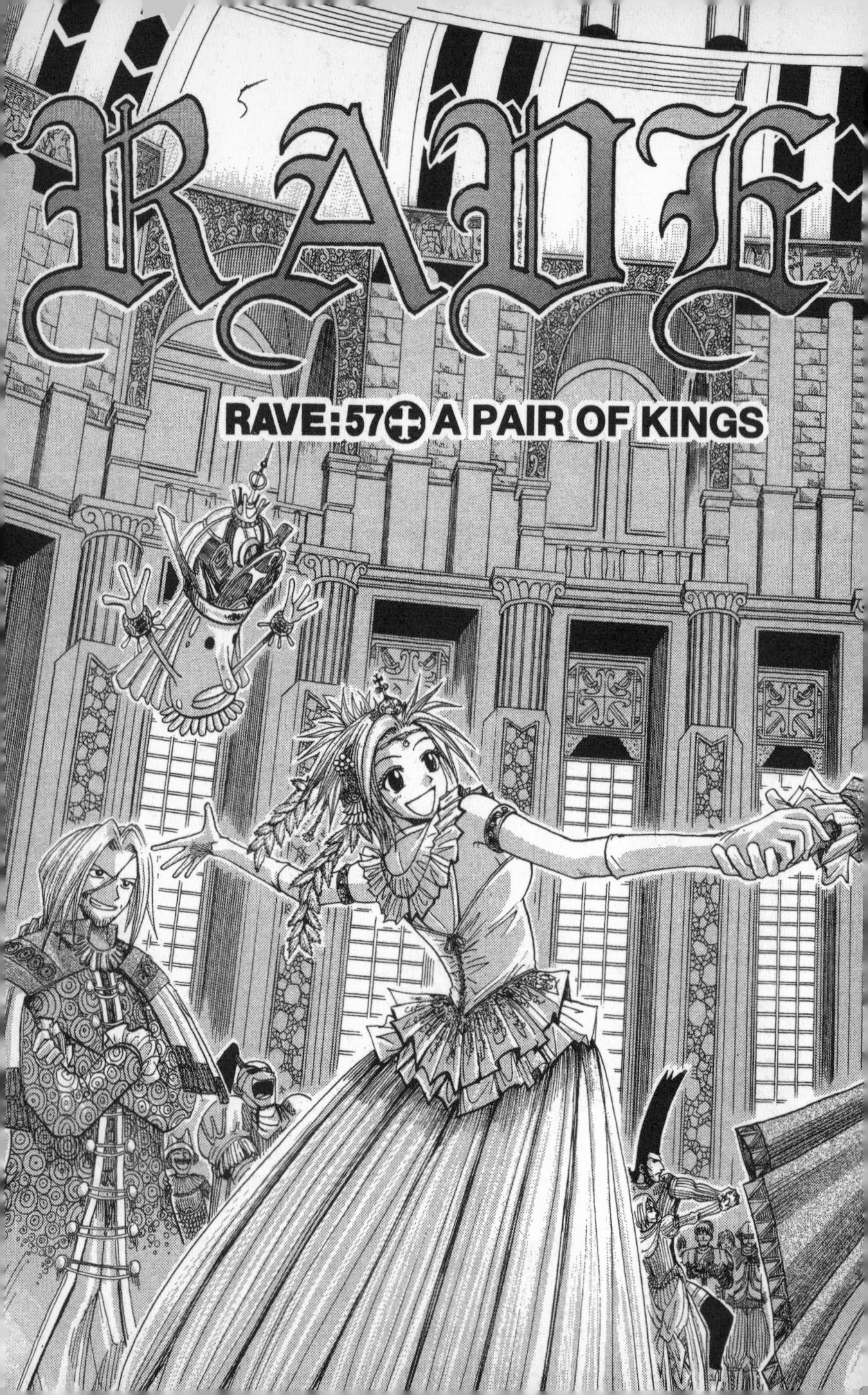
RAVE
RAVE:57 A PAIR OF KINGS

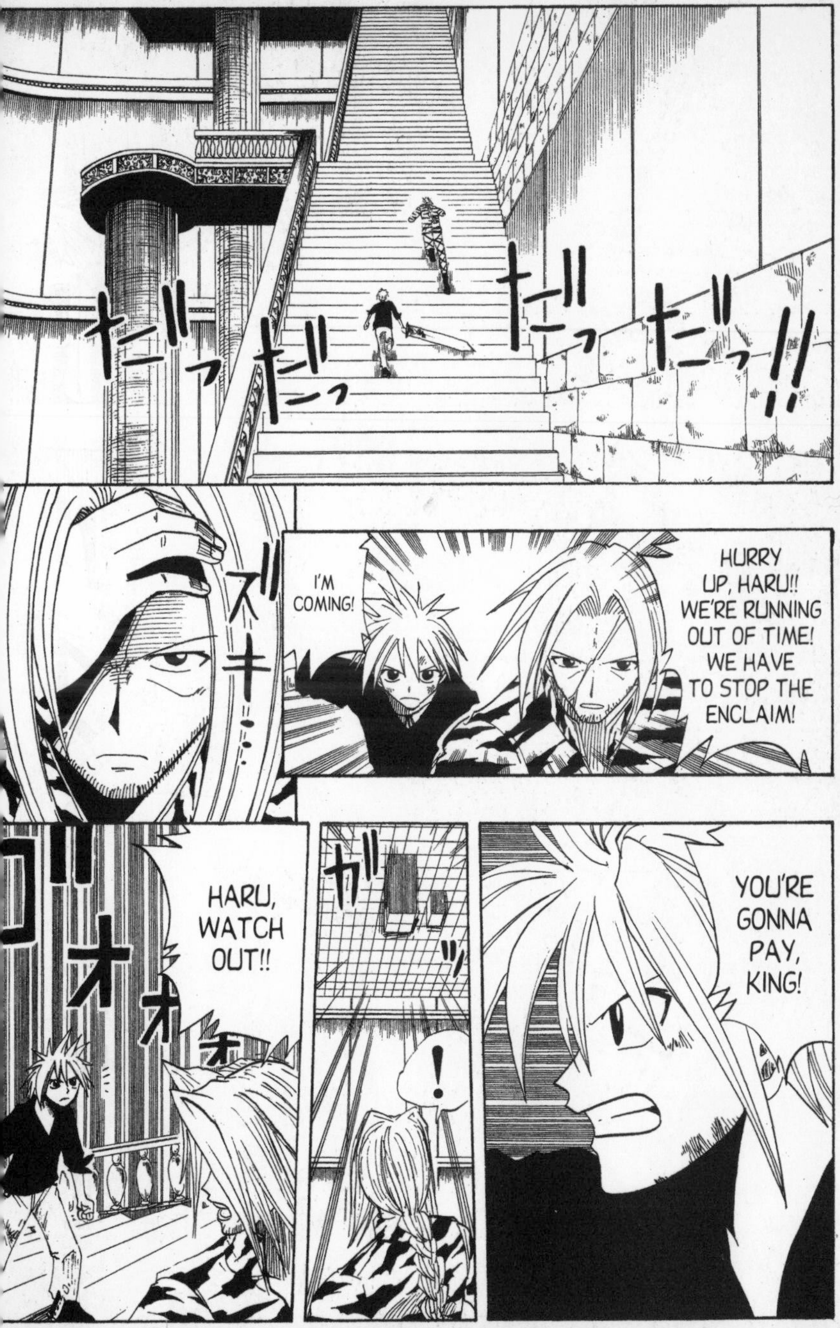
だっ だっ だっ だっ!!
HURRY UP, HARU!! WE'RE RUNNING OUT OF TIME! WE HAVE TO STOP THE ENCLAIM!
I'M COMING!
ズキ…
YOU'RE GONNA PAY, KING!
ガッ
!
HARU, WATCH OUT!!
ゴオオオ

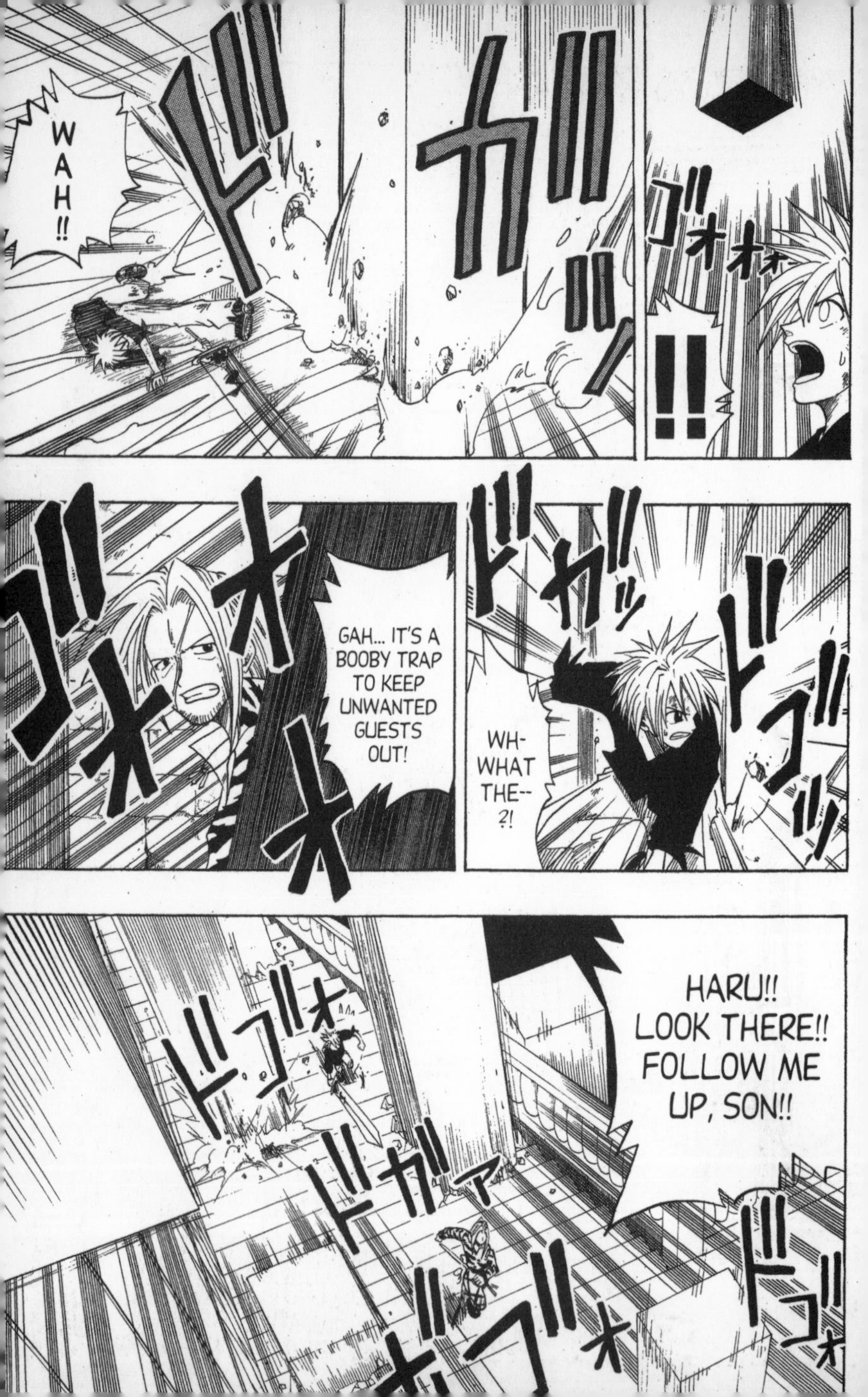
ゴォォォ
!!
ガッ
ド
WAH!!
ドガッ
ドゴッ
WH- WHAT THE-- ?!
ゴォォォ
GAH... IT'S A BOOBY TRAP TO KEEP UNWANTED GUESTS OUT!
HARU!! LOOK THERE!! FOLLOW ME UP, SON!!
ドゴォ
ドガァ
ドゴォ
ドゴォ

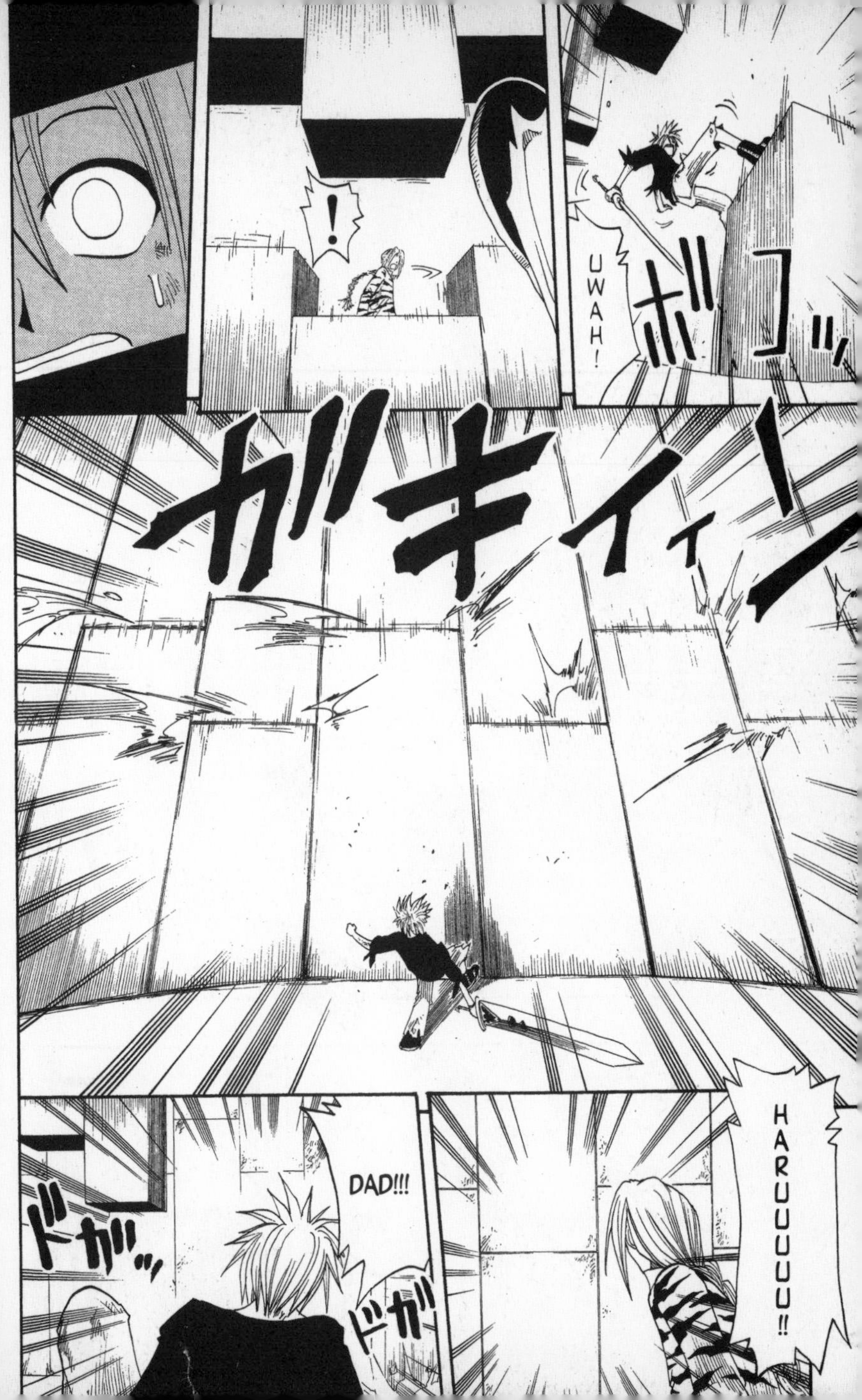
UWAH!
ボコッ
!
ガキィーン
HARUUUUUU!!
DAD!!!
ドガッ
ドガ

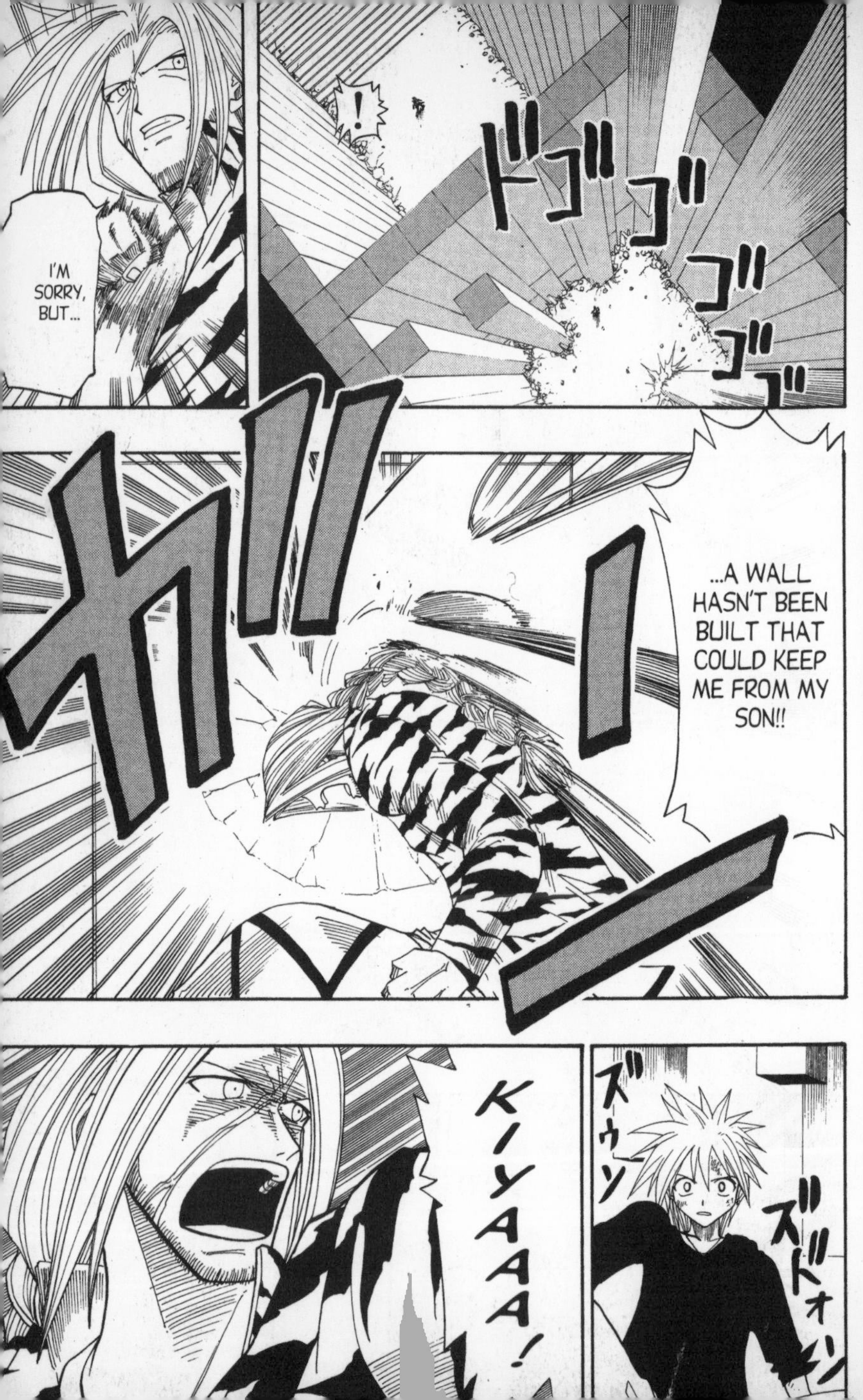
!
ドゴゴゴゴ
I'M SORRY, BUT...
...A WALL HASN'T BEEN BUILT THAT COULD KEEP ME FROM MY SON!!
ズゥン
ズドォン
KIYAAAA!

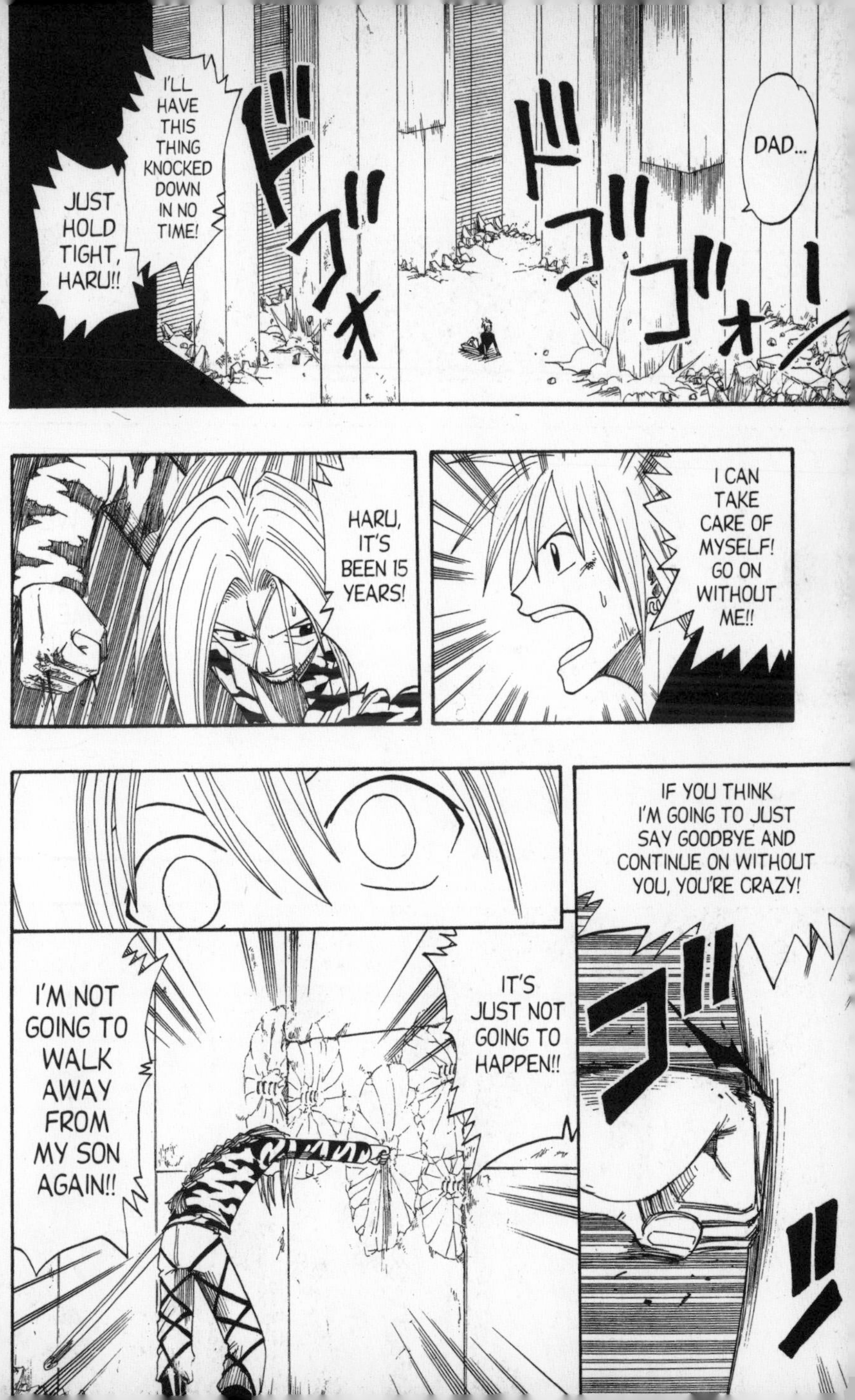
DAD...
ドゴゴォー
ドゴォ
I'LL HAVE THIS THING KNOCKED DOWN IN NO TIME!
JUST HOLD TIGHT, HARU!!
I CAN TAKE CARE OF MYSELF! GO ON WITHOUT ME!!
HARU, IT'S BEEN 15 YEARS!
IF YOU THINK I'M GOING TO JUST SAY GOODBYE AND CONTINUE ON WITHOUT YOU, YOU'RE CRAZY!
IT'S JUST NOT GOING TO HAPPEN!!
I'M NOT GOING TO WALK AWAY FROM MY SON AGAIN!!

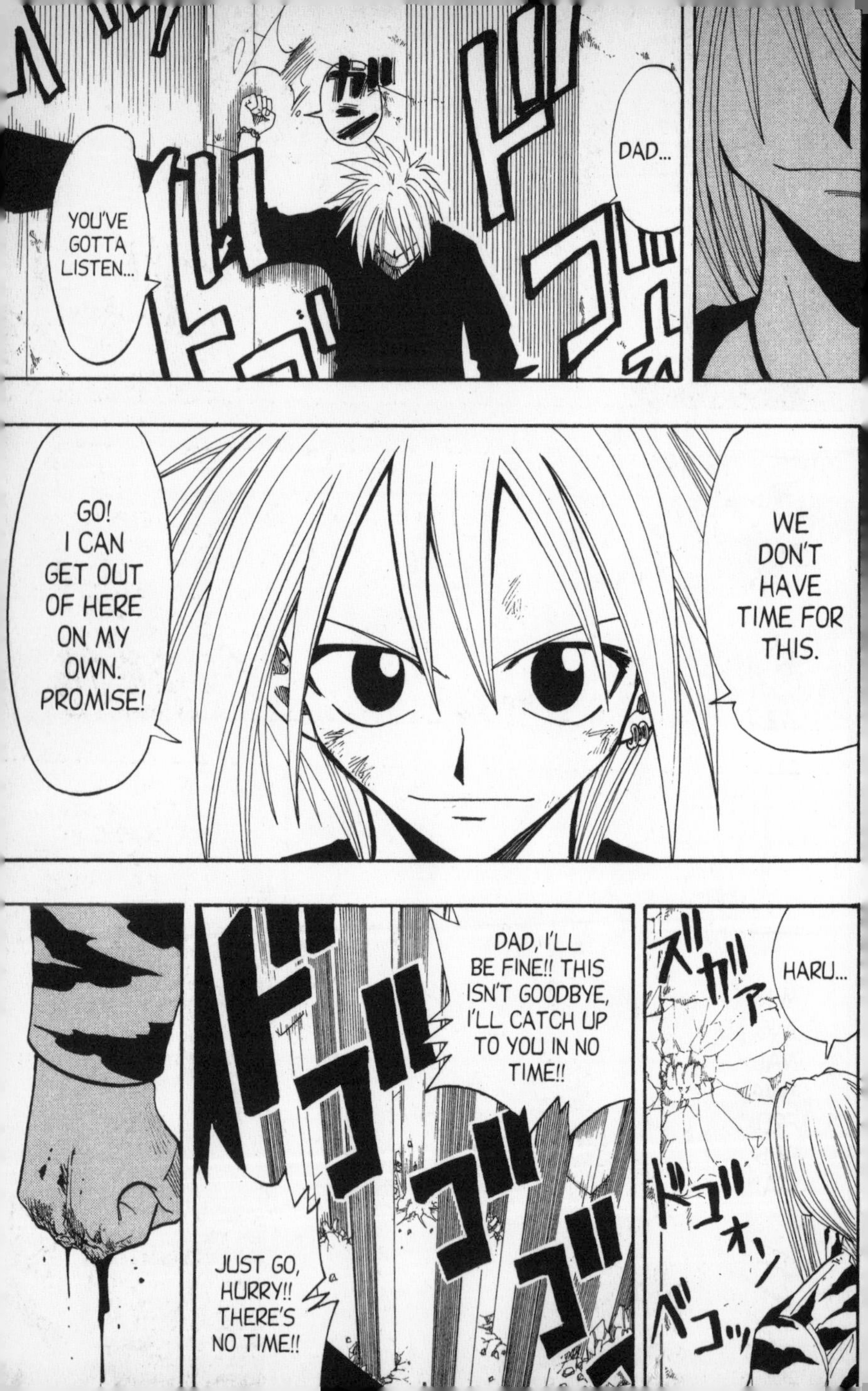
DAD...
YOU'VE GOTTA LISTEN...
WE DON'T HAVE TIME FOR THIS.
GO! I CAN GET OUT OF HERE ON MY OWN. PROMISE!
HARU...
ズガァ
ドゴォン
ベコッ
DAD, I'LL BE FINE!! THIS ISN'T GOODBYE, I'LL CATCH UP TO YOU IN NO TIME!!
JUST GO, HURRY!! THERE'S NO TIME!!

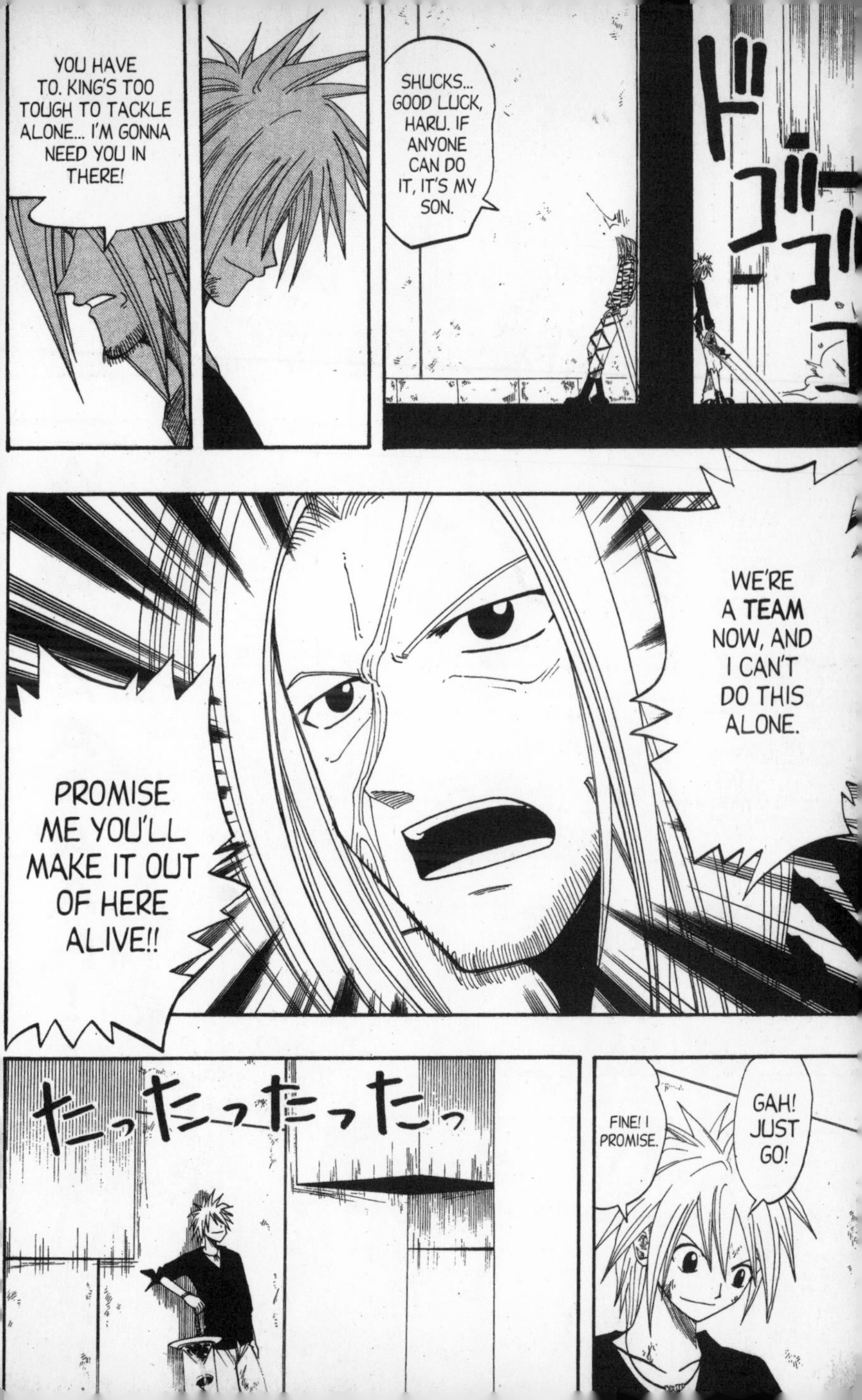
ドゴゴゴ
SHUCKS... GOOD LUCK, HARU. IF ANYONE CAN DO IT, IT'S MY SON.
YOU HAVE TO. KING'S TOO TOUGH TO TACKLE ALONE... I'M GONNA NEED YOU IN THERE!
WE'RE A **TEAM** NOW, AND I CAN'T DO THIS ALONE.
PROMISE ME YOU'LL MAKE IT OUT OF HERE ALIVE!!
GAH! JUST GO!
FINE! I PROMISE.
たったったったっ

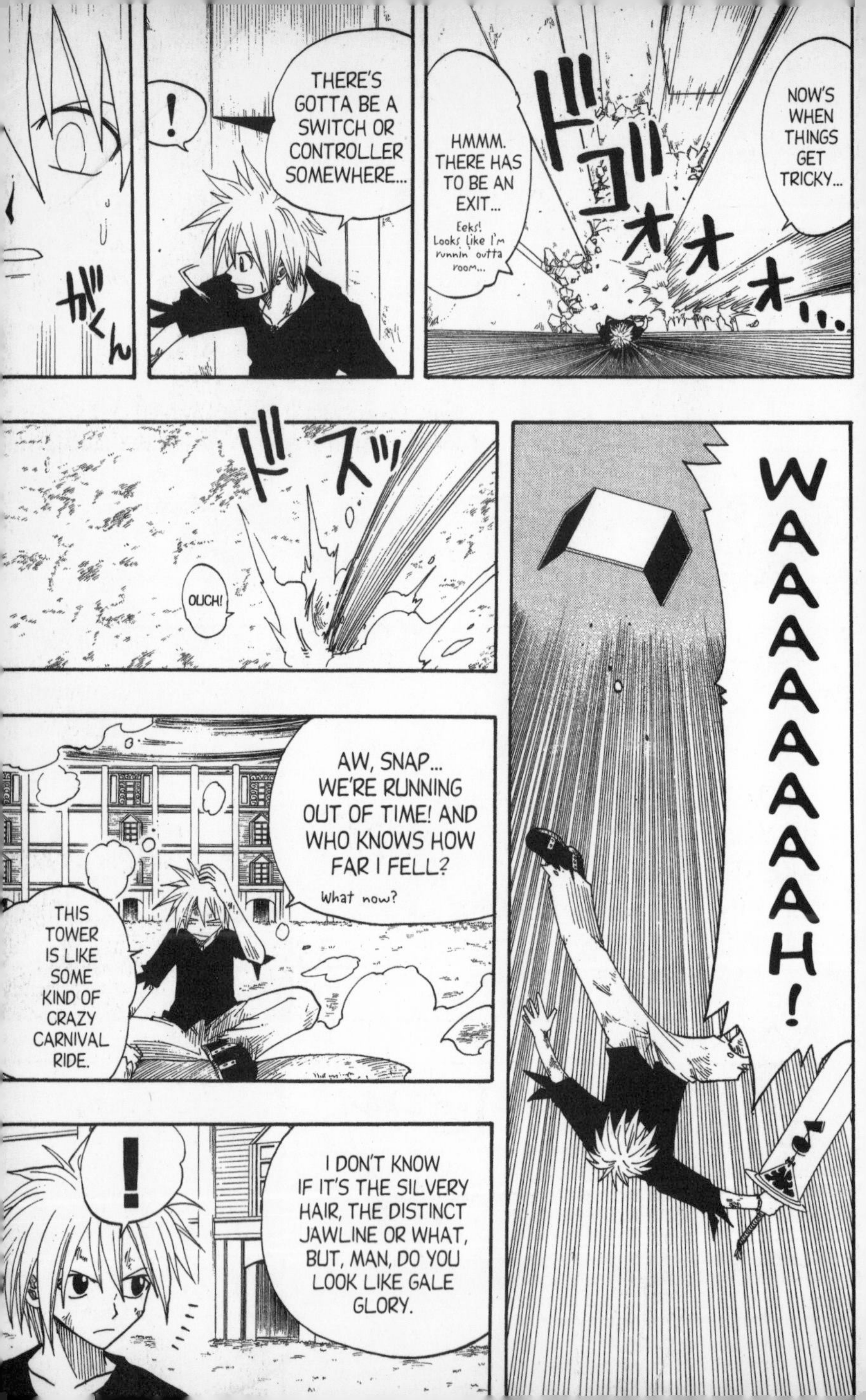
NOW'S WHEN THINGS GET TRICKY...
ドゴォォォ…
HMMM. THERE HAS TO BE AN EXIT...
Eeks! Looks like I'm runnin' outta room...
THERE'S GOTTA BE A SWITCH OR CONTROLLER SOMEWHERE...
!
がくん
WAAAAAAAAAAH!
ドズッ
OUCH!
AW, SNAP... WE'RE RUNNING OUT OF TIME! AND WHO KNOWS HOW FAR I FELL?
What now?
THIS TOWER IS LIKE SOME KIND OF CRAZY CARNIVAL RIDE.
I DON'T KNOW IF IT'S THE SILVERY HAIR, THE DISTINCT JAWLINE OR WHAT, BUT, MAN, DO YOU LOOK LIKE GALE GLORY.
!

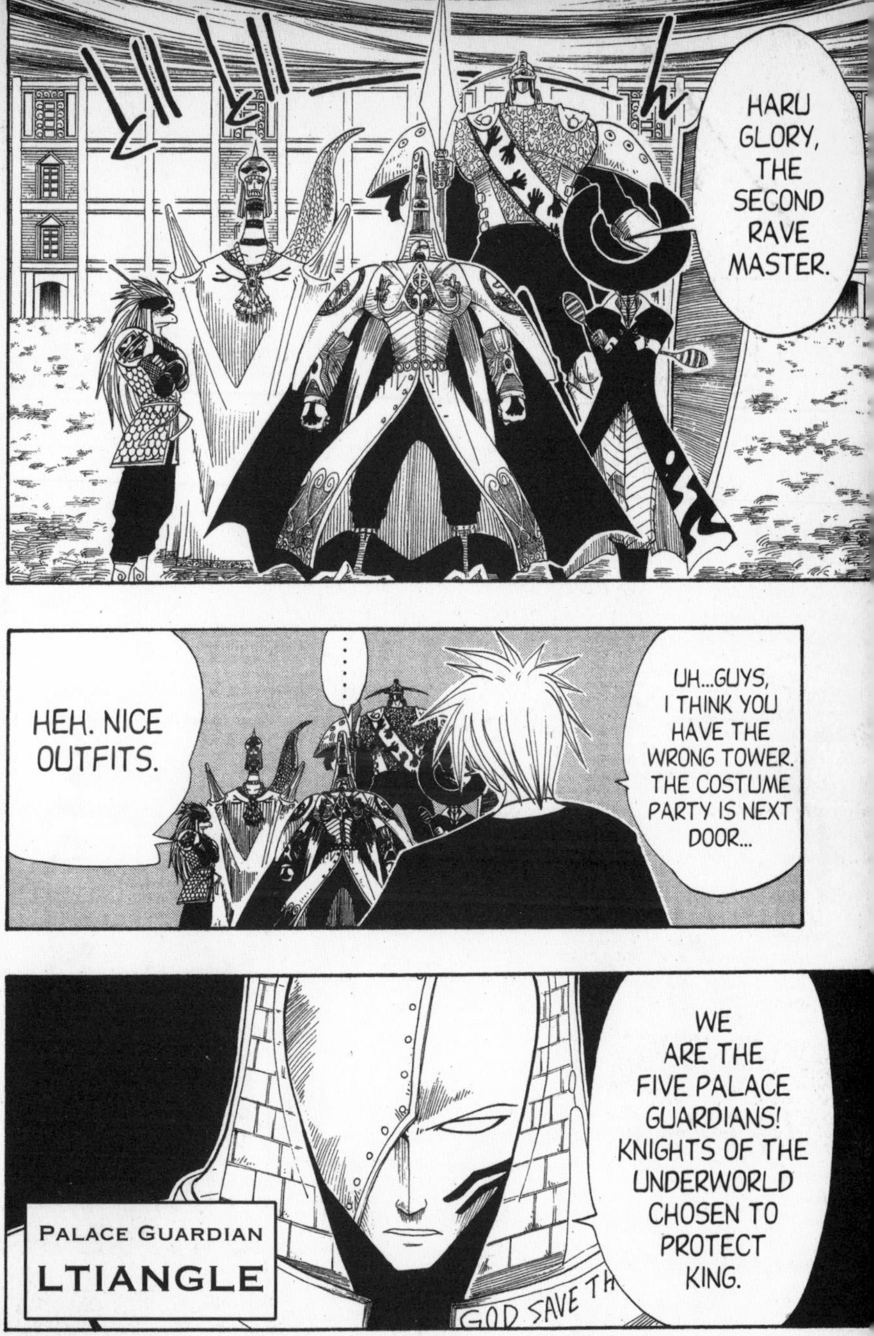
HARU GLORY, THE SECOND RAVE MASTER.
UH...GUYS, I THINK YOU HAVE THE WRONG TOWER. THE COSTUME PARTY IS NEXT DOOR...
....
HEH. NICE OUTFITS.
WE ARE THE FIVE PALACE GUARDIANS! KNIGHTS OF THE UNDERWORLD CHOSEN TO PROTECT KING.
GOD SAVE TH
PALACE GUARDIAN
LTIANGLE

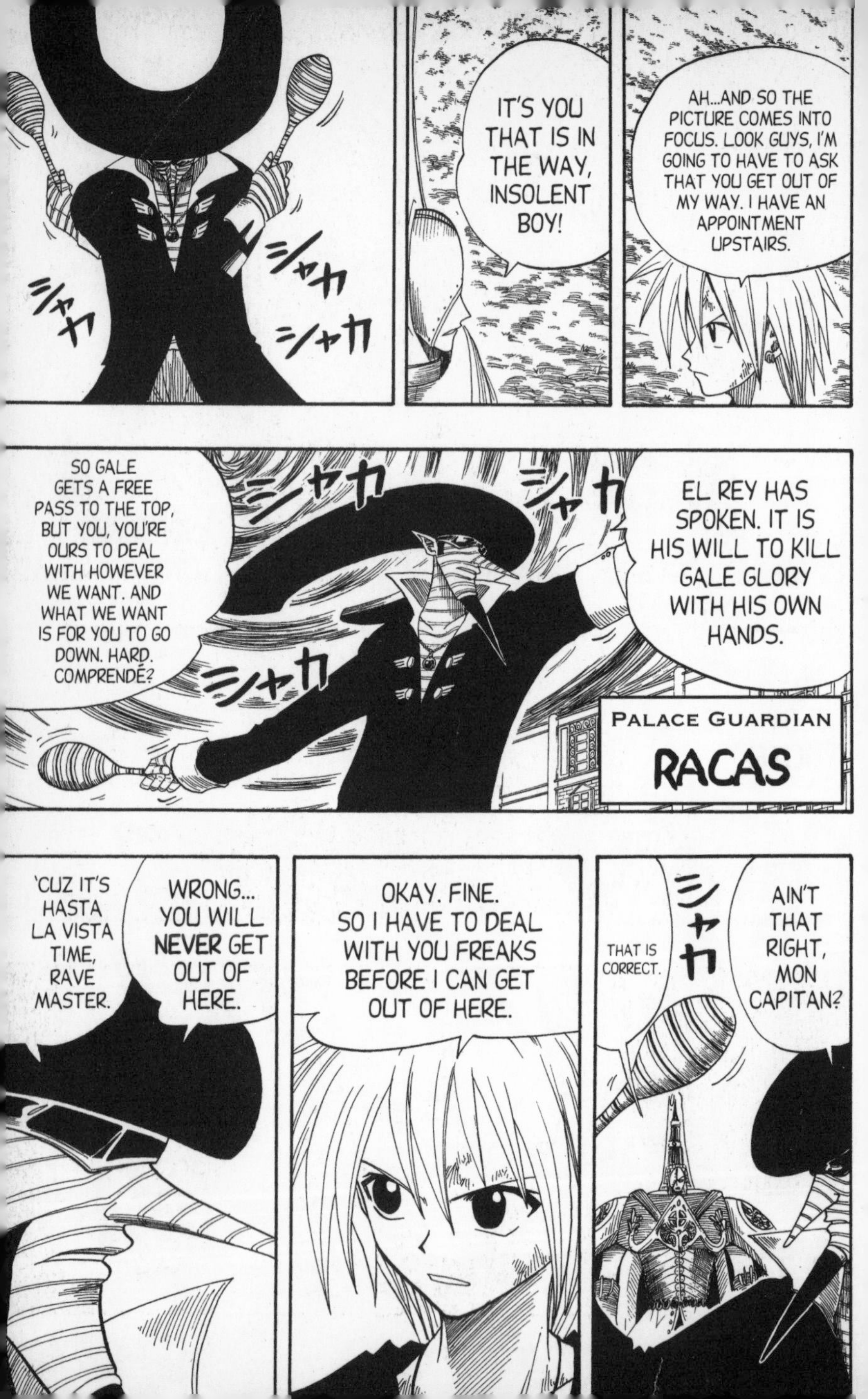
AH...AND SO THE PICTURE COMES INTO FOCUS. LOOK GUYS, I'M GOING TO HAVE TO ASK THAT YOU GET OUT OF MY WAY. I HAVE AN APPOINTMENT UPSTAIRS.
IT'S YOU THAT IS IN THE WAY, INSOLENT BOY!
シャカ
シャカ
シャカ
EL REY HAS SPOKEN. IT IS HIS WILL TO KILL GALE GLORY WITH HIS OWN HANDS.
シャカ
PALACE GUARDIAN
RACAS
シャカ
SO GALE GETS A FREE PASS TO THE TOP, BUT YOU, YOU'RE OURS TO DEAL WITH HOWEVER WE WANT. AND WHAT WE WANT IS FOR YOU TO GO DOWN. HARD. COMPRENDÉ?
シャカ
AIN'T THAT RIGHT, MON CAPITAN?
シャカ
THAT IS CORRECT.
OKAY. FINE. SO I HAVE TO DEAL WITH YOU FREAKS BEFORE I CAN GET OUT OF HERE.
WRONG... YOU WILL **NEVER** GET OUT OF HERE.
'CUZ IT'S HASTA LA VISTA TIME, RAVE MASTER.

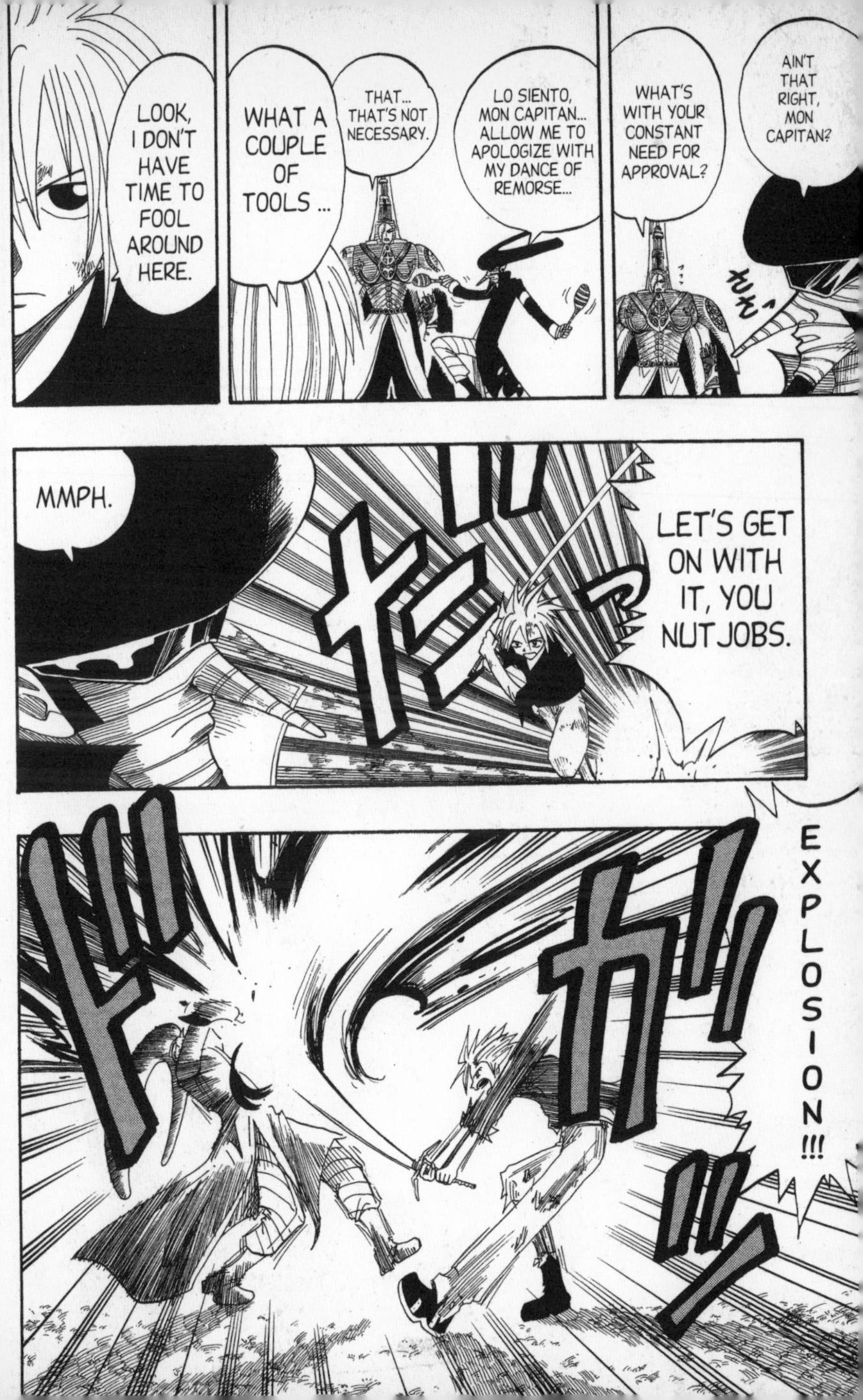
AIN'T THAT RIGHT, MON CAPITAN?
WHAT'S WITH YOUR CONSTANT NEED FOR APPROVAL?
LO SIENTO, MON CAPITAN... ALLOW ME TO APOLOGIZE WITH MY DANCE OF REMORSE...
THAT... THAT'S NOT NECESSARY.
WHAT A COUPLE OF TOOLS ...
LOOK, I DON'T HAVE TIME TO FOOL AROUND HERE.
LET'S GET ON WITH IT, YOU NUTJOBS.
MMPH.
EXPLOSION!!!

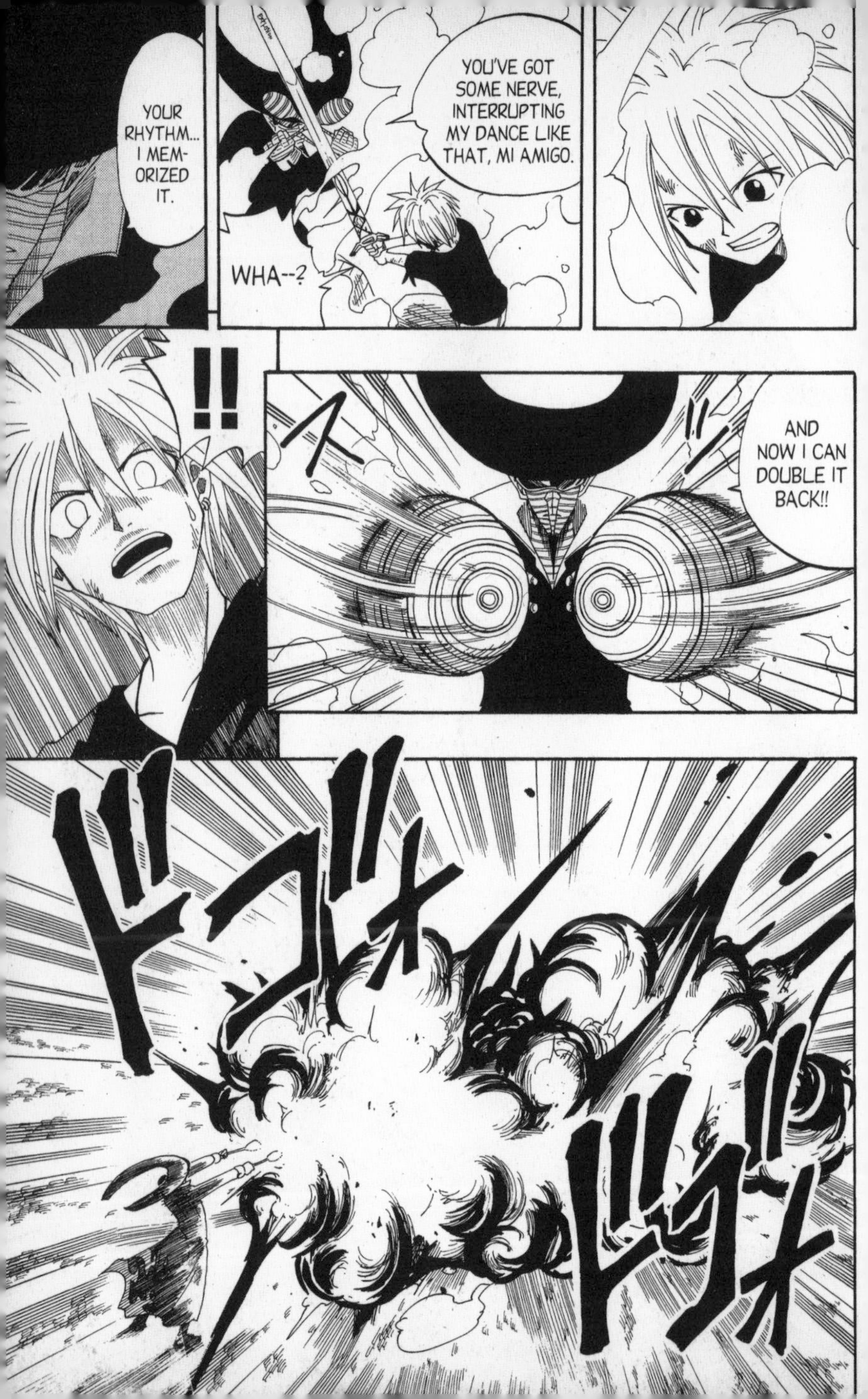
YOU'VE GOT SOME NERVE, INTERRUPTING MY DANCE LIKE THAT, MI AMIGO.
WHA--?
YOUR RHYTHM... I MEM-ORIZED IT.
AND NOW I CAN DOUBLE IT BACK!!
!!

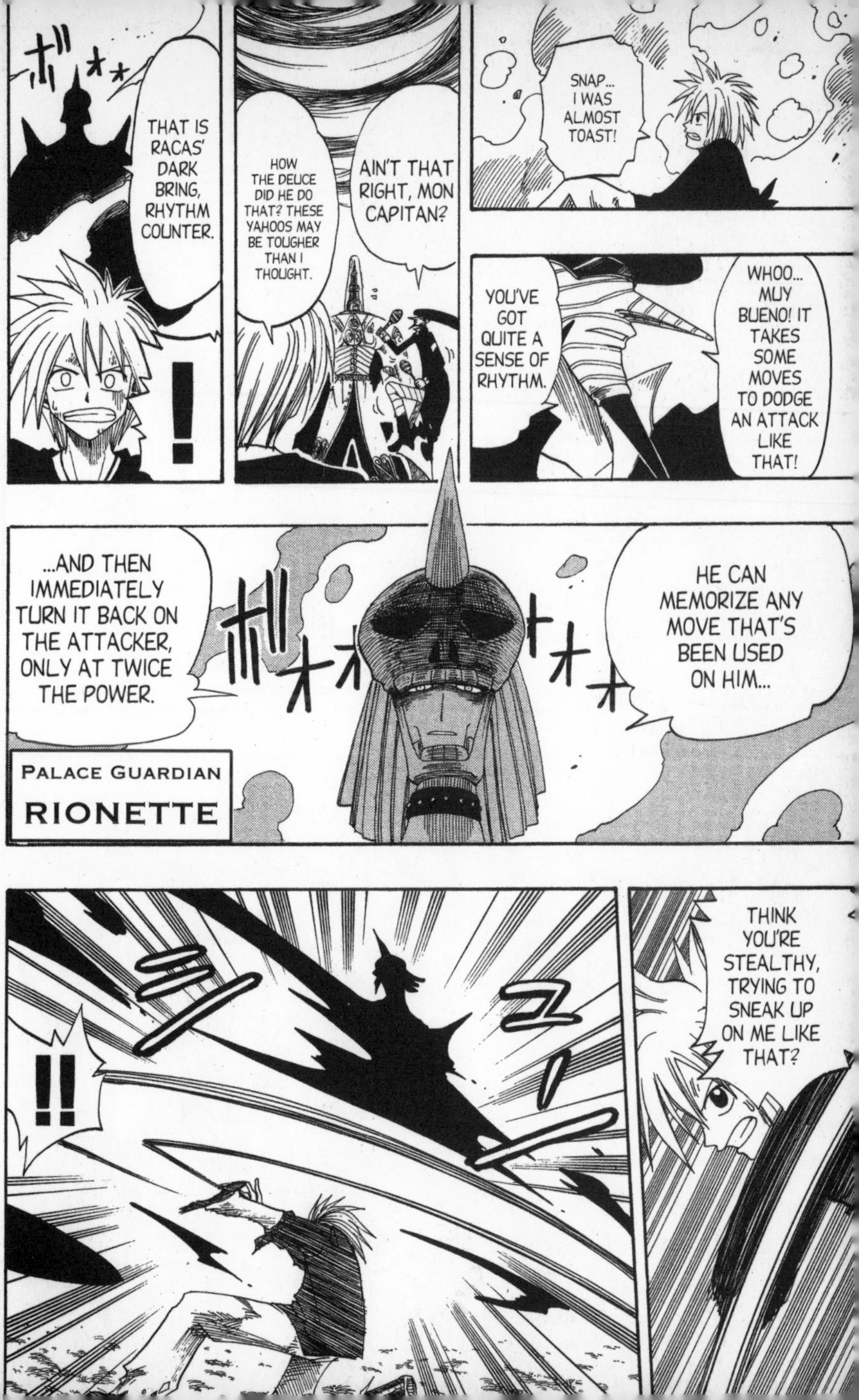
SNAP... I WAS ALMOST TOAST!
WHOO... MUY BUENO! IT TAKES SOME MOVES TO DODGE AN ATTACK LIKE THAT!
YOU'VE GOT QUITE A SENSE OF RHYTHM.
AIN'T THAT RIGHT, MON CAPITAN?
HOW THE DEUCE DID HE DO THAT? THESE YAHOOS MAY BE TOUGHER THAN I THOUGHT.
THAT IS RACAS' DARK BRING, RHYTHM COUNTER.
!
HE CAN MEMORIZE ANY MOVE THAT'S BEEN USED ON HIM...
...AND THEN IMMEDIATELY TURN IT BACK ON THE ATTACKER, ONLY AT TWICE THE POWER.
PALACE GUARDIAN
RIONETTE
THINK YOU'RE STEALTHY, TRYING TO SNEAK UP ON ME LIKE THAT?
!!

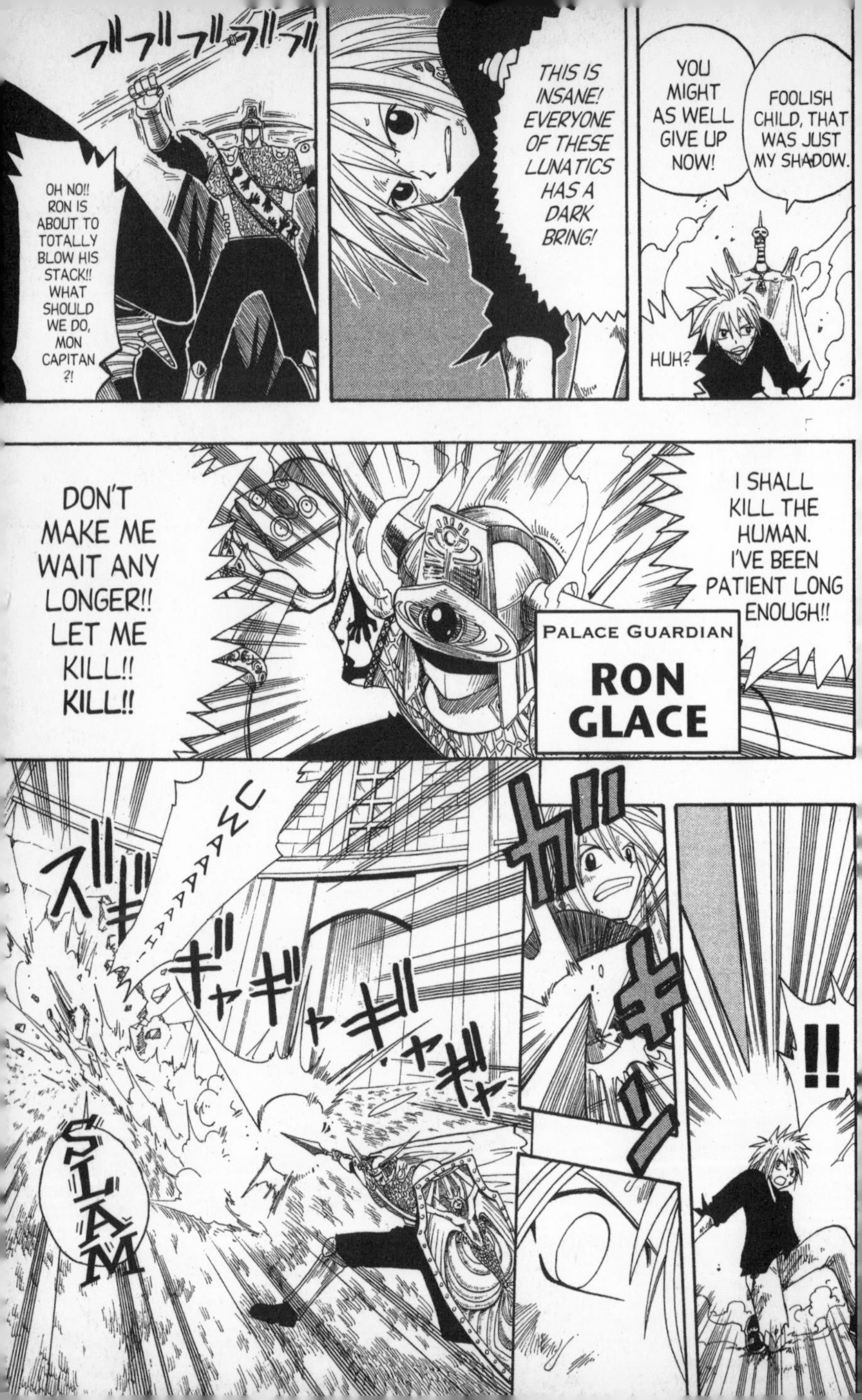

FOOLISH CHILD, THAT WAS JUST MY SHADOW.
YOU MIGHT AS WELL GIVE UP NOW!
HUH?
THIS IS INSANE! EVERYONE OF THESE LUNATICS HAS A DARK BRING!
OH NO!! RON IS ABOUT TO TOTALLY BLOW HIS STACK!! WHAT SHOULD WE DO, MON CAPITAN?!
I SHALL KILL THE HUMAN. I'VE BEEN PATIENT LONG ENOUGH!!
PALACE GUARDIAN
RON GLACE
DON'T MAKE ME WAIT ANY LONGER!! LET ME KILL!! KILL!!
!!
SLAM

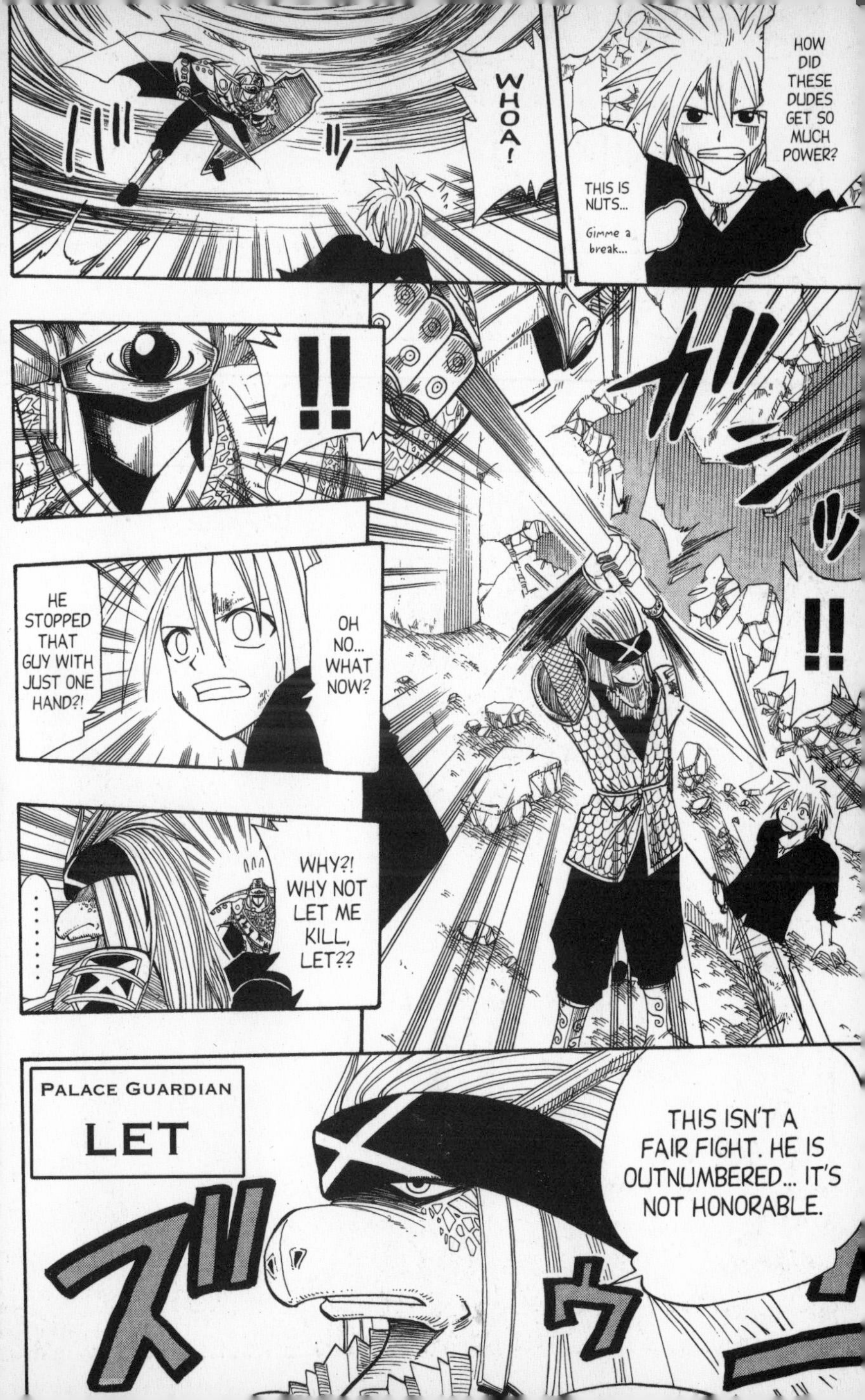
HOW DID THESE DUDES GET SO MUCH POWER?
THIS IS NUTS...
Gimme a break...
WHOA!
!!
!!
OH NO... WHAT NOW?
HE STOPPED THAT GUY WITH JUST ONE HAND?!
WHY?! WHY NOT LET ME KILL, LET??
....
THIS ISN'T A FAIR FIGHT. HE IS OUTNUMBERED... IT'S NOT HONORABLE.
PALACE GUARDIAN
LET

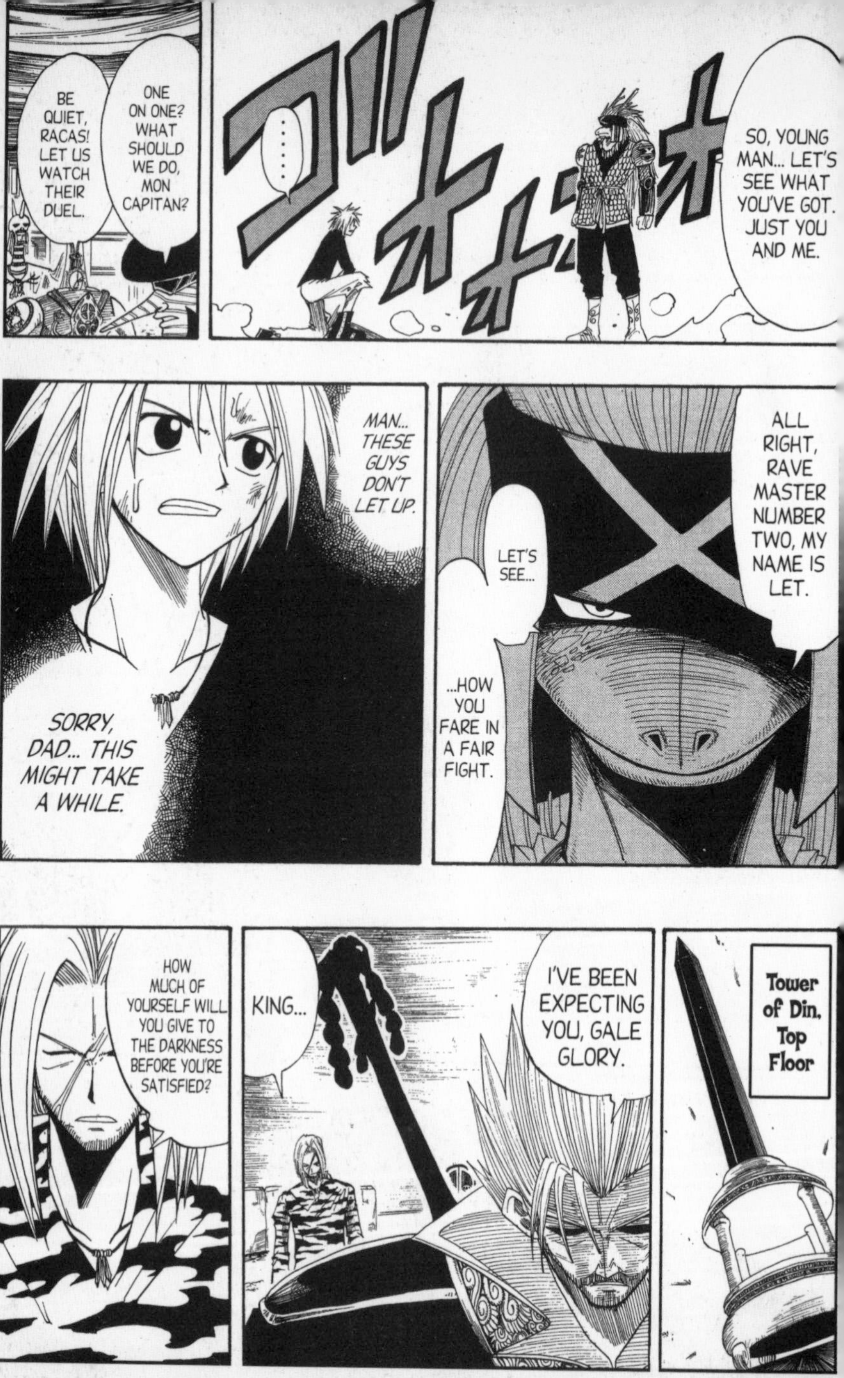
SO, YOUNG MAN... LET'S SEE WHAT YOU'VE GOT. JUST YOU AND ME.
......
ONE ON ONE? WHAT SHOULD WE DO, MON CAPITAN?
BE QUIET, RACAS! LET US WATCH THEIR DUEL.
ALL RIGHT, RAVE MASTER NUMBER TWO, MY NAME IS LET.
LET'S SEE...
...HOW YOU FARE IN A FAIR FIGHT.
MAN... THESE GUYS DON'T LET UP.
SORRY, DAD... THIS MIGHT TAKE A WHILE.
Tower of Din, Top Floor
I'VE BEEN EXPECTING YOU, GALE GLORY.
KING...
HOW MUCH OF YOURSELF WILL YOU GIVE TO THE DARKNESS BEFORE YOU'RE SATISFIED?

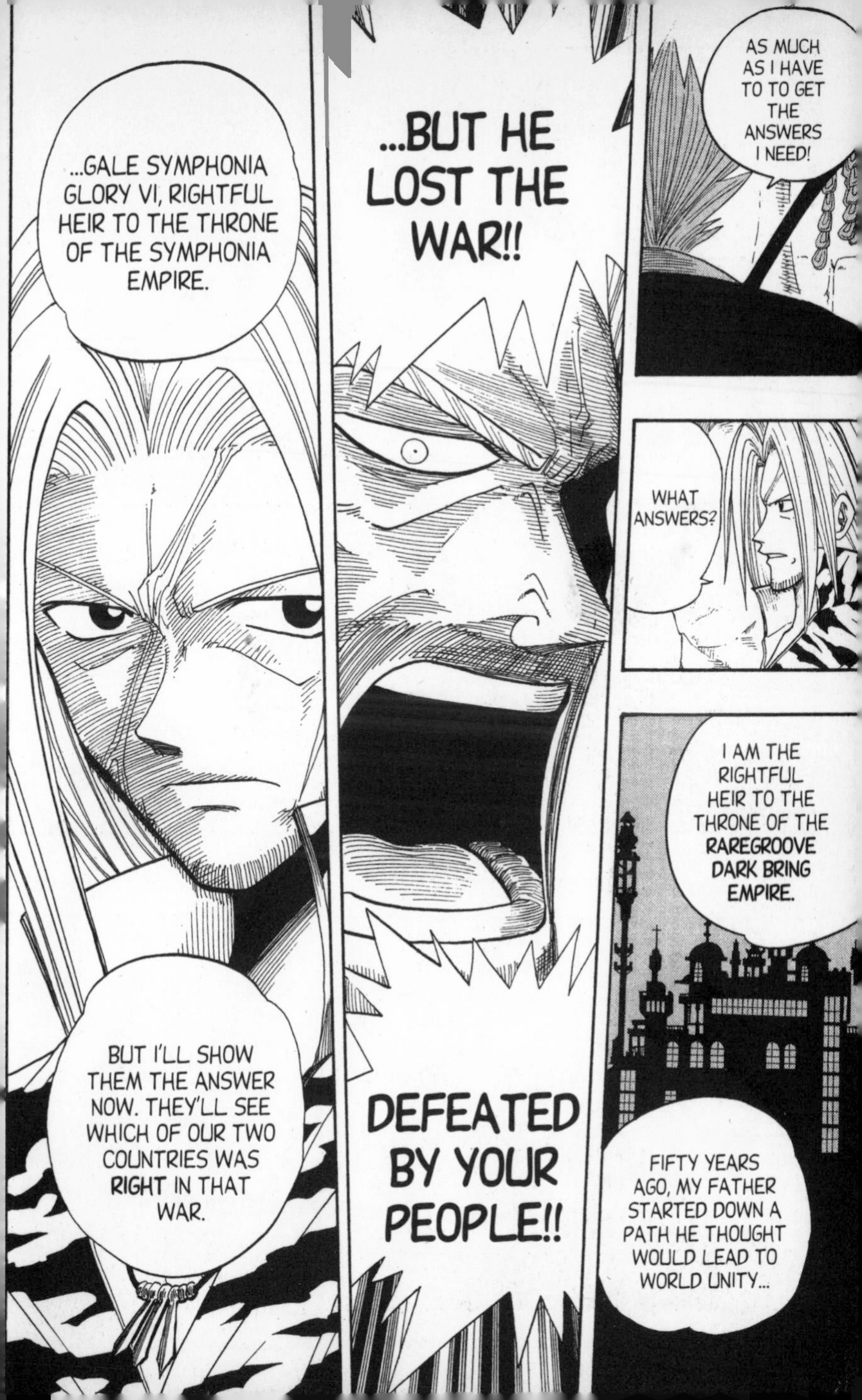
AS MUCH AS I HAVE TO TO GET THE ANSWERS I NEED!
WHAT ANSWERS?
I AM THE RIGHTFUL HEIR TO THE THRONE OF THE **RAREGROOVE DARK BRING EMPIRE.**
FIFTY YEARS AGO, MY FATHER STARTED DOWN A PATH HE THOUGHT WOULD LEAD TO WORLD UNITY...
...BUT HE LOST THE WAR!!
DEFEATED BY YOUR PEOPLE!!
...GALE SYMPHONIA GLORY VI, RIGHTFUL HEIR TO THE THRONE OF THE SYMPHONIA EMPIRE.
BUT I'LL SHOW THEM THE ANSWER NOW. THEY'LL SEE WHICH OF OUR TWO COUNTRIES WAS **RIGHT** IN THAT WAR.

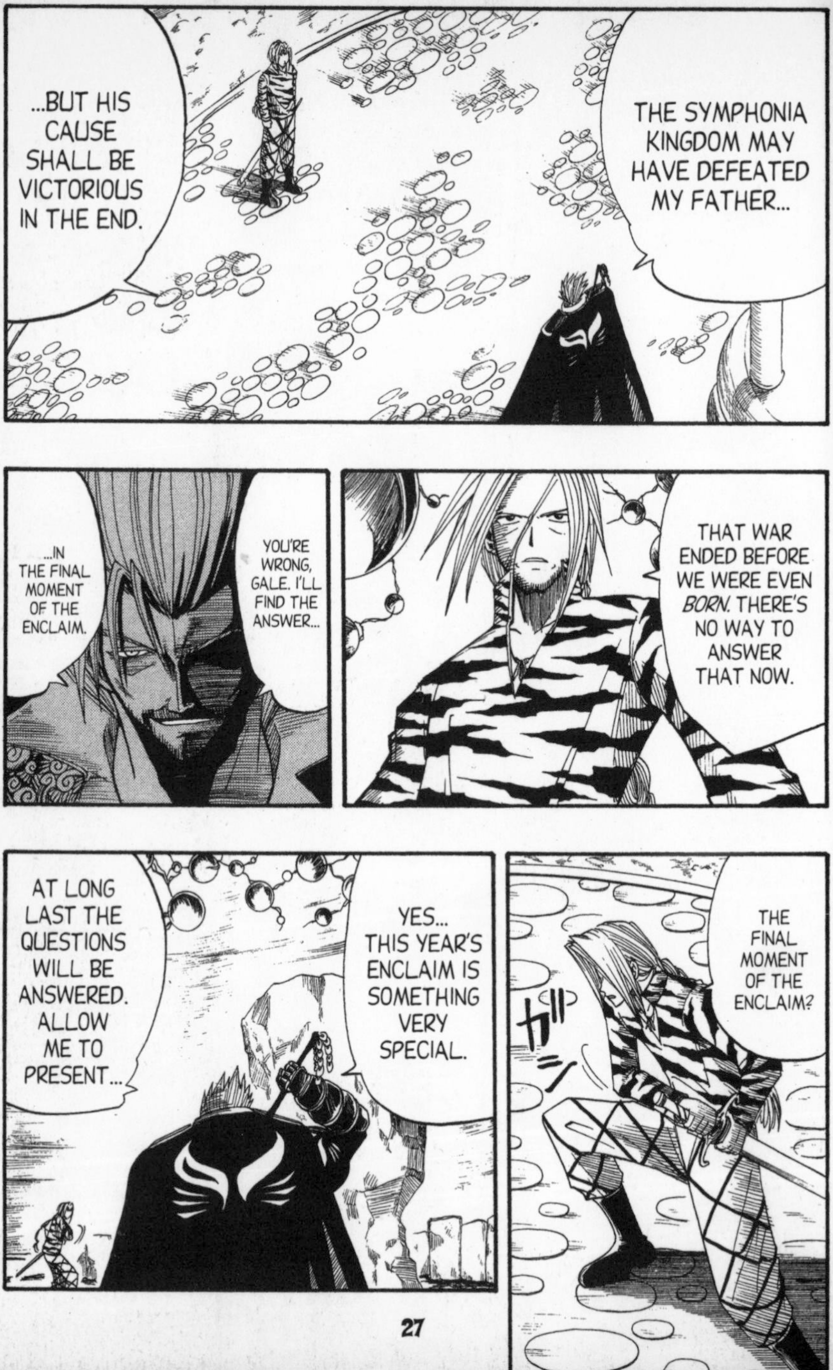
THE SYMPHONIA KINGDOM MAY HAVE DEFEATED MY FATHER...
...BUT HIS CAUSE SHALL BE VICTORIOUS IN THE END.
THAT WAR ENDED BEFORE WE WERE EVEN *BORN.* THERE'S NO WAY TO ANSWER THAT NOW.
YOU'RE WRONG, GALE. I'LL FIND THE ANSWER...
...IN THE FINAL MOMENT OF THE ENCLAIM.
THE FINAL MOMENT OF THE ENCLAIM?
YES... THIS YEAR'S ENCLAIM IS SOMETHING VERY SPECIAL.
AT LONG LAST THE QUESTIONS WILL BE ANSWERED. ALLOW ME TO PRESENT...

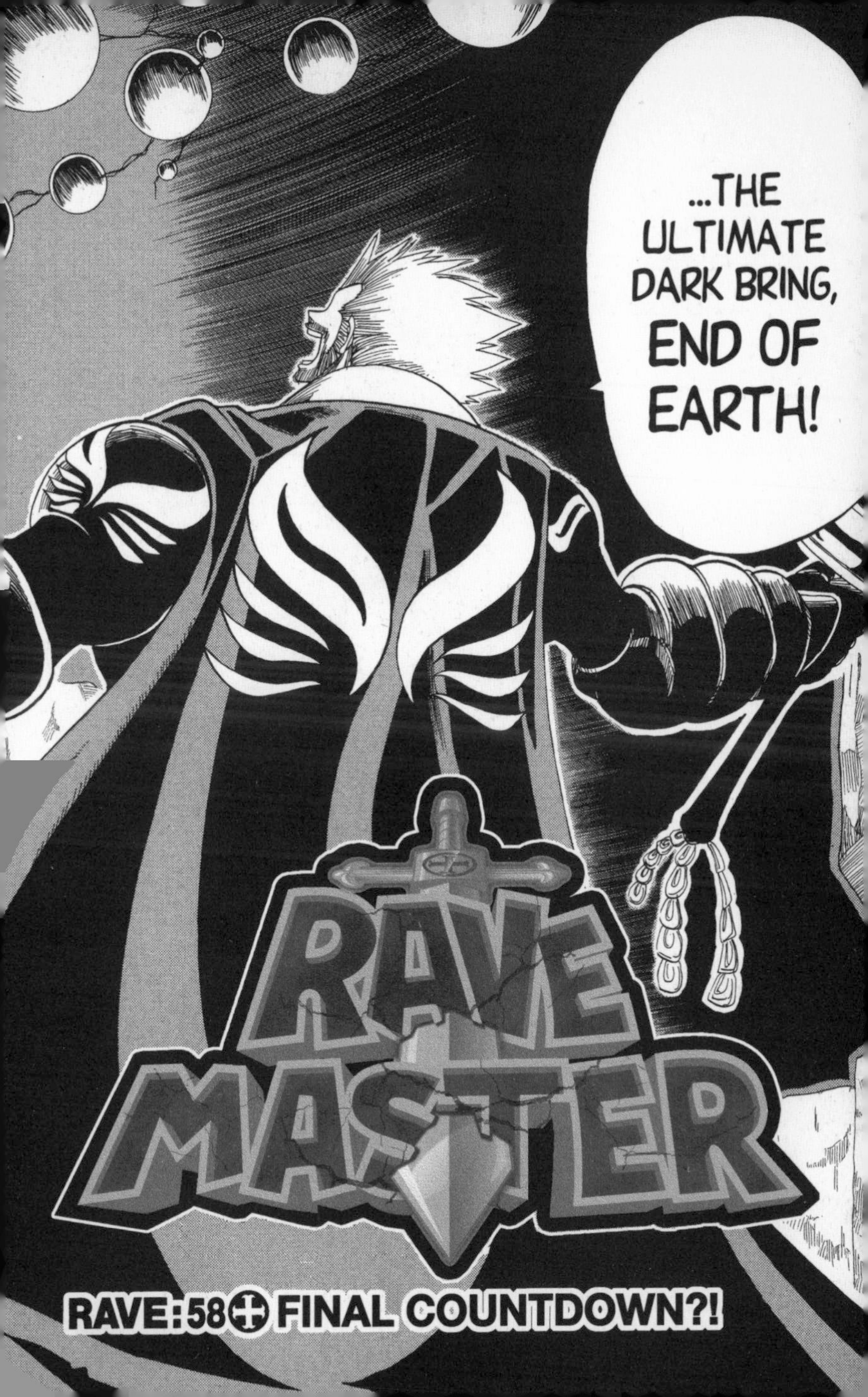
...THE ULTIMATE DARK BRING, END OF EARTH!
RAVE MASTER
RAVE:58 FINAL COUNTDOWN?!

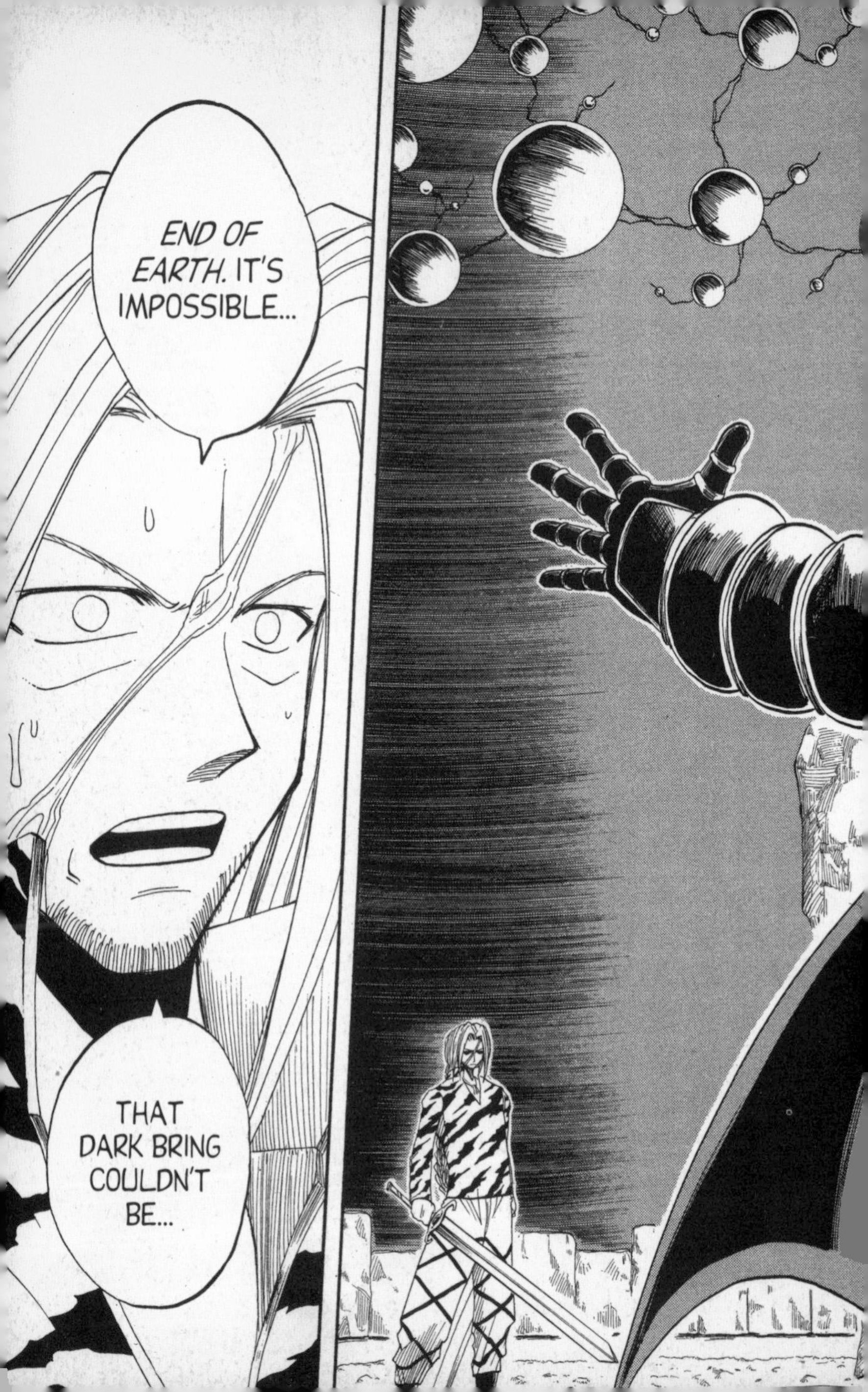
END OF EARTH. IT'S IMPOSSIBLE...
THAT DARK BRING COULDN'T BE...

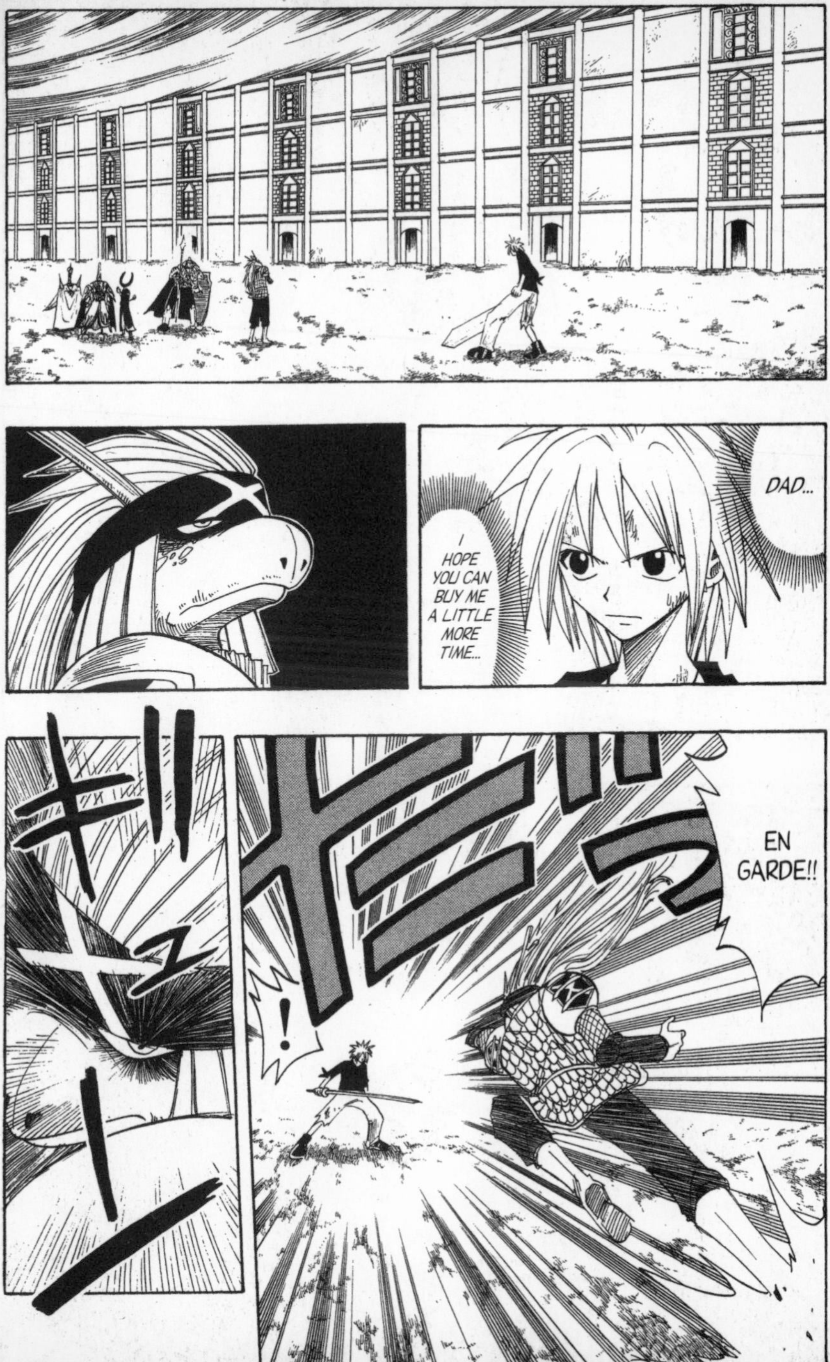
DAD...
I HOPE YOU CAN BUY ME A LITTLE MORE TIME...
EN GARDE!!
!

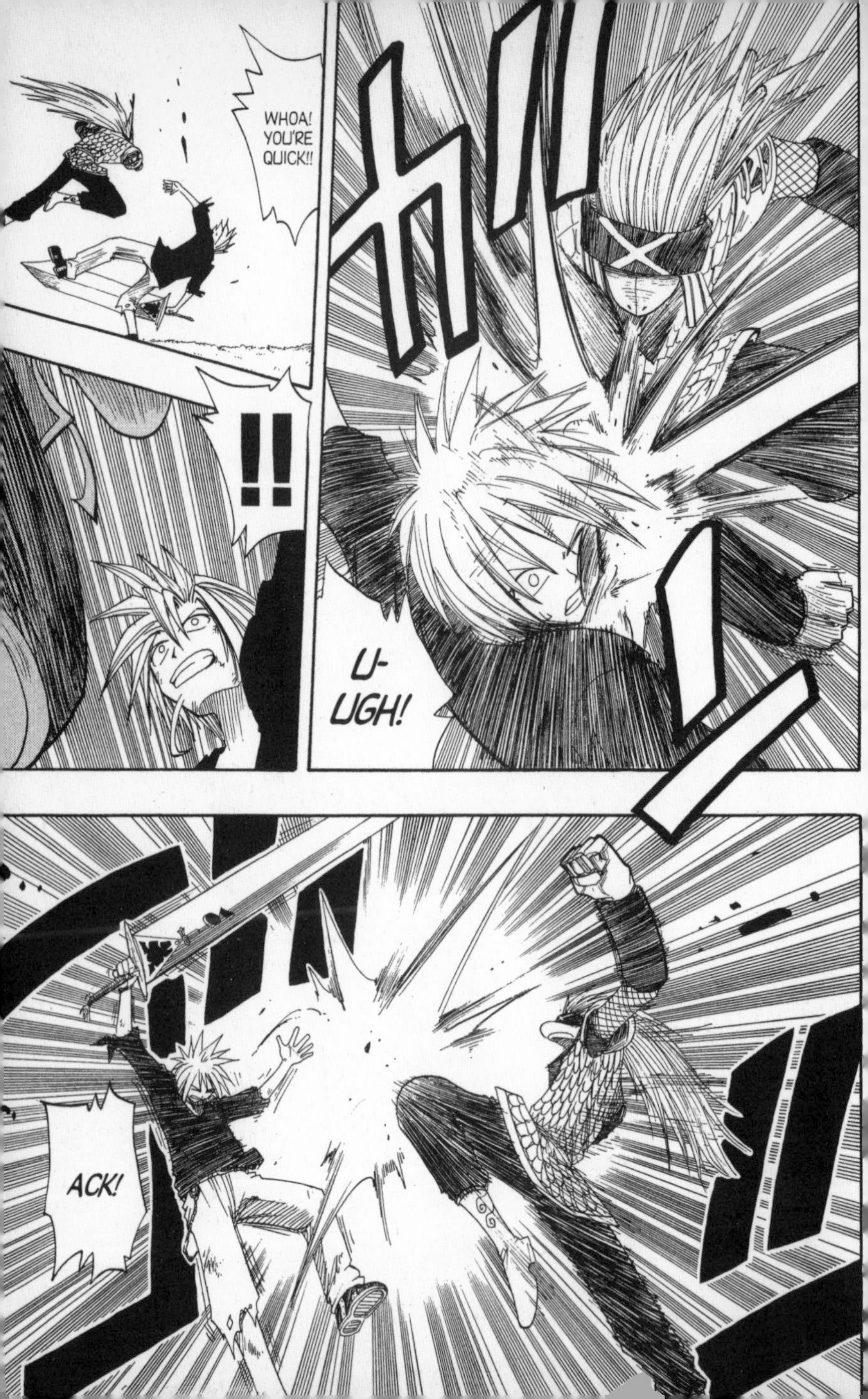
U-
UGH!
WHOA! YOU'RE QUICK!!
!!
ACK!

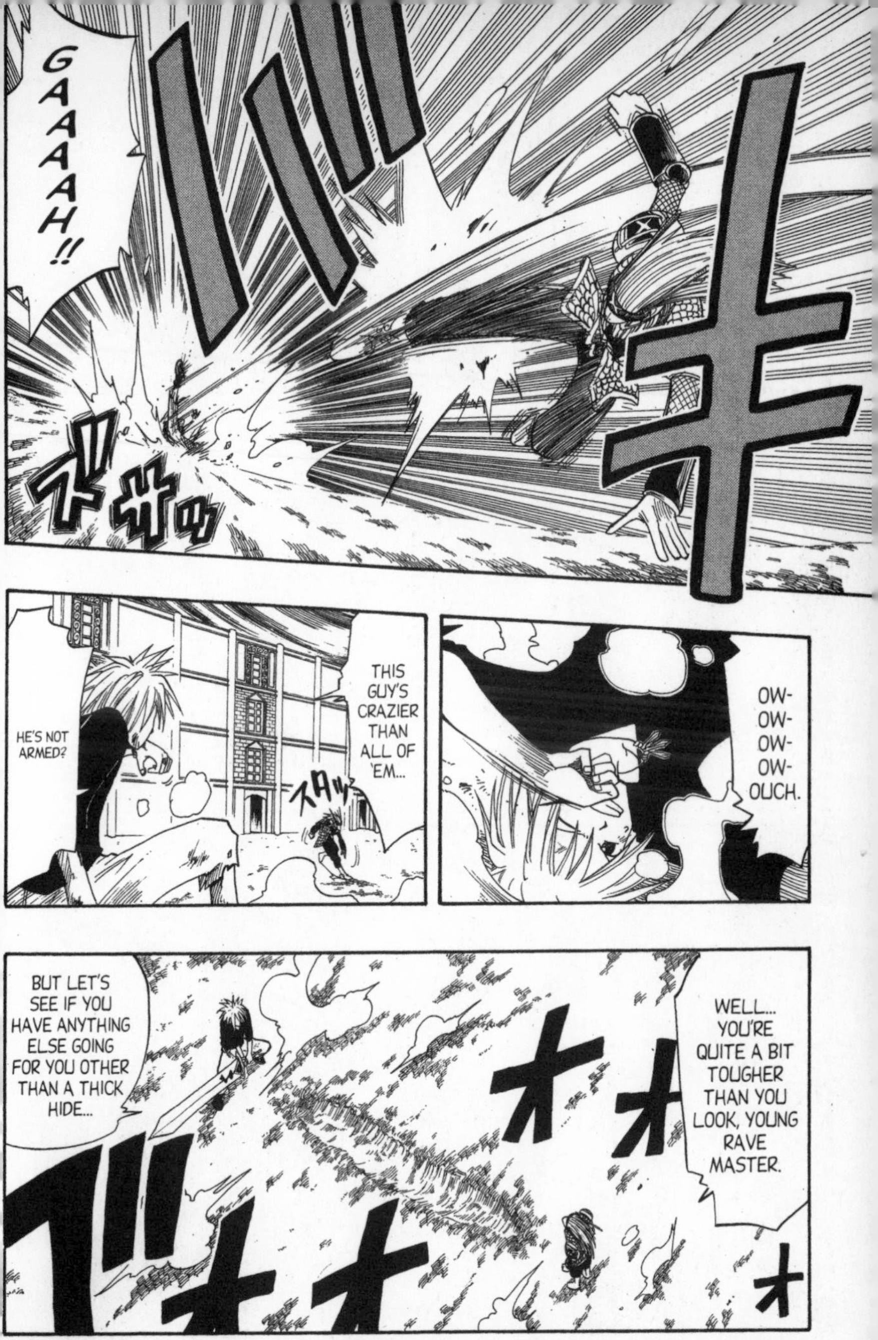
GAAAAAH!!
OW-OW-OW-OW-OUCH.
THIS GUY'S CRAZIER THAN ALL OF 'EM...
HE'S NOT ARMED?
WELL... YOU'RE QUITE A BIT TOUGHER THAN YOU LOOK, YOUNG RAVE MASTER.
BUT LET'S SEE IF YOU HAVE ANYTHING ELSE GOING FOR YOU OTHER THAN A THICK HIDE...

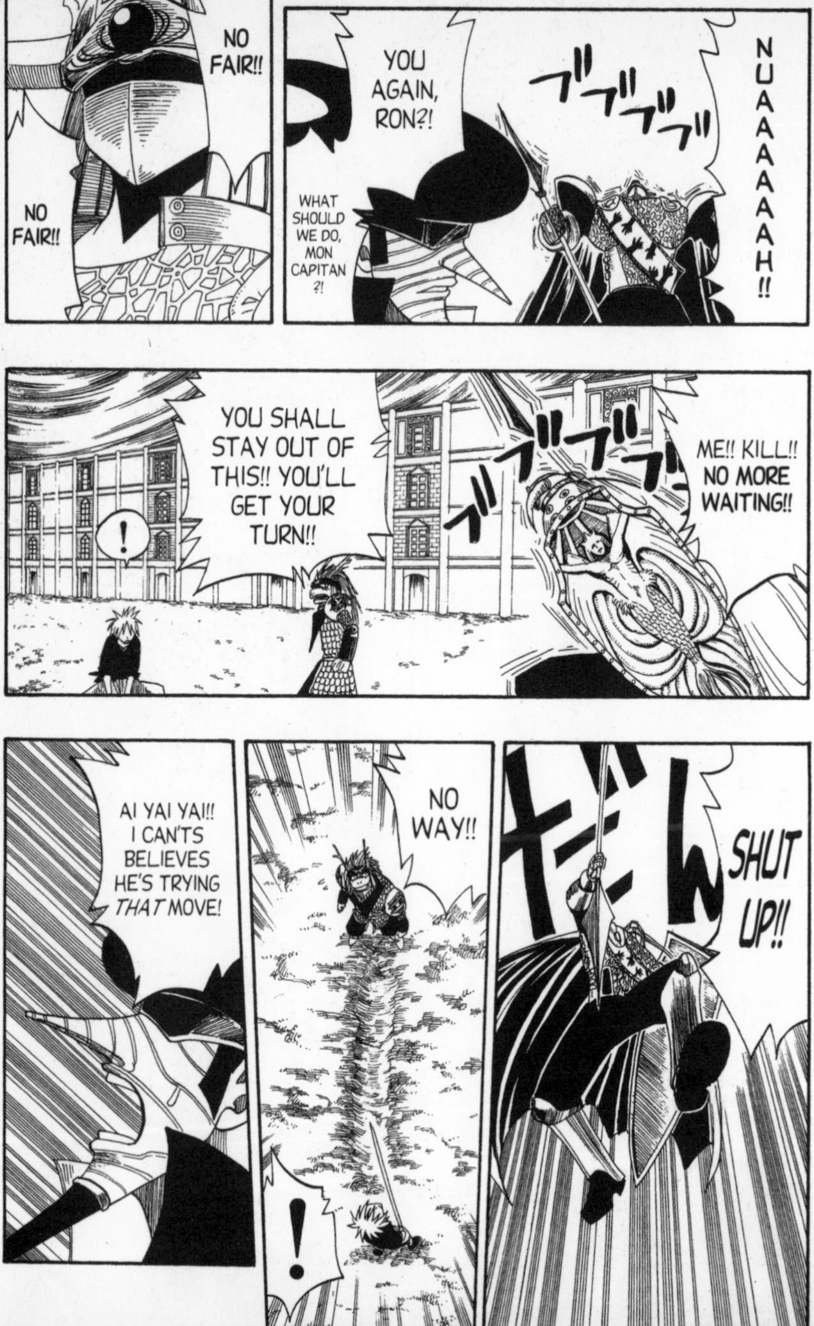

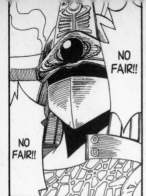

NUAAAAAAH!!
ブブブブ
YOU AGAIN, RON?!
WHAT SHOULD WE DO, MON CAPITAN?!
NO FAIR!!
NO FAIR!!
ME!! KILL!! NO MORE WAITING!!
ブブブブ
YOU SHALL STAY OUT OF THIS!! YOU'LL GET YOUR TURN!!
!
SHUT UP!!
キーん
NO WAY!!
!
AI YAI YAI!! I CAN'TS BELIEVES HE'S TRYING *THAT* MOVE!

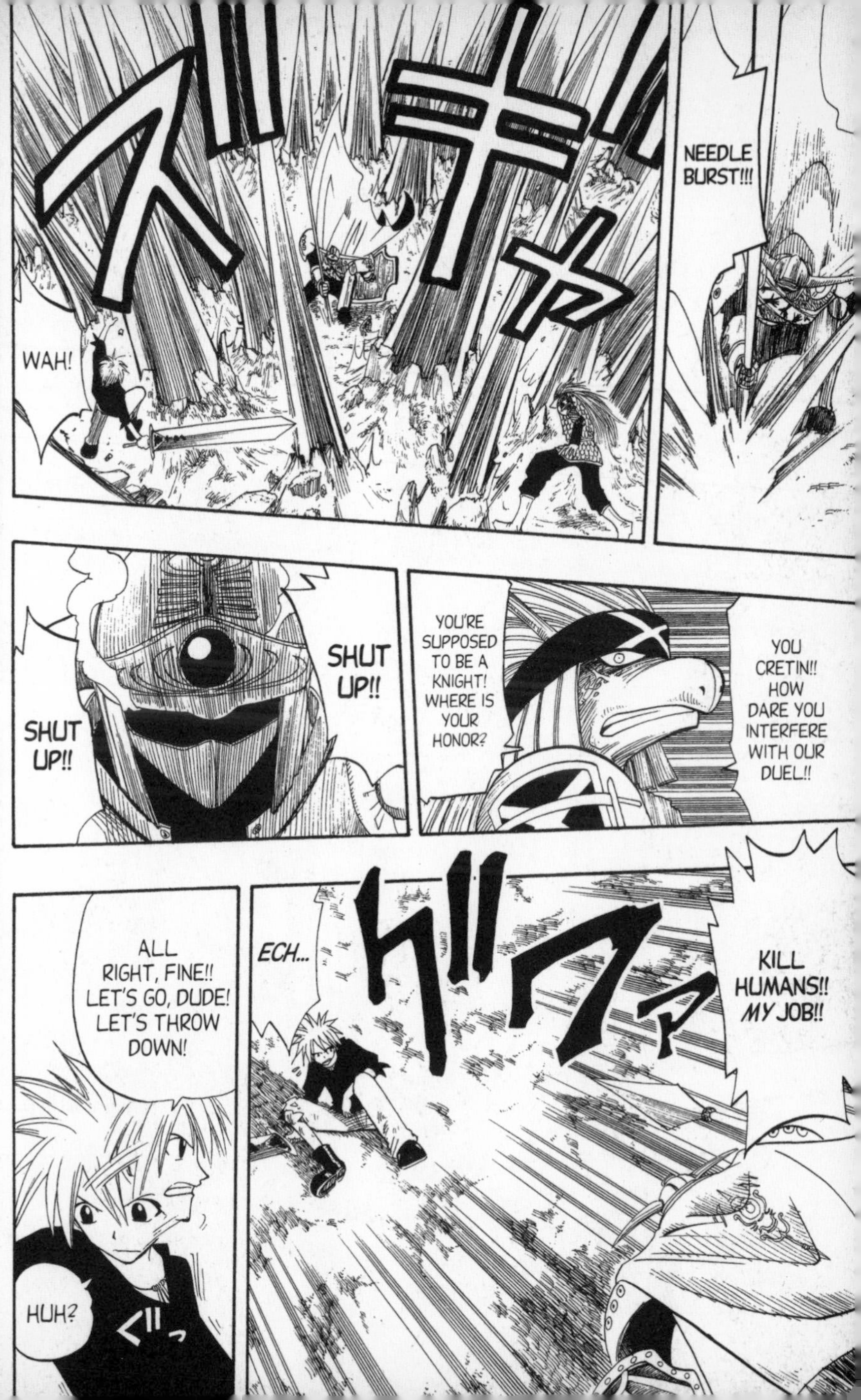
NEEDLE BURST!!!
WAH!
YOU CRETIN!! HOW DARE YOU INTERFERE WITH OUR DUEL!!
YOU'RE SUPPOSED TO BE A KNIGHT! WHERE IS YOUR HONOR?
SHUT UP!!
SHUT UP!!
KILL HUMANS!! MY JOB!!
ECH...
ALL RIGHT, FINE!! LET'S GO, DUDE! LET'S THROW DOWN!
HUH?

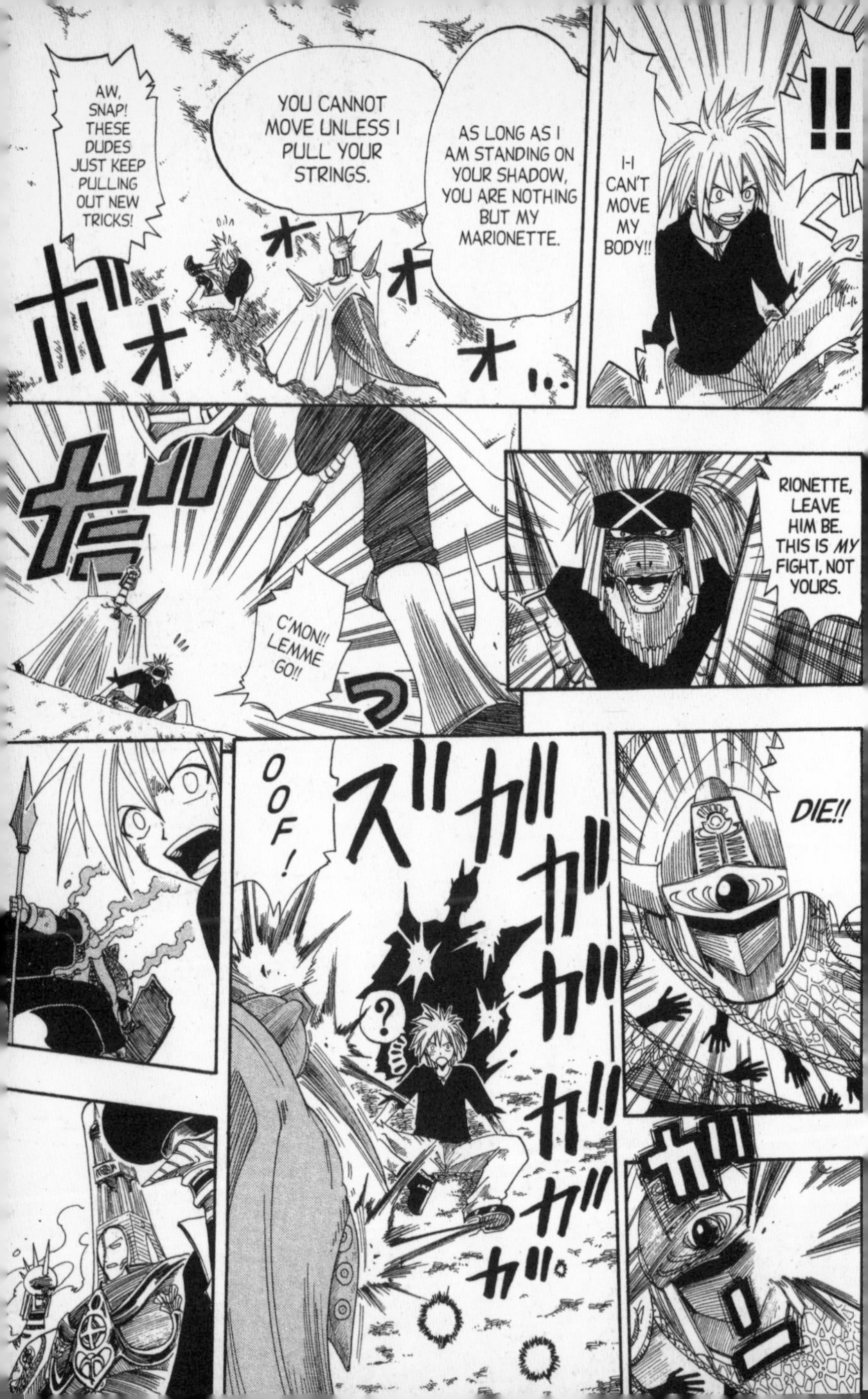
!!
I-I CAN'T MOVE MY BODY!!
AS LONG AS I AM STANDING ON YOUR SHADOW, YOU ARE NOTHING BUT MY MARIONETTE.
YOU CANNOT MOVE UNLESS I PULL YOUR STRINGS.
AW, SNAP! THESE DUDES JUST KEEP PULLING OUT NEW TRICKS!
RIONETTE, LEAVE HIM BE. THIS IS *MY* FIGHT, NOT YOURS.
C'MON!! LEMME GO!!
DIE!!
OOF!
?

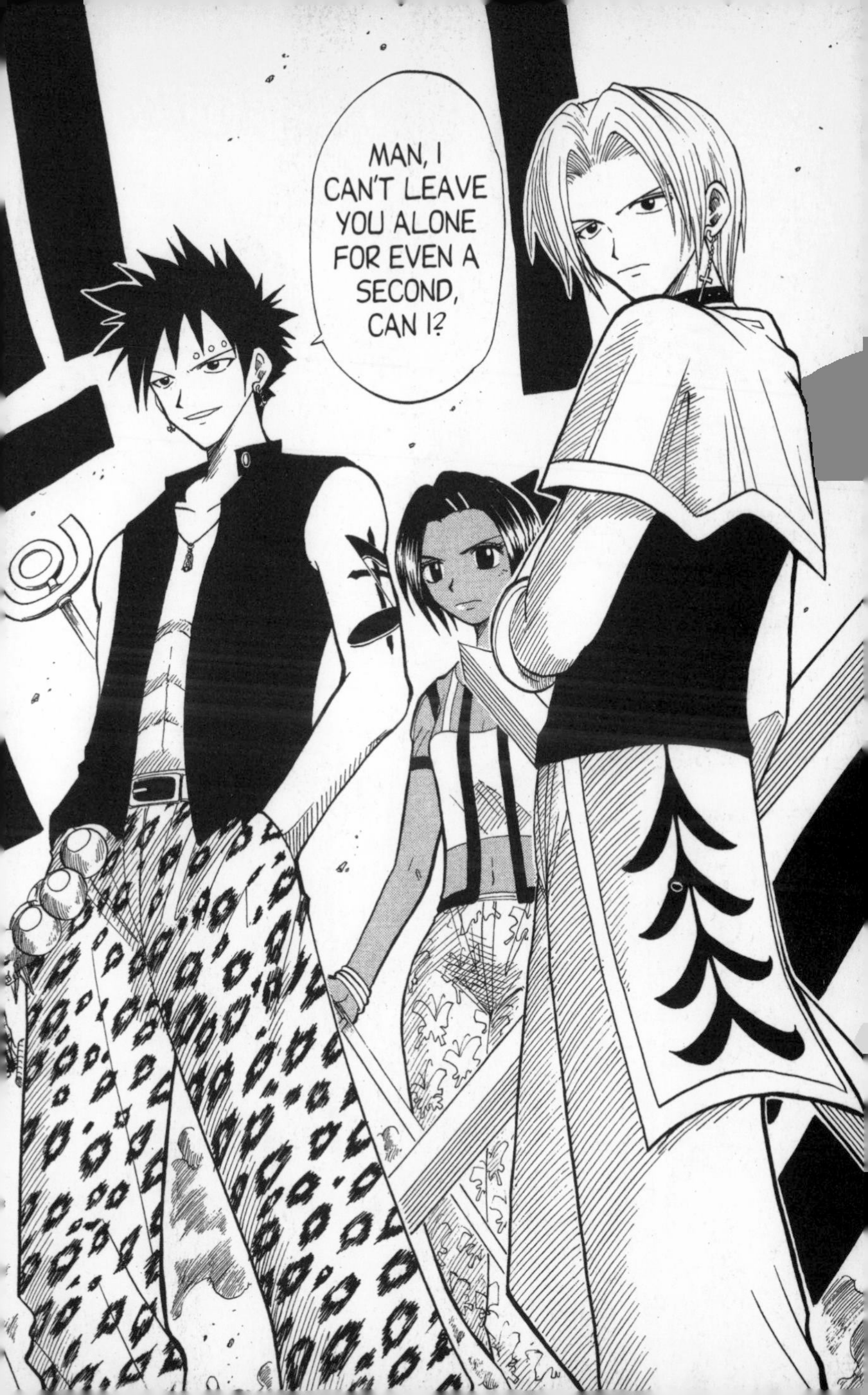
MAN, I CAN'T LEAVE YOU ALONE FOR EVEN A SECOND, CAN I?

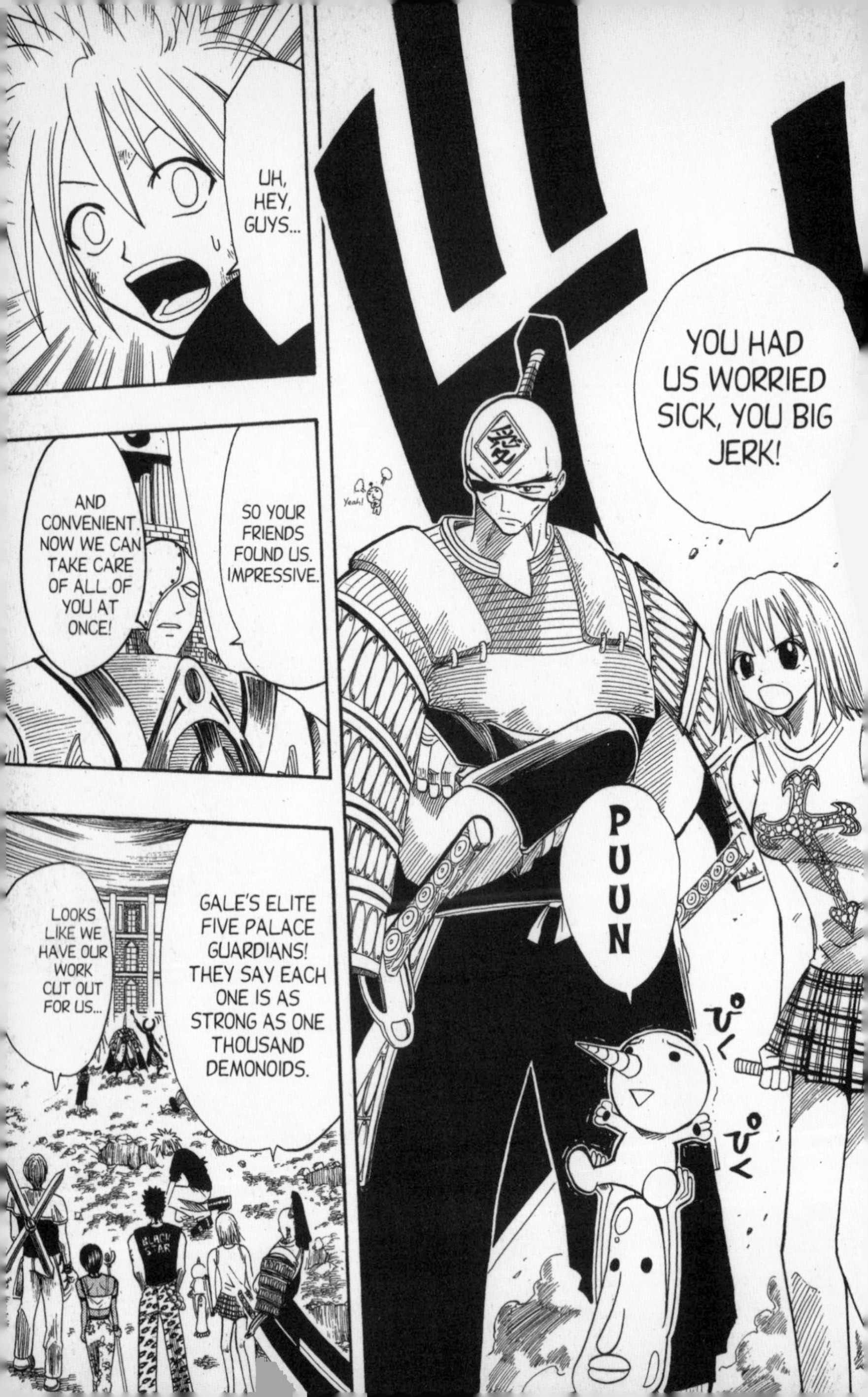
YOU HAD US WORRIED SICK, YOU BIG JERK!
Yeah!
PUUN
ぴくぴく
ぴくぴく
UH, HEY, GUYS...
SO YOUR FRIENDS FOUND US. IMPRESSIVE.
AND CONVENIENT. NOW WE CAN TAKE CARE OF ALL OF YOU AT ONCE!
GALE'S ELITE FIVE PALACE GUARDIANS! THEY SAY EACH ONE IS AS STRONG AS ONE THOUSAND DEMONOIDS.
LOOKS LIKE WE HAVE OUR WORK CUT OUT FOR US...
BLACK STAR

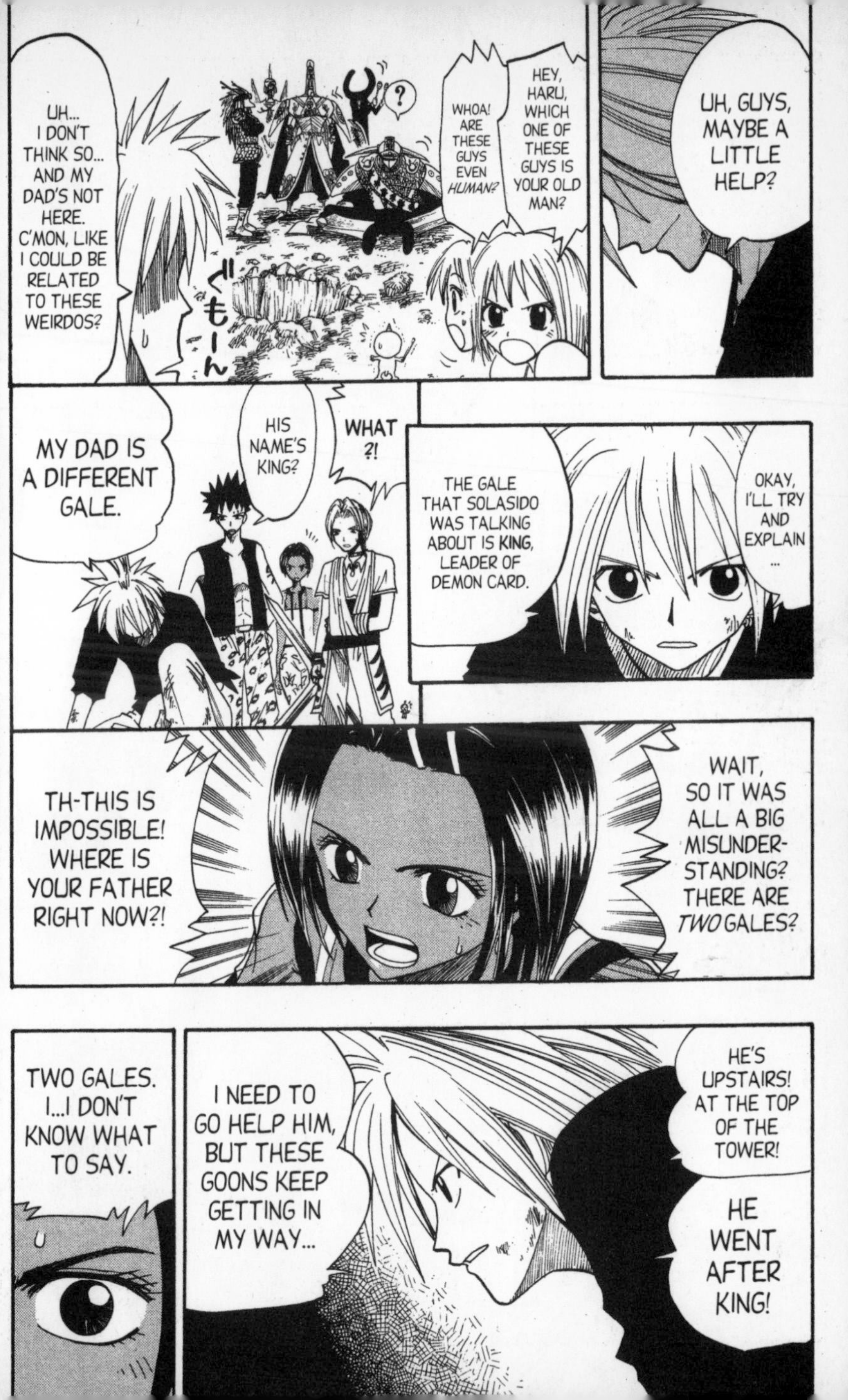
UH, GUYS, MAYBE A LITTLE HELP?
HEY, HARU, WHICH ONE OF THESE GUYS IS YOUR OLD MAN?
WHOA! ARE THESE GUYS EVEN *HUMAN*?
UH... I DON'T THINK SO... AND MY DAD'S NOT HERE. C'MON, LIKE I COULD BE RELATED TO THESE WEIRDOS?
OKAY, I'LL TRY AND EXPLAIN ...
THE GALE THAT SOLASIDO WAS TALKING ABOUT IS **KING**, LEADER OF DEMON CARD.
WHAT ?!
HIS NAME'S KING?
MY DAD IS A DIFFERENT GALE.
WAIT, SO IT WAS ALL A BIG MISUNDERSTANDING? THERE ARE *TWO* GALES?
TH-THIS IS IMPOSSIBLE! WHERE IS YOUR FATHER RIGHT NOW?!
HE'S UPSTAIRS! AT THE TOP OF THE TOWER!
HE WENT AFTER KING!
I NEED TO GO HELP HIM, BUT THESE GOONS KEEP GETTING IN MY WAY...
TWO GALES. I...I DON'T KNOW WHAT TO SAY.

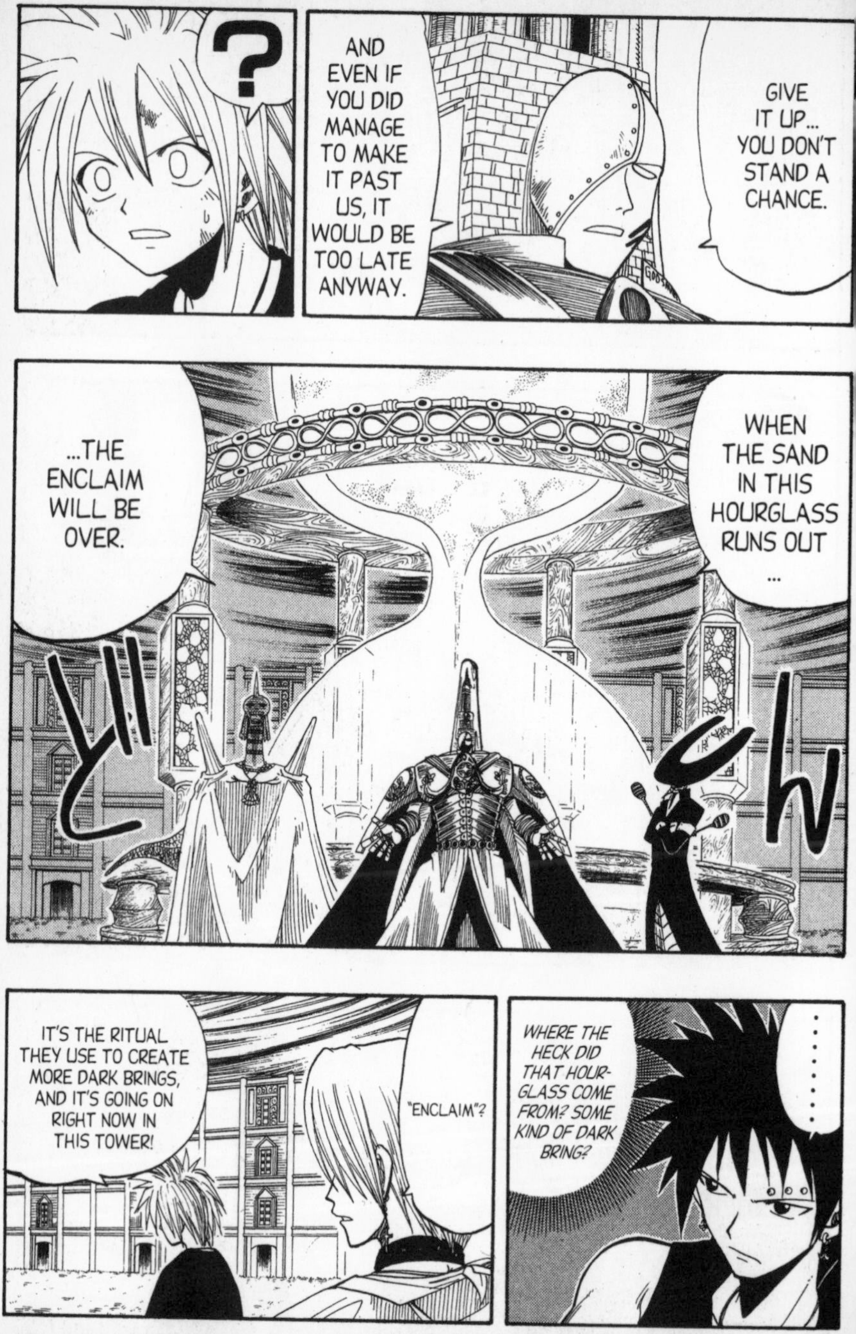
GIVE IT UP... YOU DON'T STAND A CHANCE.
AND EVEN IF YOU DID MANAGE TO MAKE IT PAST US, IT WOULD BE TOO LATE ANYWAY.
?
WHEN THE SAND IN THIS HOURGLASS RUNS OUT ...
...THE ENCLAIM WILL BE OVER.
どん
......
WHERE THE HECK DID THAT HOUR-GLASS COME FROM? SOME KIND OF DARK BRING?
"ENCLAIM"?
IT'S THE RITUAL THEY USE TO CREATE MORE DARK BRINGS, AND IT'S GOING ON RIGHT NOW IN THIS TOWER!

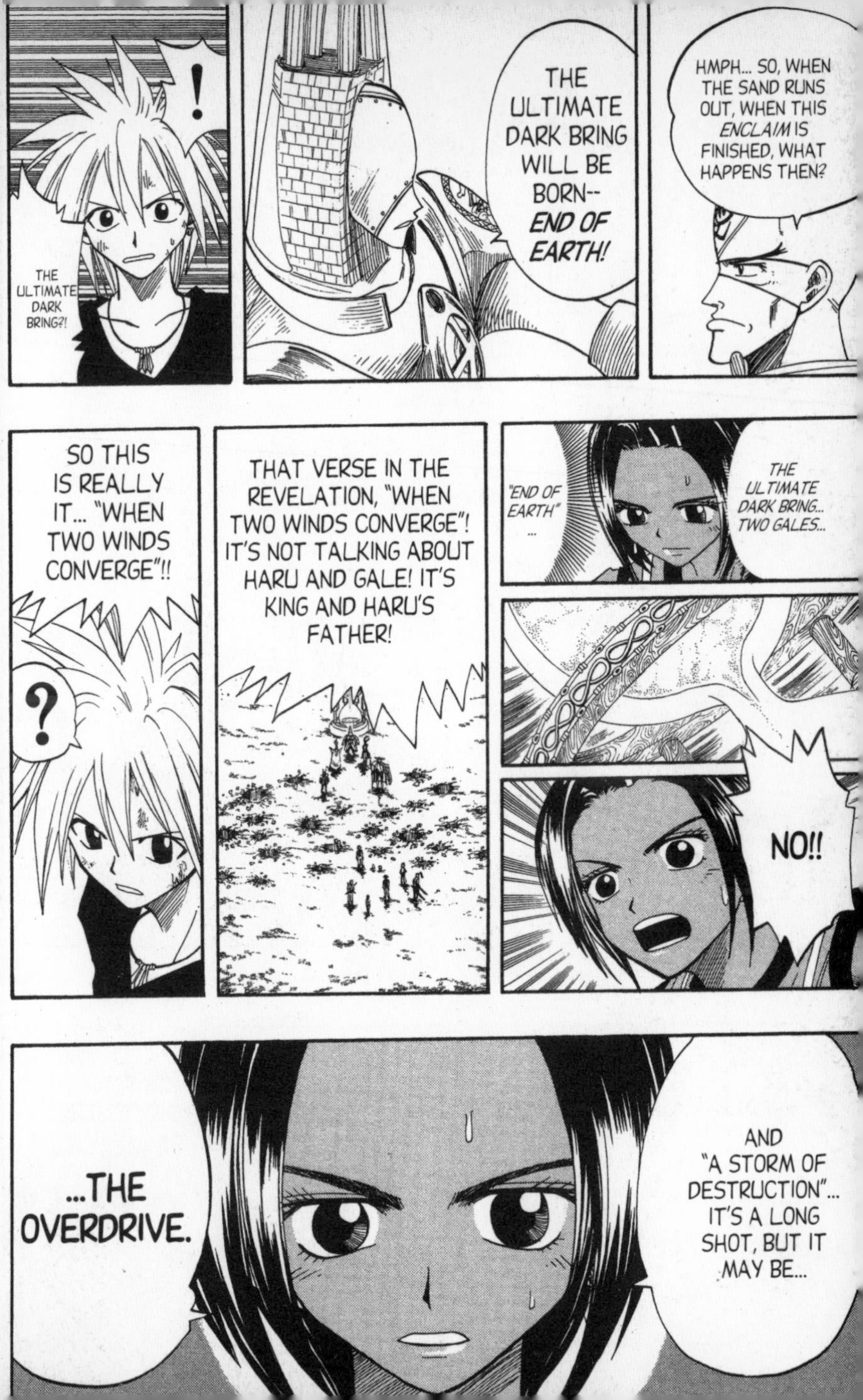
HMPH... SO, WHEN THE SAND RUNS OUT, WHEN THIS *ENCLAIM* IS FINISHED, WHAT HAPPENS THEN?
THE ULTIMATE DARK BRING WILL BE BORN-- *END OF EARTH!*
!
THE ULTIMATE DARK BRING?!
THE ULTIMATE DARK BRING... TWO GALES...
"END OF EARTH" ...
NO!!
THAT VERSE IN THE REVELATION, "WHEN TWO WINDS CONVERGE"! IT'S NOT TALKING ABOUT HARU AND GALE! IT'S KING AND HARU'S FATHER!
SO THIS IS REALLY IT... "WHEN TWO WINDS CONVERGE"!!
?
AND "A STORM OF DESTRUCTION"... IT'S A LONG SHOT, BUT IT MAY BE...
...THE OVERDRIVE.

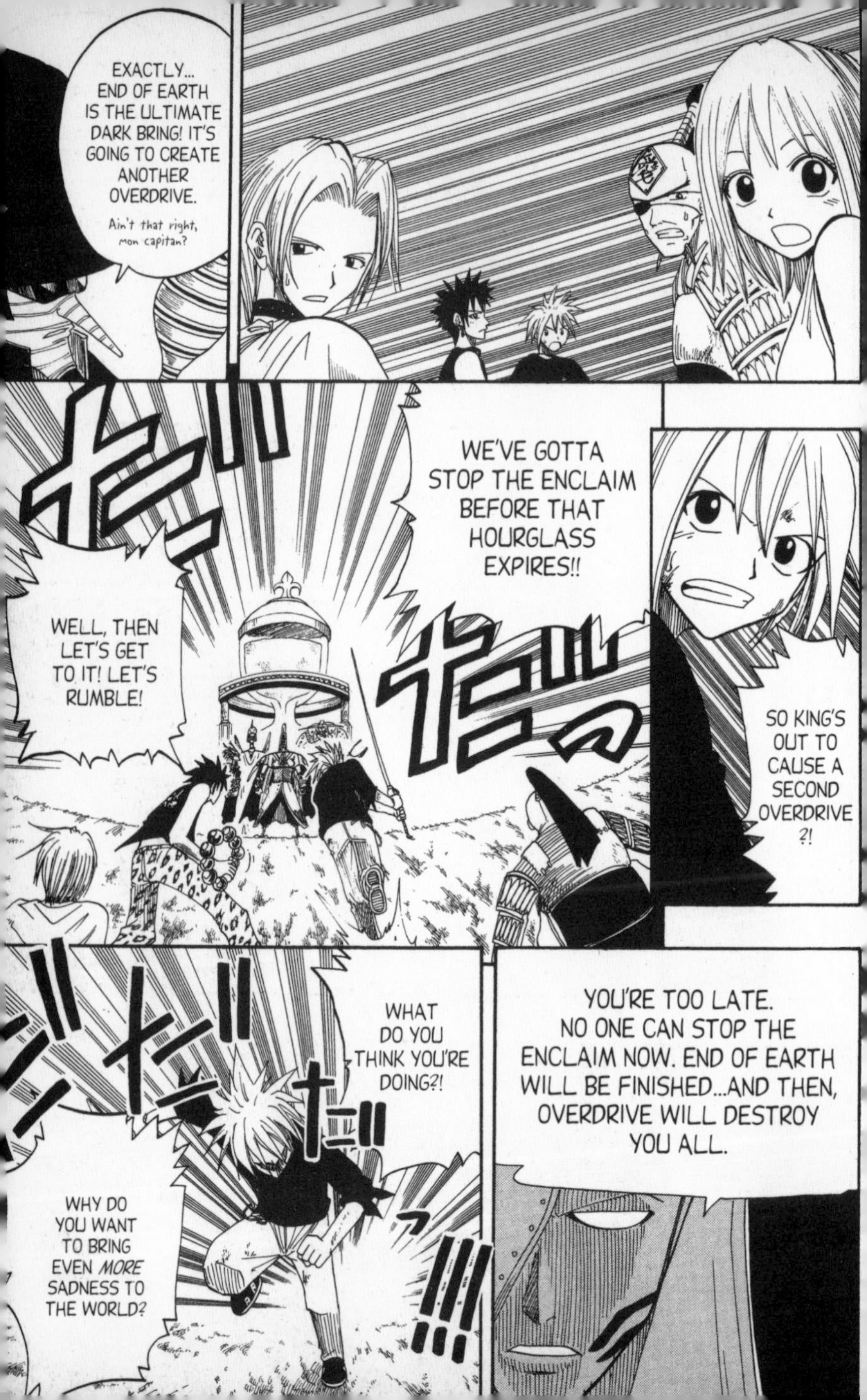
EXACTLY... END OF EARTH IS THE ULTIMATE DARK BRING! IT'S GOING TO CREATE ANOTHER OVERDRIVE.
Ain't that right, mon capitan?
SO KING'S OUT TO CAUSE A SECOND OVERDRIVE ?!
WE'VE GOTTA STOP THE ENCLAIM BEFORE THAT HOURGLASS EXPIRES!!
WELL, THEN LET'S GET TO IT! LET'S RUMBLE!
YOU'RE TOO LATE. NO ONE CAN STOP THE ENCLAIM NOW. END OF EARTH WILL BE FINISHED...AND THEN, OVERDRIVE WILL DESTROY YOU ALL.
WHAT DO YOU THINK YOU'RE DOING?!
WHY DO YOU WANT TO BRING EVEN *MORE* SADNESS TO THE WORLD?

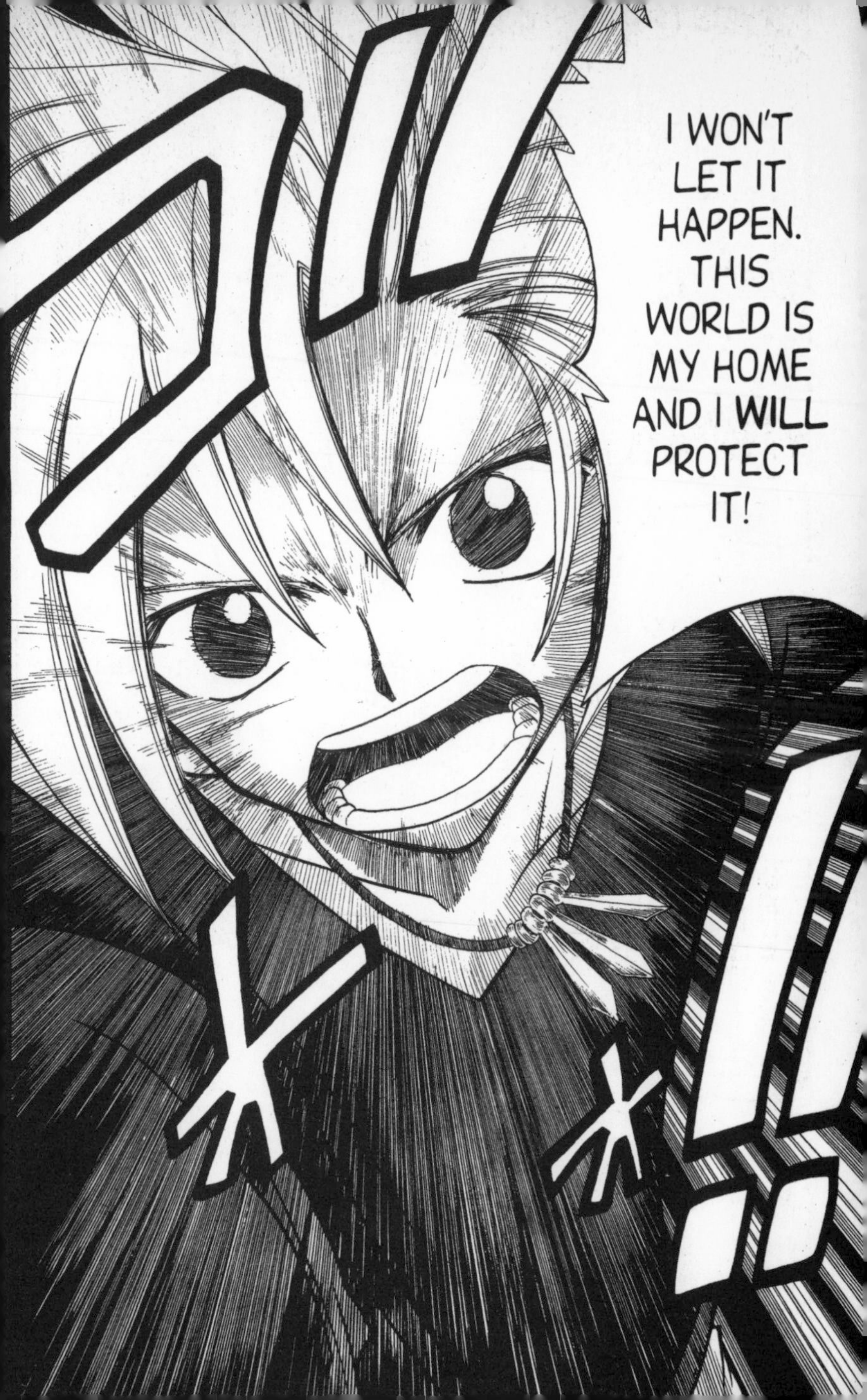
I WON'T LET IT HAPPEN. THIS WORLD IS MY HOME AND I WILL PROTECT IT!

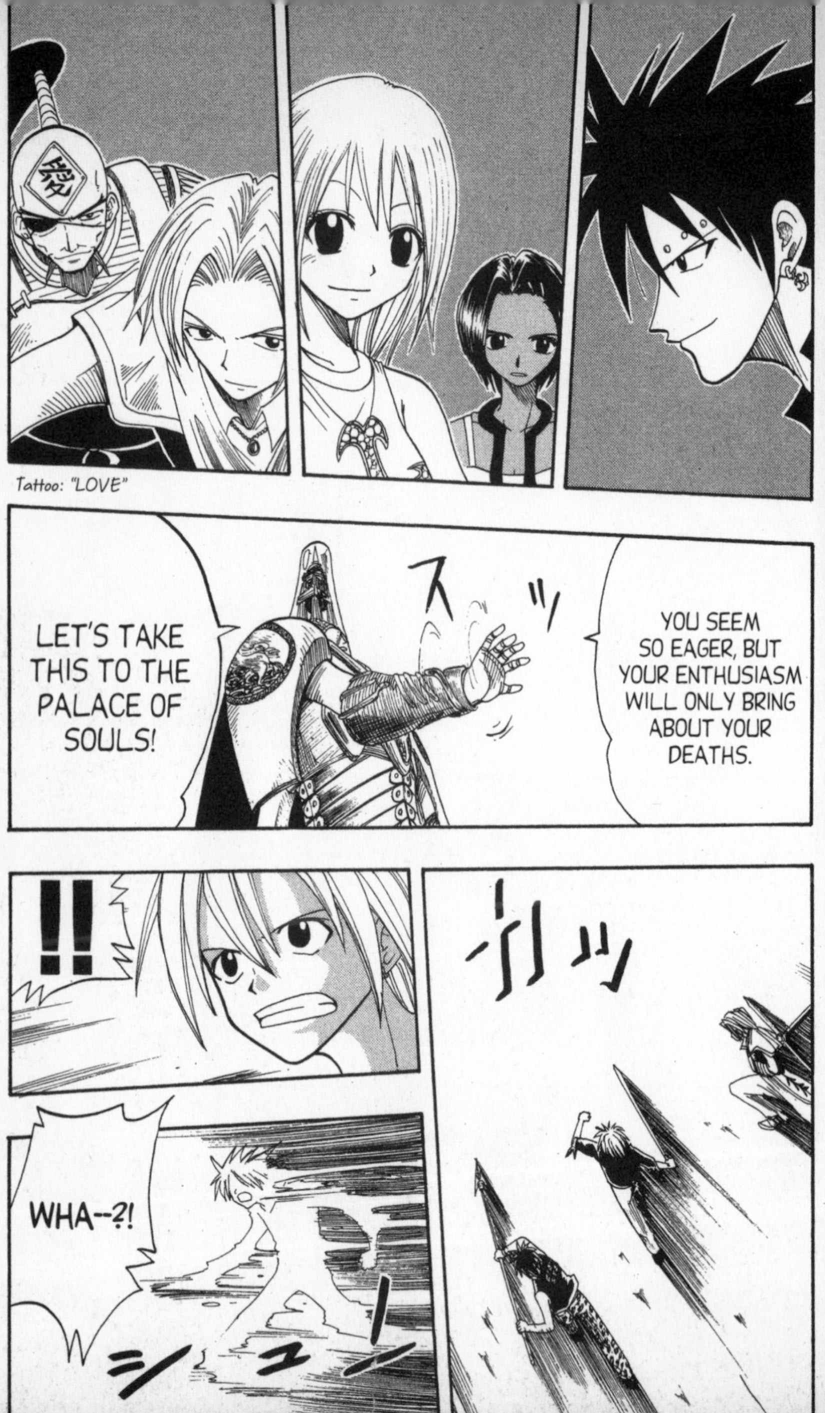
Tattoo: "LOVE"
YOU SEEM SO EAGER, BUT YOUR ENTHUSIASM WILL ONLY BRING ABOUT YOUR DEATHS.
スッ
LET'S TAKE THIS TO THE PALACE OF SOULS!
!!
WHA--?!

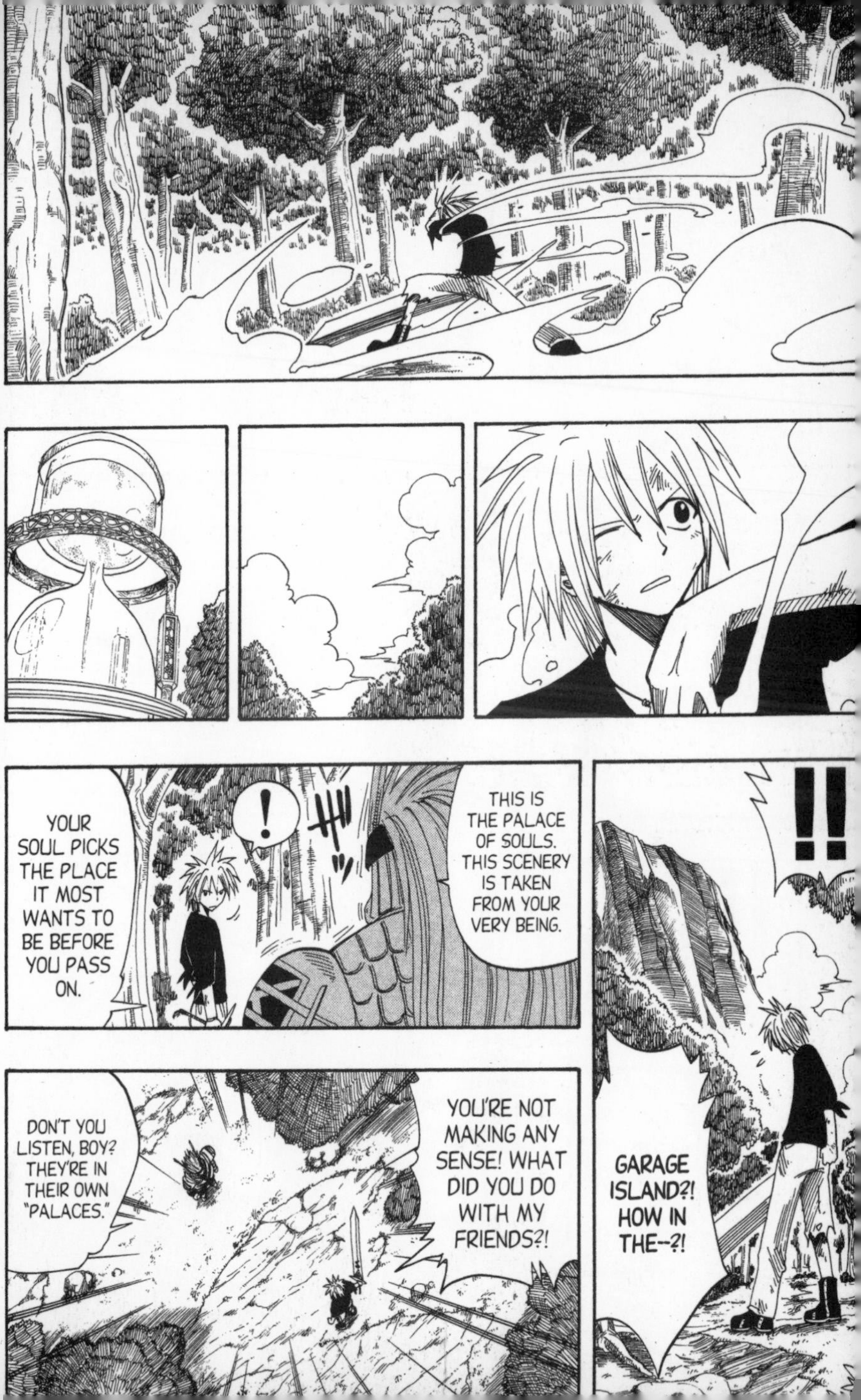
!!
GARAGE ISLAND?! HOW IN THE--?!
THIS IS THE PALACE OF SOULS. THIS SCENERY IS TAKEN FROM YOUR VERY BEING.
!
YOUR SOUL PICKS THE PLACE IT MOST WANTS TO BE BEFORE YOU PASS ON.
YOU'RE NOT MAKING ANY SENSE! WHAT DID YOU DO WITH MY FRIENDS?!
DON'T YOU LISTEN, BOY? THEY'RE IN THEIR OWN "PALACES."

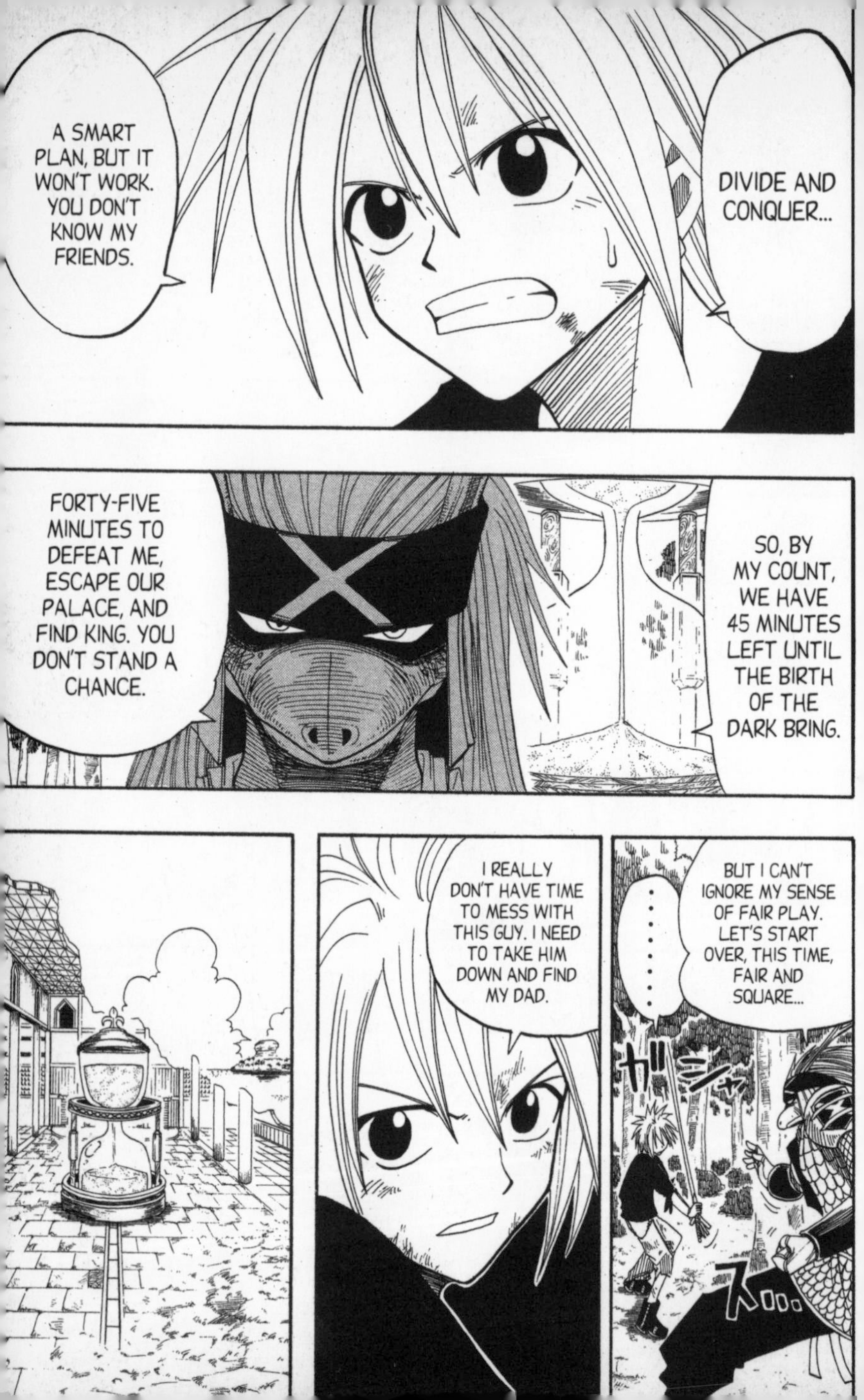
DIVIDE AND CONQUER...
A SMART PLAN, BUT IT WON'T WORK. YOU DON'T KNOW MY FRIENDS.
SO, BY MY COUNT, WE HAVE 45 MINUTES LEFT UNTIL THE BIRTH OF THE DARK BRING.
FORTY-FIVE MINUTES TO DEFEAT ME, ESCAPE OUR PALACE, AND FIND KING. YOU DON'T STAND A CHANCE.
BUT I CAN'T IGNORE MY SENSE OF FAIR PLAY. LET'S START OVER, THIS TIME, FAIR AND SQUARE...
......
I REALLY DON'T HAVE TIME TO MESS WITH THIS GUY. I NEED TO TAKE HIM DOWN AND FIND MY DAD.

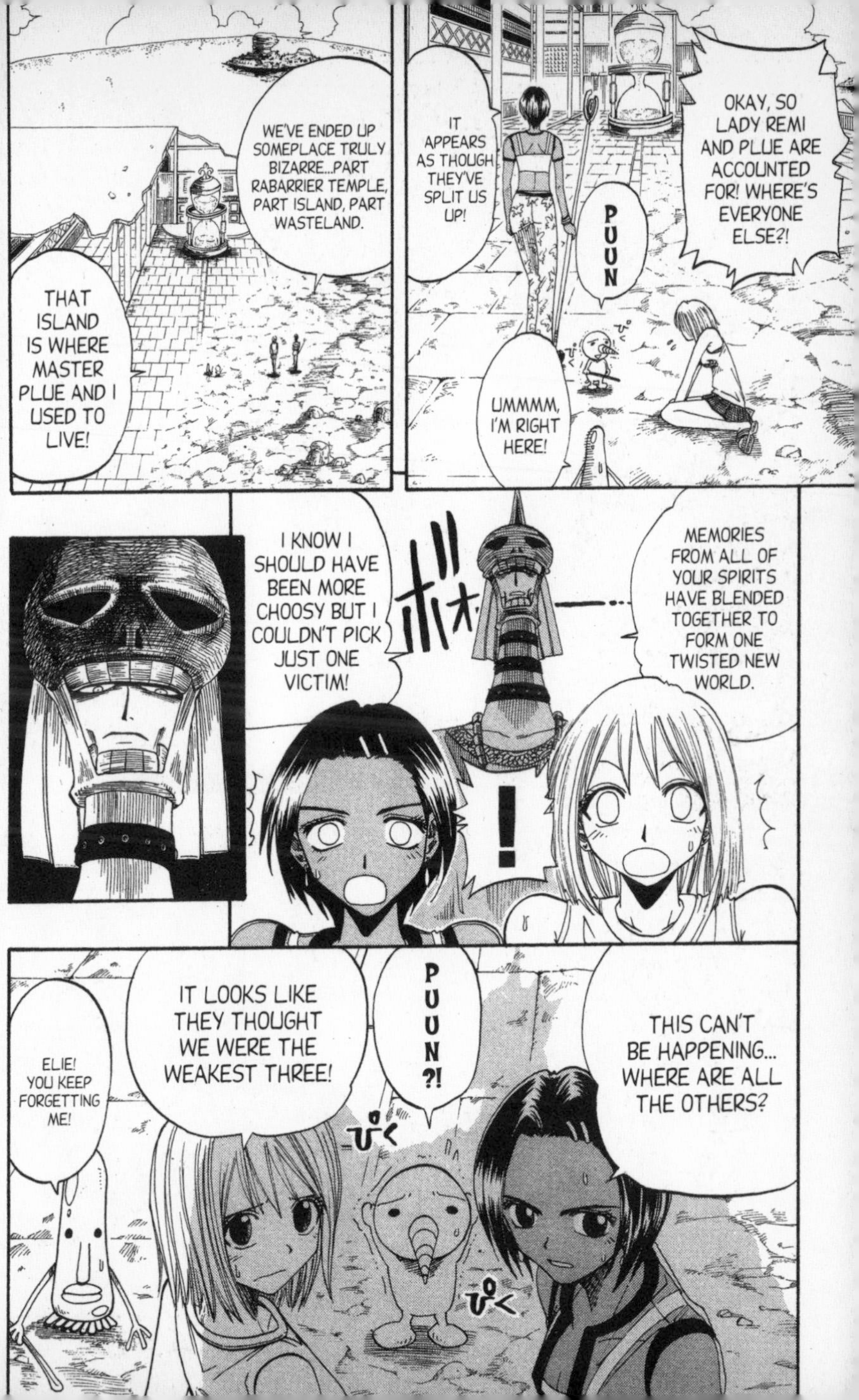
OKAY, SO LADY REMI AND PLUE ARE ACCOUNTED FOR! WHERE'S EVERYONE ELSE?!
IT APPEARS AS THOUGH THEY'VE SPLIT US UP!
PUUN
UMMMM, I'M RIGHT HERE!
WE'VE ENDED UP SOMEPLACE TRULY BIZARRE...PART RABARRIER TEMPLE, PART ISLAND, PART WASTELAND.
THAT ISLAND IS WHERE MASTER PLUE AND I USED TO LIVE!
MEMORIES FROM ALL OF YOUR SPIRITS HAVE BLENDED TOGETHER TO FORM ONE TWISTED NEW WORLD.
I KNOW I SHOULD HAVE BEEN MORE CHOOSY BUT I COULDN'T PICK JUST ONE VICTIM!
!
THIS CAN'T BE HAPPENING... WHERE ARE ALL THE OTHERS?
PUUN?!
IT LOOKS LIKE THEY THOUGHT WE WERE THE WEAKEST THREE!
ELIE! YOU KEEP FORGETTING ME!

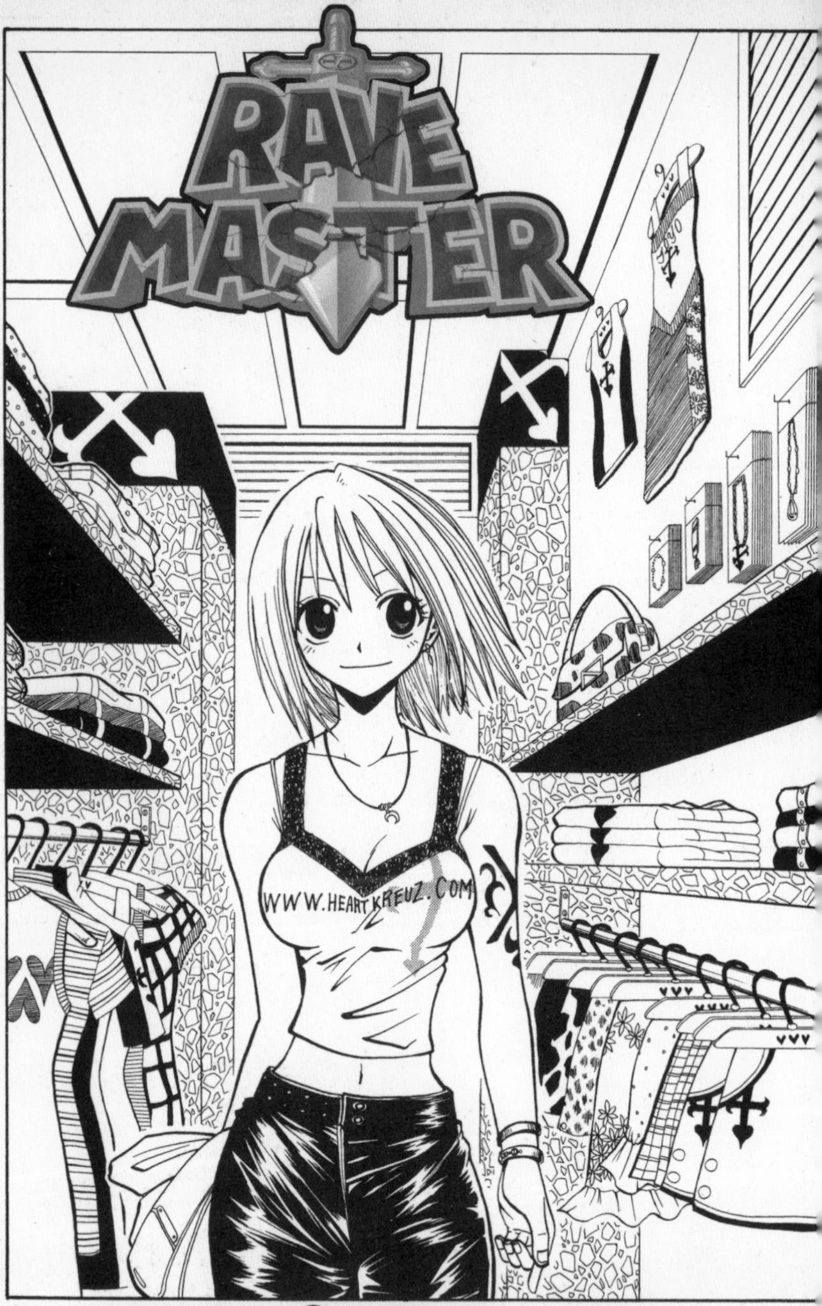
RAVE MASTER
WWW.HEARTKREUZ.COM

RAVE:59 INFINITE RESOLVE

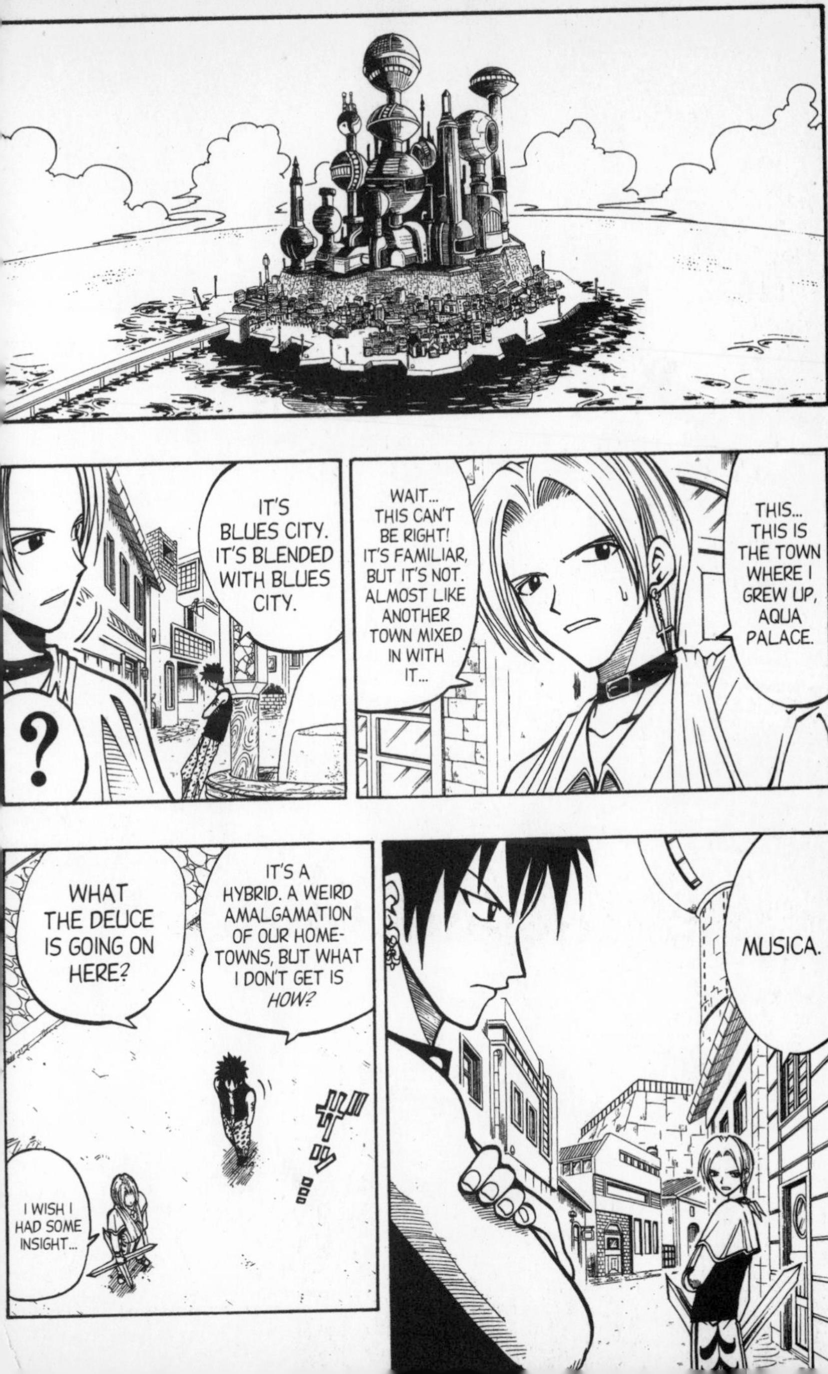
THIS... THIS IS THE TOWN WHERE I GREW UP, AQUA PALACE.
WAIT... THIS CAN'T BE RIGHT! IT'S FAMILIAR, BUT IT'S NOT. ALMOST LIKE ANOTHER TOWN MIXED IN WITH IT...
IT'S BLUES CITY. IT'S BLENDED WITH BLUES CITY.
?
MUSICA.
IT'S A HYBRID. A WEIRD AMALGAMATION OF OUR HOME-TOWNS, BUT WHAT I DON'T GET IS *HOW?*
WHAT THE DEUCE IS GOING ON HERE?
I WISH I HAD SOME INSIGHT...

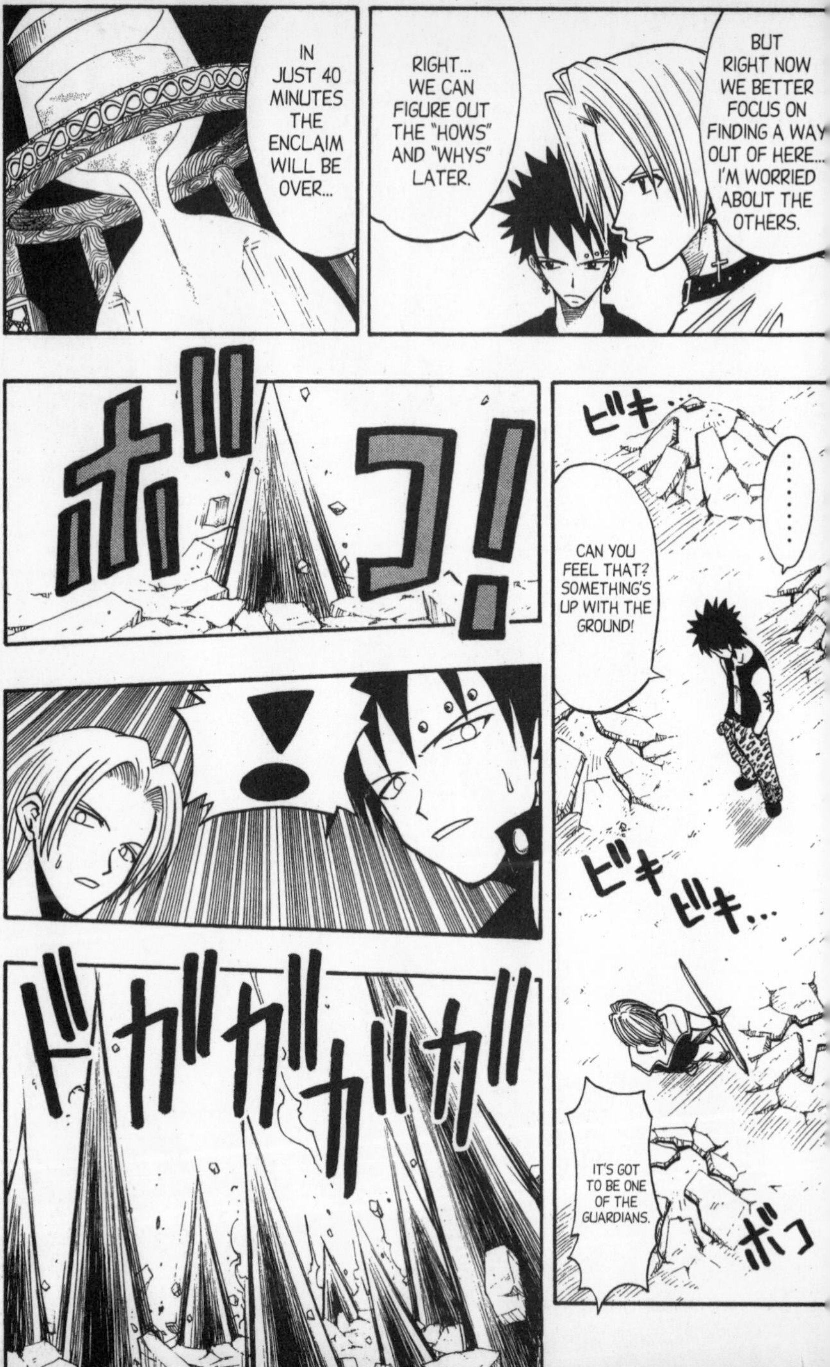
BUT RIGHT NOW WE BETTER FOCUS ON FINDING A WAY OUT OF HERE... I'M WORRIED ABOUT THE OTHERS.
RIGHT... WE CAN FIGURE OUT THE "HOWS" AND "WHYS" LATER.
IN JUST 40 MINUTES THE ENCLAIM WILL BE OVER...
ビキ...
....
CAN YOU FEEL THAT? SOMETHING'S UP WITH THE GROUND!
ビキ ビキ...
IT'S GOT TO BE ONE OF THE GUARDIANS.
ボコ
ボコ!
ドガガガガ

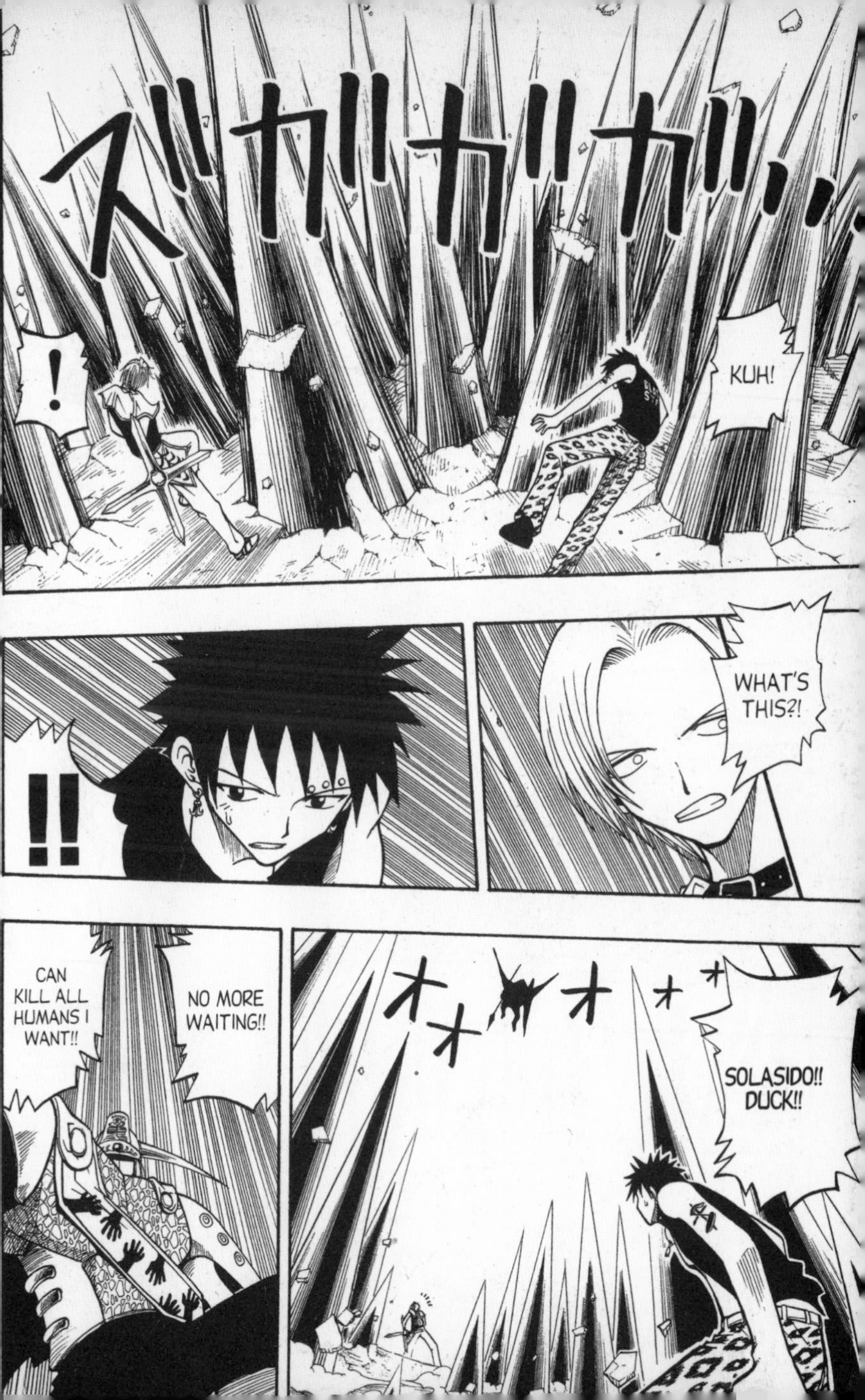

ズカカカ…
KUH!
!
WHAT'S THIS?!
!!
SOLASIDO!! DUCK!!
オオオオオ
NO MORE WAITING!!
CAN KILL ALL HUMANS I WANT!!

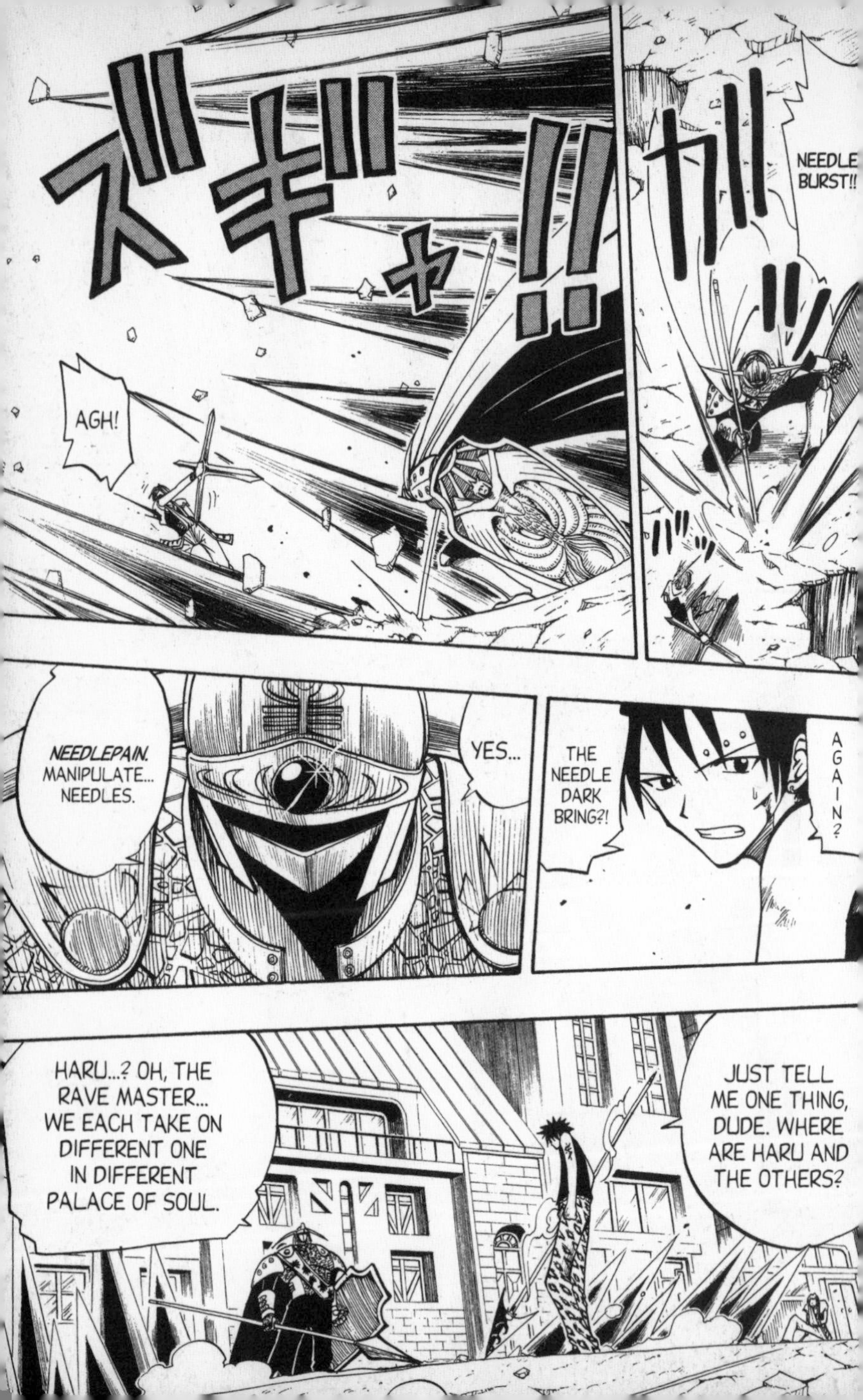
NEEDLE BURST!!
ズギャ!!
AGH!
AGAIN?
THE NEEDLE DARK BRING?!
YES...
NEEDLEPAIN. MANIPULATE... NEEDLES.
JUST TELL ME ONE THING, DUDE. WHERE ARE HARU AND THE OTHERS?
HARU...? OH, THE RAVE MASTER... WE EACH TAKE ON DIFFERENT ONE IN DIFFERENT PALACE OF SOUL.

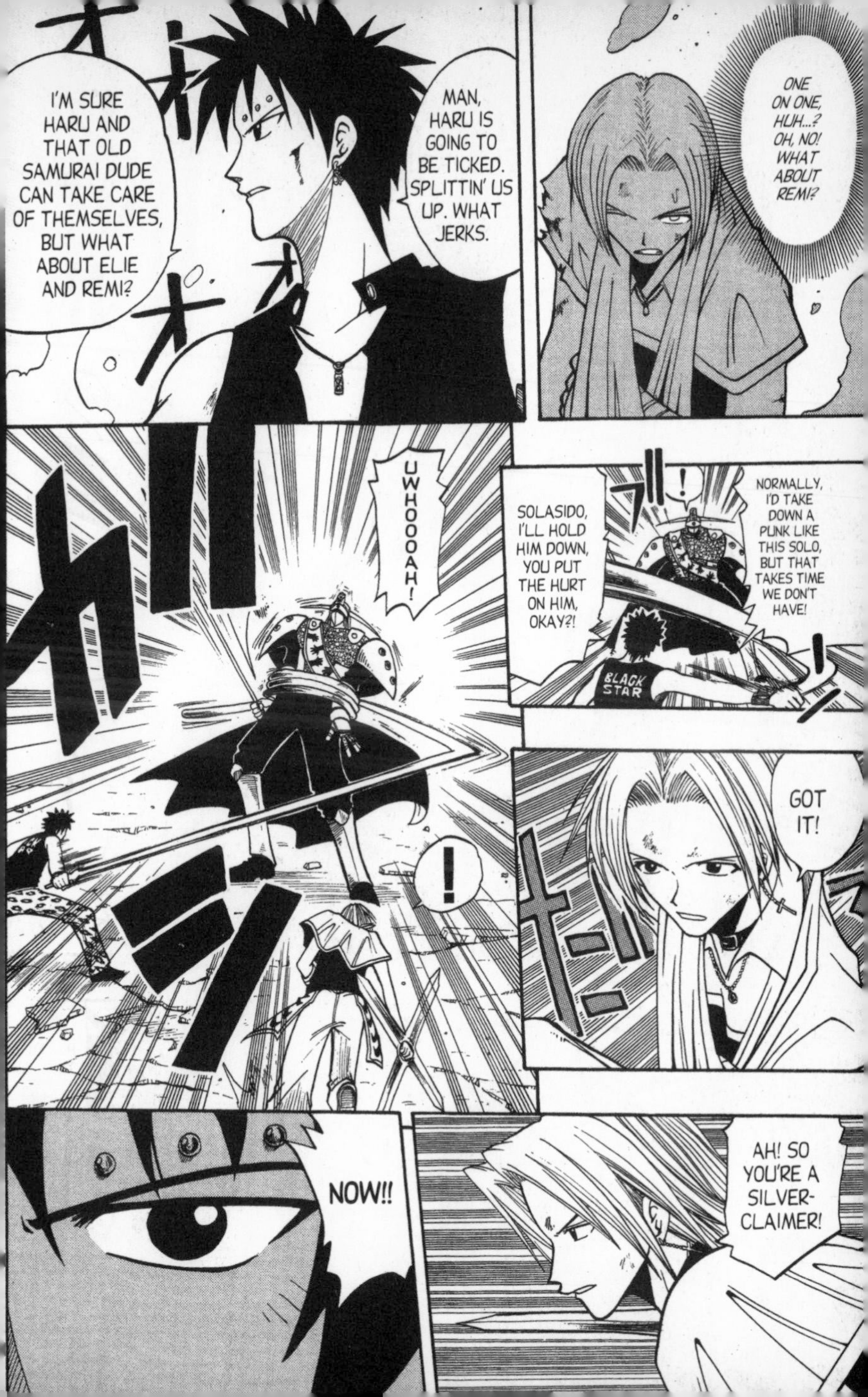

ONE ON ONE, HUH...? OH, NO! WHAT ABOUT REMI?
MAN, HARU IS GOING TO BE TICKED. SPLITTIN' US UP. WHAT JERKS.
I'M SURE HARU AND THAT OLD SAMURAI DUDE CAN TAKE CARE OF THEMSELVES, BUT WHAT ABOUT ELIE AND REMI?
NORMALLY, I'D TAKE DOWN A PUNK LIKE THIS SOLO, BUT THAT TAKES TIME WE DON'T HAVE!
!
SOLASIDO, I'LL HOLD HIM DOWN, YOU PUT THE HURT ON HIM, OKAY?!
BLACK STAR
GOT IT!
UWHOOOOAH!
!
AH! SO YOU'RE A SILVER-CLAIMER!
NOW!!

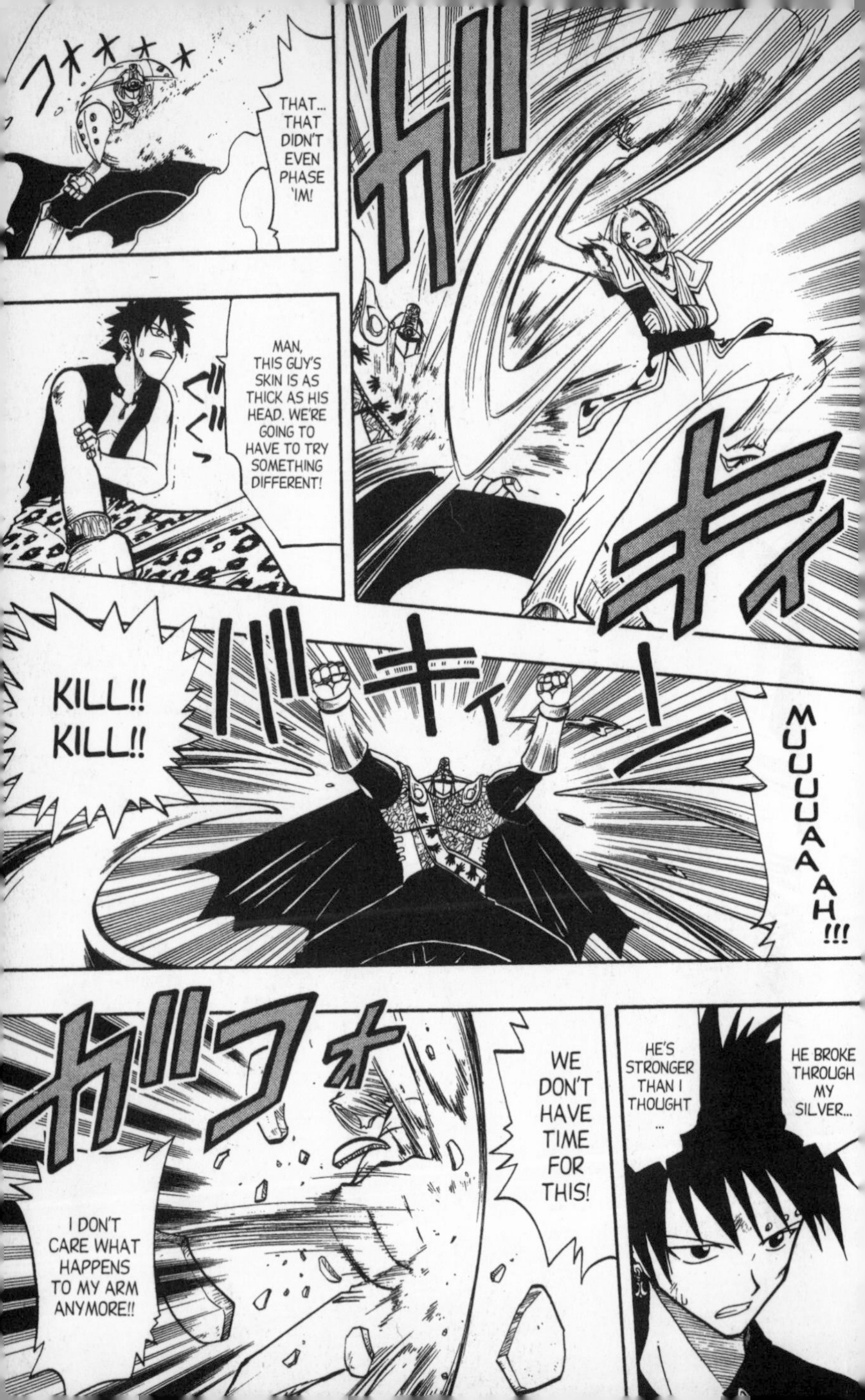
ガッ
キィ
THAT... THAT DIDN'T EVEN PHASE 'IM!
MAN, THIS GUY'S SKIN IS AS THICK AS HIS HEAD. WE'RE GOING TO HAVE TO TRY SOMETHING DIFFERENT!
MUUUUAAAH!!!
バキィーー
KILL!! KILL!!
HE BROKE THROUGH MY SILVER...
HE'S STRONGER THAN I THOUGHT...
WE DON'T HAVE TIME FOR THIS!
ガッフォ
I DON'T CARE WHAT HAPPENS TO MY ARM ANYMORE!!

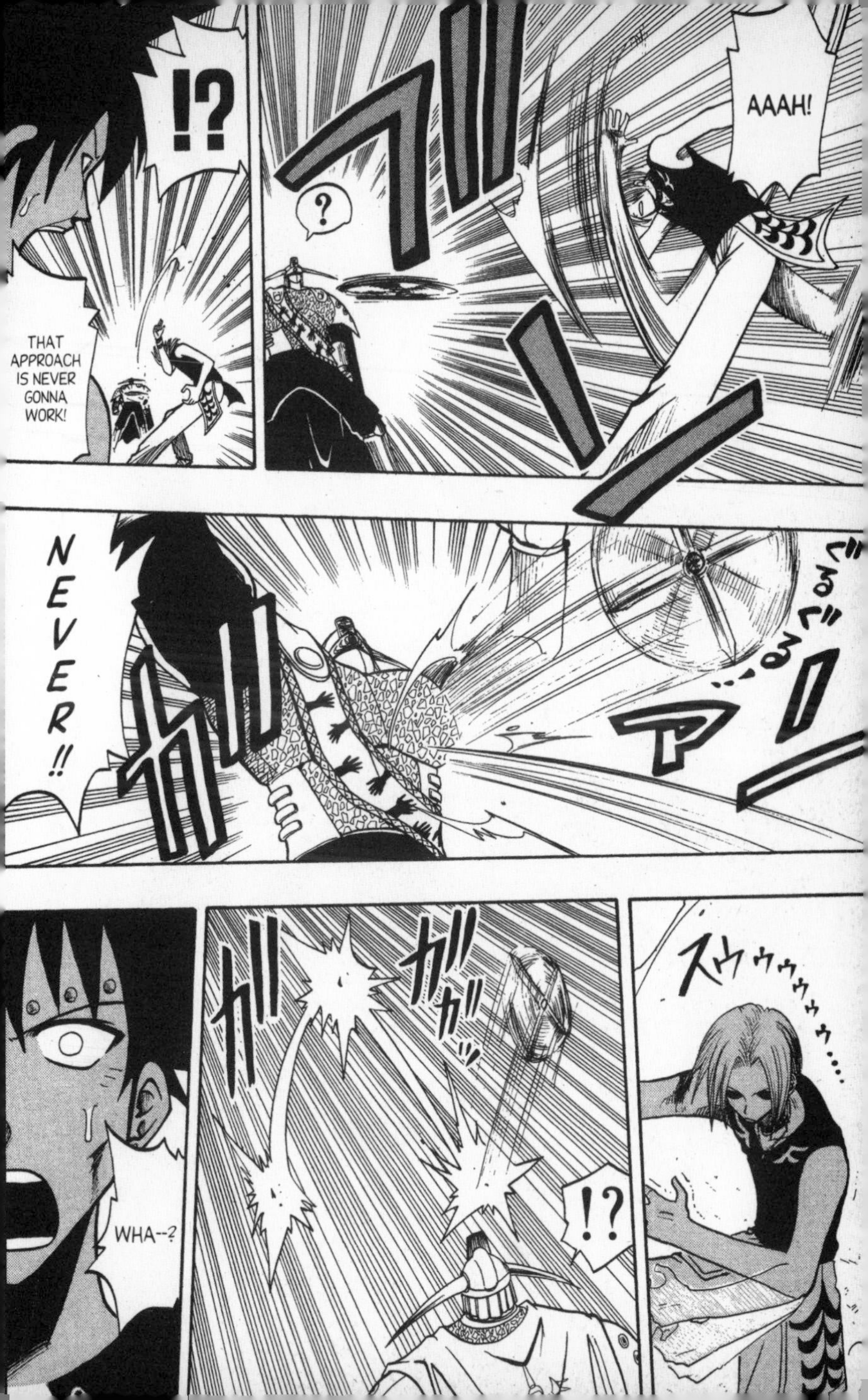
AAAH!
?
!?
THAT APPROACH IS NEVER GONNA WORK!
NEVER!!
!?
WHA--?

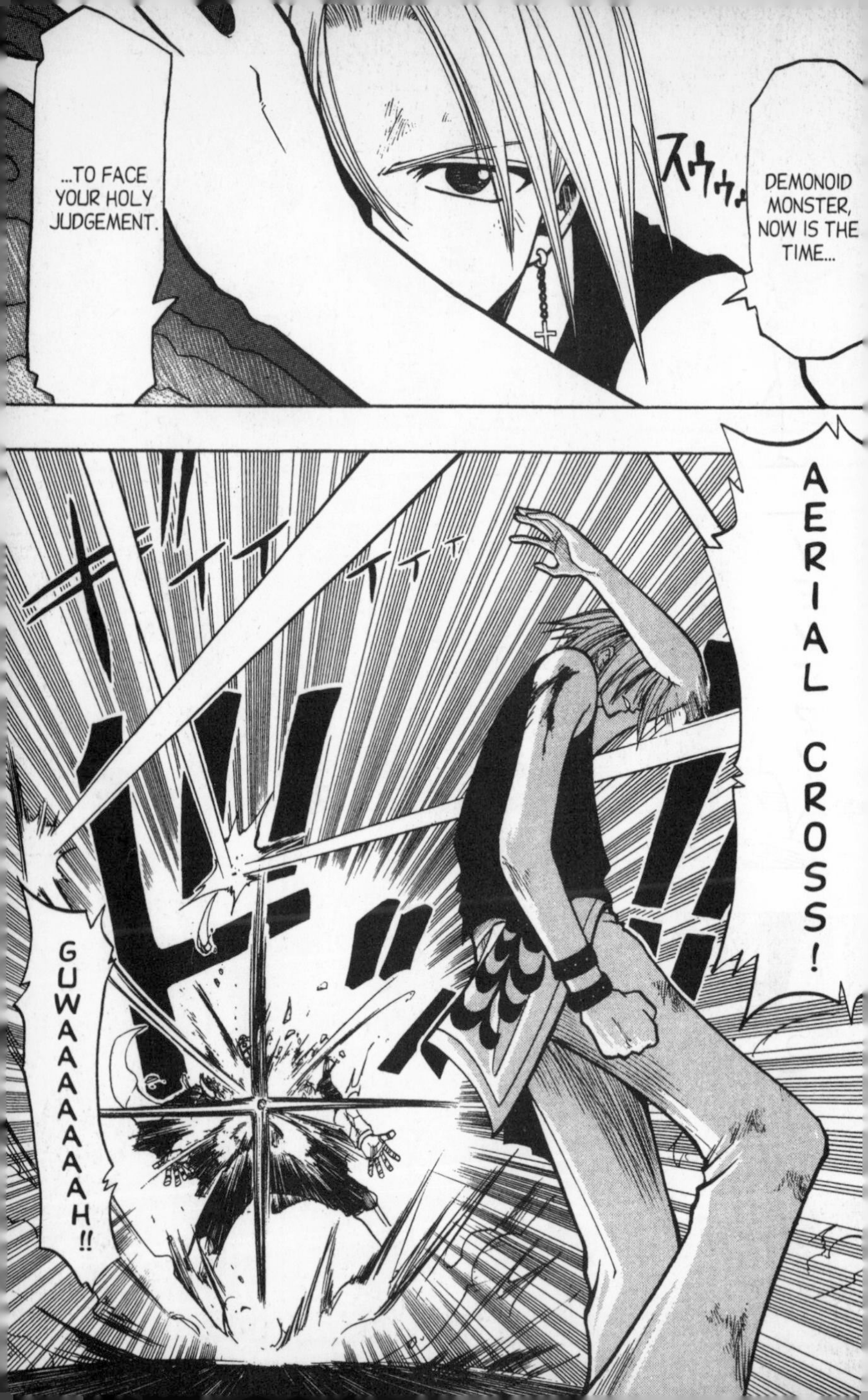
DEMONOID MONSTER, NOW IS THE TIME...
...TO FACE YOUR HOLY JUDGEMENT.
AERIAL CROSS!
GUWAAAAAAAAAH!!

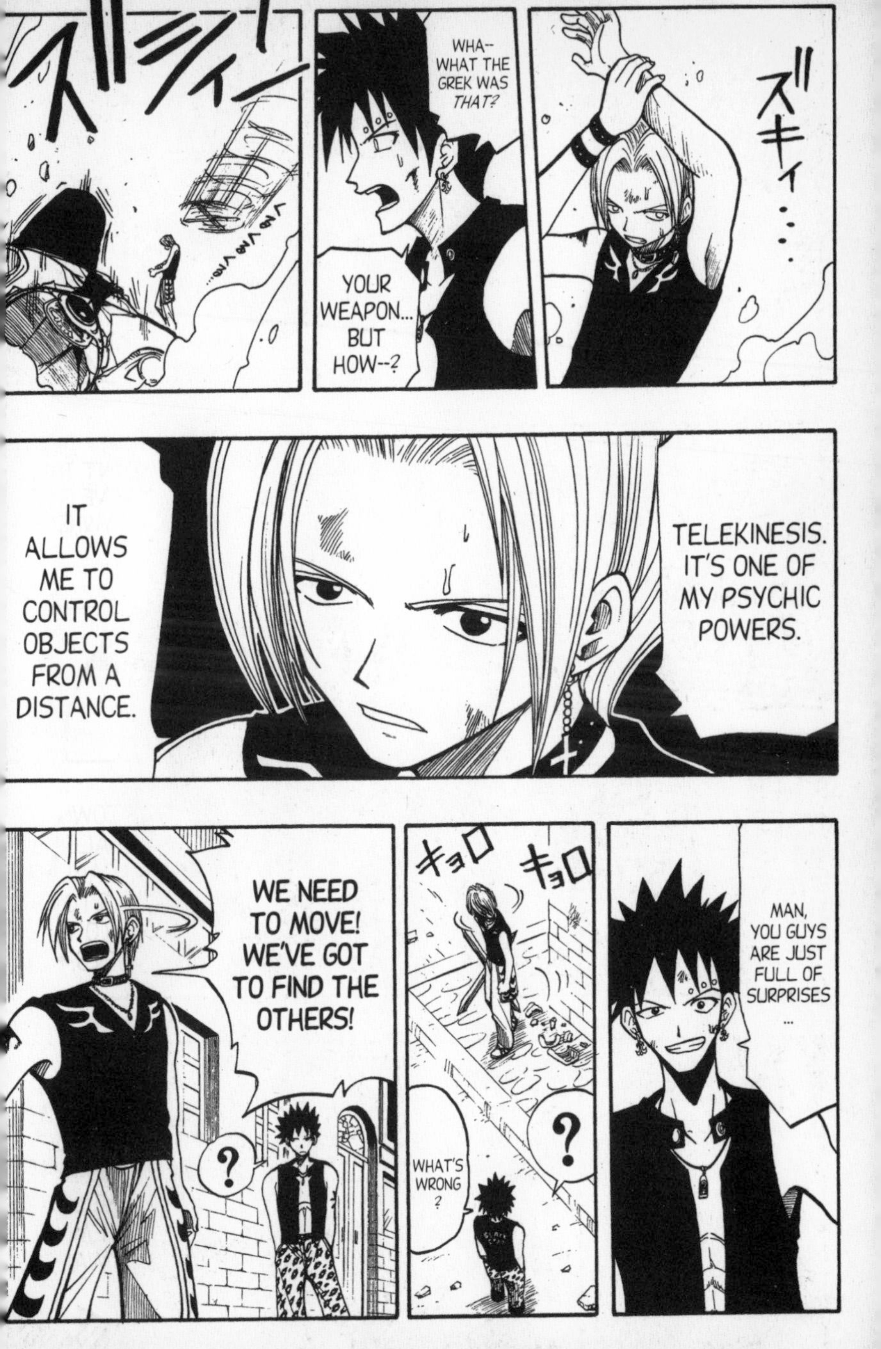
ズキィ・・・
WHA-- WHAT THE GREK WAS THAT?
YOUR WEAPON... BUT HOW--?
ズシィー!
TELEKINESIS. IT'S ONE OF MY PSYCHIC POWERS.
IT ALLOWS ME TO CONTROL OBJECTS FROM A DISTANCE.
MAN, YOU GUYS ARE JUST FULL OF SURPRISES ...
キョロ
キョロ
?
WHAT'S WRONG?
WE NEED TO MOVE! WE'VE GOT TO FIND THE OTHERS!
?

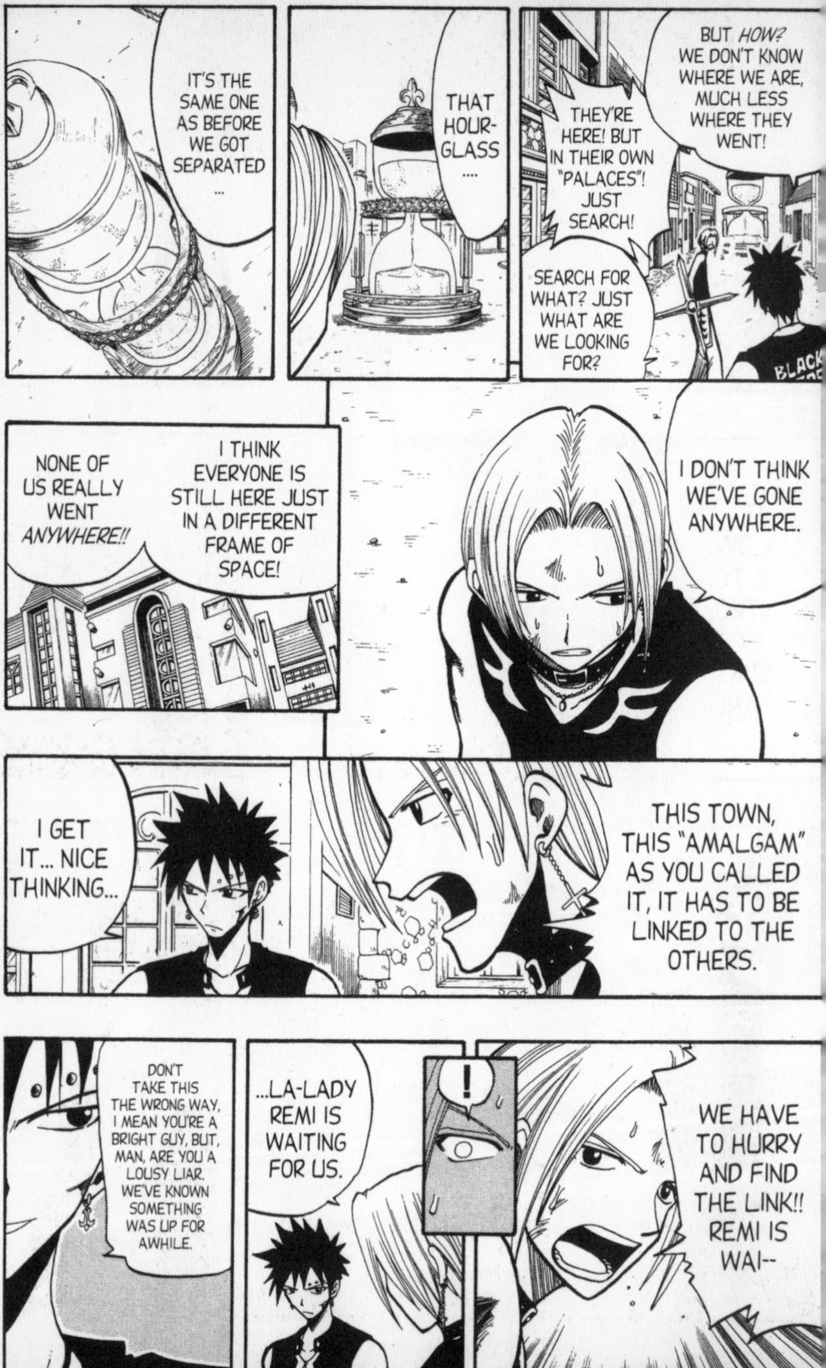
BUT *HOW?* WE DON'T KNOW WHERE WE ARE, MUCH LESS WHERE THEY WENT!
THEY'RE HERE! BUT IN THEIR OWN "PALACES"! JUST SEARCH!
SEARCH FOR WHAT? JUST WHAT ARE WE LOOKING FOR?
THAT HOUR-GLASS ....
IT'S THE SAME ONE AS BEFORE WE GOT SEPARATED ...
I DON'T THINK WE'VE GONE ANYWHERE.
I THINK EVERYONE IS STILL HERE JUST IN A DIFFERENT FRAME OF SPACE!
NONE OF US REALLY WENT *ANYWHERE!!*
THIS TOWN, THIS "AMALGAM" AS YOU CALLED IT, IT HAS TO BE LINKED TO THE OTHERS.
I GET IT... NICE THINKING...
WE HAVE TO HURRY AND FIND THE LINK!! REMI IS WAI--
!
...LA-LADY REMI IS WAITING FOR US.
DON'T TAKE THIS THE WRONG WAY, I MEAN YOU'RE A BRIGHT GUY, BUT, MAN, ARE YOU A LOUSY LIAR. WE'VE KNOWN SOMETHING WAS UP FOR AWHILE.

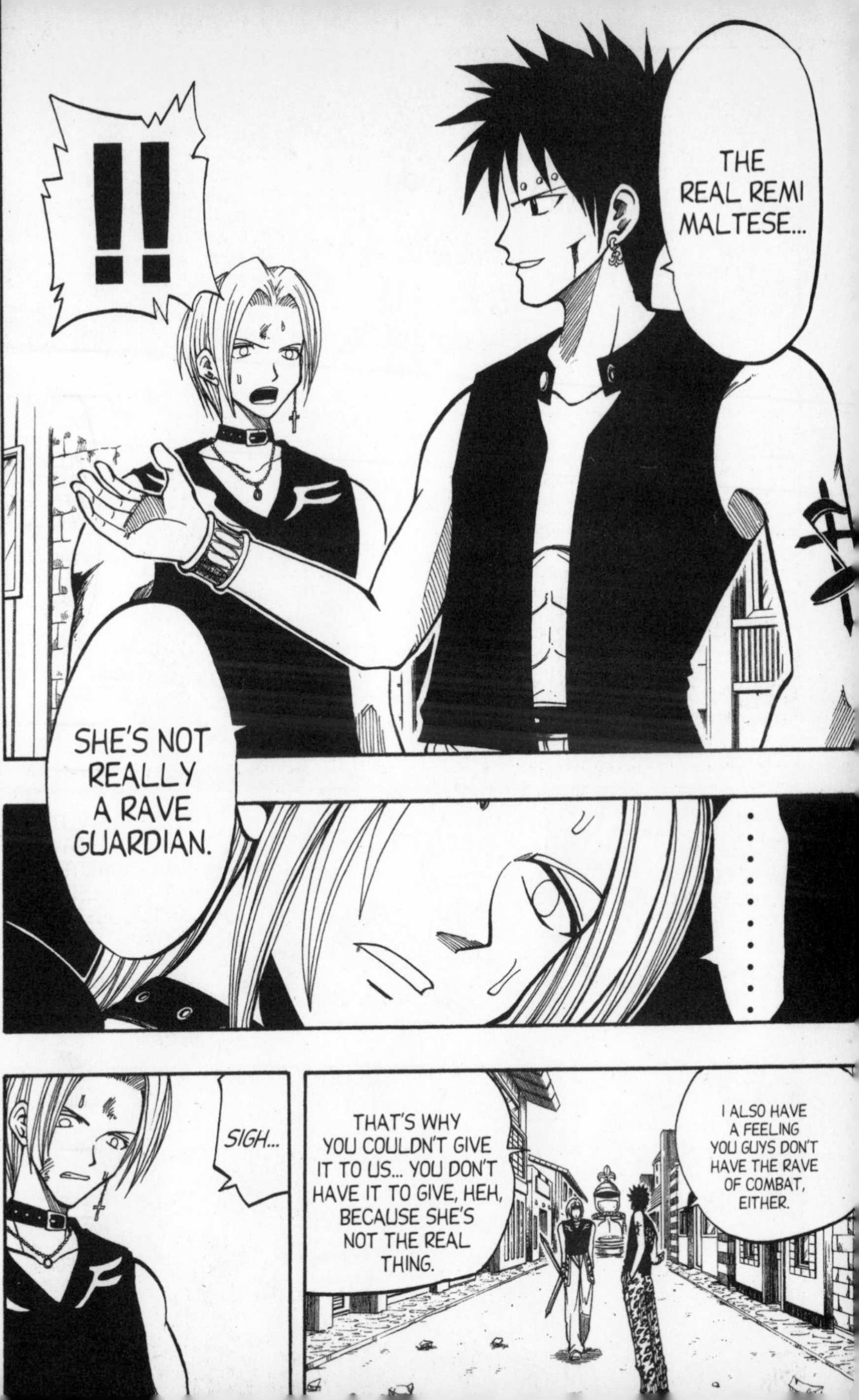
THE REAL REMI MALTESE...
!!
SHE'S NOT REALLY A RAVE GUARDIAN.
....
I ALSO HAVE A FEELING YOU GUYS DON'T HAVE THE RAVE OF COMBAT, EITHER.
THAT'S WHY YOU COULDN'T GIVE IT TO US... YOU DON'T HAVE IT TO GIVE, HEH, BECAUSE SHE'S NOT THE REAL THING.
SIGH...

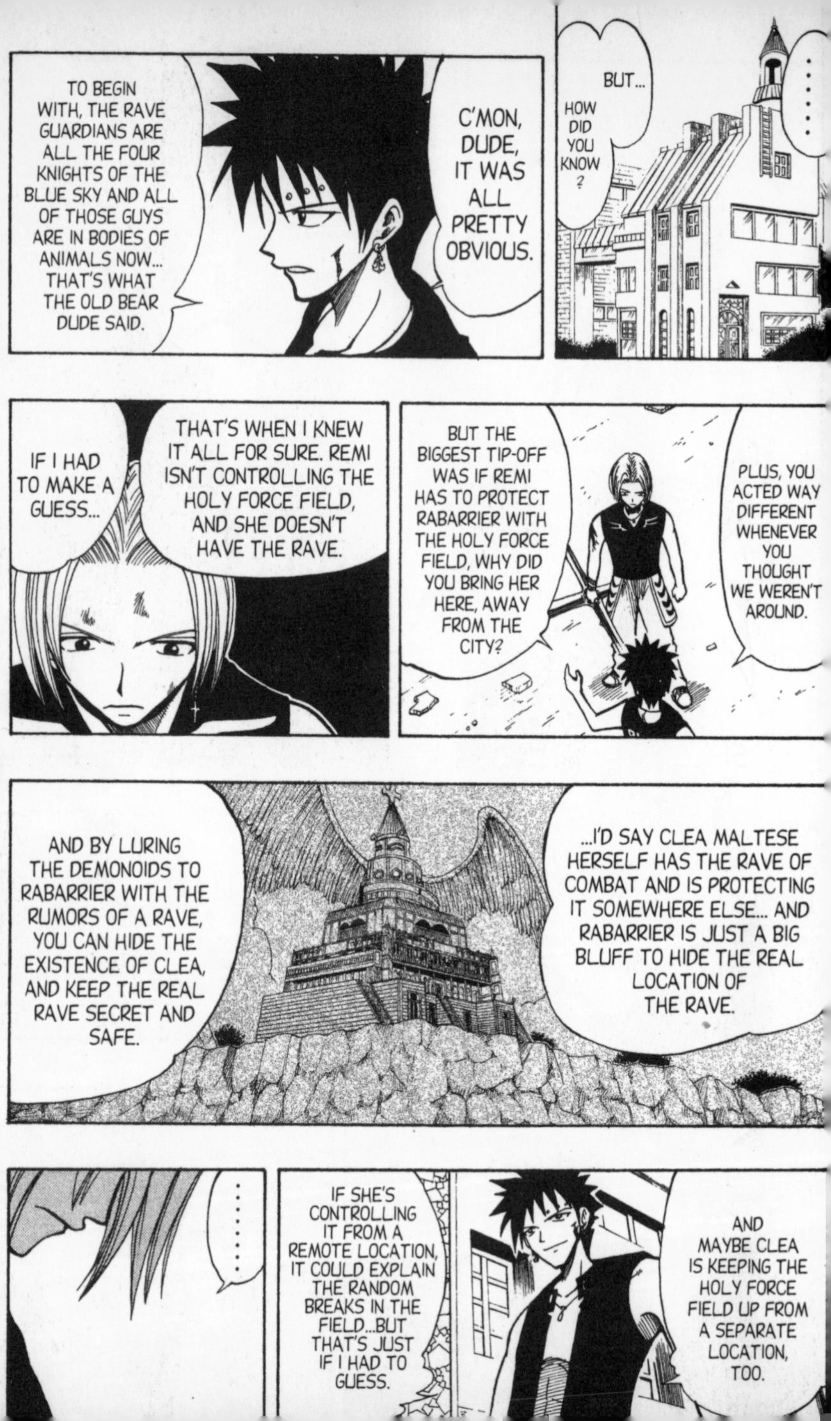
......
BUT...
HOW DID YOU KNOW?
C'MON, DUDE, IT WAS ALL PRETTY OBVIOUS.
TO BEGIN WITH, THE RAVE GUARDIANS ARE ALL THE FOUR KNIGHTS OF THE BLUE SKY AND ALL OF THOSE GUYS ARE IN BODIES OF ANIMALS NOW... THAT'S WHAT THE OLD BEAR DUDE SAID.
PLUS, YOU ACTED WAY DIFFERENT WHENEVER YOU THOUGHT WE WEREN'T AROUND.
BUT THE BIGGEST TIP-OFF WAS IF REMI HAS TO PROTECT RABARRIER WITH THE HOLY FORCE FIELD, WHY DID YOU BRING HER HERE, AWAY FROM THE CITY?
THAT'S WHEN I KNEW IT ALL FOR SURE. REMI ISN'T CONTROLLING THE HOLY FORCE FIELD, AND SHE DOESN'T HAVE THE RAVE.
IF I HAD TO MAKE A GUESS...
...I'D SAY CLEA MALTESE HERSELF HAS THE RAVE OF COMBAT AND IS PROTECTING IT SOMEWHERE ELSE... AND RABARRIER IS JUST A BIG BLUFF TO HIDE THE REAL LOCATION OF THE RAVE.
AND BY LURING THE DEMONOIDS TO RABARRIER WITH THE RUMORS OF A RAVE, YOU CAN HIDE THE EXISTENCE OF CLEA, AND KEEP THE REAL RAVE SECRET AND SAFE.
AND MAYBE CLEA IS KEEPING THE HOLY FORCE FIELD UP FROM A SEPARATE LOCATION, TOO.
IF SHE'S CONTROLLING IT FROM A REMOTE LOCATION, IT COULD EXPLAIN THE RANDOM BREAKS IN THE FIELD...BUT THAT'S JUST IF I HAD TO GUESS.
......

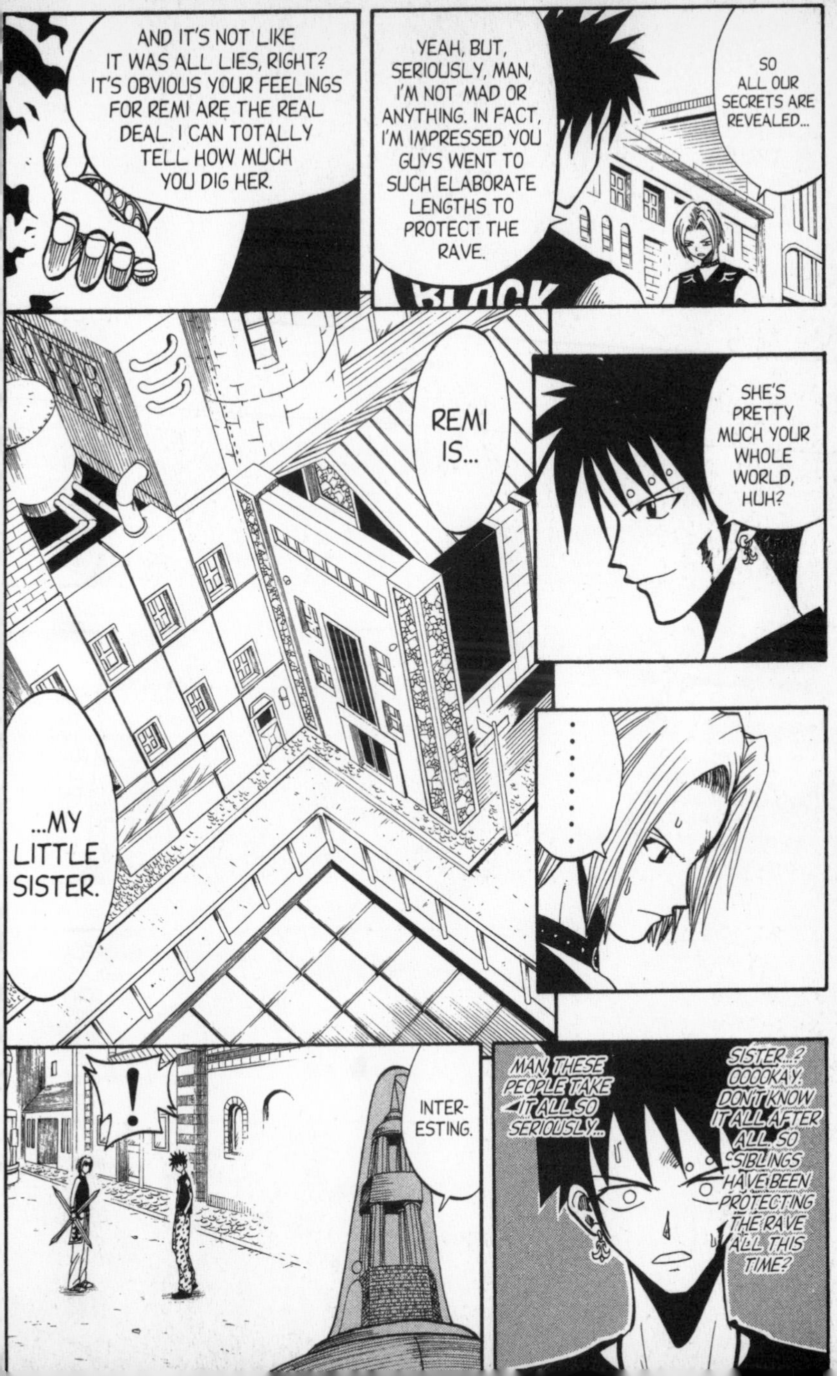
SO ALL OUR SECRETS ARE REVEALED...
YEAH, BUT, SERIOUSLY, MAN, I'M NOT MAD OR ANYTHING. IN FACT, I'M IMPRESSED YOU GUYS WENT TO SUCH ELABORATE LENGTHS TO PROTECT THE RAVE.
AND IT'S NOT LIKE IT WAS ALL LIES, RIGHT? IT'S OBVIOUS YOUR FEELINGS FOR REMI ARE THE REAL DEAL. I CAN TOTALLY TELL HOW MUCH YOU DIG HER.
SHE'S PRETTY MUCH YOUR WHOLE WORLD, HUH?
....
REMI IS...
...MY LITTLE SISTER.
SISTER...? OOOOKAY. DON'T KNOW IT ALL AFTER ALL. SO SIBLINGS HAVE BEEN PROTECTING THE RAVE ALL THIS TIME?
MAN, THESE PEOPLE TAKE IT ALL SO SERIOUSLY...
!
INTER-ESTING.

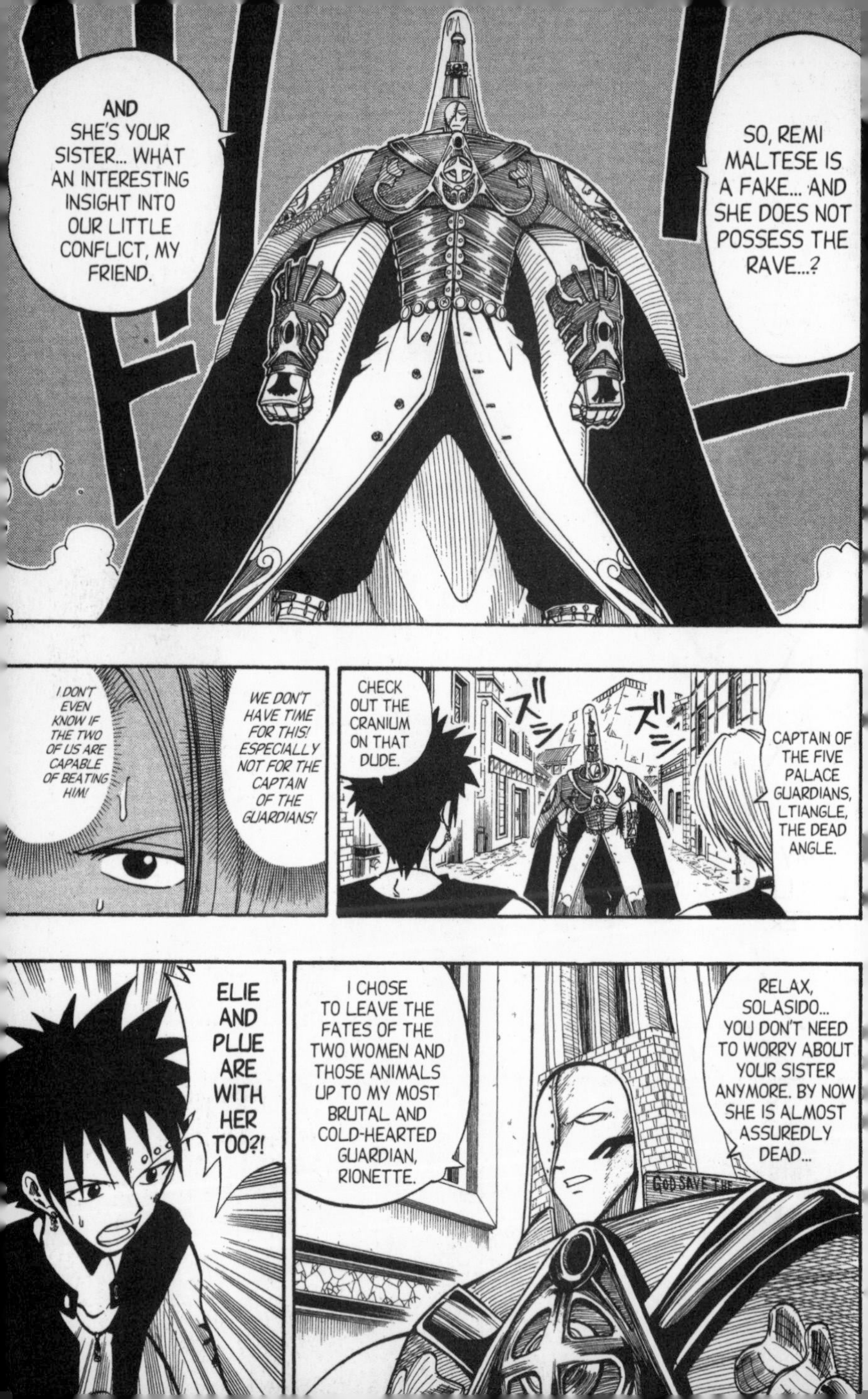
SO, REMI MALTESE IS A FAKE... AND SHE DOES NOT POSSESS THE RAVE...?
AND SHE'S YOUR SISTER... WHAT AN INTERESTING INSIGHT INTO OUR LITTLE CONFLICT, MY FRIEND.
CAPTAIN OF THE FIVE PALACE GUARDIANS, LTIANGLE, THE DEAD ANGLE.
CHECK OUT THE CRANIUM ON THAT DUDE.
WE DON'T HAVE TIME FOR THIS! ESPECIALLY NOT FOR THE CAPTAIN OF THE GUARDIANS!
I DON'T EVEN KNOW IF THE TWO OF US ARE CAPABLE OF BEATING HIM!
RELAX, SOLASIDO... YOU DON'T NEED TO WORRY ABOUT YOUR SISTER ANYMORE. BY NOW SHE IS ALMOST ASSUREDLY DEAD...
I CHOSE TO LEAVE THE FATES OF THE TWO WOMEN AND THOSE ANIMALS UP TO MY MOST BRUTAL AND COLD-HEARTED GUARDIAN, RIONETTE.
GOD SAVE THE
ELIE AND PLUE ARE WITH HER TOO?!

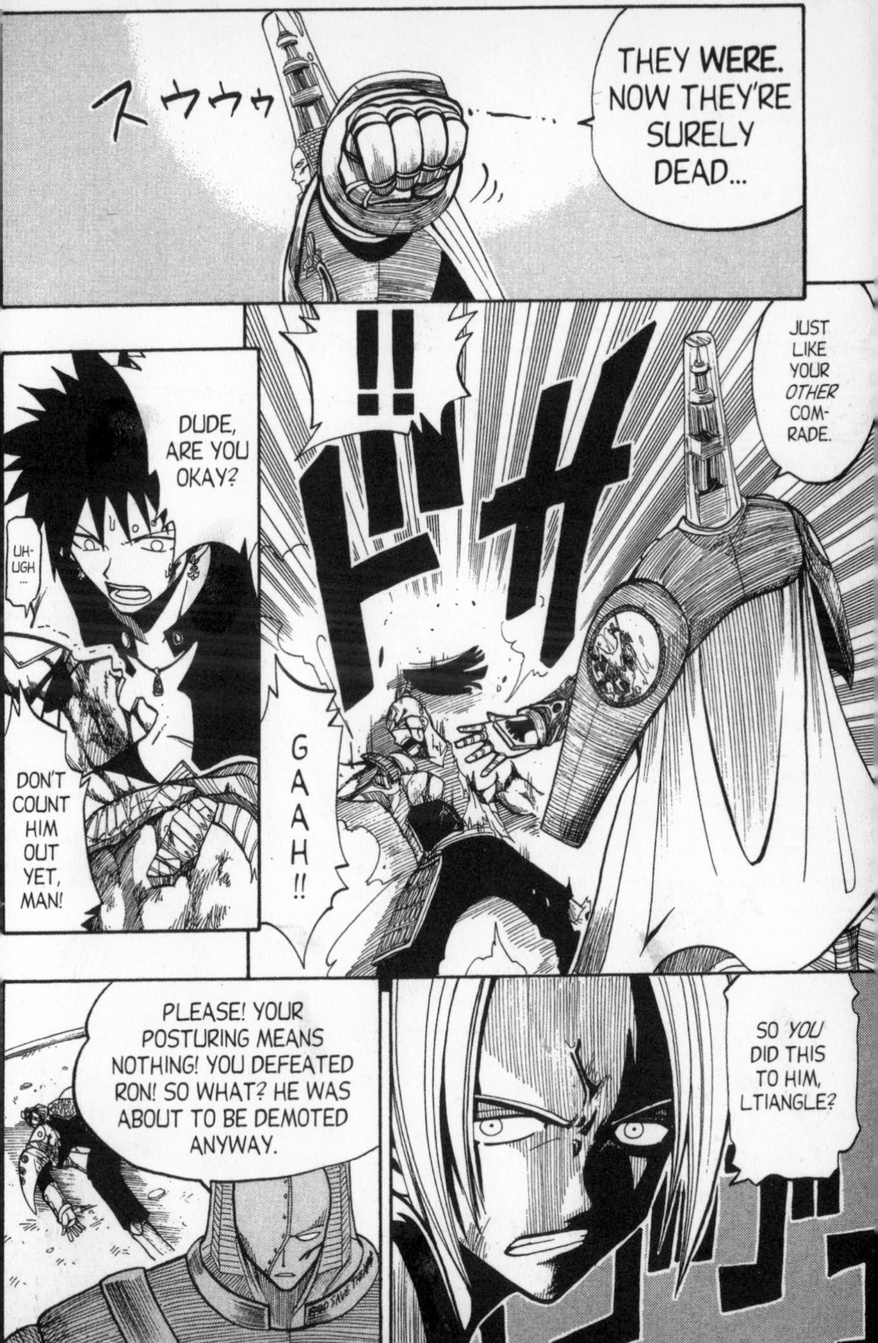
THEY WERE. NOW THEY'RE SURELY DEAD...
スウウゥ
JUST LIKE YOUR OTHER COMRADE.
!!
ドサ
GAAAH!!
DUDE, ARE YOU OKAY?
UH-UGH...
DON'T COUNT HIM OUT YET, MAN!
SO YOU DID THIS TO HIM, LTIANGLE?
PLEASE! YOUR POSTURING MEANS NOTHING! YOU DEFEATED RON! SO WHAT? HE WAS ABOUT TO BE DEMOTED ANYWAY.

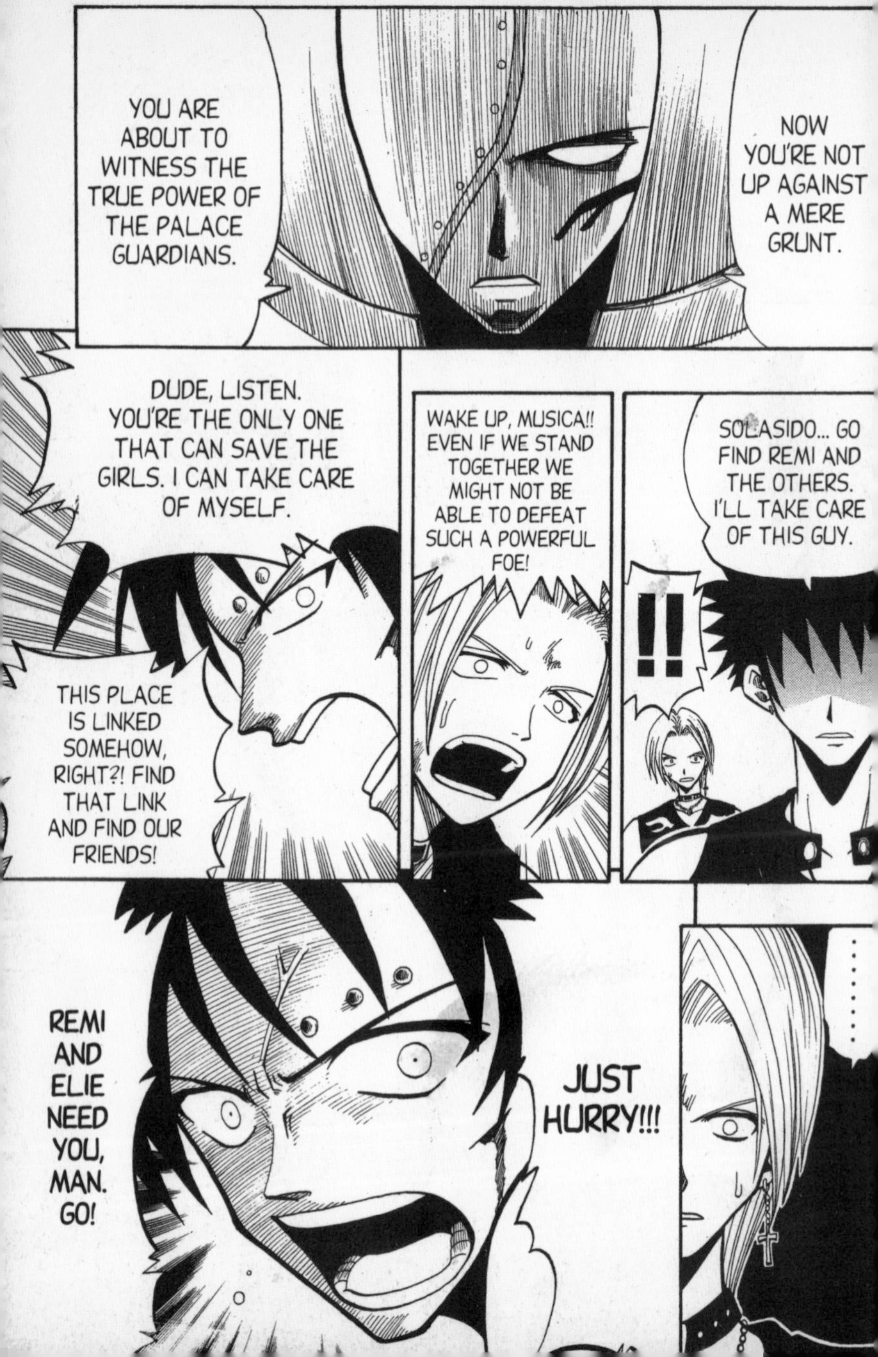
NOW YOU'RE NOT UP AGAINST A MERE GRUNT.
YOU ARE ABOUT TO WITNESS THE TRUE POWER OF THE PALACE GUARDIANS.
SOLASIDO... GO FIND REMI AND THE OTHERS. I'LL TAKE CARE OF THIS GUY.
!!
WAKE UP, MUSICA!! EVEN IF WE STAND TOGETHER WE MIGHT NOT BE ABLE TO DEFEAT SUCH A POWERFUL FOE!
DUDE, LISTEN. YOU'RE THE ONLY ONE THAT CAN SAVE THE GIRLS. I CAN TAKE CARE OF MYSELF.
THIS PLACE IS LINKED SOMEHOW, RIGHT?! FIND THAT LINK AND FIND OUR FRIENDS!
......
REMI AND ELIE NEED YOU, MAN. GO!
JUST HURRY!!!

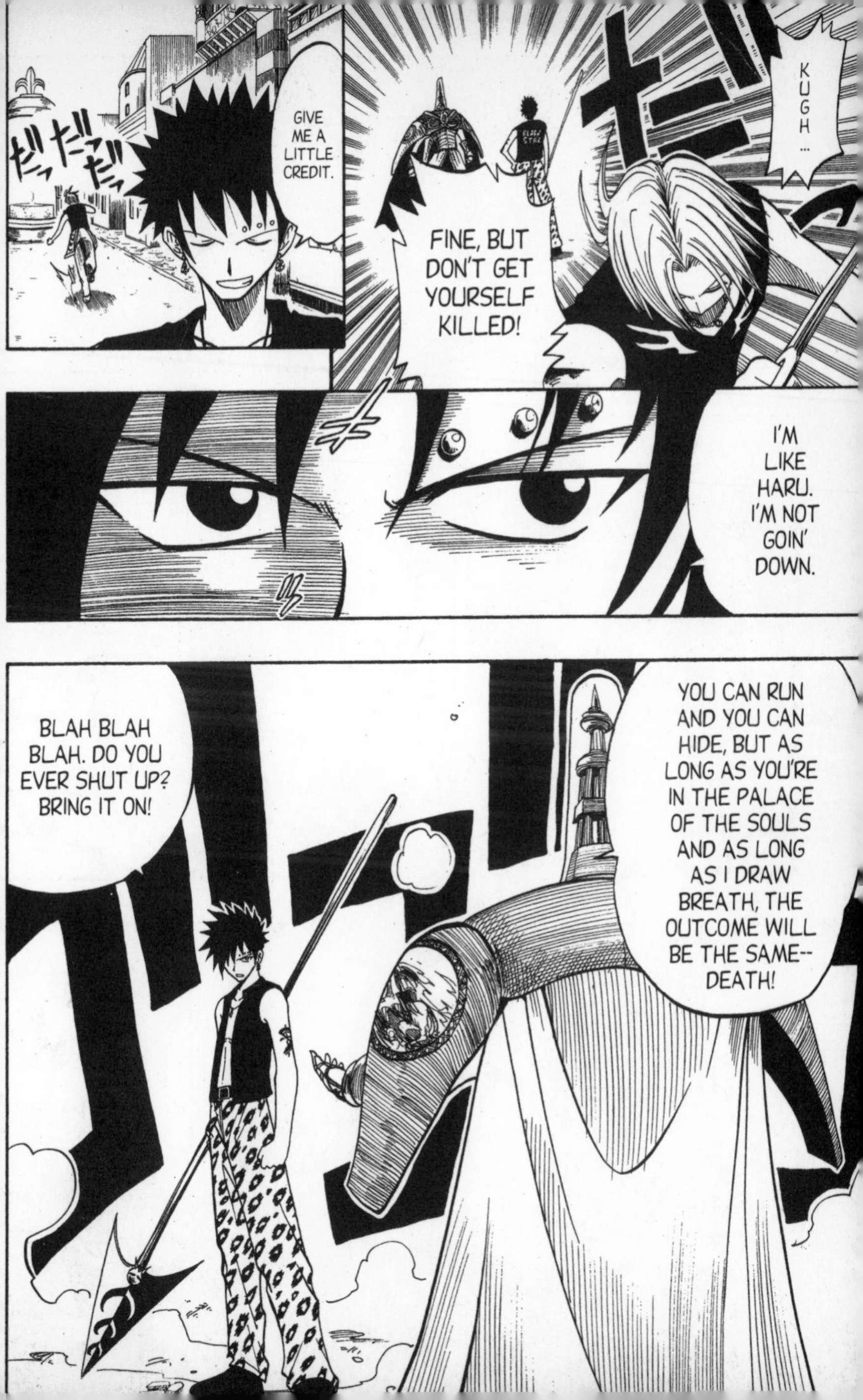
KUGH...
FINE, BUT DON'T GET YOURSELF KILLED!
GIVE ME A LITTLE CREDIT.
I'M LIKE HARU. I'M NOT GOIN' DOWN.
YOU CAN RUN AND YOU CAN HIDE, BUT AS LONG AS YOU'RE IN THE PALACE OF THE SOULS AND AS LONG AS I DRAW BREATH, THE OUTCOME WILL BE THE SAME--DEATH!
BLAH BLAH BLAH. DO YOU EVER SHUT UP? BRING IT ON!

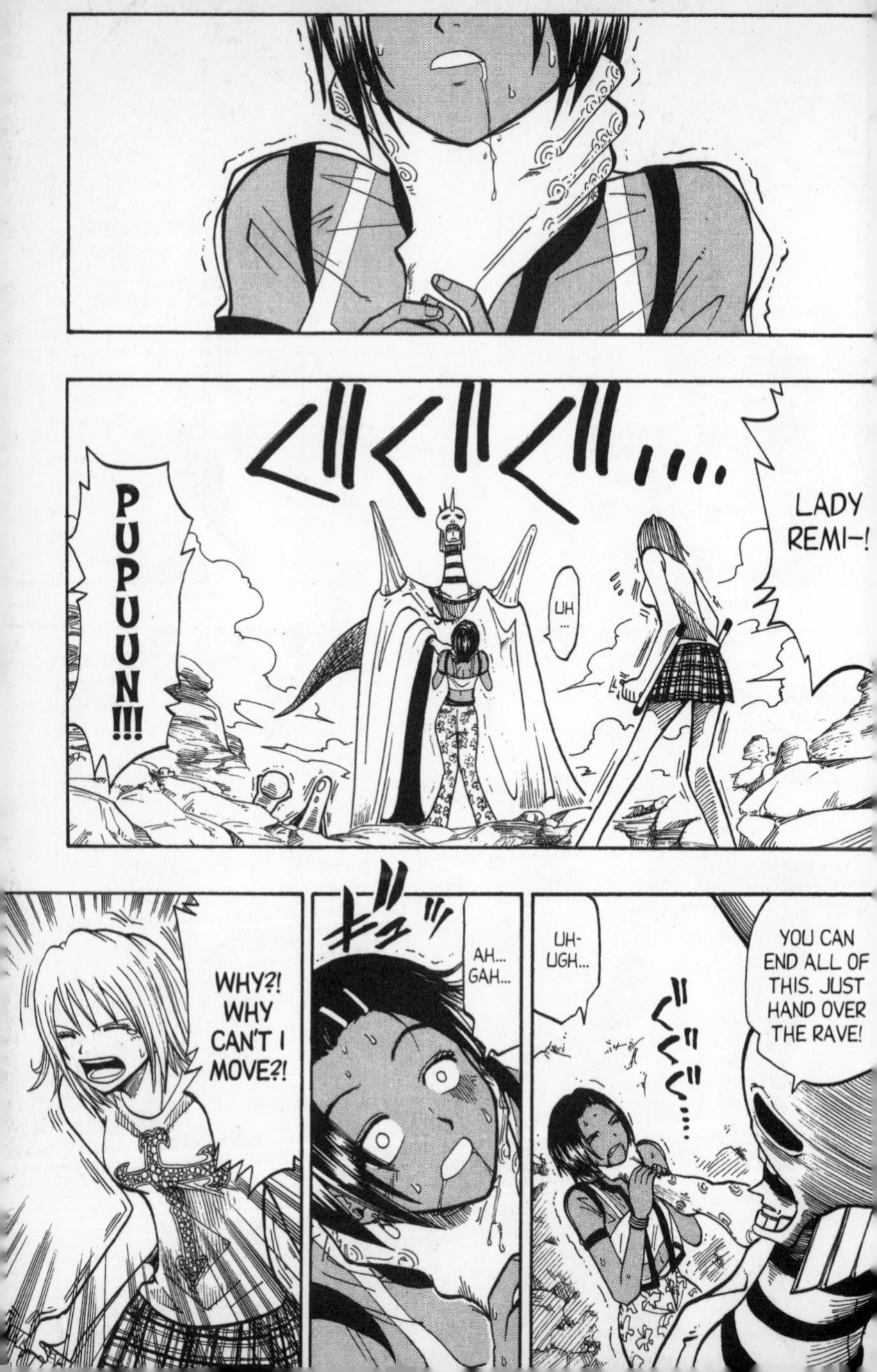
LADY REMI–!
UH ...
PUPUUUN!!!
YOU CAN END ALL OF THIS. JUST HAND OVER THE RAVE!
UH-UGH...
AH... GAH...
WHY?! WHY CAN'T I MOVE?!

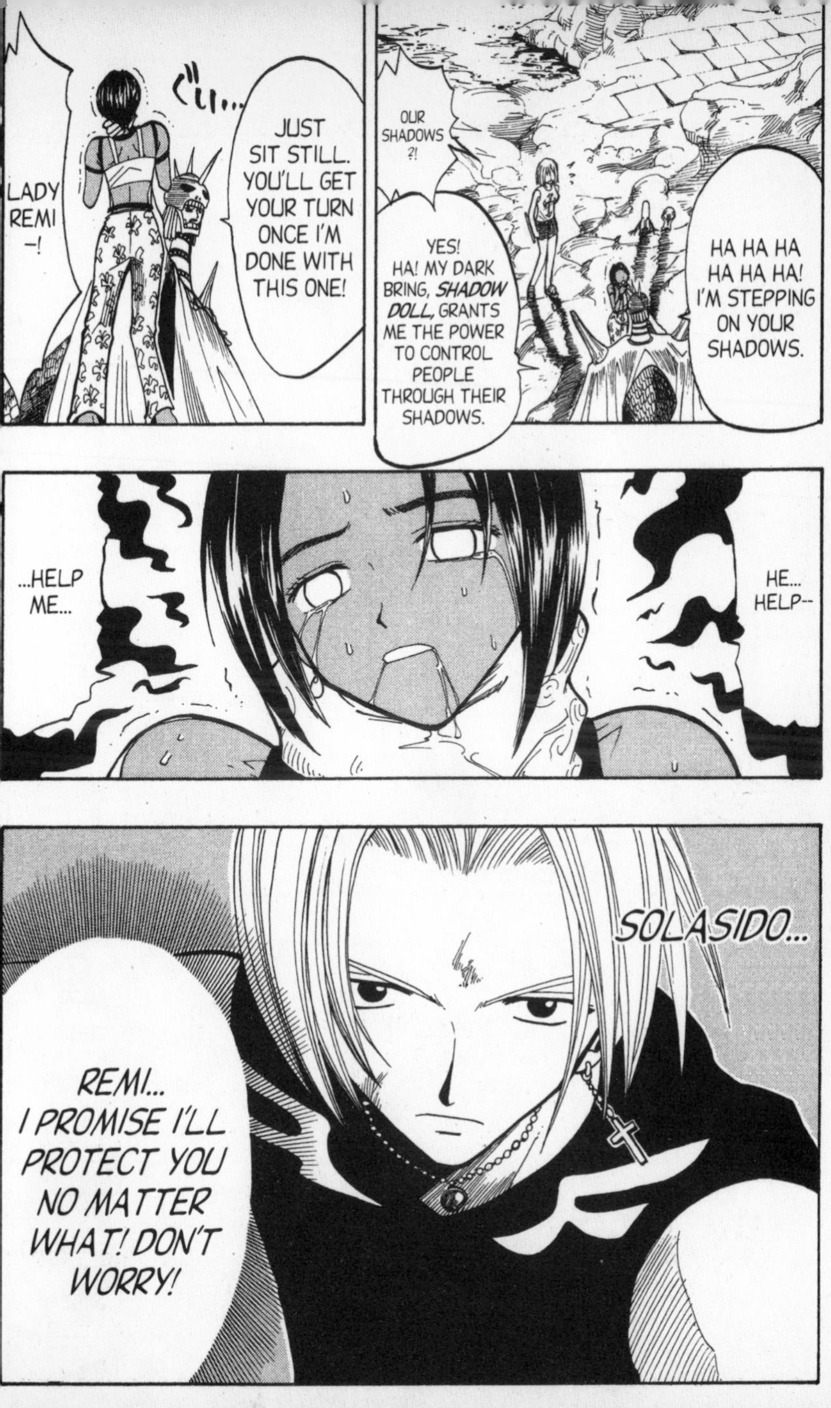
OUR SHADOWS ?!
HA HA HA HA HA HA! I'M STEPPING ON YOUR SHADOWS.
YES! HA! MY DARK BRING, SHADOW DOLL, GRANTS ME THE POWER TO CONTROL PEOPLE THROUGH THEIR SHADOWS.
JUST SIT STILL. YOU'LL GET YOUR TURN ONCE I'M DONE WITH THIS ONE!
ぐい…
LADY REMI —!
HE... HELP--
...HELP ME...
SOLASIDO...
REMI... I PROMISE I'LL PROTECT YOU NO MATTER WHAT! DON'T WORRY!

RAVE MASTER

◎ GALE GLORY

GALE SYMPHONIA GLORY VI, HEIR OF SYMPHONIA, COUNTRY OF RAVE. FATHER TO HARU.

VS

EXACTLY WHAT HAPPENED IN THE PAST BETWEEN THESE TWO?

◎ KING

GALE RAREGROOVE, HEIR OF RAREGROOVE EMPIRE. CURRENTLY SUPREME COMMANDER OF DEMON CARD. CARRIES FIVE DARK BRINGS.

| DIN TOWER | HURRY AND COME HELP ME! | WANTS TO CATCH UP TO DAD AND JOIN HIM! | 40 MINUTES LEFT UNTIL THE ULTIMATE DARK BRING IS COMPLETE! |
| PALACE OF SOULS | | | |

◎ RACAS

WHERE IS HE?

◎ HARU

IN HIS WAY →

VS

← WANTS A 1-ON-1 FIGHT

◎ LET

◎ SOLASIDO

◎ MUSICA

VS

◎ LTIANGLE
CAPTAIN

◎ RON--DOWN

◎ FUA--DOWN

HEADS TO HELP (PSYCHICALLY LINKED?)

?

◎ CLEA MALTESE
ONE OF FOUR KNIGHTS OF THE BLUE SKY. HAS RAVE?

↕ SIBLINGS

◎ REMI
BLUFFED TO HIDE THE REAL MALTESE.

◎ ELIE
HAS FAINT RECOLLECTION OF DIN TOWER.

◎ PLUE

◎ GRIFF

VS

◎ RIONETTE

RAVE: 60 ✚ THOUGHTS OF TOMORROW

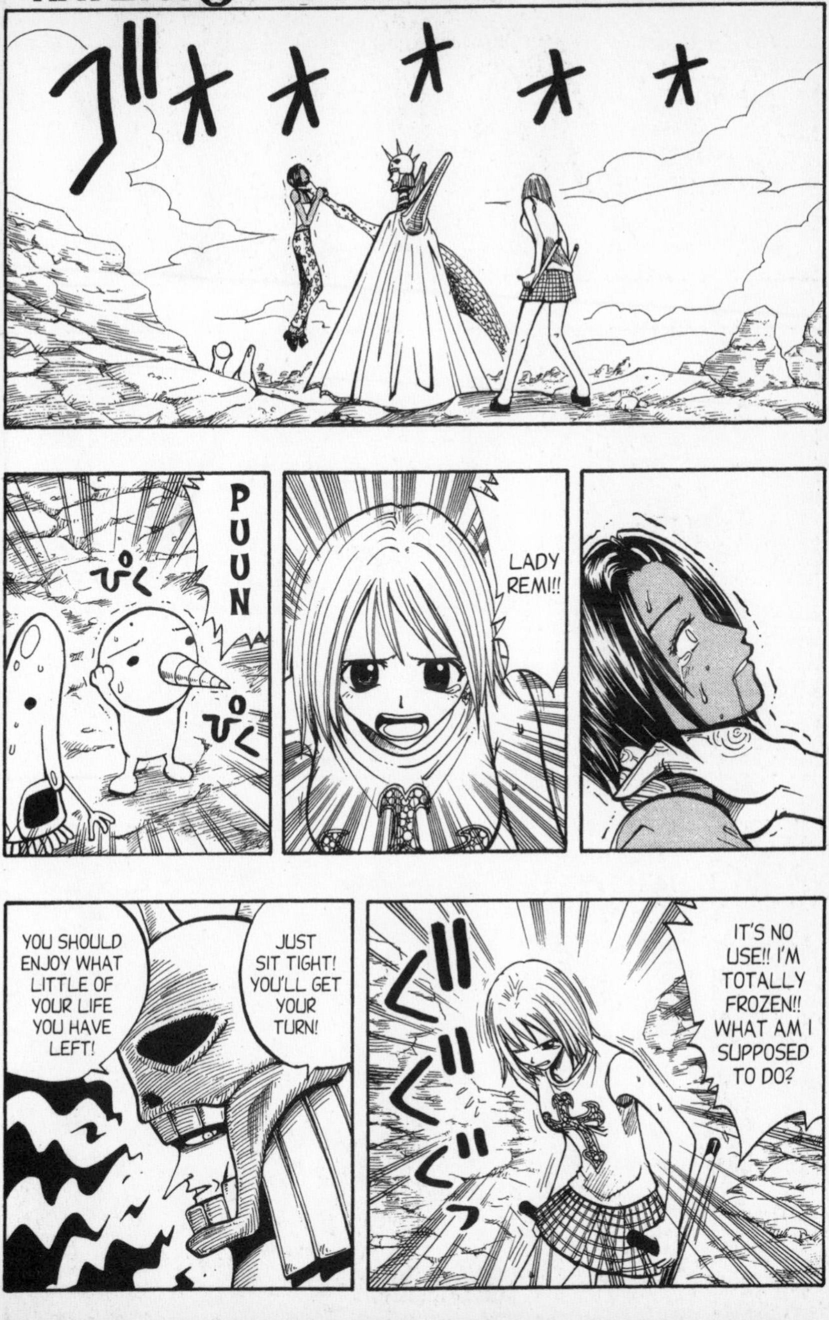
ゴォォォォォ
LADY REMI!!
PUUN
ぴく
ぴく
IT'S NO USE!! I'M TOTALLY FROZEN!! WHAT AM I SUPPOSED TO DO?
ぐぐぐぐっ
JUST SIT TIGHT! YOU'LL GET YOUR TURN!
YOU SHOULD ENJOY WHAT LITTLE OF YOUR LIFE YOU HAVE LEFT!

THIS IS IT...I'M SORRY I LIED TO EVERYONE... EVEN IF IT WAS TO PROTECT THE RAVE...

I'M SO SORRY...I CAN'T GO ON ANY LONGER...

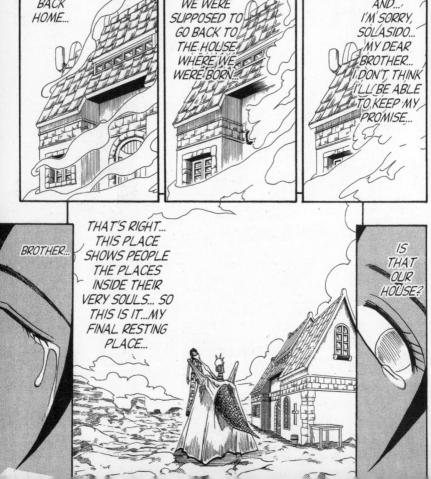

BACK HOME...

WE WERE SUPPOSED TO GO BACK TO THE HOUSE WHERE WE WERE BORN...

AND... I'M SORRY, SOLASIDO... MY DEAR BROTHER... I DON'T THINK I'LL BE ABLE TO KEEP MY PROMISE...

BROTHER...

THAT'S RIGHT... THIS PLACE SHOWS PEOPLE THE PLACES INSIDE THEIR VERY SOULS... SO THIS IS IT...MY FINAL RESTING PLACE...

IS THAT OUR HOUSE?

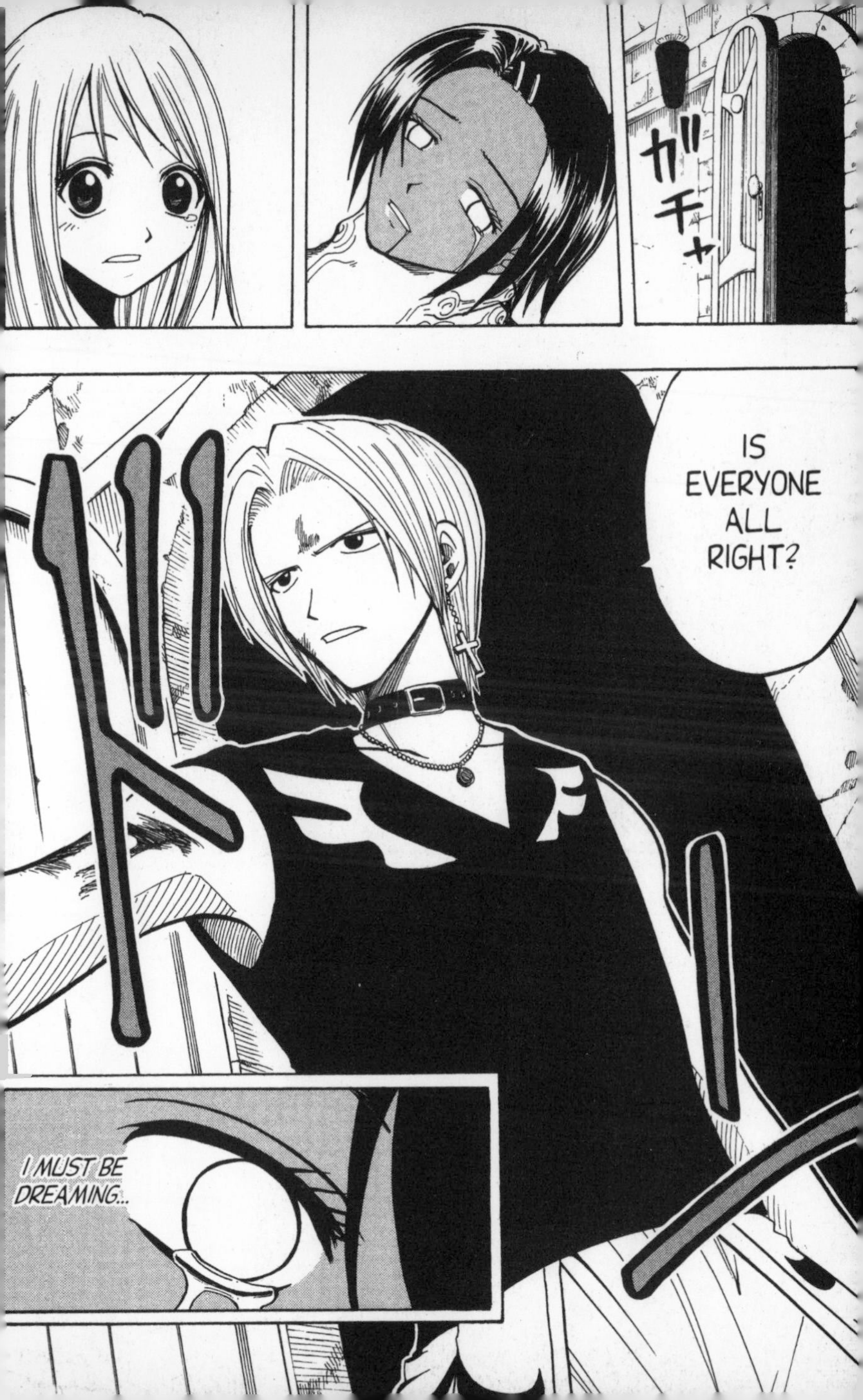

ガチャ
IS EVERYONE ALL RIGHT?
I MUST BE DREAMING...

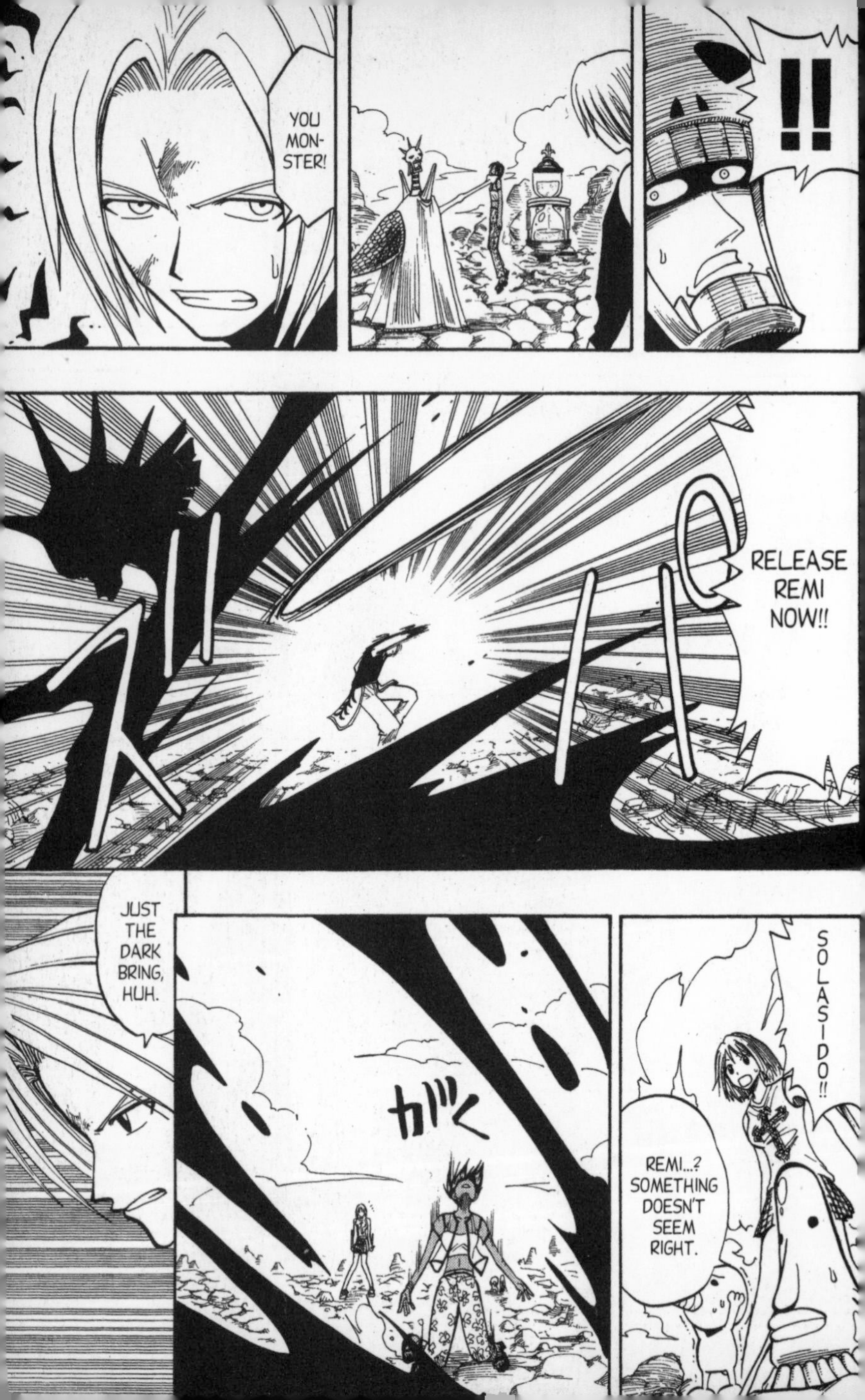
!!
YOU MONSTER!
RELEASE REMI NOW!!
SOLASIDO!!
REMI...? SOMETHING DOESN'T SEEM RIGHT.
ガく
JUST THE DARK BRING, HUH.

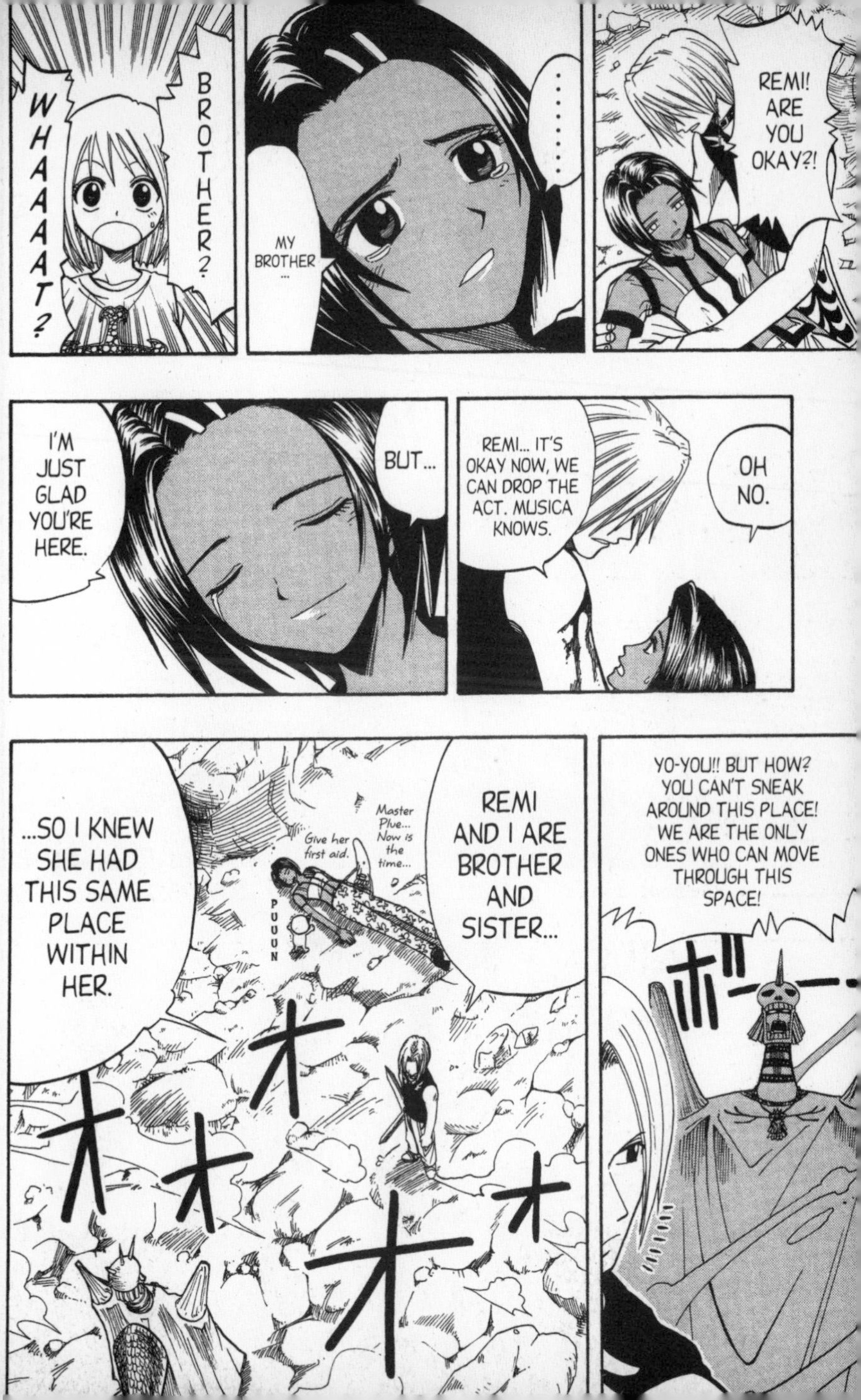

REMI! ARE YOU OKAY?!
......
MY BROTHER ...
BROTHER?
WHAAAAAT?
OH NO.
REMI... IT'S OKAY NOW, WE CAN DROP THE ACT. MUSICA KNOWS.
BUT...
I'M JUST GLAD YOU'RE HERE.
YO-YOU!! BUT HOW? YOU CAN'T SNEAK AROUND THIS PLACE! WE ARE THE ONLY ONES WHO CAN MOVE THROUGH THIS SPACE!
ボー
REMI AND I ARE BROTHER AND SISTER...
Master Plue... Now is the time...
Give her first aid.
PUUUN
...SO I KNEW SHE HAD THIS SAME PLACE WITHIN HER.
オオオオ

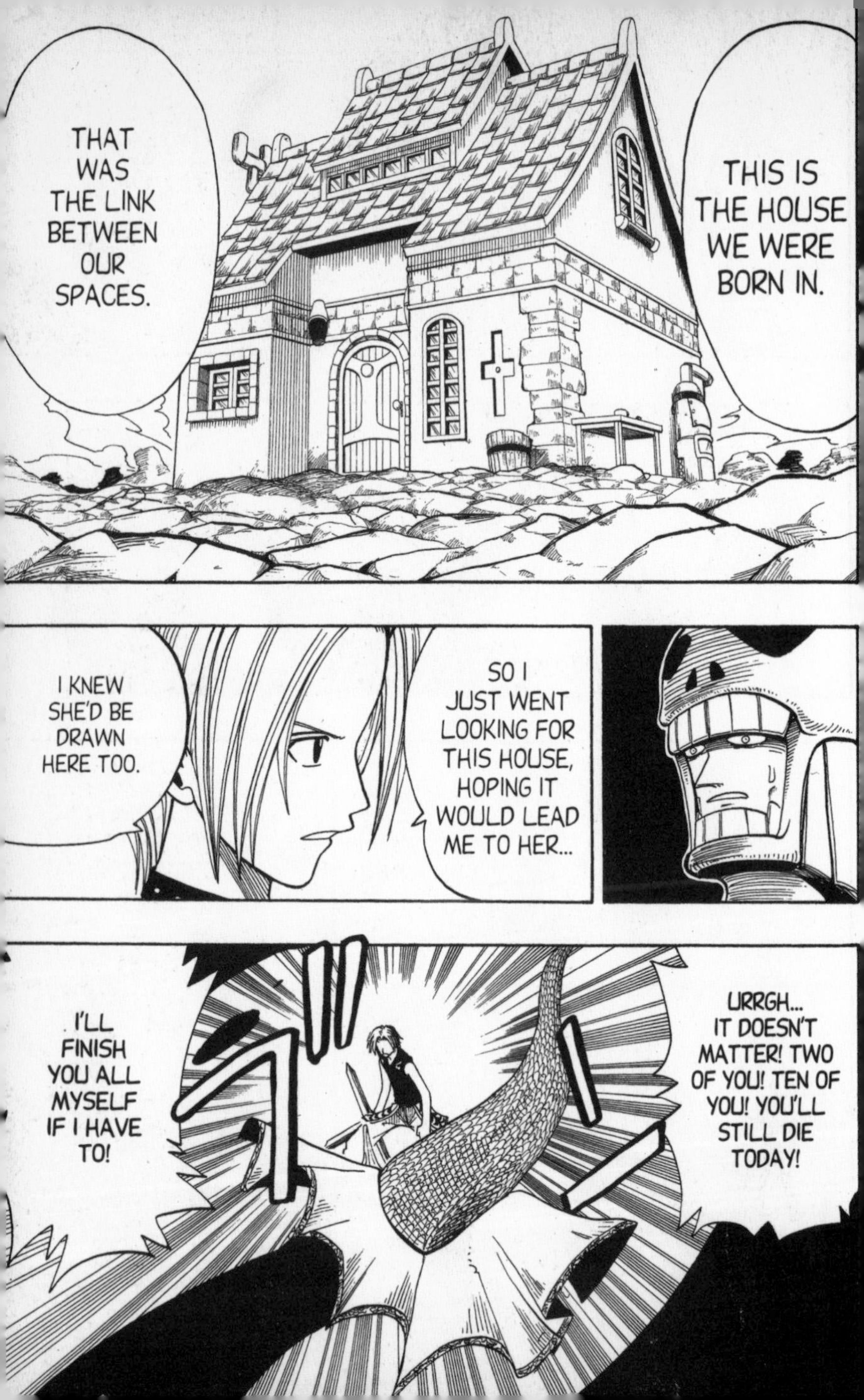
THIS IS THE HOUSE WE WERE BORN IN.
THAT WAS THE LINK BETWEEN OUR SPACES.
SO I JUST WENT LOOKING FOR THIS HOUSE, HOPING IT WOULD LEAD ME TO HER...
I KNEW SHE'D BE DRAWN HERE TOO.
URRGH... IT DOESN'T MATTER! TWO OF YOU! TEN OF YOU! YOU'LL STILL DIE TODAY!
I'LL FINISH YOU ALL MYSELF IF I HAVE TO!

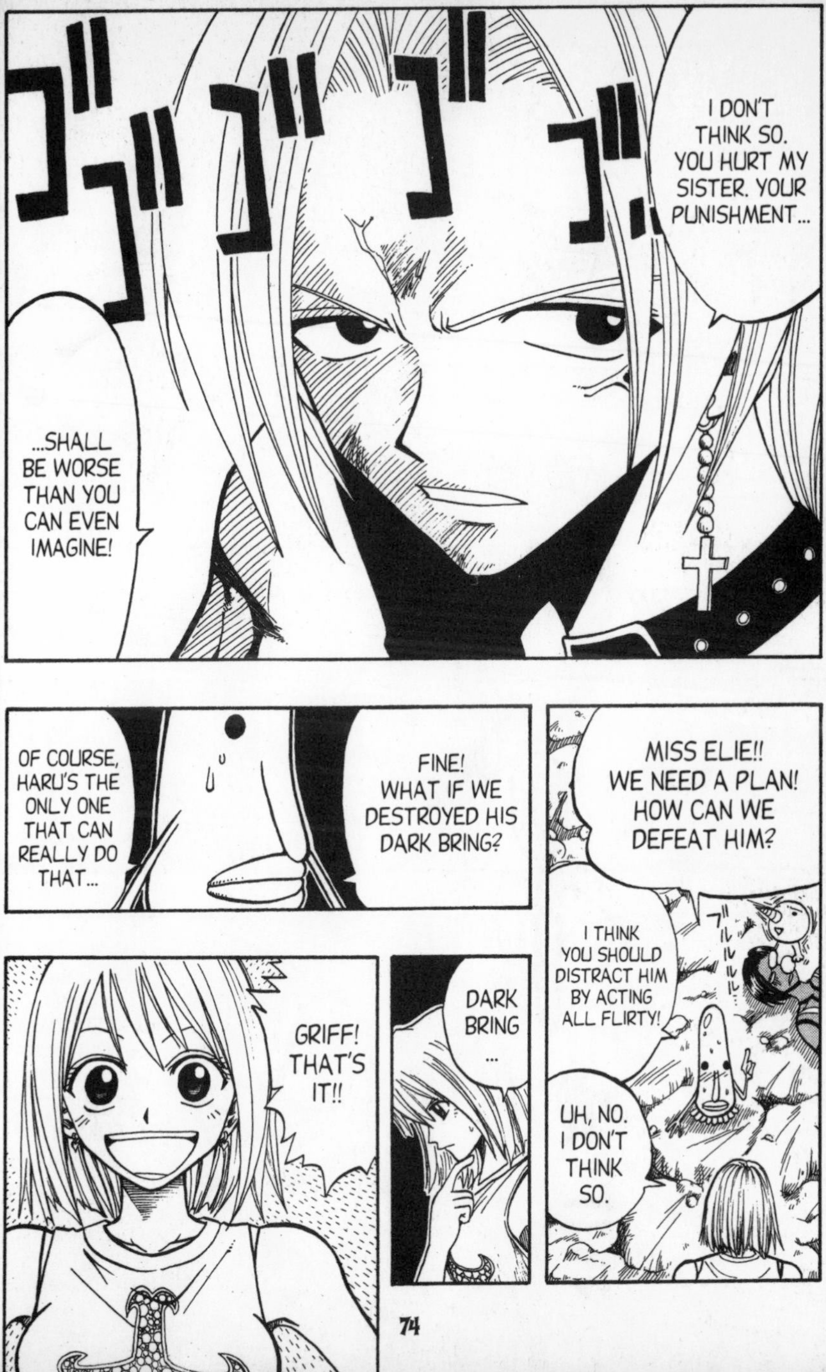
ゴゴゴゴ
I DON'T THINK SO. YOU HURT MY SISTER. YOUR PUNISHMENT...
...SHALL BE WORSE THAN YOU CAN EVEN IMAGINE!
MISS ELIE!! WE NEED A PLAN! HOW CAN WE DEFEAT HIM?
I THINK YOU SHOULD DISTRACT HIM BY ACTING ALL FLIRTY!
ブルルル...
UH, NO. I DON'T THINK SO.
FINE! WHAT IF WE DESTROYED HIS DARK BRING?
OF COURSE, HARU'S THE ONLY ONE THAT CAN REALLY DO THAT...
DARK BRING ...
GRIFF! THAT'S IT!!

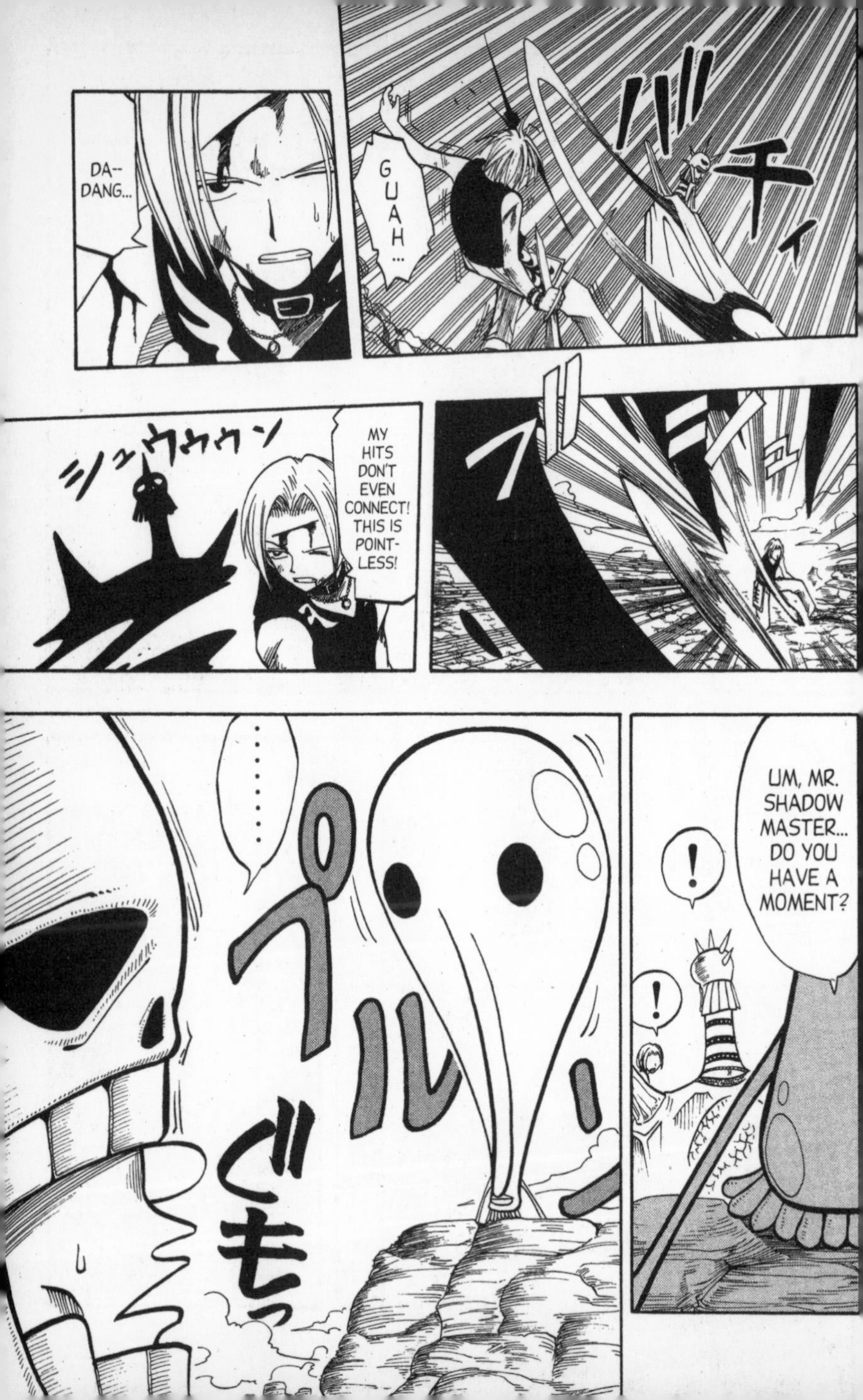
バチィ
GUAH...
DA-- DANG...
MY HITS DON'T EVEN CONNECT! THIS IS POINTLESS!
シュウゥゥン
UM, MR. SHADOW MASTER... DO YOU HAVE A MOMENT?
!
!
......
プルーン
ぐもっ

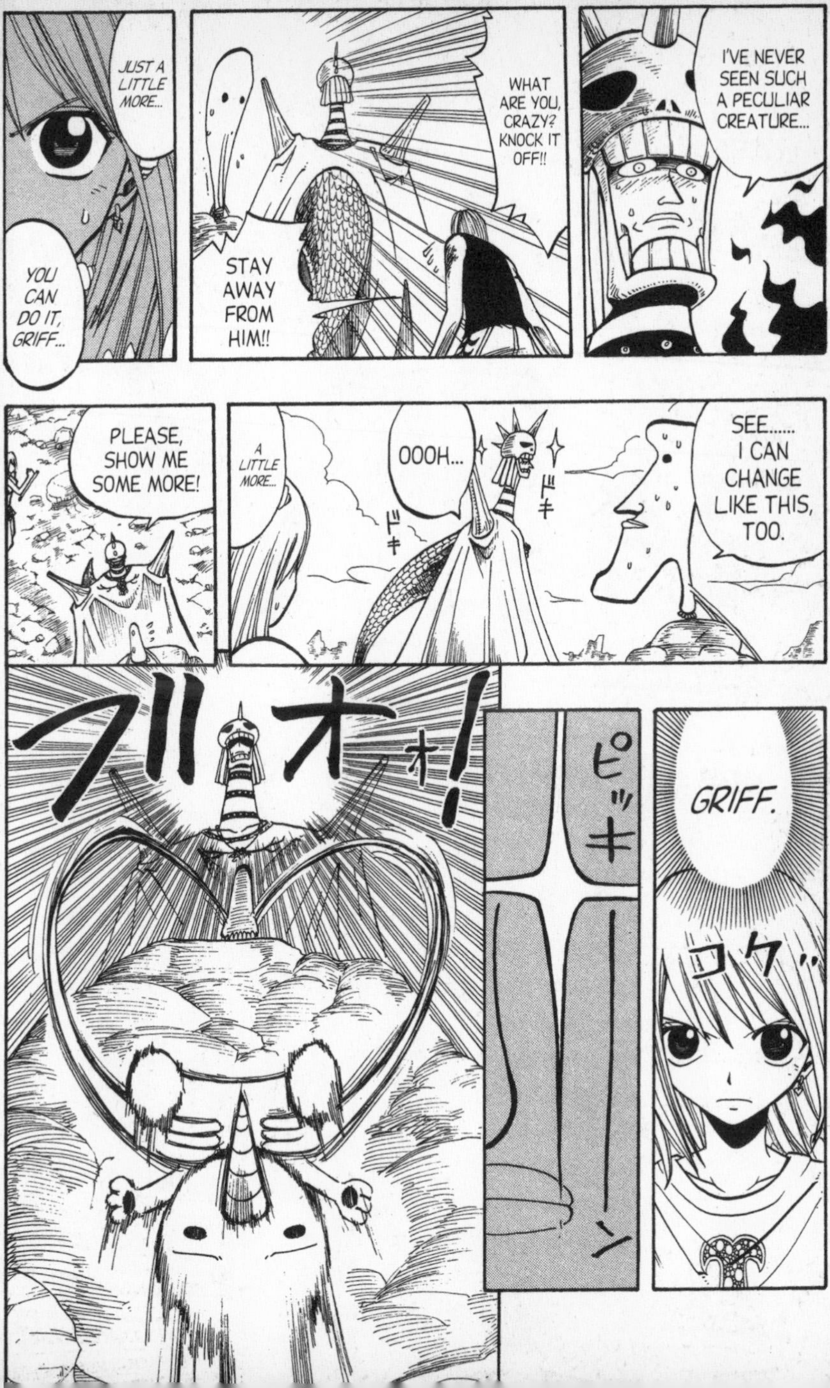

I'VE NEVER SEEN SUCH A PECULIAR CREATURE...
WHAT ARE YOU, CRAZY? KNOCK IT OFF!!
STAY AWAY FROM HIM!!
JUST A LITTLE MORE...
YOU CAN DO IT, GRIFF...
SEE...... I CAN CHANGE LIKE THIS, TOO.
ドキ
OOOH...
ドキ
A LITTLE MORE...
PLEASE, SHOW ME SOME MORE!
GRIFF.
コク"
ピッキーン
フルオーォ!

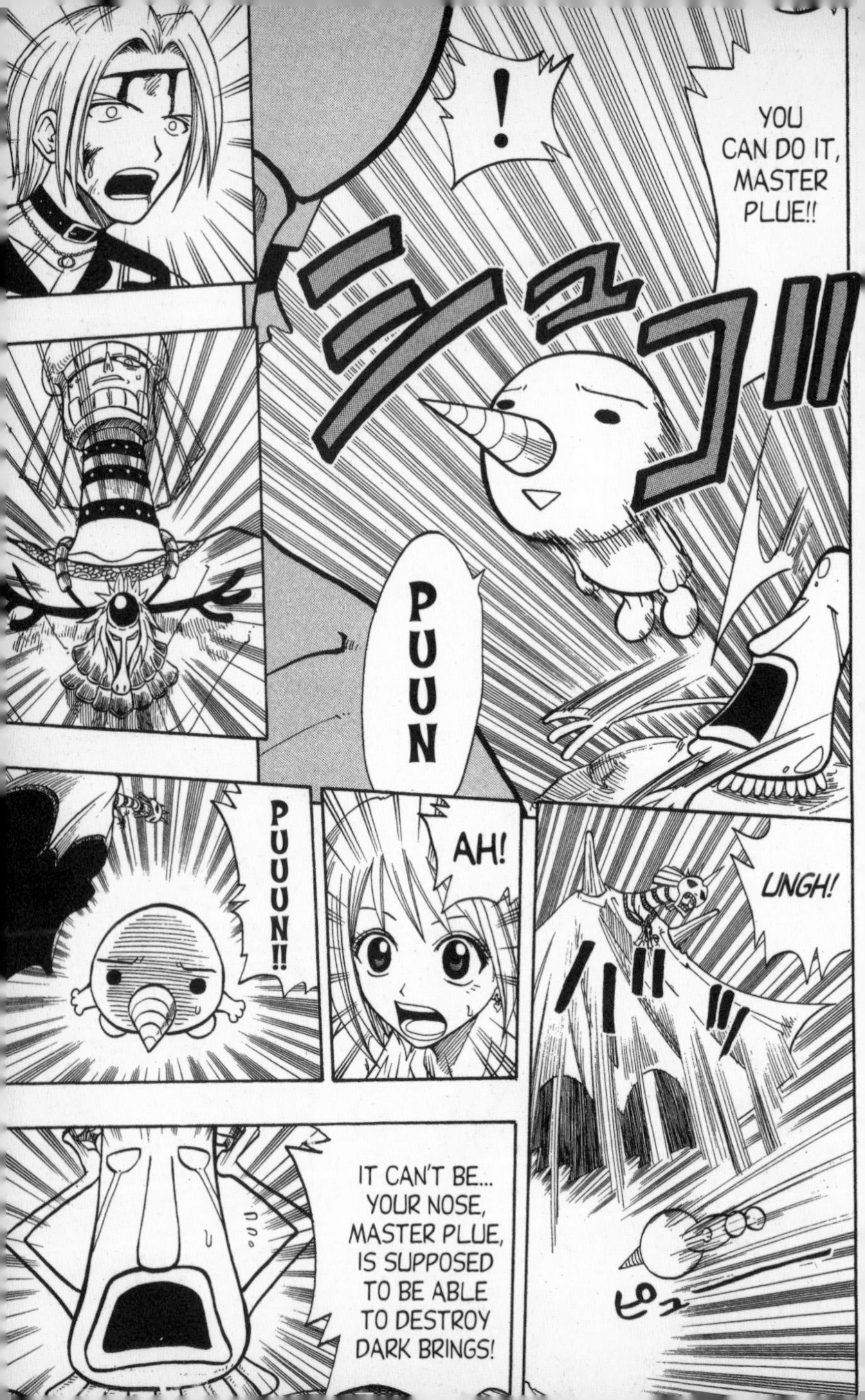
YOU CAN DO IT, MASTER PLUE!!
!
PUUN
UNGH!
AH!
PUUUUN!!
IT CAN'T BE... YOUR NOSE, MASTER PLUE, IS SUPPOSED TO BE ABLE TO DESTROY DARK BRINGS!

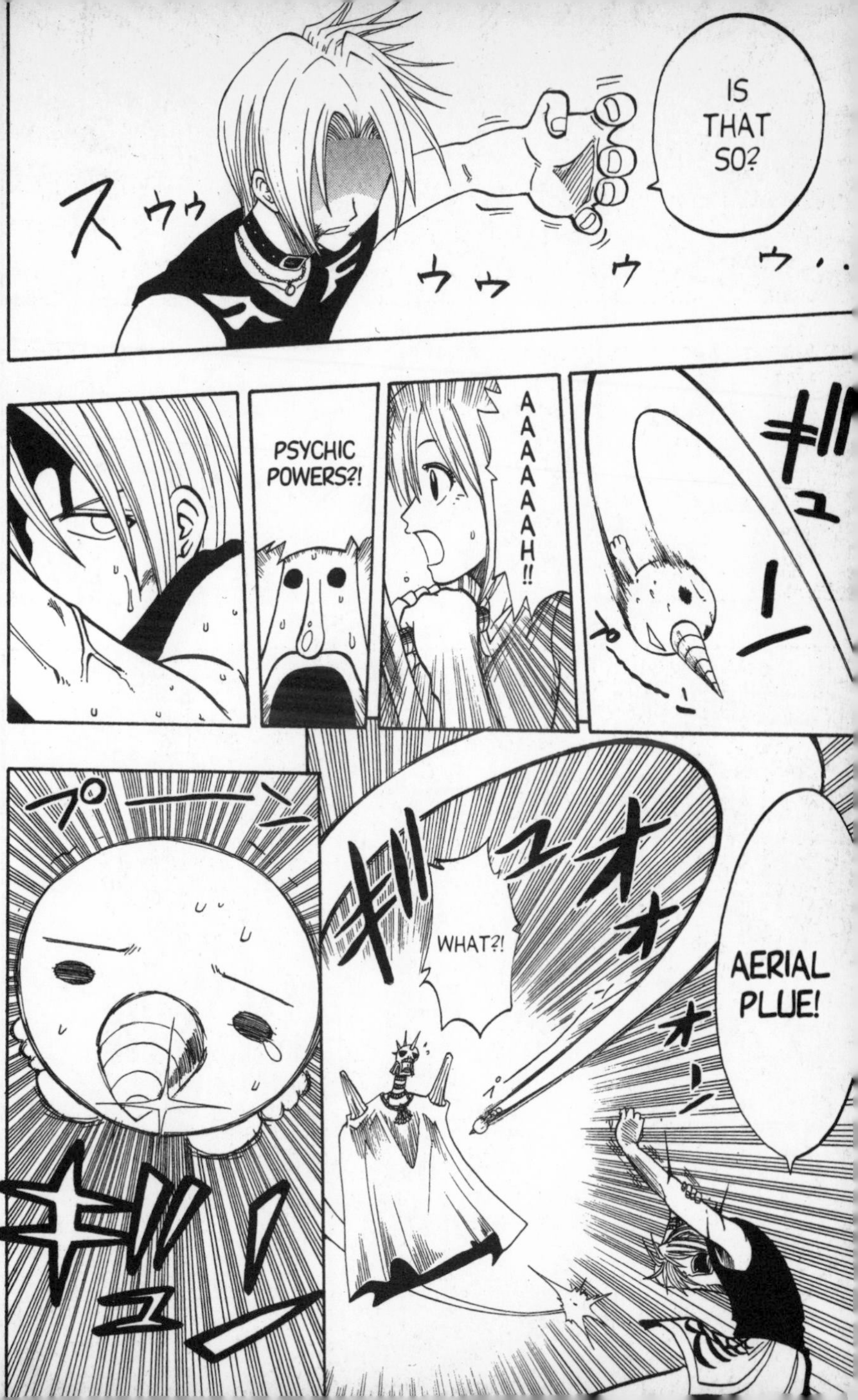
IS THAT SO?
スウゥ
ウゥ
ウ
ウ・・
ギュ
ーン
AAAAAAAAAH!!
PSYCHIC POWERS?!
AERIAL PLUE!
ギュオオォーン
WHAT?!
プーーン
ギュン

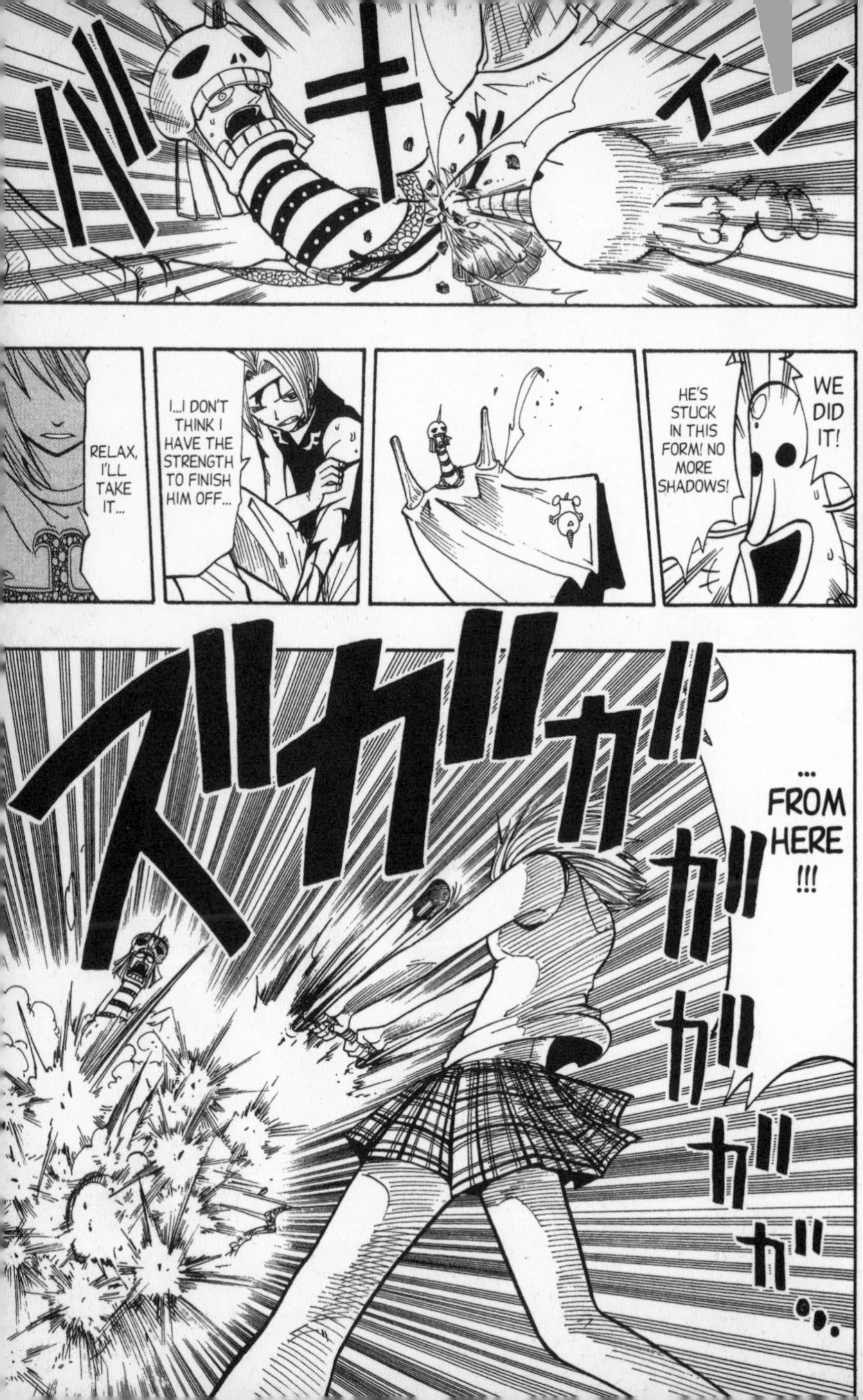
WE DID IT!
HE'S STUCK IN THIS FORM! NO MORE SHADOWS!
I...I DON'T THINK I HAVE THE STRENGTH TO FINISH HIM OFF...
RELAX, I'LL TAKE IT...
...FROM HERE!!!

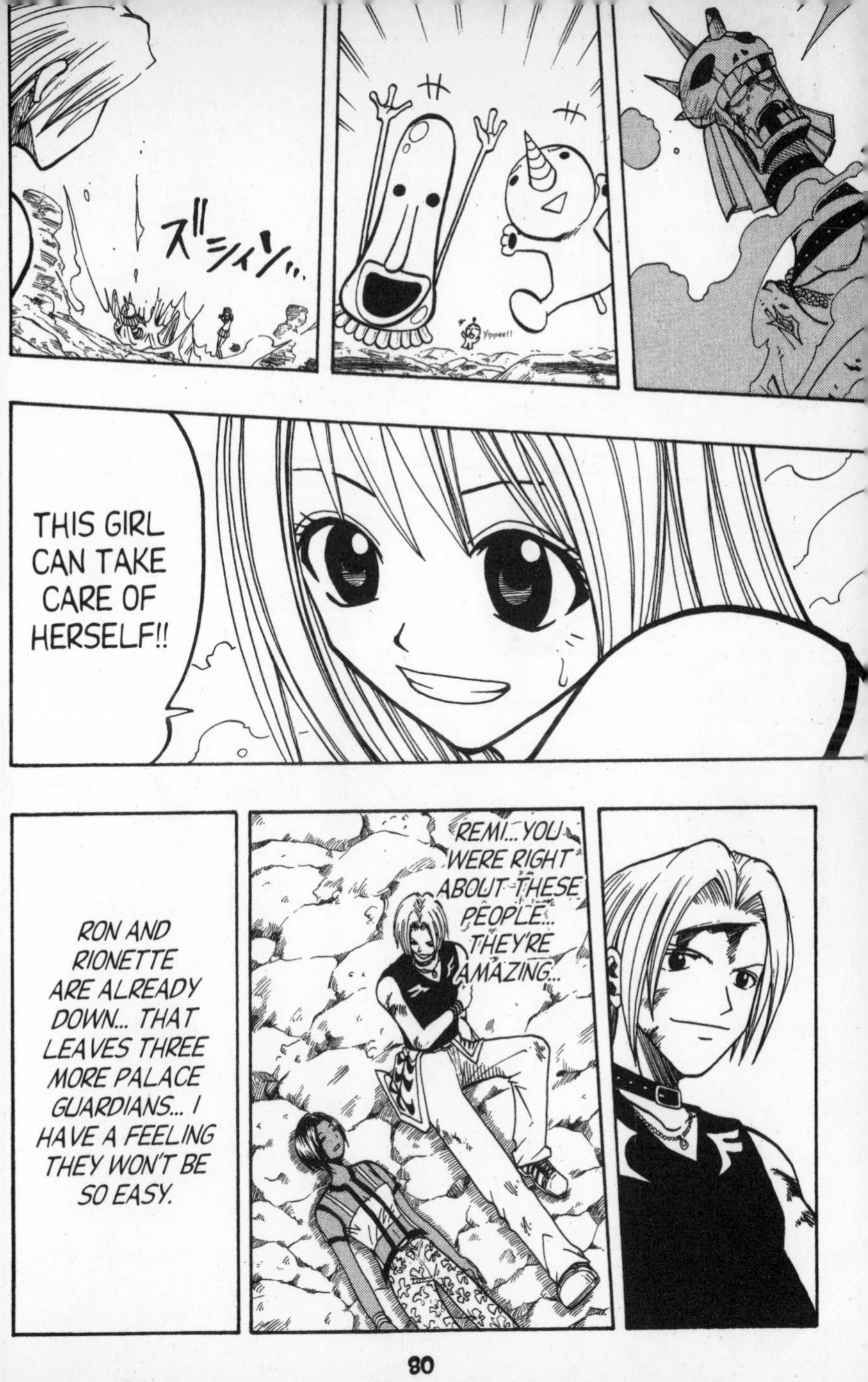
Yippee!!
ズシィン…
THIS GIRL CAN TAKE CARE OF HERSELF!!
REMI... YOU WERE RIGHT ABOUT THESE PEOPLE... THEY'RE AMAZING...
RON AND RIONETTE ARE ALREADY DOWN... THAT LEAVES THREE MORE PALACE GUARDIANS... I HAVE A FEELING THEY WON'T BE SO EASY.

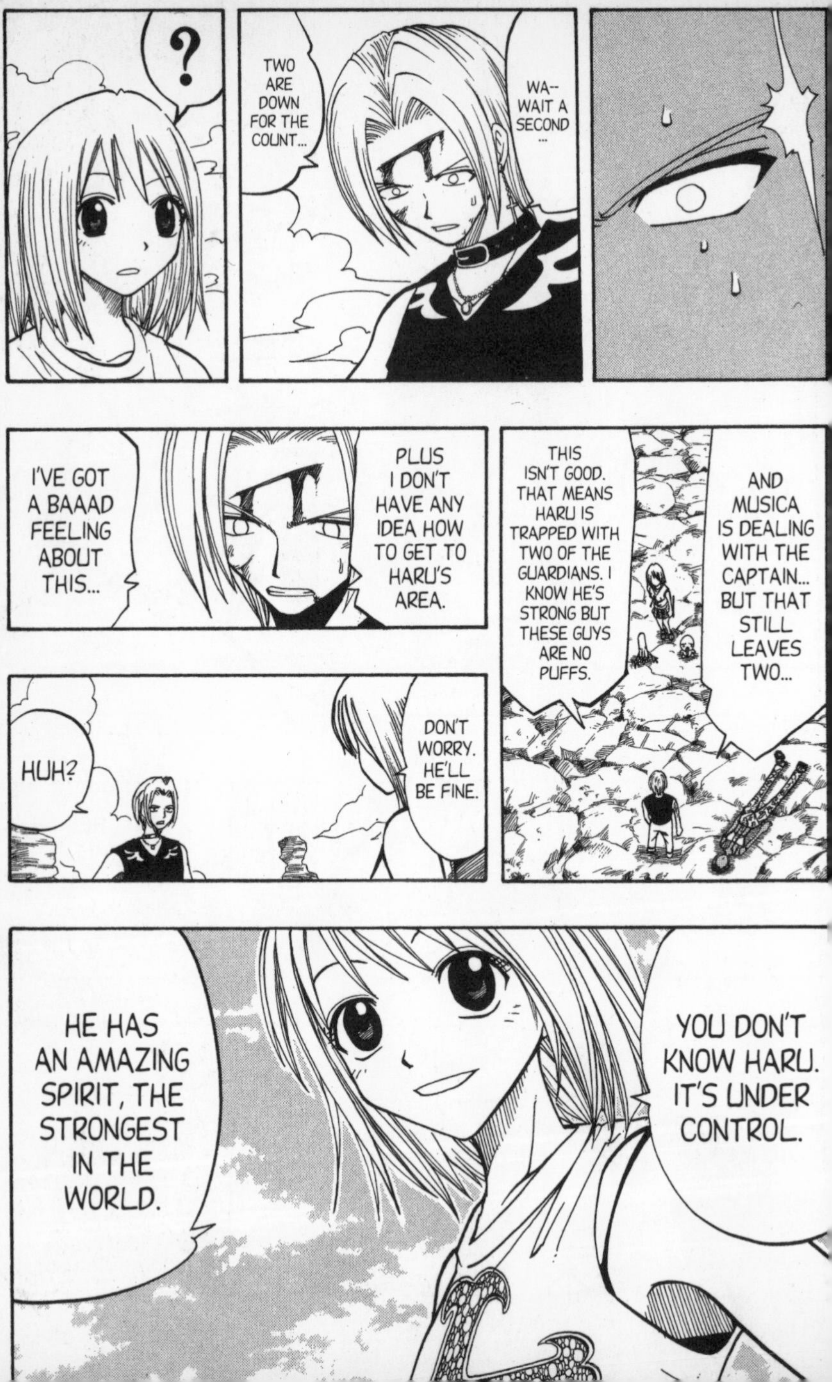
WA-- WAIT A SECOND ...
TWO ARE DOWN FOR THE COUNT...
?
AND MUSICA IS DEALING WITH THE CAPTAIN... BUT THAT STILL LEAVES TWO...
THIS ISN'T GOOD. THAT MEANS HARU IS TRAPPED WITH TWO OF THE GUARDIANS. I KNOW HE'S STRONG BUT THESE GUYS ARE NO PUFFS.
PLUS I DON'T HAVE ANY IDEA HOW TO GET TO HARU'S AREA.
I'VE GOT A BAAAD FEELING ABOUT THIS...
DON'T WORRY. HE'LL BE FINE.
HUH?
YOU DON'T KNOW HARU. IT'S UNDER CONTROL.
HE HAS AN AMAZING SPIRIT, THE STRONGEST IN THE WORLD.

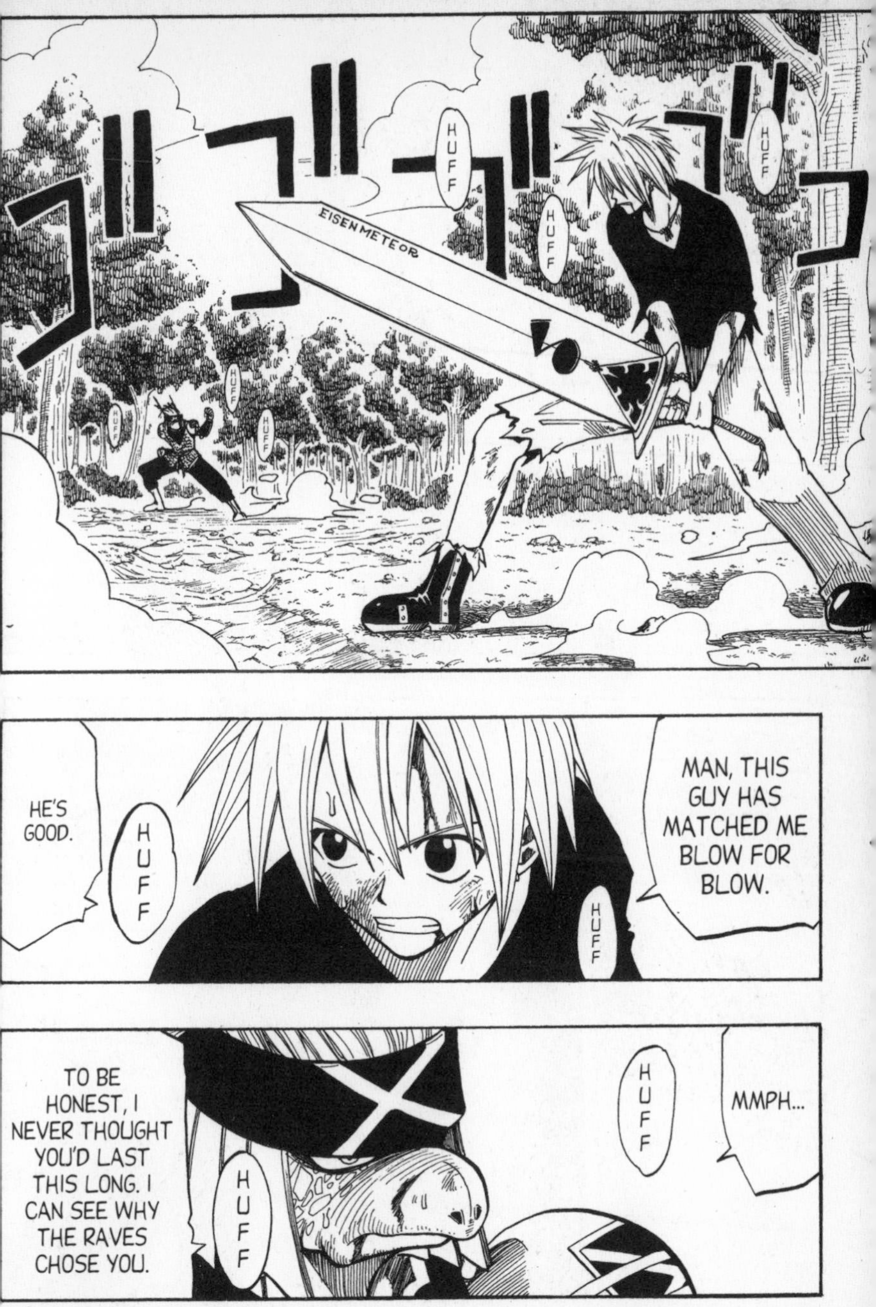
HUFF
HUFF
HUFF
EISENMETEOR
HUFF
HUFF
HUFF
MAN, THIS GUY HAS MATCHED ME BLOW FOR BLOW.
HUFF
HUFF
HE'S GOOD.
MMPH...
HUFF
HUFF
TO BE HONEST, I NEVER THOUGHT YOU'D LAST THIS LONG. I CAN SEE WHY THE RAVES CHOSE YOU.

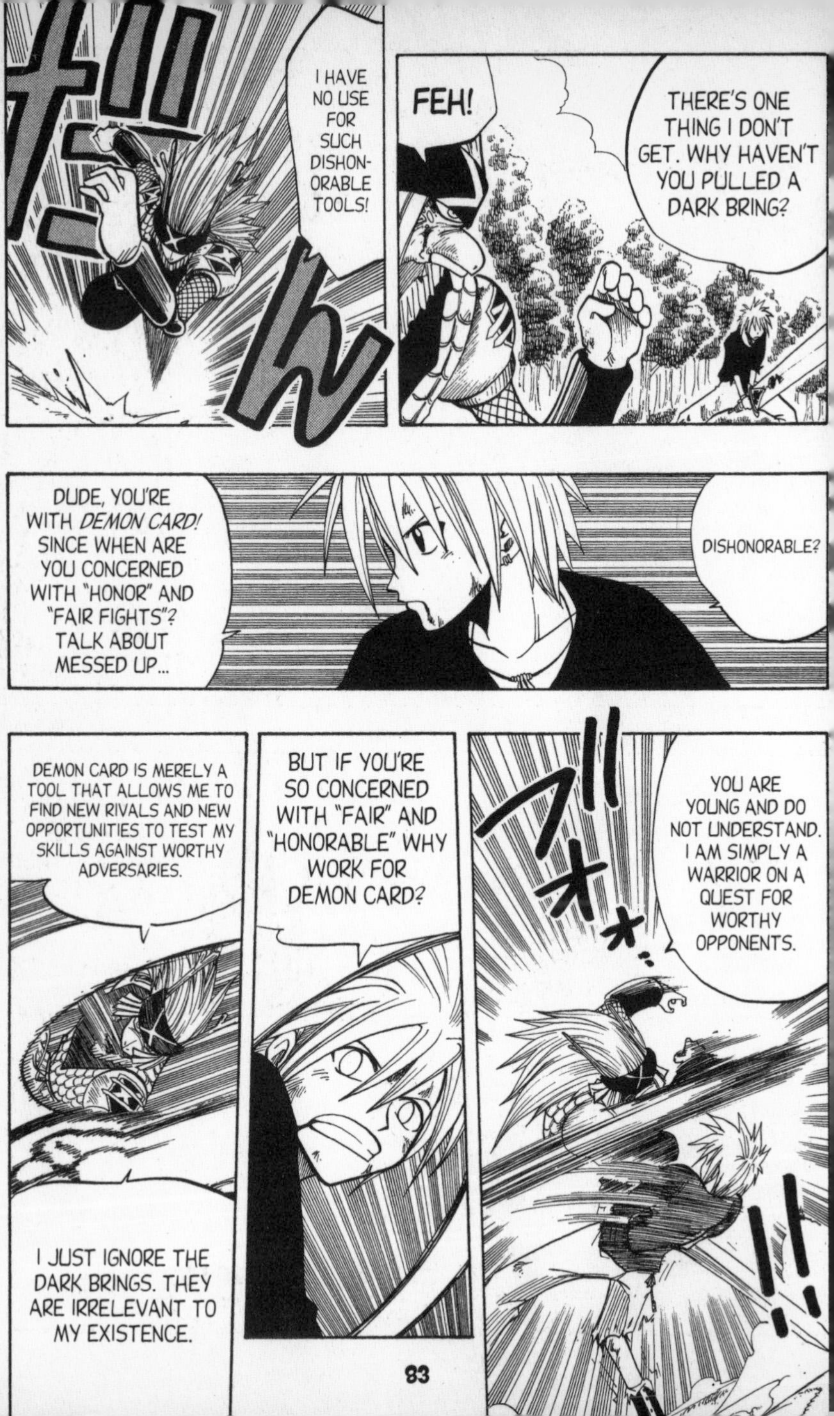
THERE'S ONE THING I DON'T GET. WHY HAVEN'T YOU PULLED A DARK BRING?
FEH!
I HAVE NO USE FOR SUCH DISHON-ORABLE TOOLS!
DISHONORABLE?
DUDE, YOU'RE WITH *DEMON CARD!* SINCE WHEN ARE YOU CONCERNED WITH "HONOR" AND "FAIR FIGHTS"? TALK ABOUT MESSED UP...
YOU ARE YOUNG AND DO NOT UNDERSTAND. I AM SIMPLY A WARRIOR ON A QUEST FOR WORTHY OPPONENTS.
BUT IF YOU'RE SO CONCERNED WITH "FAIR" AND "HONORABLE" WHY WORK FOR DEMON CARD?
DEMON CARD IS MERELY A TOOL THAT ALLOWS ME TO FIND NEW RIVALS AND NEW OPPORTUNITIES TO TEST MY SKILLS AGAINST WORTHY ADVERSARIES.
I JUST IGNORE THE DARK BRINGS. THEY ARE IRRELEVANT TO MY EXISTENCE.

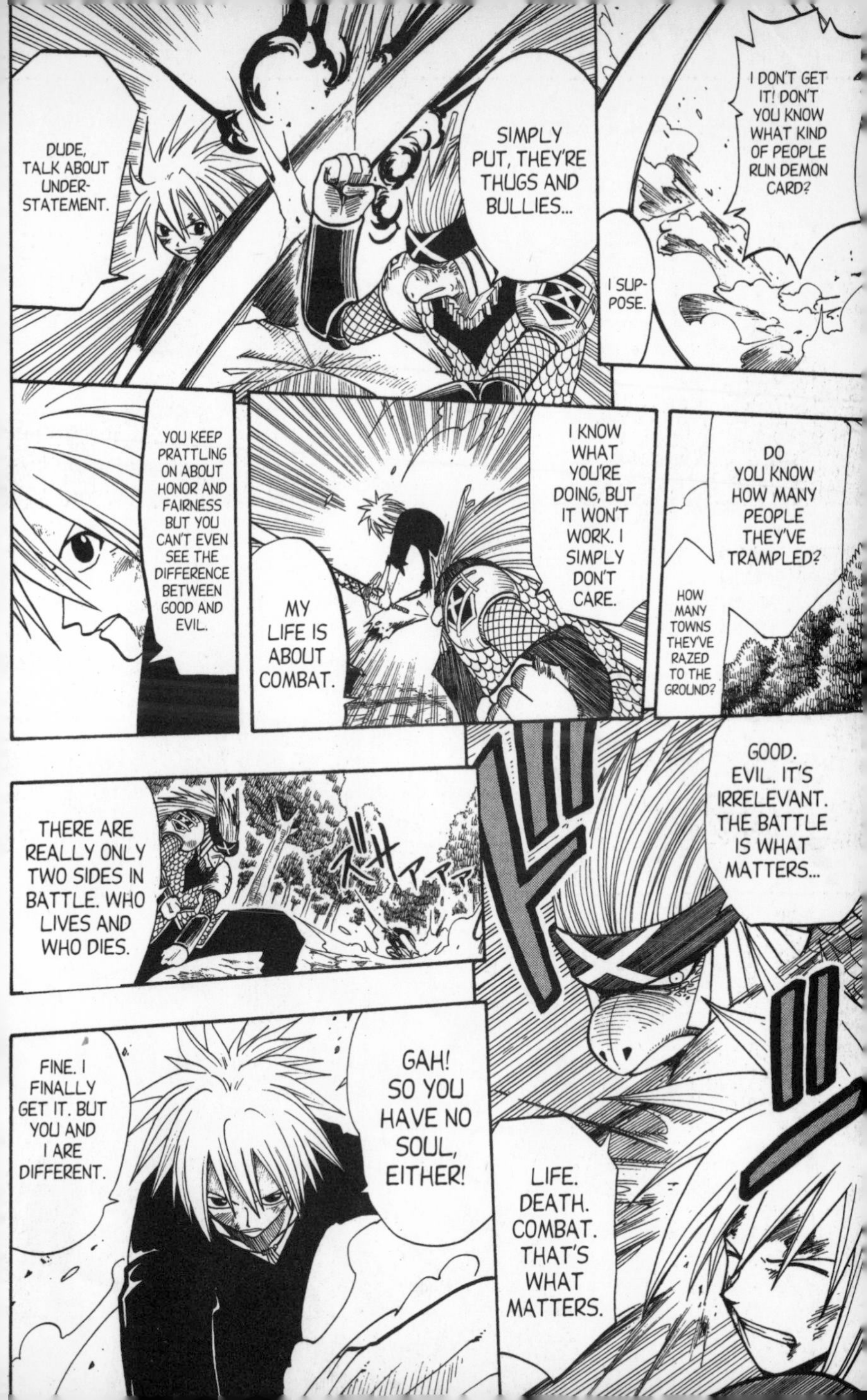
I DON'T GET IT! DON'T YOU KNOW WHAT KIND OF PEOPLE RUN DEMON CARD?
I SUPPOSE.
SIMPLY PUT, THEY'RE THUGS AND BULLIES...
DUDE, TALK ABOUT UNDERSTATEMENT.
DO YOU KNOW HOW MANY PEOPLE THEY'VE TRAMPLED?
HOW MANY TOWNS THEY'VE RAZED TO THE GROUND?
I KNOW WHAT YOU'RE DOING, BUT IT WON'T WORK. I SIMPLY DON'T CARE.
MY LIFE IS ABOUT COMBAT.
YOU KEEP PRATTLING ON ABOUT HONOR AND FAIRNESS BUT YOU CAN'T EVEN SEE THE DIFFERENCE BETWEEN GOOD AND EVIL.
GOOD. EVIL. IT'S IRRELEVANT. THE BATTLE IS WHAT MATTERS...
LIFE. DEATH. COMBAT. THAT'S WHAT MATTERS.
THERE ARE REALLY ONLY TWO SIDES IN BATTLE. WHO LIVES AND WHO DIES.
GAH! SO YOU HAVE NO SOUL, EITHER!
FINE. I FINALLY GET IT. BUT YOU AND I ARE DIFFERENT.

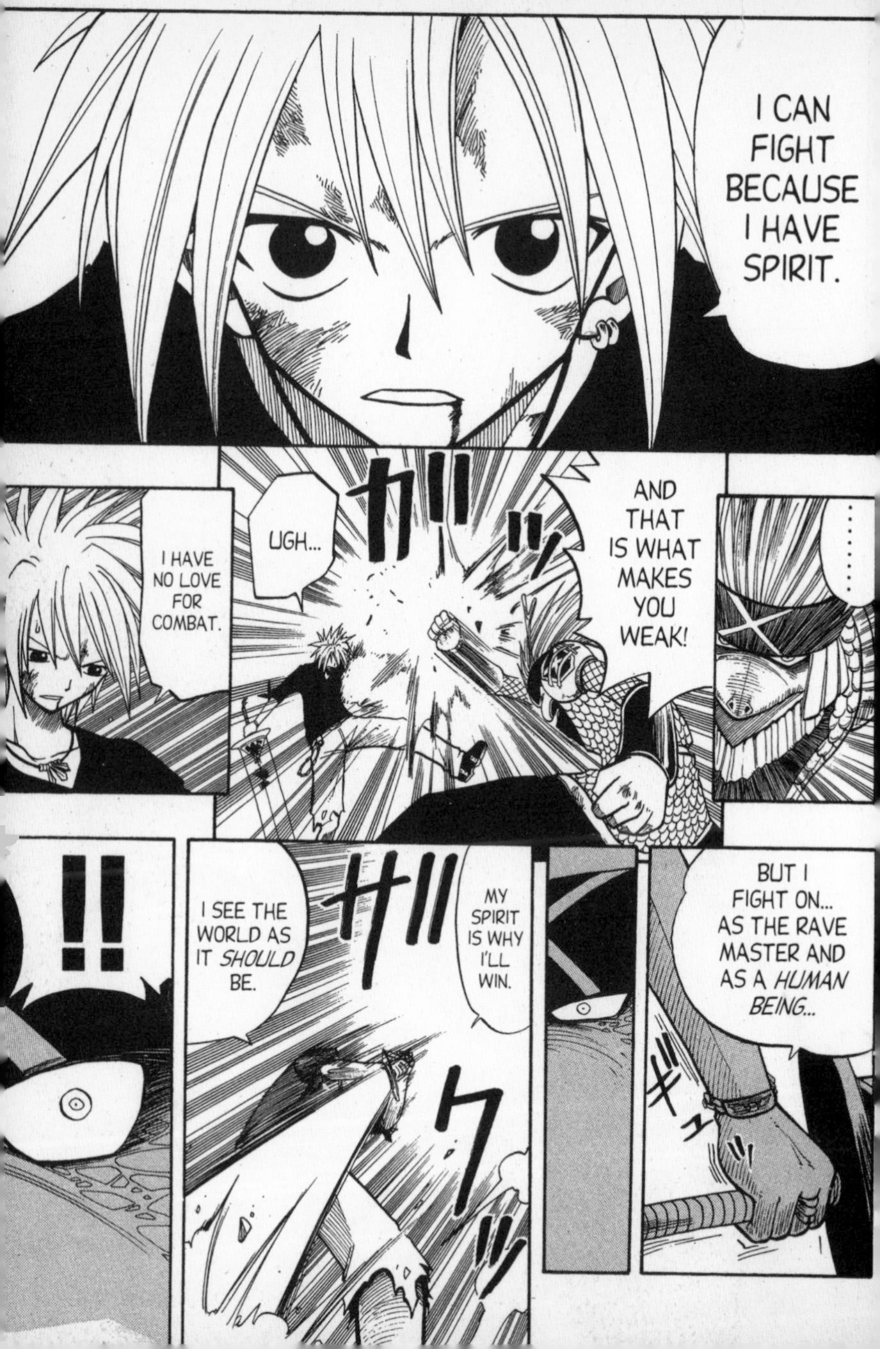
I CAN FIGHT BECAUSE I HAVE SPIRIT.
....
AND THAT IS WHAT MAKES YOU WEAK!
ガッ
UGH...
I HAVE NO LOVE FOR COMBAT.
BUT I FIGHT ON... AS THE RAVE MASTER AND AS A *HUMAN BEING*...
ギュッ
MY SPIRIT IS WHY I'LL WIN.
ザクッ
I SEE THE WORLD AS IT *SHOULD* BE.
!!

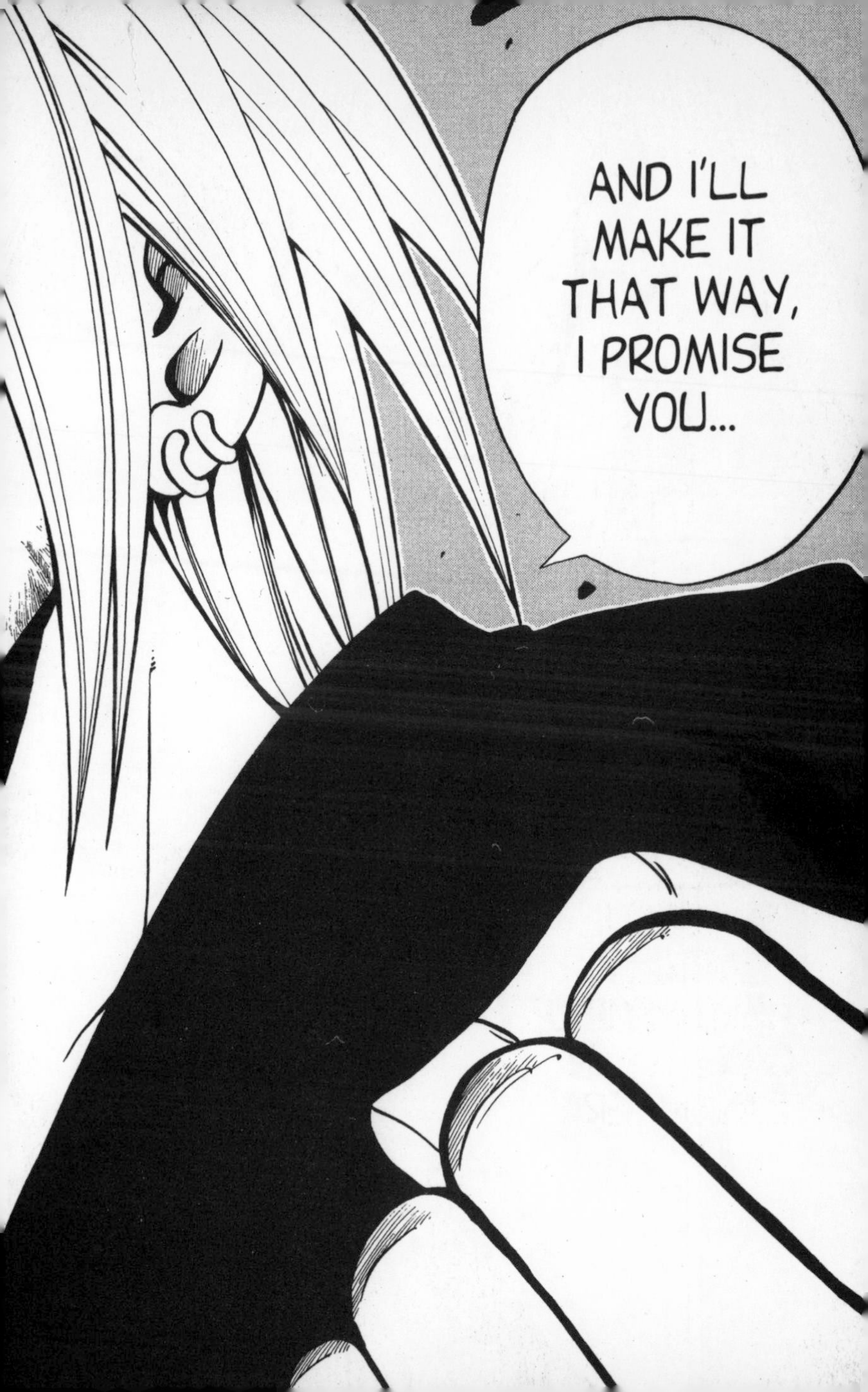
AND I'LL MAKE IT THAT WAY, I PROMISE YOU...

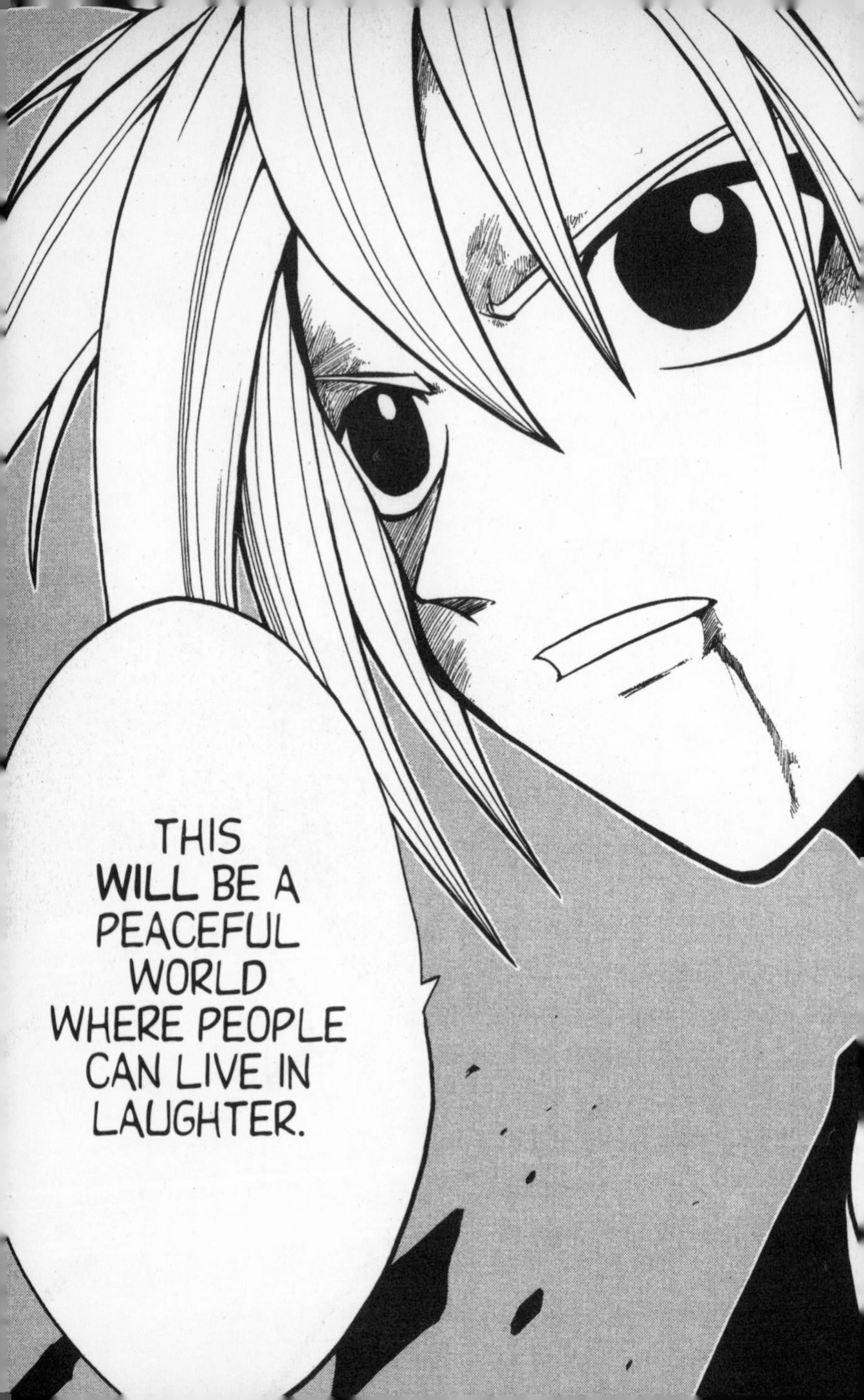
THIS WILL BE A PEACEFUL WORLD WHERE PEOPLE CAN LIVE IN LAUGHTER.

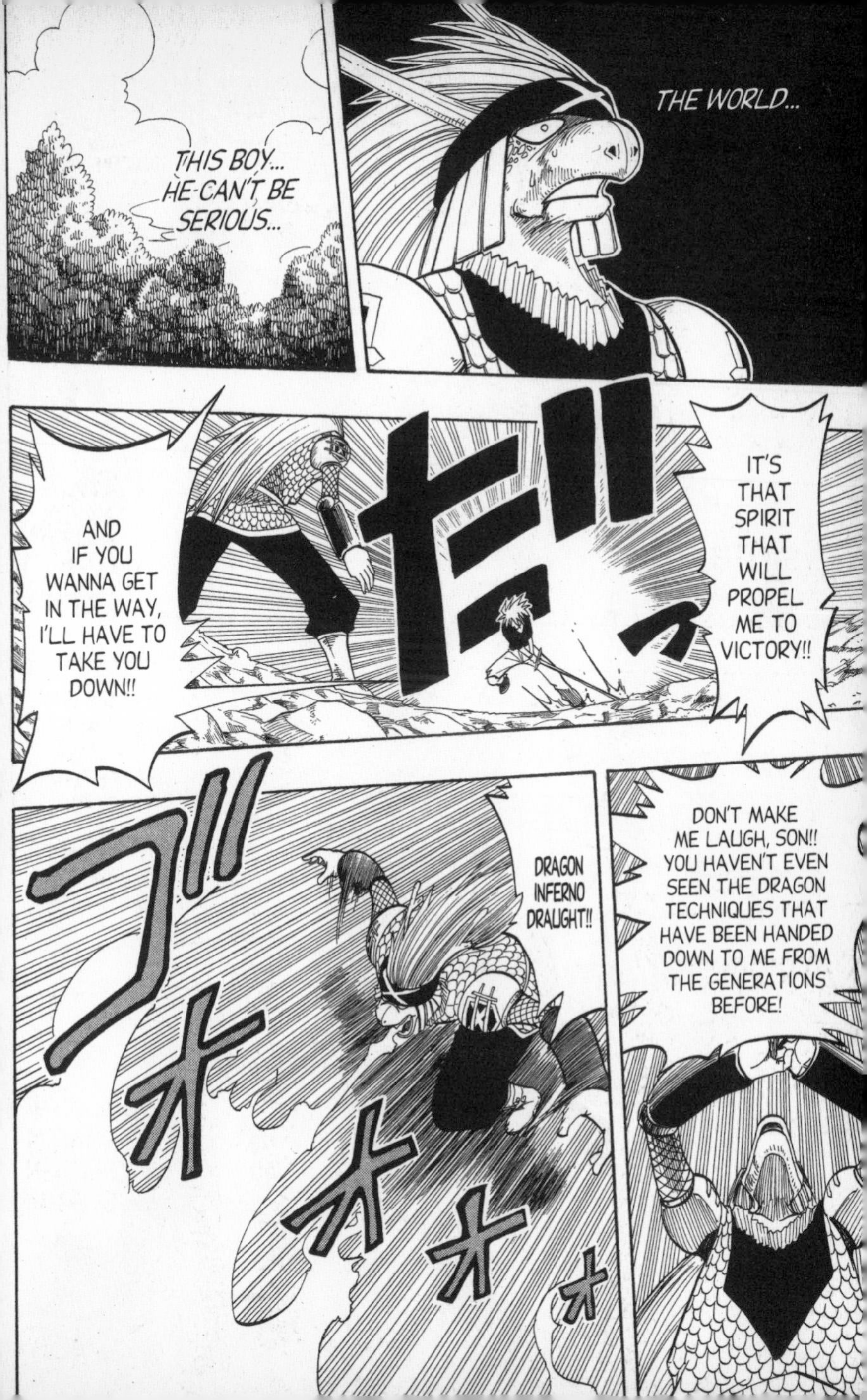
THE WORLD...
THIS BOY... HE CAN'T BE SERIOUS...
IT'S THAT SPIRIT THAT WILL PROPEL ME TO VICTORY!!
AND IF YOU WANNA GET IN THE WAY, I'LL HAVE TO TAKE YOU DOWN!!
DON'T MAKE ME LAUGH, SON!! YOU HAVEN'T EVEN SEEN THE DRAGON TECHNIQUES THAT HAVE BEEN HANDED DOWN TO ME FROM THE GENERATIONS BEFORE!
DRAGON INFERNO DRAUGHT!!

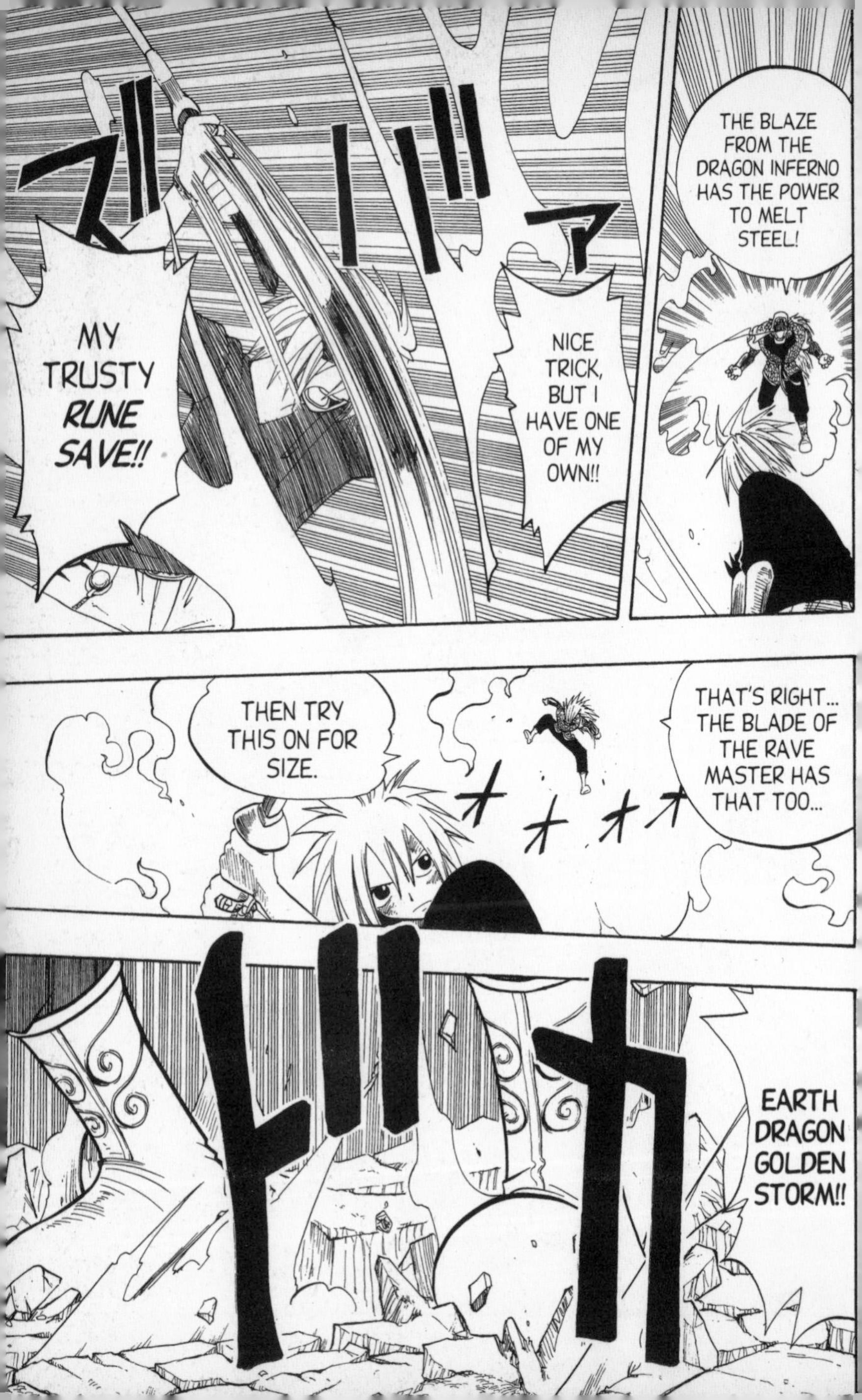
THE BLAZE FROM THE DRAGON INFERNO HAS THE POWER TO MELT STEEL!
NICE TRICK, BUT I HAVE ONE OF MY OWN!!
MY TRUSTY *RUNE SAVE!!*
THAT'S RIGHT... THE BLADE OF THE RAVE MASTER HAS THAT TOO...
THEN TRY THIS ON FOR SIZE.
EARTH DRAGON GOLDEN STORM!!

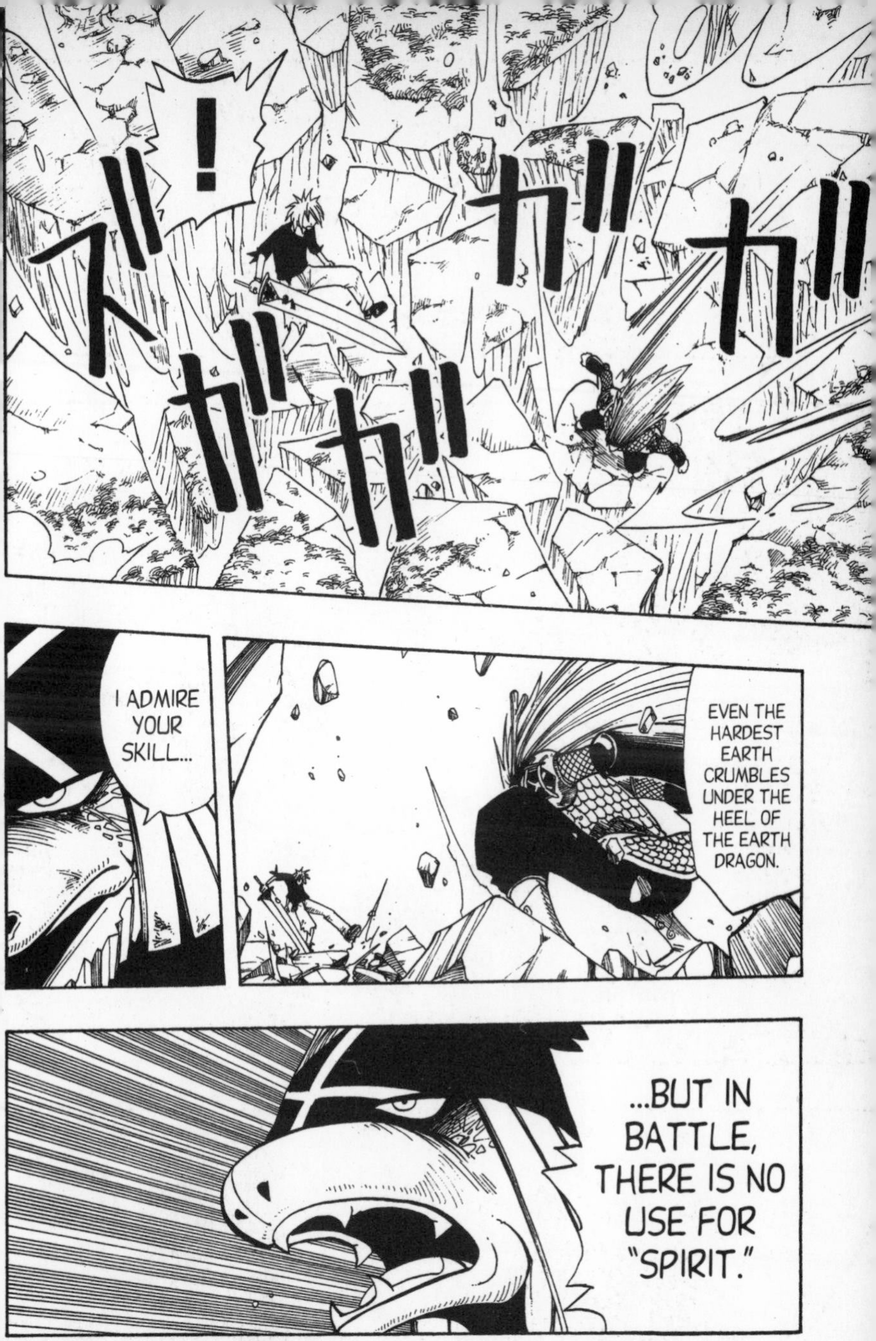
ガガ
ガガ
ズ
!
EVEN THE HARDEST EARTH CRUMBLES UNDER THE HEEL OF THE EARTH DRAGON.
I ADMIRE YOUR SKILL...
...BUT IN BATTLE, THERE IS NO USE FOR "SPIRIT."

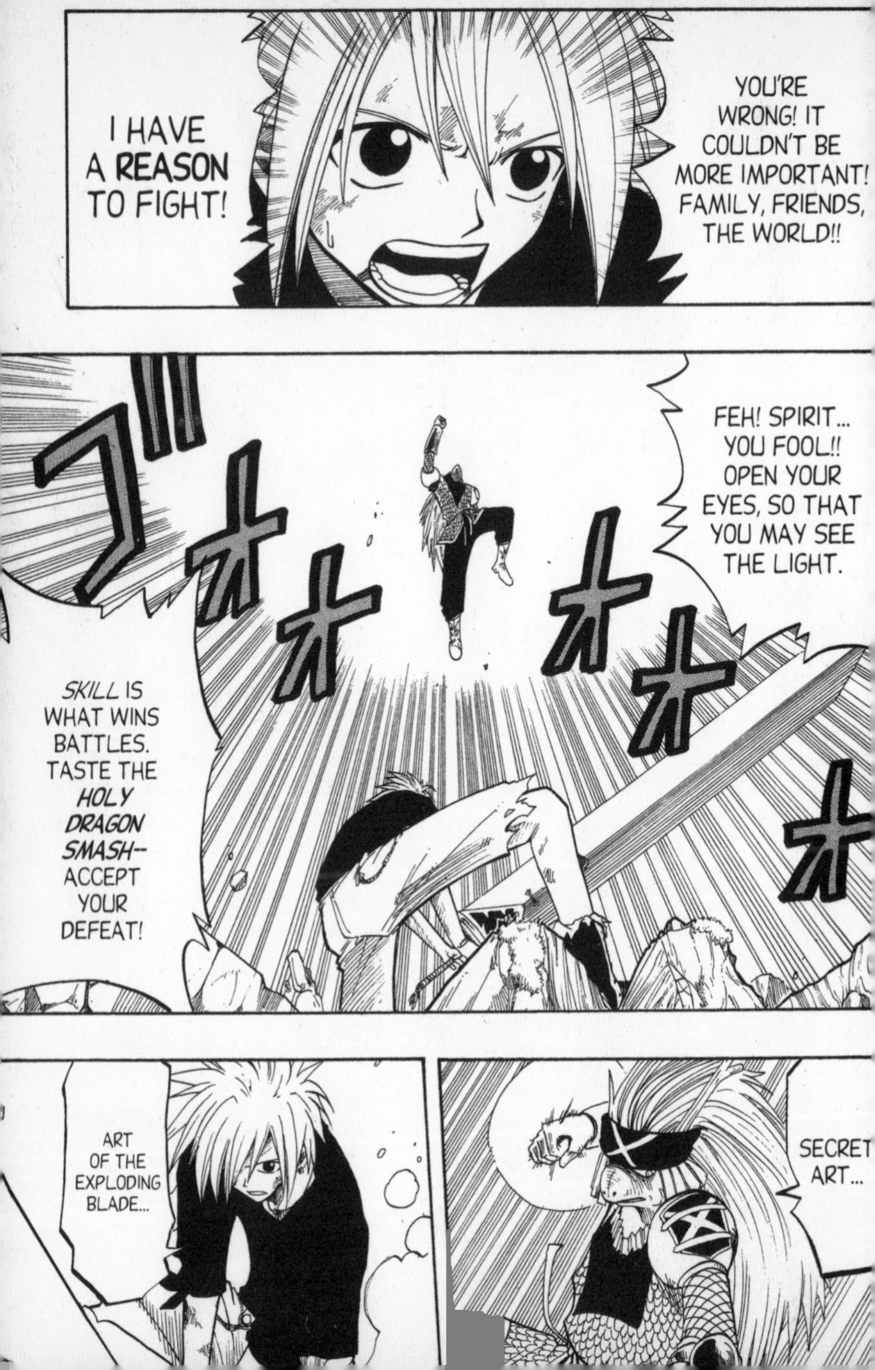
YOU'RE WRONG! IT COULDN'T BE MORE IMPORTANT! FAMILY, FRIENDS, THE WORLD!!
I HAVE A **REASON** TO FIGHT!
ゴオオオオオ
FEH! SPIRIT... YOU FOOL!! OPEN YOUR EYES, SO THAT YOU MAY SEE THE LIGHT.
SKILL IS WHAT WINS BATTLES. TASTE THE *HOLY DRAGON SMASH*-- ACCEPT YOUR DEFEAT!
SECRET ART...
ART OF THE EXPLODING BLADE...

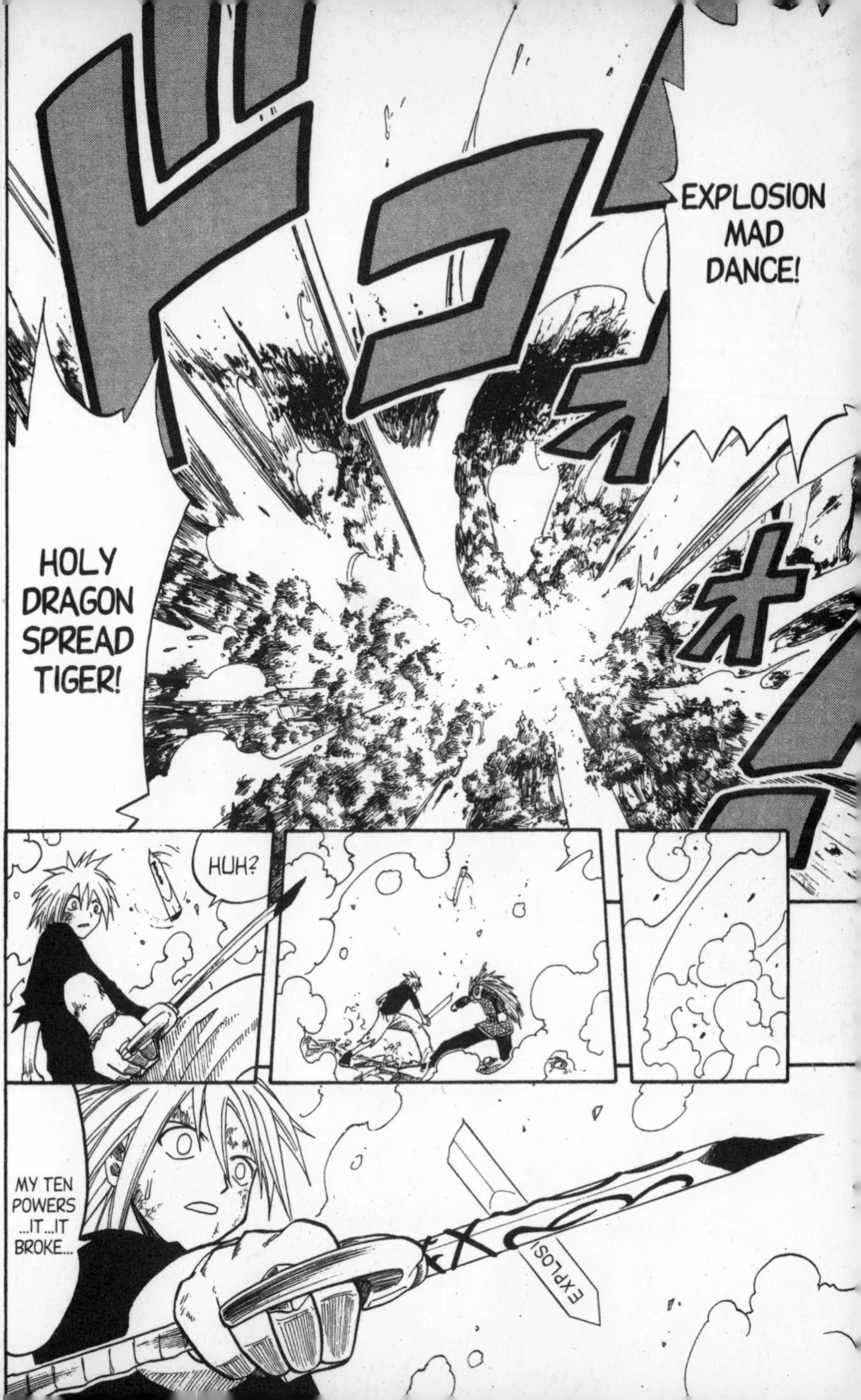
EXPLOSION MAD DANCE!
HOLY DRAGON SPREAD TIGER!
HUH?
MY TEN POWERS ...IT...IT BROKE...
EXPLOSI

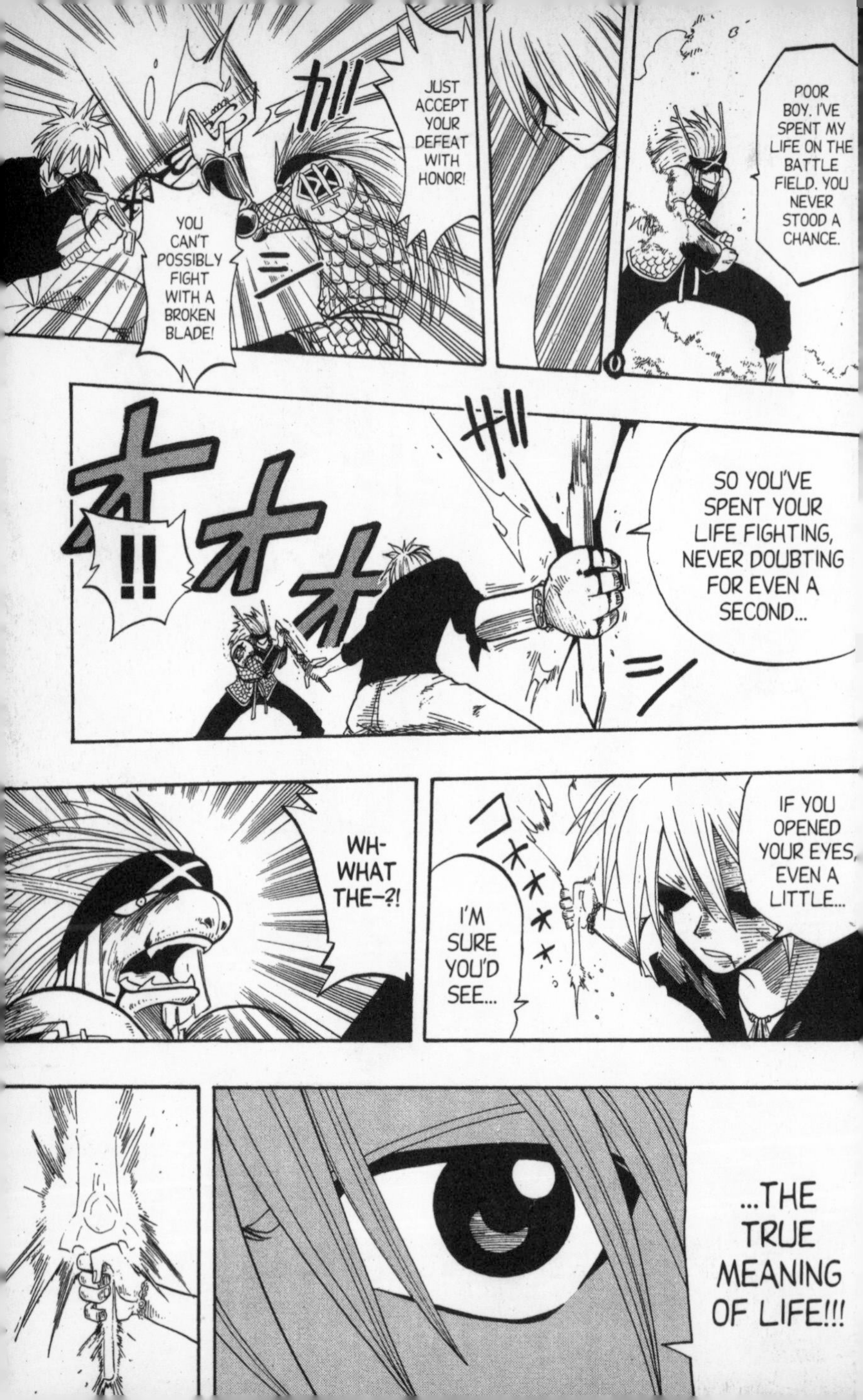
POOR BOY. I'VE SPENT MY LIFE ON THE BATTLE FIELD. YOU NEVER STOOD A CHANCE.
JUST ACCEPT YOUR DEFEAT WITH HONOR!
YOU CAN'T POSSIBLY FIGHT WITH A BROKEN BLADE!
SO YOU'VE SPENT YOUR LIFE FIGHTING, NEVER DOUBTING FOR EVEN A SECOND...
!!
IF YOU OPENED YOUR EYES, EVEN A LITTLE...
I'M SURE YOU'D SEE...
WH- WHAT THE-?!
...THE TRUE MEANING OF LIFE!!!

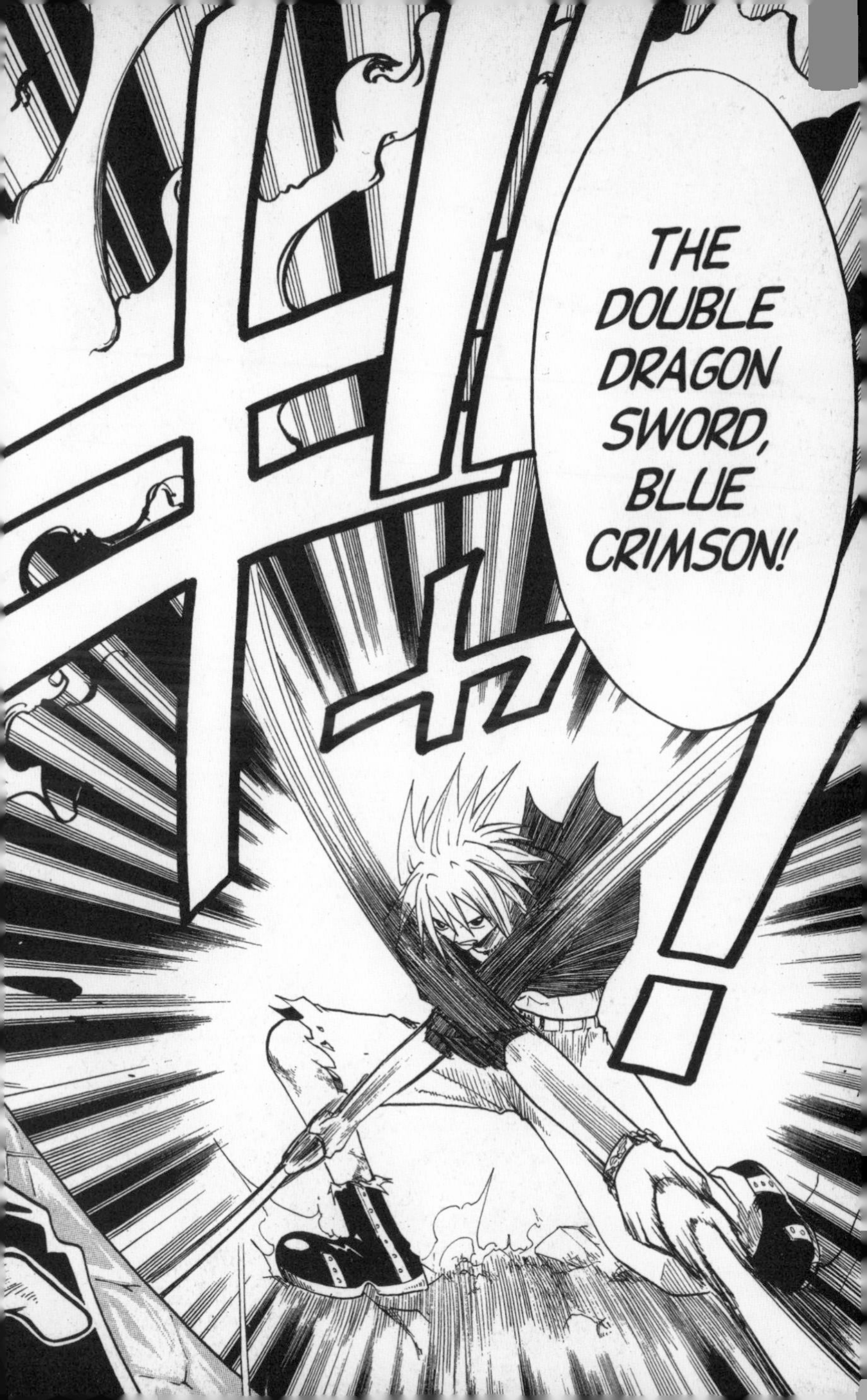
THE DOUBLE DRAGON SWORD, BLUE CRIMSON!

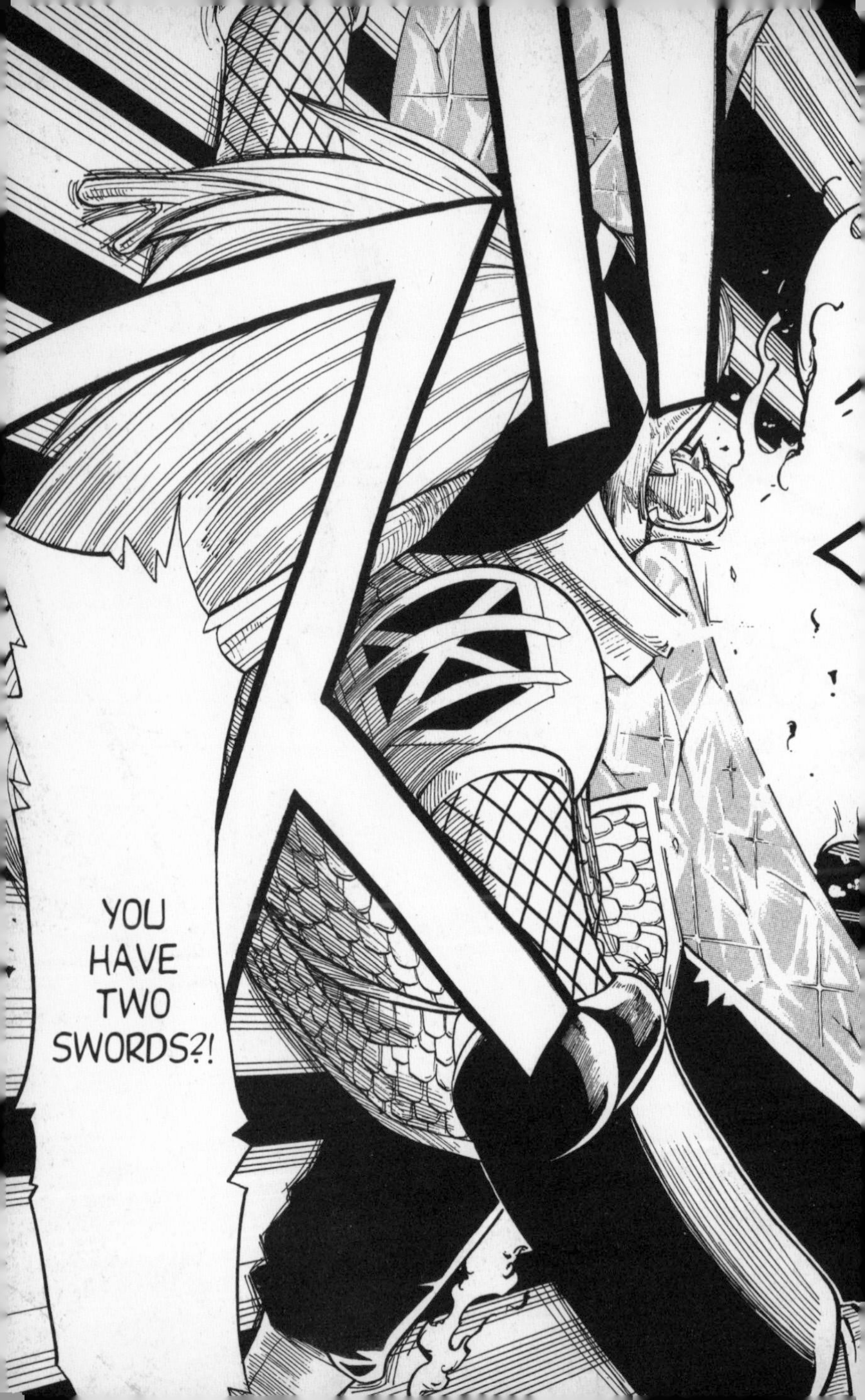
YOU HAVE TWO SWORDS?!

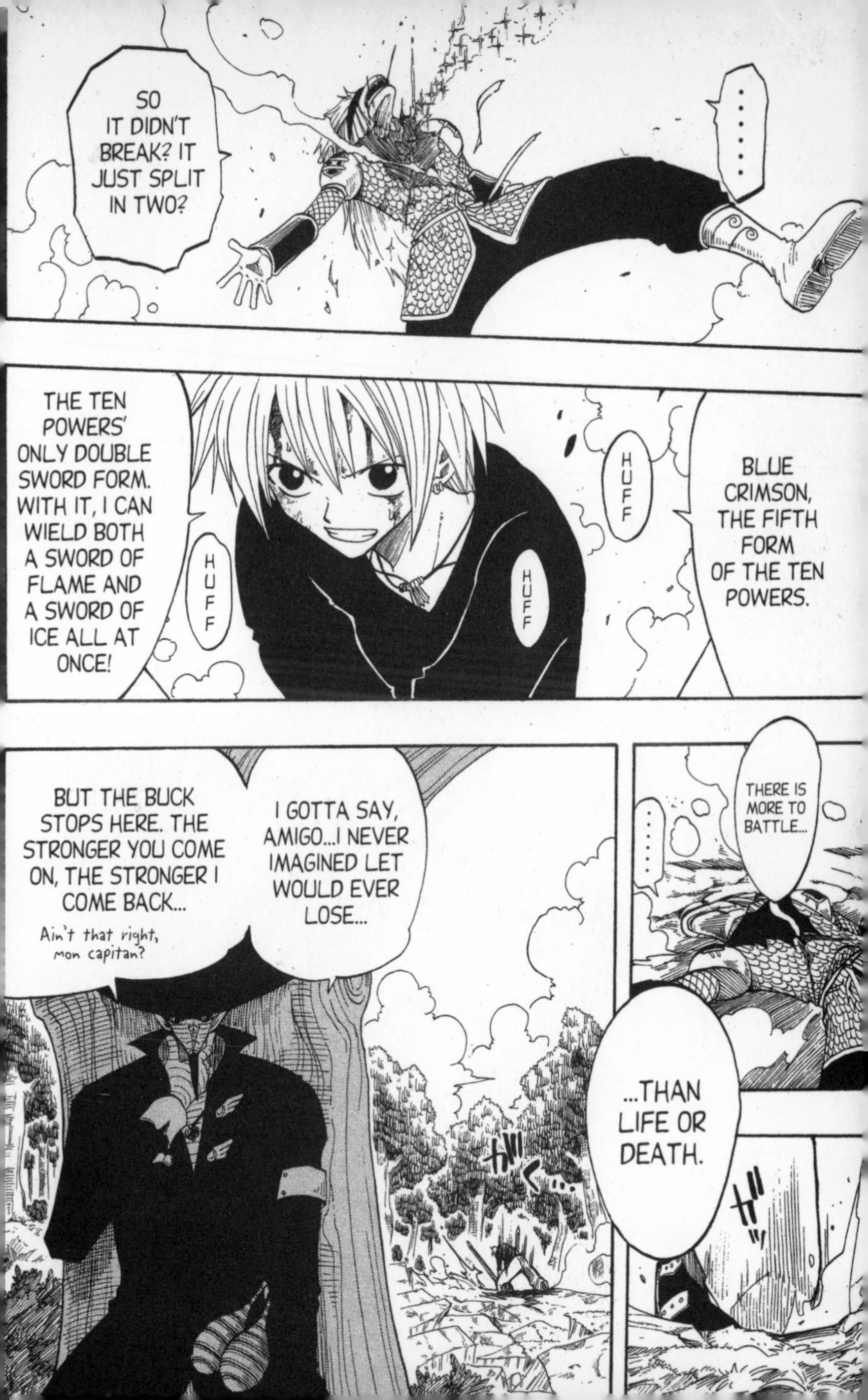
......
SO IT DIDN'T BREAK? IT JUST SPLIT IN TWO?
BLUE CRIMSON, THE FIFTH FORM OF THE TEN POWERS.
HUFF
HUFF
HUFF
THE TEN POWERS' ONLY DOUBLE SWORD FORM. WITH IT, I CAN WIELD BOTH A SWORD OF FLAME AND A SWORD OF ICE ALL AT ONCE!
THERE IS MORE TO BATTLE...
......
...THAN LIFE OR DEATH.
I GOTTA SAY, AMIGO...I NEVER IMAGINED LET WOULD EVER LOSE...
BUT THE BUCK STOPS HERE. THE STRONGER YOU COME ON, THE STRONGER I COME BACK...
Ain't that right, mon capitan?

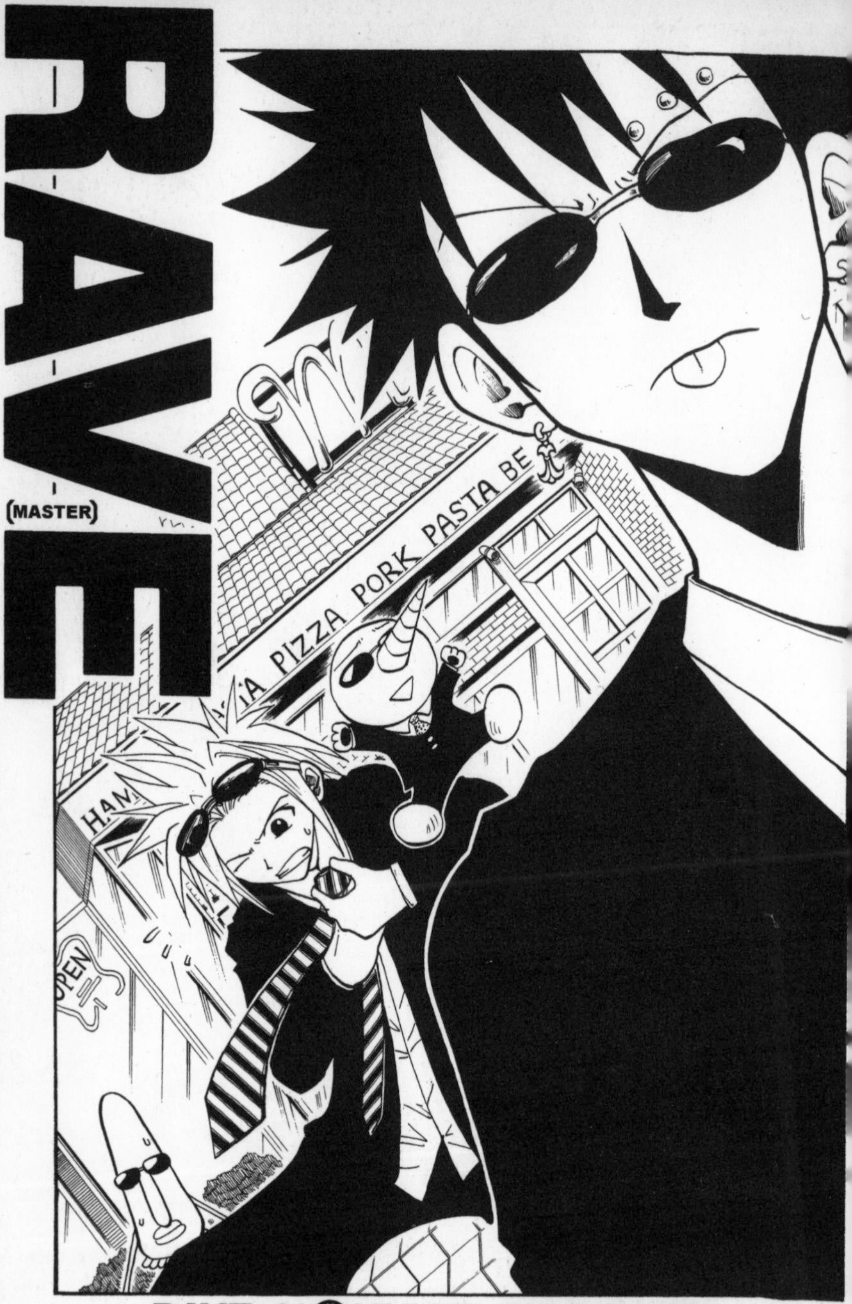
RAVE (MASTER)
IA PIZZA PORK PASTA BE
HAM
OPEN

RAVE:61 ✠ UNYIELDING FAITH

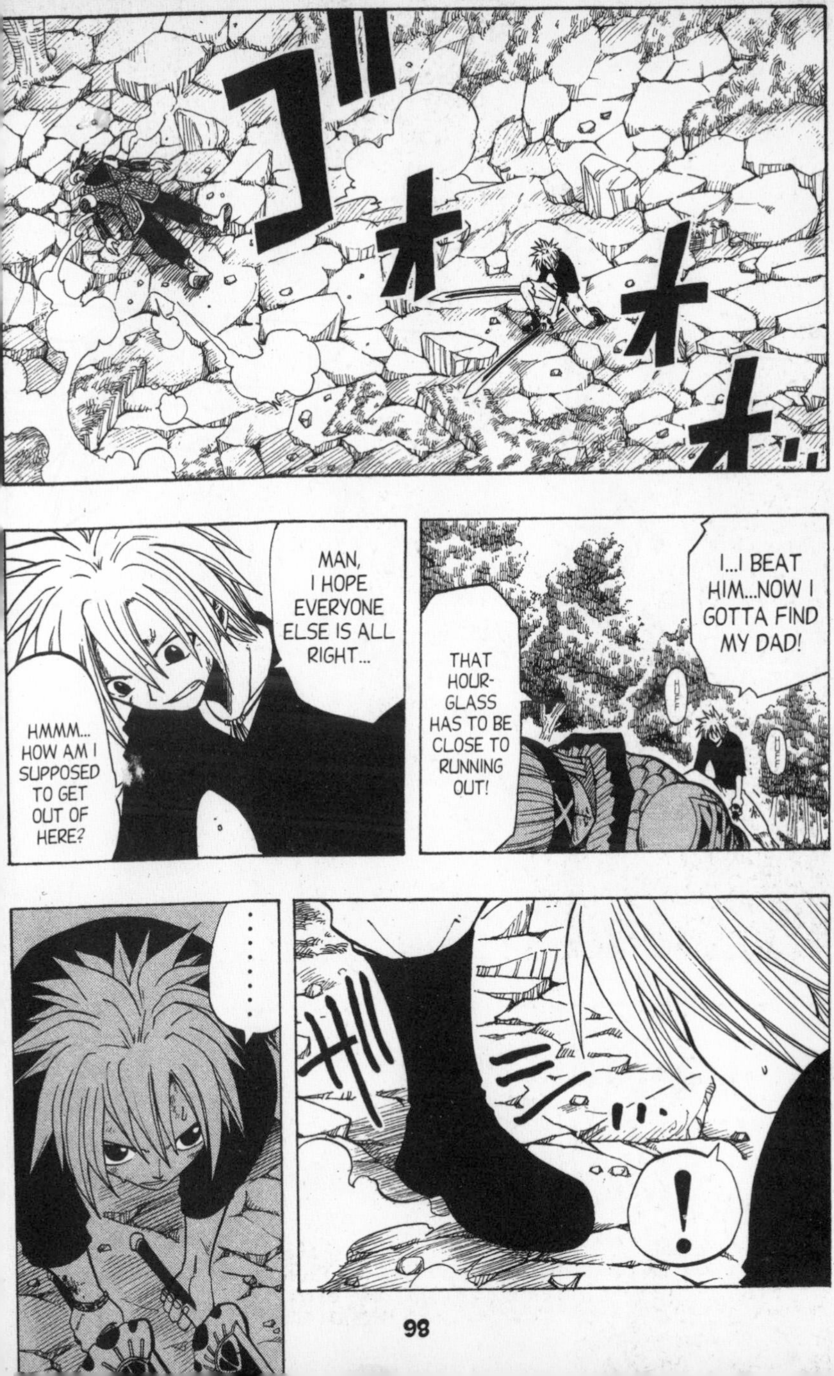
ゴオオオッ
I...I BEAT HIM...NOW I GOTTA FIND MY DAD!
HUFF
HUFF
THAT HOUR-GLASS HAS TO BE CLOSE TO RUNNING OUT!
MAN, I HOPE EVERYONE ELSE IS ALL RIGHT...
HMMM... HOW AM I SUPPOSED TO GET OUT OF HERE?
ザッ
!
......

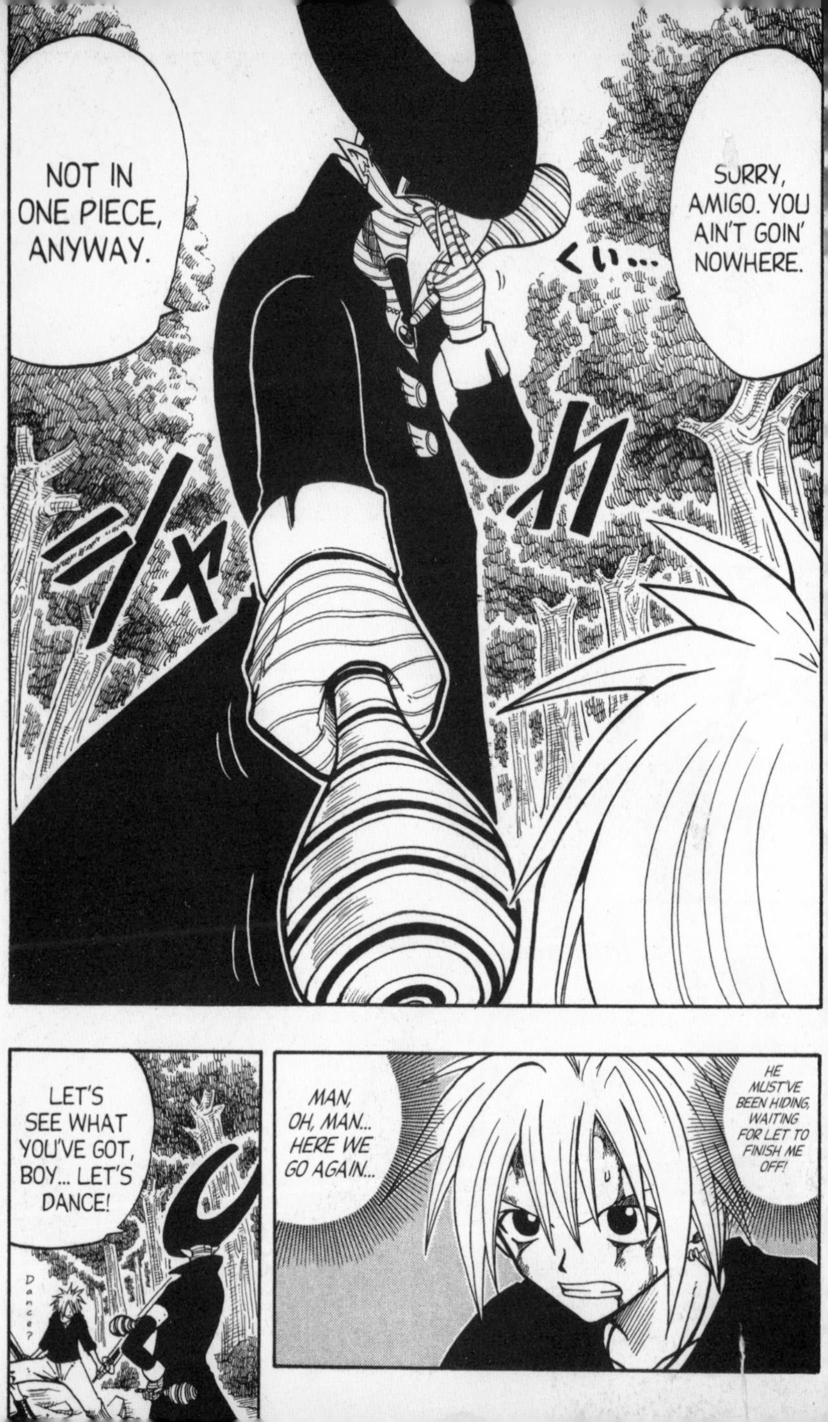
SORRY, AMIGO. YOU AIN'T GOIN' NOWHERE.
くい...
NOT IN ONE PIECE, ANYWAY.
ニヤ
HE MUST'VE BEEN HIDING, WAITING FOR LET TO FINISH ME OFF!
MAN, OH, MAN... HERE WE GO AGAIN...
LET'S SEE WHAT YOU'VE GOT, BOY... LET'S DANCE!
Dance?

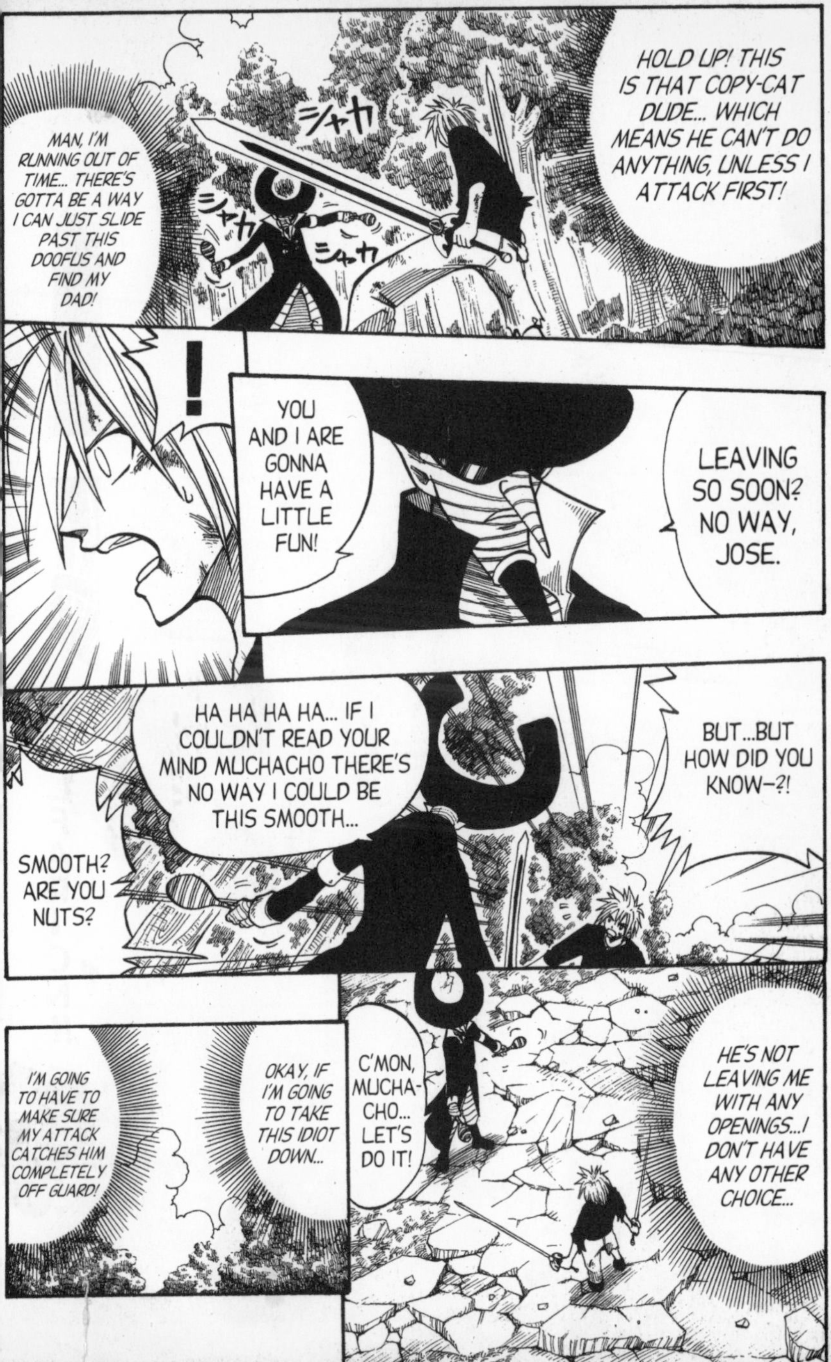
HOLD UP! THIS IS THAT COPY-CAT DUDE... WHICH MEANS HE CAN'T DO ANYTHING, UNLESS I ATTACK FIRST!
シャカ
シャカ
シャカ
MAN, I'M RUNNING OUT OF TIME... THERE'S GOTTA BE A WAY I CAN JUST SLIDE PAST THIS DOOFUS AND FIND MY DAD!
LEAVING SO SOON? NO WAY, JOSE.
YOU AND I ARE GONNA HAVE A LITTLE FUN!
!
BUT...BUT HOW DID YOU KNOW-?!
HA HA HA HA... IF I COULDN'T READ YOUR MIND MUCHACHO THERE'S NO WAY I COULD BE THIS SMOOTH...
SMOOTH? ARE YOU NUTS?
HE'S NOT LEAVING ME WITH ANY OPENINGS...I DON'T HAVE ANY OTHER CHOICE...
C'MON, MUCHA-CHO... LET'S DO IT!
OKAY, IF I'M GOING TO TAKE THIS IDIOT DOWN...
I'M GOING TO HAVE TO MAKE SURE MY ATTACK CATCHES HIM COMPLETELY OFF GUARD!

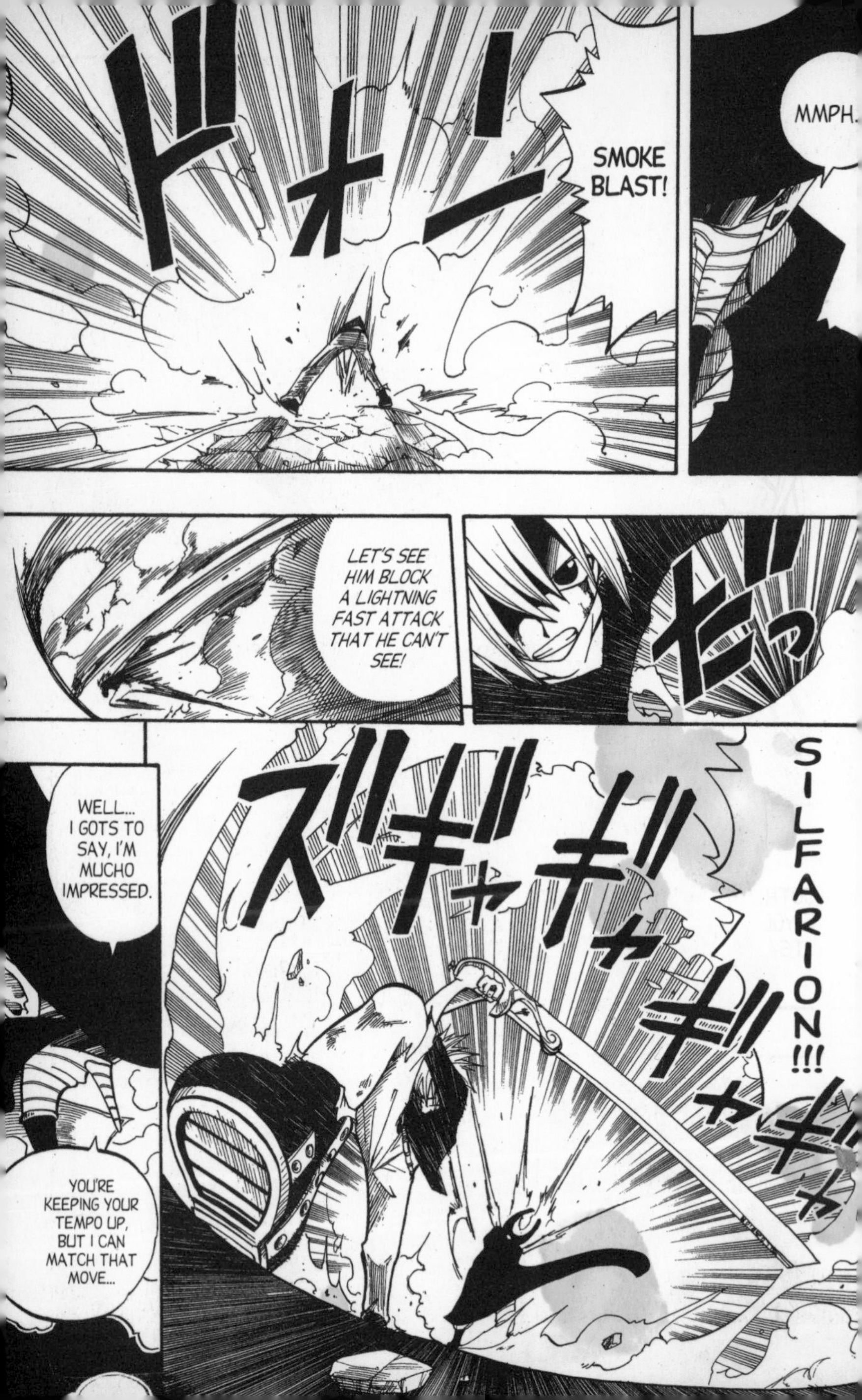
MMPH.
SMOKE BLAST!
ドオー
たっ
LET'S SEE HIM BLOCK A LIGHTNING FAST ATTACK THAT HE CAN'T SEE!
SILFARION!!!
ズギャギャギャギャ
WELL... I GOTS TO SAY, I'M MUCHO IMPRESSED.
YOU'RE KEEPING YOUR TEMPO UP, BUT I CAN MATCH THAT MOVE...

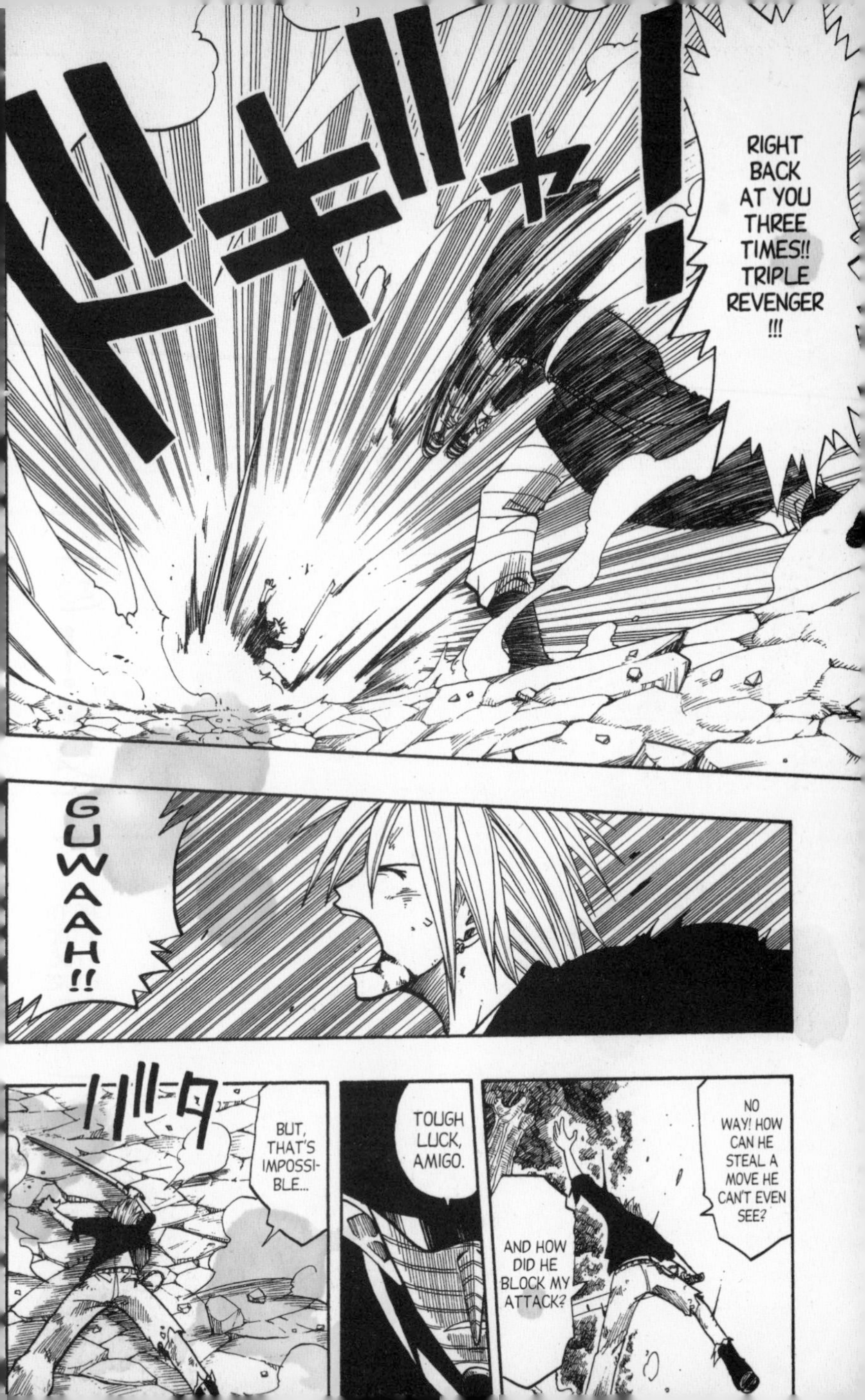
RIGHT BACK AT YOU THREE TIMES!! TRIPLE REVENGER !!!
GUWAAH!!
NO WAY! HOW CAN HE STEAL A MOVE HE CAN'T EVEN SEE?
AND HOW DID HE BLOCK MY ATTACK?
TOUGH LUCK, AMIGO.
BUT, THAT'S IMPOSSI-BLE...

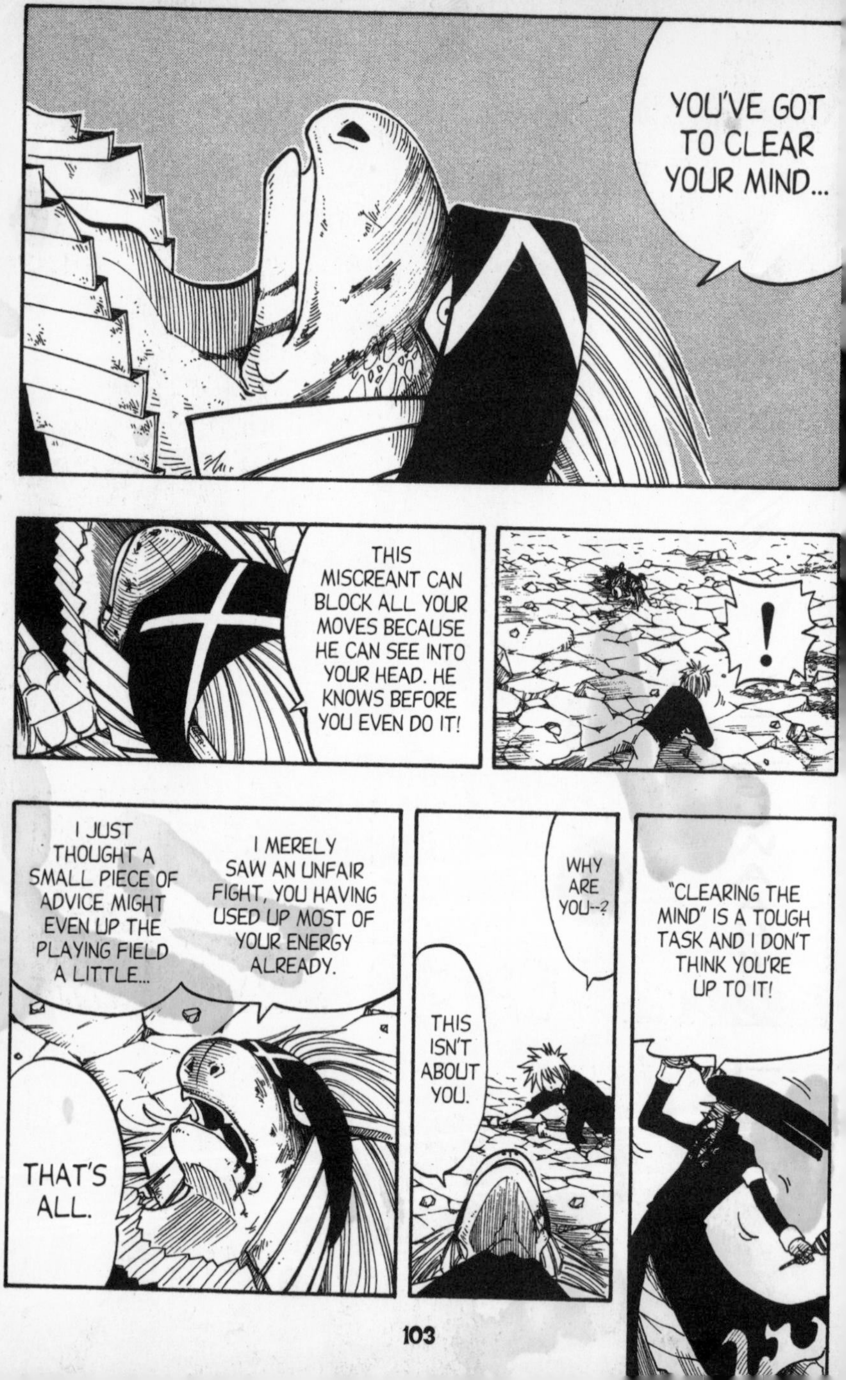
YOU'VE GOT TO CLEAR YOUR MIND...
!
THIS MISCREANT CAN BLOCK ALL YOUR MOVES BECAUSE HE CAN SEE INTO YOUR HEAD. HE KNOWS BEFORE YOU EVEN DO IT!
"CLEARING THE MIND" IS A TOUGH TASK AND I DON'T THINK YOU'RE UP TO IT!
WHY ARE YOU--?
THIS ISN'T ABOUT YOU.
I MERELY SAW AN UNFAIR FIGHT, YOU HAVING USED UP MOST OF YOUR ENERGY ALREADY.
I JUST THOUGHT A SMALL PIECE OF ADVICE MIGHT EVEN UP THE PLAYING FIELD A LITTLE...
THAT'S ALL.

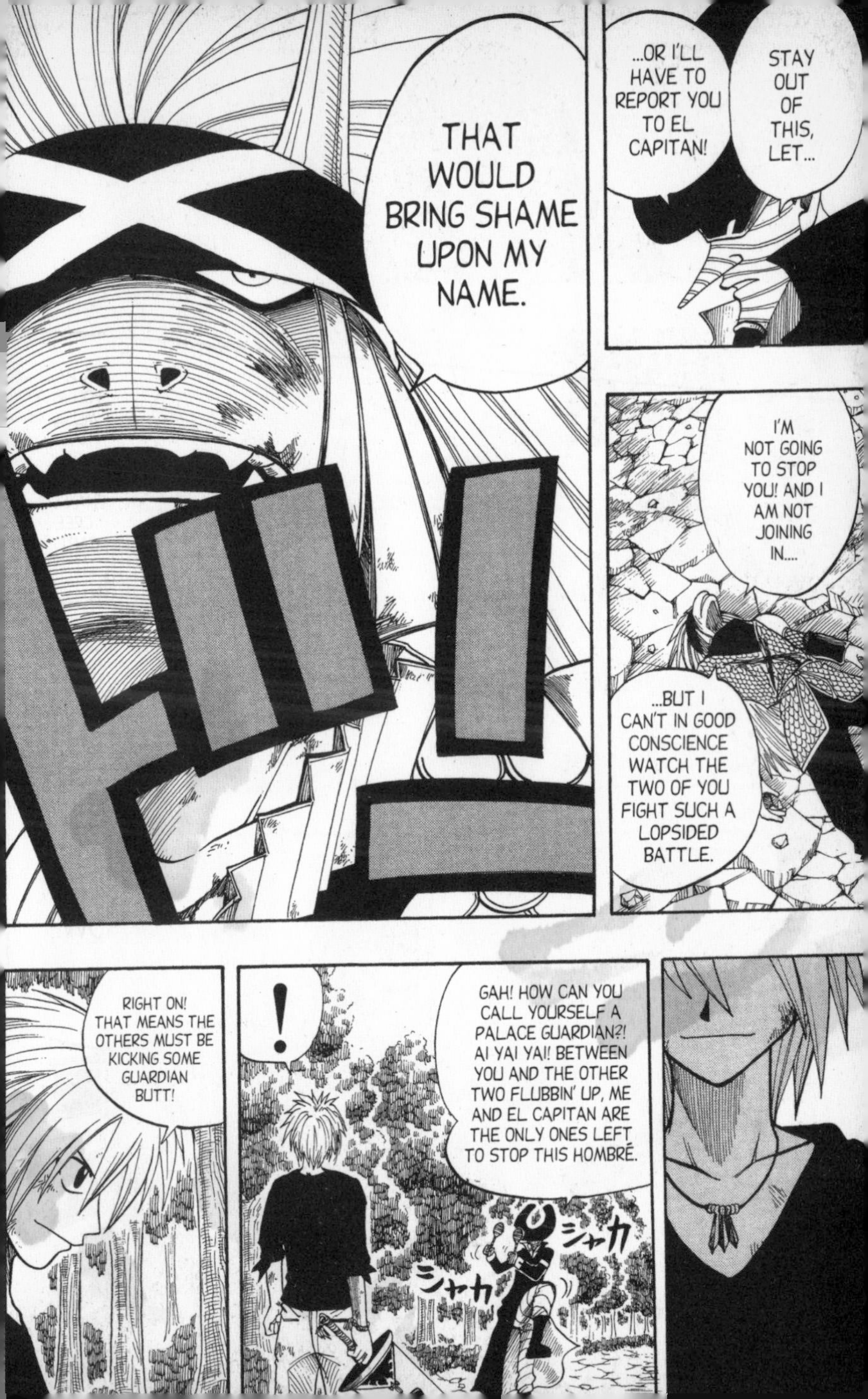
STAY OUT OF THIS, LET...
...OR I'LL HAVE TO REPORT YOU TO EL CAPITAN!
I'M NOT GOING TO STOP YOU! AND I AM NOT JOINING IN....
...BUT I CAN'T IN GOOD CONSCIENCE WATCH THE TWO OF YOU FIGHT SUCH A LOPSIDED BATTLE.
THAT WOULD BRING SHAME UPON MY NAME.
GAH! HOW CAN YOU CALL YOURSELF A PALACE GUARDIAN?! AI YAI YAI! BETWEEN YOU AND THE OTHER TWO FLUBBIN' UP, ME AND EL CAPITAN ARE THE ONLY ONES LEFT TO STOP THIS HOMBRÉ.
!
シャカ
シャカ
RIGHT ON! THAT MEANS THE OTHERS MUST BE KICKING SOME GUARDIAN BUTT!

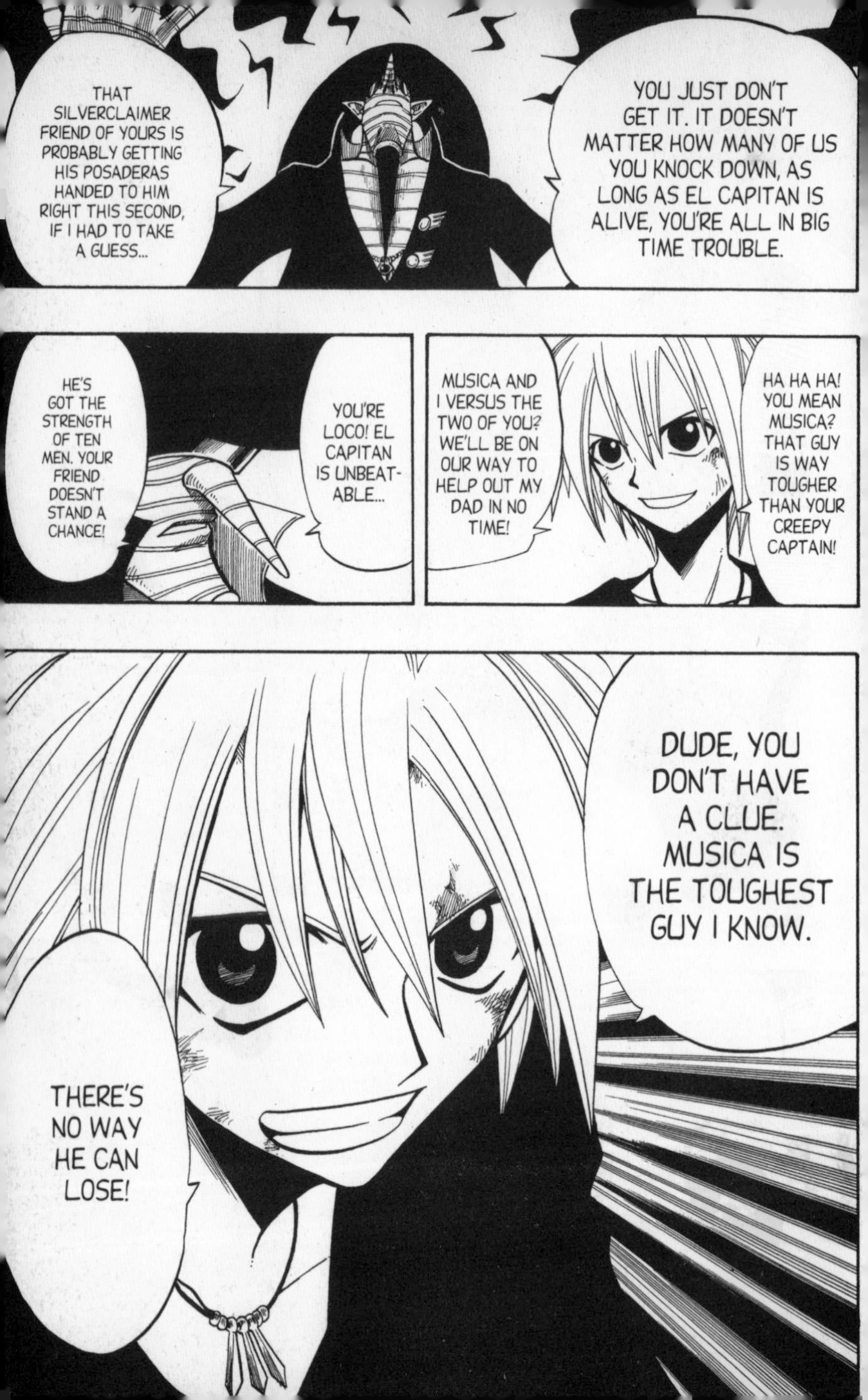
YOU JUST DON'T GET IT. IT DOESN'T MATTER HOW MANY OF US YOU KNOCK DOWN, AS LONG AS EL CAPITAN IS ALIVE, YOU'RE ALL IN BIG TIME TROUBLE.
THAT SILVERCLAIMER FRIEND OF YOURS IS PROBABLY GETTING HIS POSADERAS HANDED TO HIM RIGHT THIS SECOND, IF I HAD TO TAKE A GUESS...
HA HA HA! YOU MEAN MUSICA? THAT GUY IS WAY TOUGHER THAN YOUR CREEPY CAPTAIN!
MUSICA AND I VERSUS THE TWO OF YOU? WE'LL BE ON OUR WAY TO HELP OUT MY DAD IN NO TIME!
YOU'RE LOCO! EL CAPITAN IS UNBEAT-ABLE...
HE'S GOT THE STRENGTH OF TEN MEN. YOUR FRIEND DOESN'T STAND A CHANCE!
DUDE, YOU DON'T HAVE A CLUE. MUSICA IS THE TOUGHEST GUY I KNOW.
THERE'S NO WAY HE CAN LOSE!

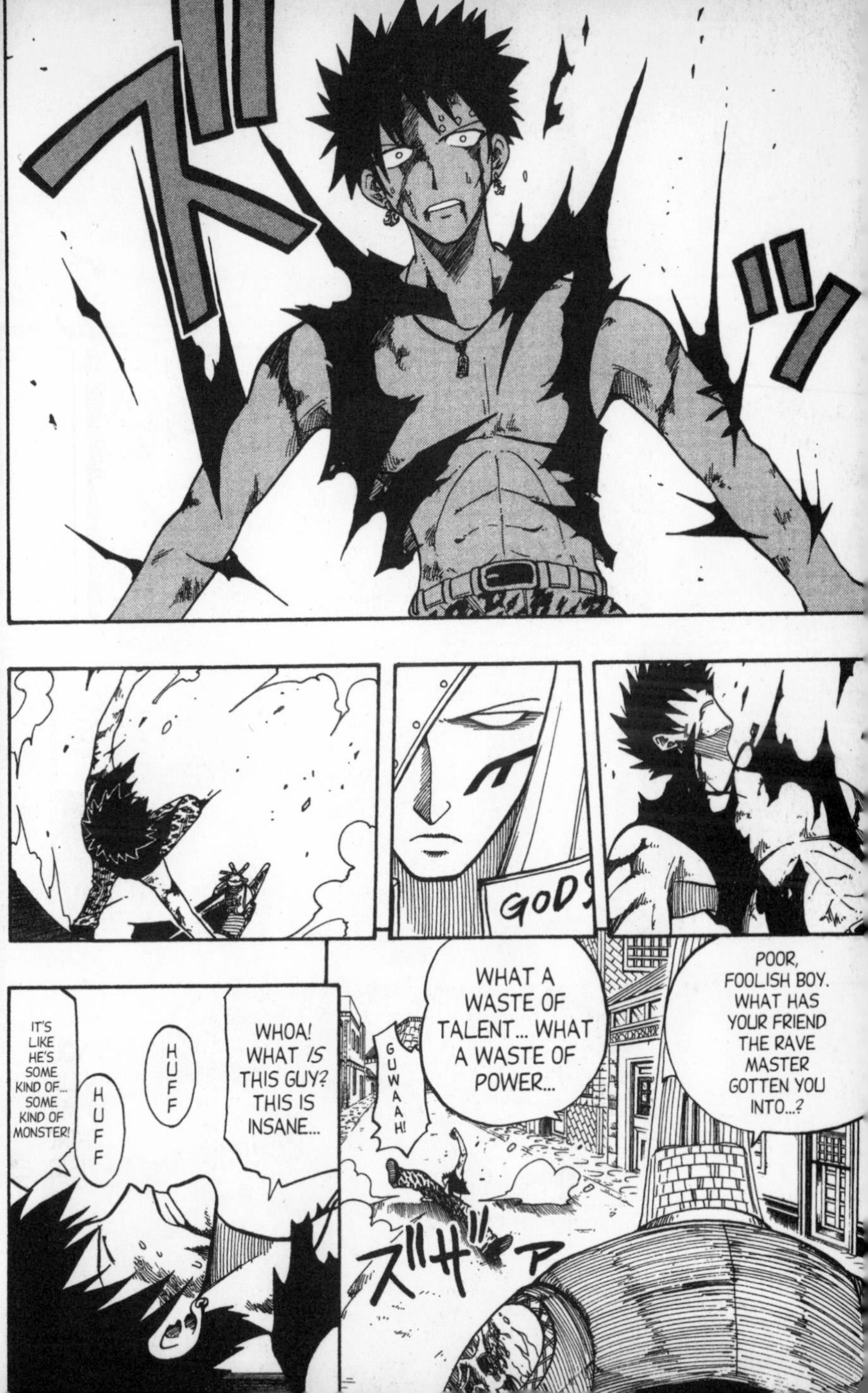
GODS
POOR, FOOLISH BOY. WHAT HAS YOUR FRIEND THE RAVE MASTER GOTTEN YOU INTO...?
WHAT A WASTE OF TALENT... WHAT A WASTE OF POWER...
GUWAAH!
WHOA! WHAT *IS* THIS GUY? THIS IS INSANE...
HUFF
HUFF
IT'S LIKE HE'S SOME KIND OF... SOME KIND OF MONSTER!

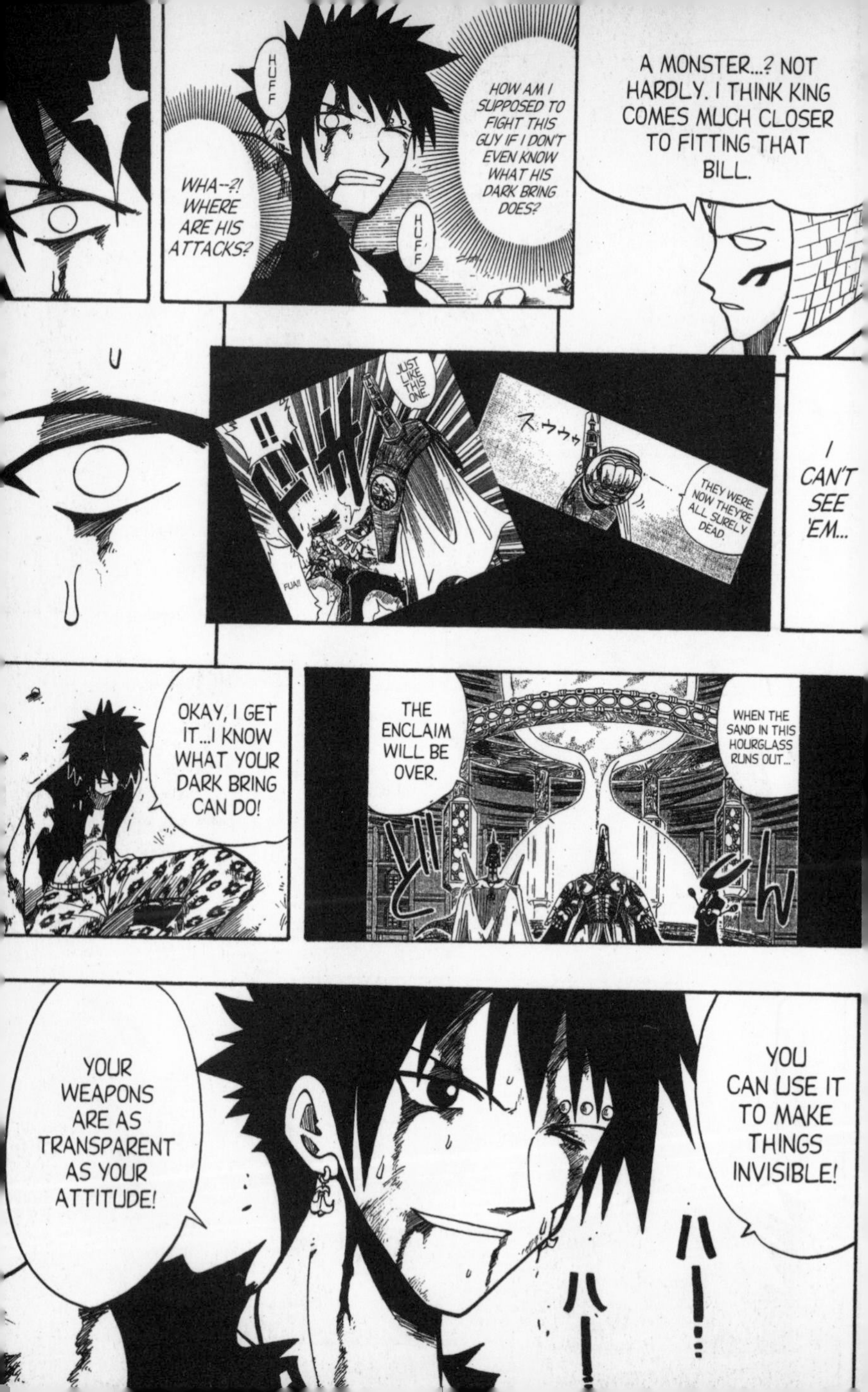
A MONSTER...? NOT HARDLY. I THINK KING COMES MUCH CLOSER TO FITTING THAT BILL.
HUFF
HOW AM I SUPPOSED TO FIGHT THIS GUY IF I DON'T EVEN KNOW WHAT HIS DARK BRING DOES?
HUFF
WHA--?! WHERE ARE HIS ATTACKS?
I CAN'T SEE 'EM...
スウゥゥ
THEY WERE. NOW THEY'RE ALL SURELY DEAD.
JUST LIKE THIS ONE.
!!
FUA!!
U
WHEN THE SAND IN THIS HOURGLASS RUNS OUT...
THE ENCLAIM WILL BE OVER.
OKAY, I GET IT...I KNOW WHAT YOUR DARK BRING CAN DO!
YOU CAN USE IT TO MAKE THINGS INVISIBLE!
YOUR WEAPONS ARE AS TRANSPARENT AS YOUR ATTITUDE!

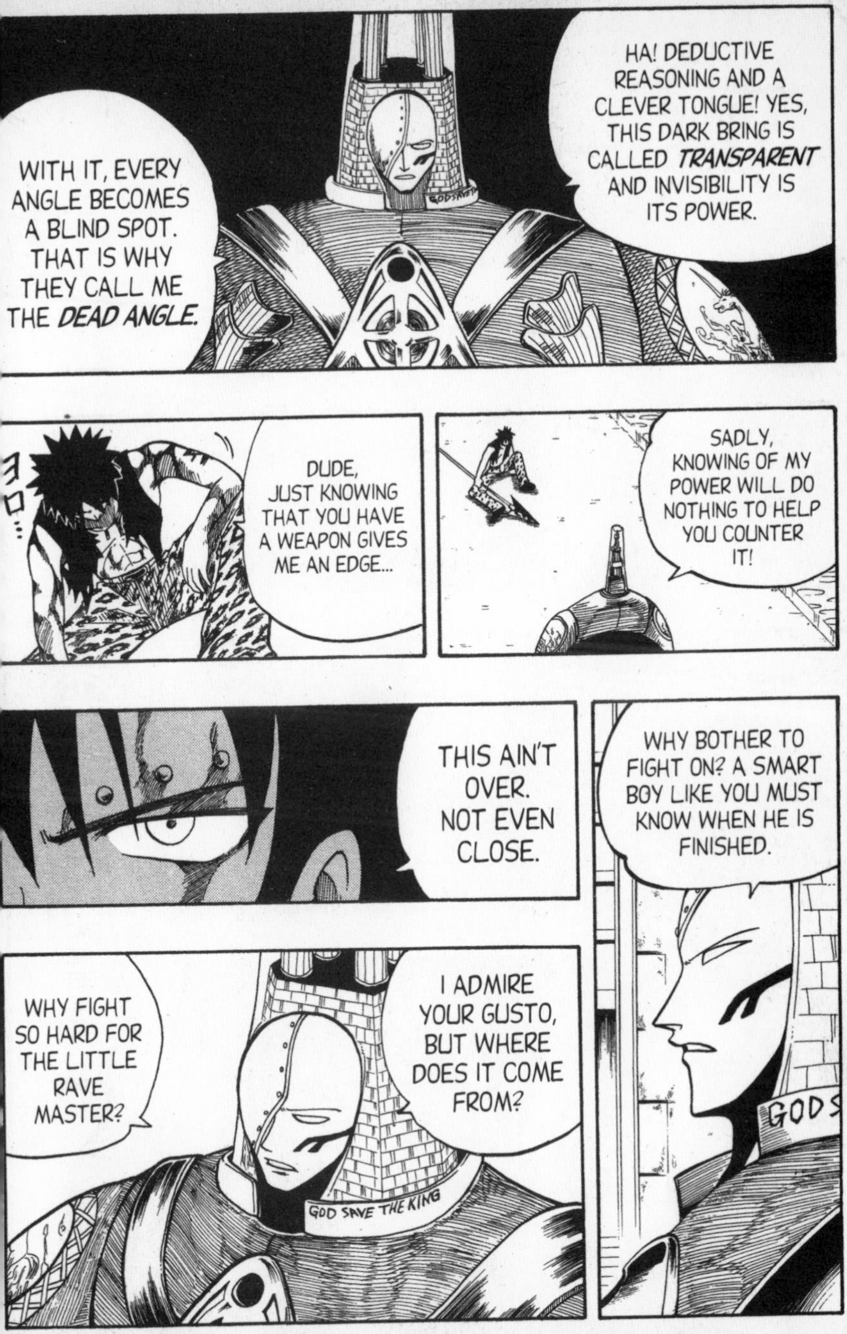
HA! DEDUCTIVE REASONING AND A CLEVER TONGUE! YES, THIS DARK BRING IS CALLED *TRANSPARENT* AND INVISIBILITY IS ITS POWER.
WITH IT, EVERY ANGLE BECOMES A BLIND SPOT. THAT IS WHY THEY CALL ME THE *DEAD ANGLE*.
SADLY, KNOWING OF MY POWER WILL DO NOTHING TO HELP YOU COUNTER IT!
DUDE, JUST KNOWING THAT YOU HAVE A WEAPON GIVES ME AN EDGE...
ヨロ…
WHY BOTHER TO FIGHT ON? A SMART BOY LIKE YOU MUST KNOW WHEN HE IS FINISHED.
GODS
THIS AIN'T OVER. NOT EVEN CLOSE.
I ADMIRE YOUR GUSTO, BUT WHERE DOES IT COME FROM?
WHY FIGHT SO HARD FOR THE LITTLE RAVE MASTER?
GOD SAVE THE KING

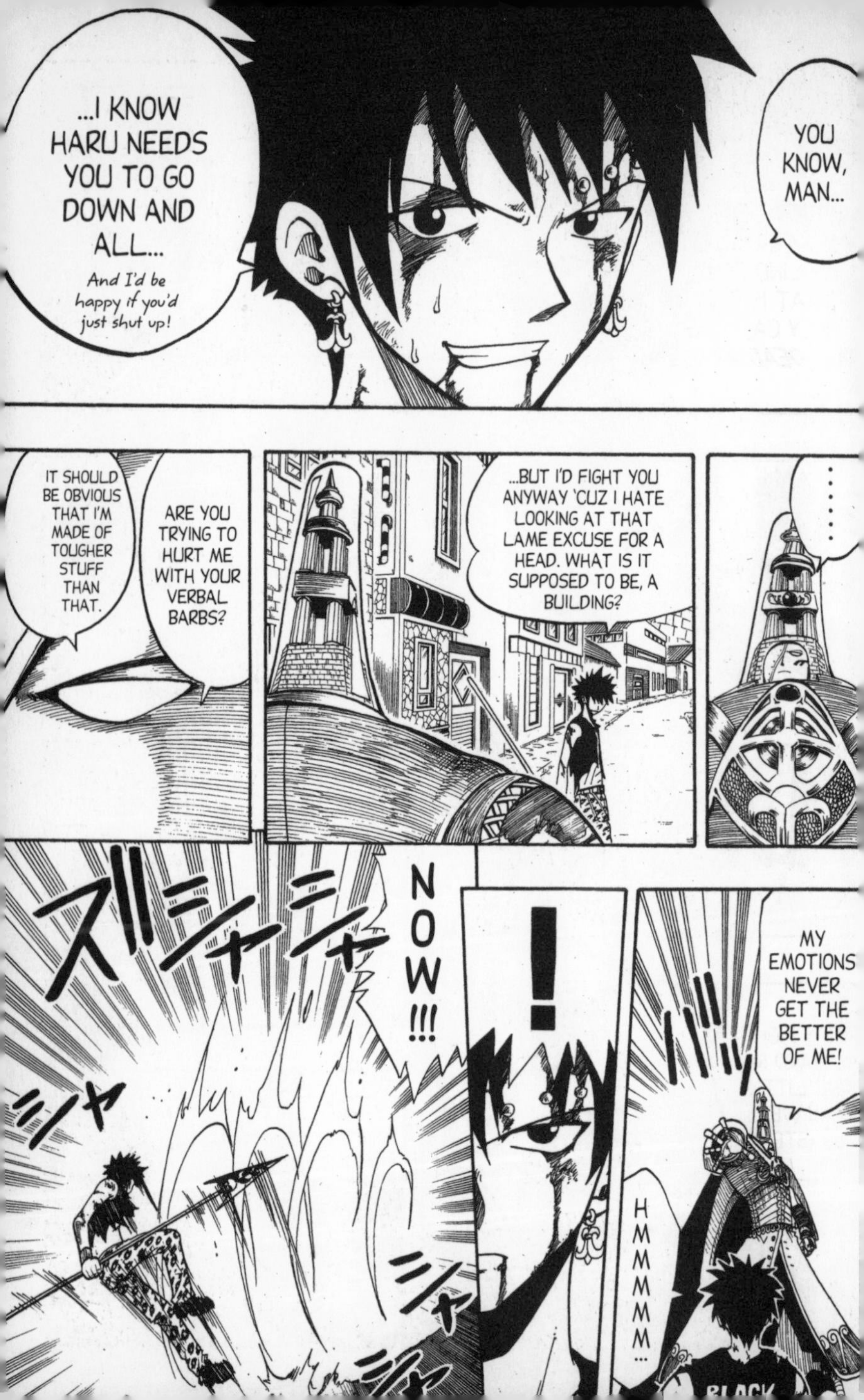
YOU KNOW, MAN...
...I KNOW HARU NEEDS YOU TO GO DOWN AND ALL...
And I'd be happy if you'd just shut up!
......
...BUT I'D FIGHT YOU ANYWAY 'CUZ I HATE LOOKING AT THAT LAME EXCUSE FOR A HEAD. WHAT IS IT SUPPOSED TO BE, A BUILDING?
ARE YOU TRYING TO HURT ME WITH YOUR VERBAL BARBS?
IT SHOULD BE OBVIOUS THAT I'M MADE OF TOUGHER STUFF THAN THAT.
MY EMOTIONS NEVER GET THE BETTER OF ME!
HMMMMM...
!
NOW!!!

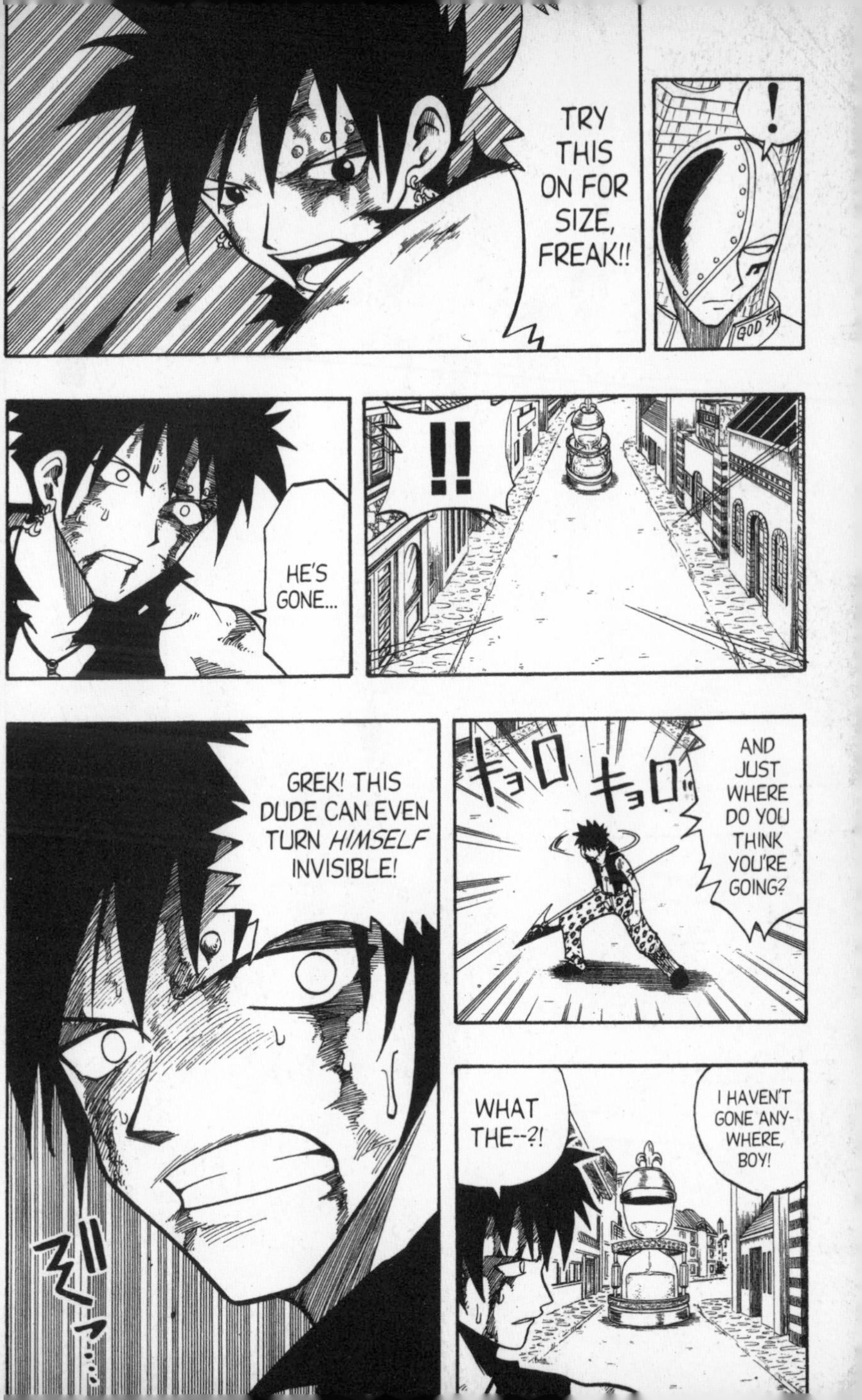
!
TRY THIS ON FOR SIZE, FREAK!!
!!
HE'S GONE...
AND JUST WHERE DO YOU THINK YOU'RE GOING?
キョロ キョロ
I HAVEN'T GONE ANY-WHERE, BOY!
WHAT THE--?!
GREK! THIS DUDE CAN EVEN TURN *HIMSELF* INVISIBLE!

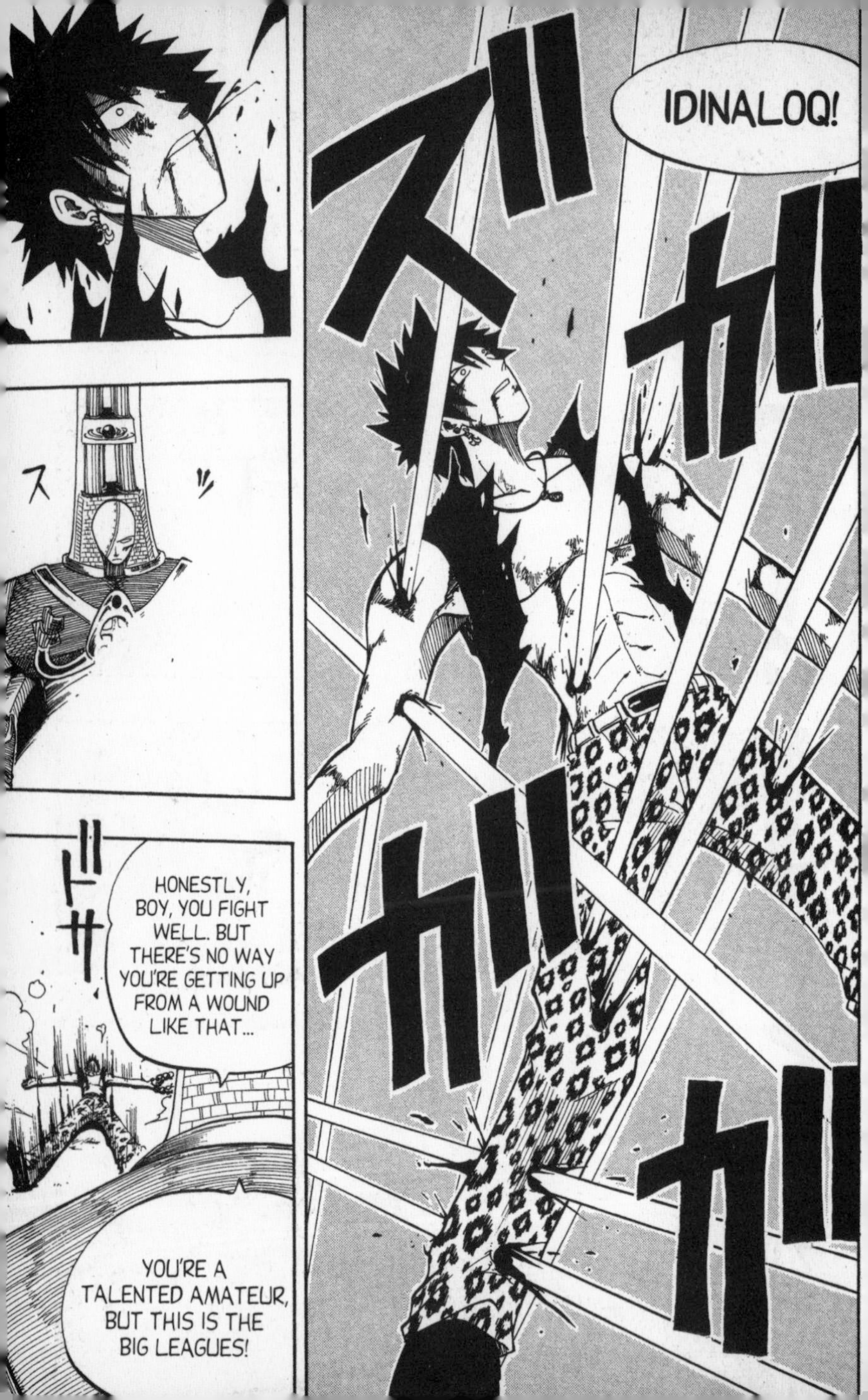
IDINALOQ!
HONESTLY, BOY, YOU FIGHT WELL. BUT THERE'S NO WAY YOU'RE GETTING UP FROM A WOUND LIKE THAT...
YOU'RE A TALENTED AMATEUR, BUT THIS IS THE BIG LEAGUES!

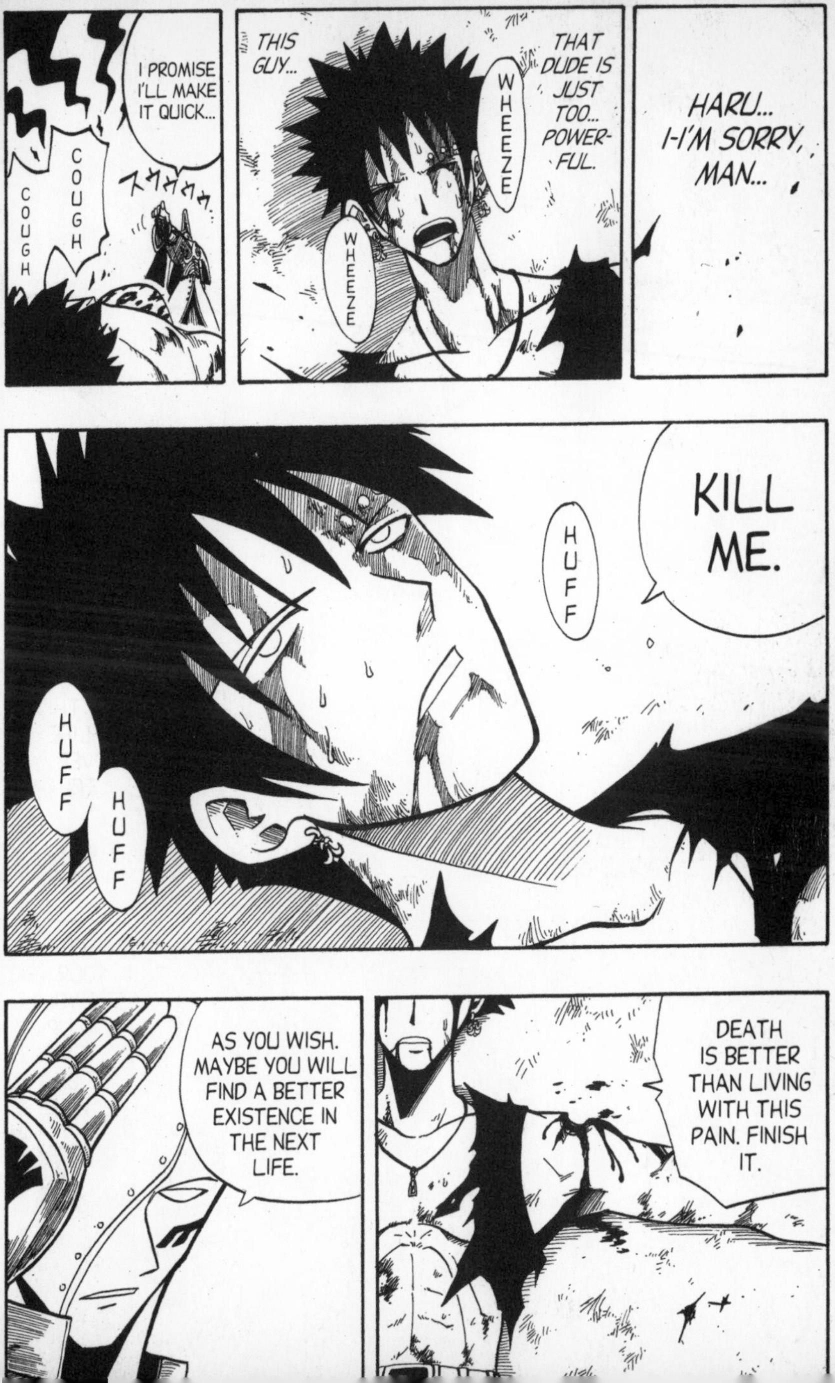
HARU... I-I'M SORRY, MAN...
THAT DUDE IS JUST TOO... POWER-FUL.
WHEEZE
THIS GUY...
WHEEZE
I PROMISE I'LL MAKE IT QUICK...
COUGH
COUGH
KILL ME.
HUFF
HUFF
HUFF
DEATH IS BETTER THAN LIVING WITH THIS PAIN. FINISH IT.
AS YOU WISH. MAYBE YOU WILL FIND A BETTER EXISTENCE IN THE NEXT LIFE.

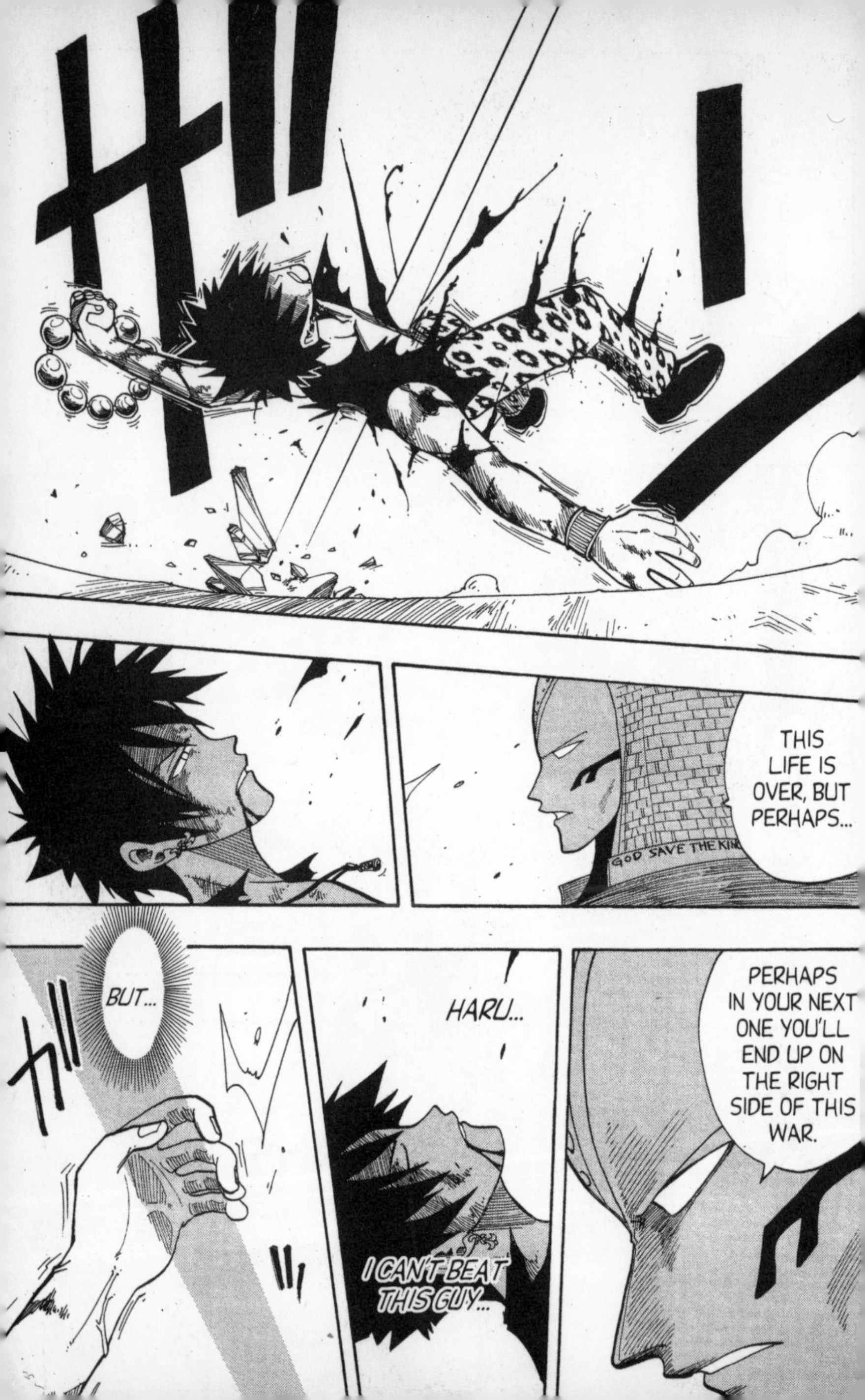
THIS LIFE IS OVER, BUT PERHAPS...
PERHAPS IN YOUR NEXT ONE YOU'LL END UP ON THE RIGHT SIDE OF THIS WAR.
HARU...
I CAN'T BEAT THIS GUY...
BUT...

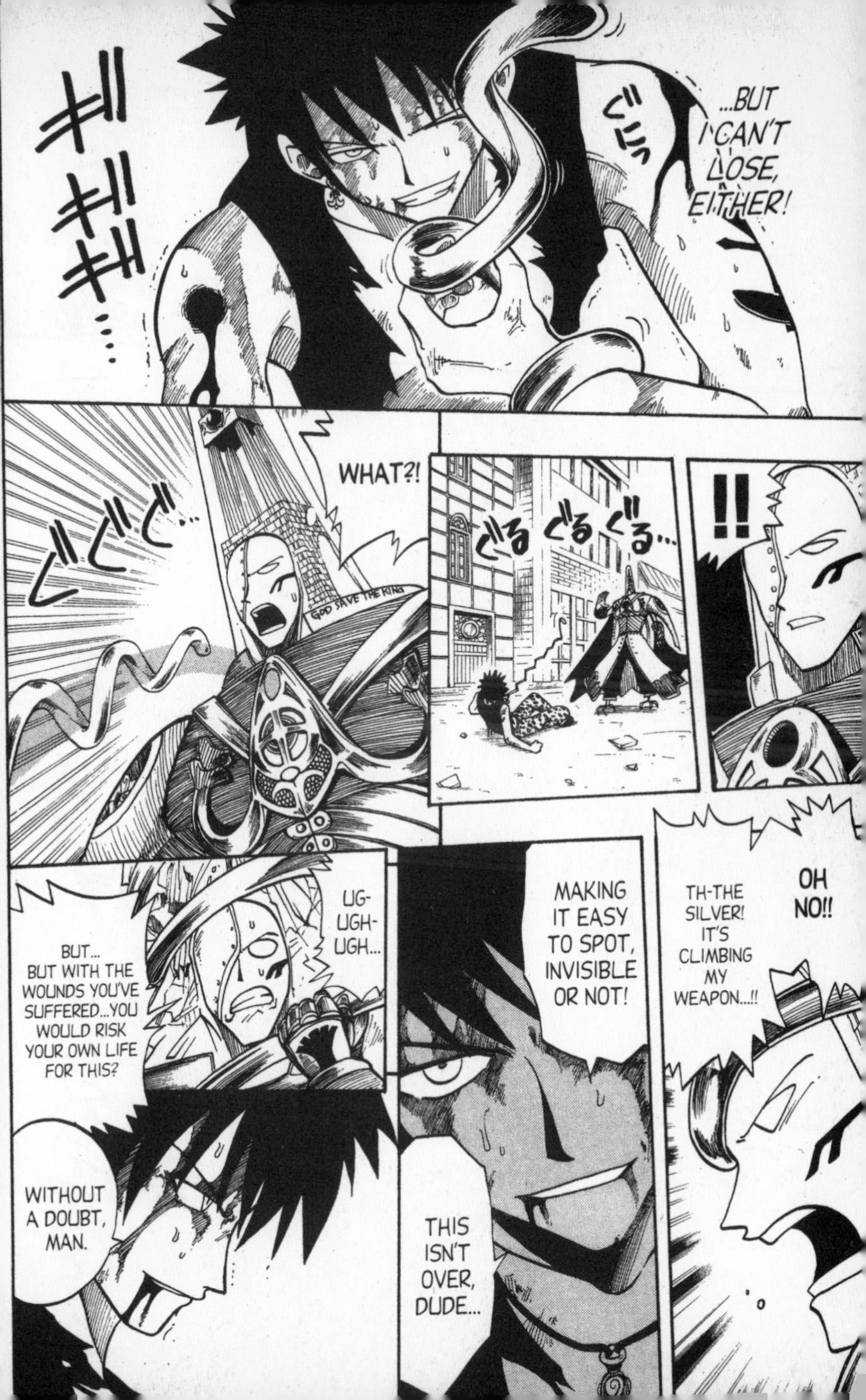

...BUT I CAN'T LOSE, EITHER!
!!
ぐる ぐる ぐる...
WHAT?!
GOD SAVE THE KING
OH NO!!
TH-THE SILVER! IT'S CLIMBING MY WEAPON...!!
MAKING IT EASY TO SPOT, INVISIBLE OR NOT!
THIS ISN'T OVER, DUDE...
UG-UGH-UGH...
BUT... BUT WITH THE WOUNDS YOU'VE SUFFERED...YOU WOULD RISK YOUR OWN LIFE FOR THIS?
WITHOUT A DOUBT, MAN.

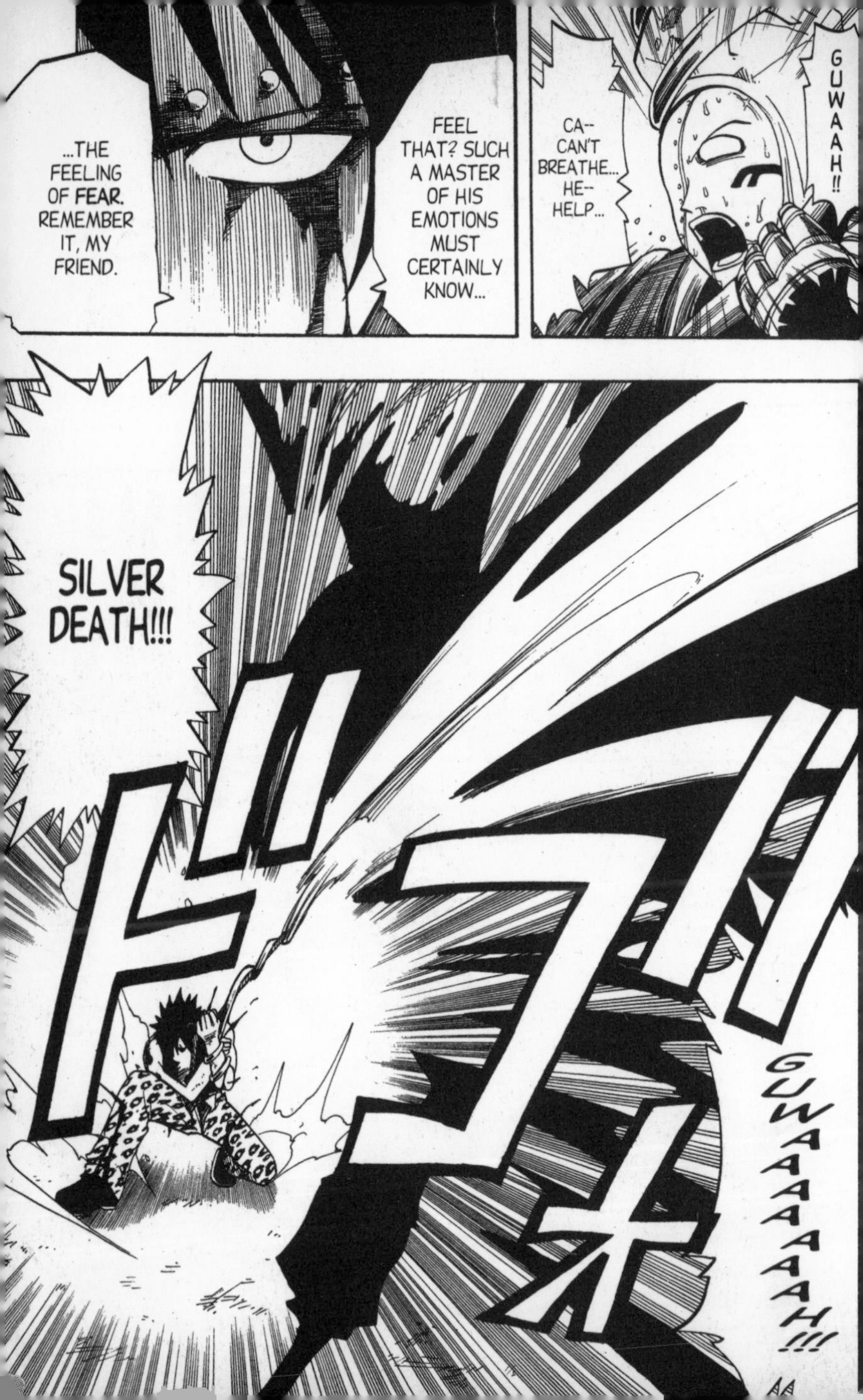
GUWAAH!!
CA-- CAN'T BREATHE... HE-- HELP...
FEEL THAT? SUCH A MASTER OF HIS EMOTIONS MUST CERTAINLY KNOW...
...THE FEELING OF FEAR. REMEMBER IT, MY FRIEND.
SILVER DEATH!!!
GUWAAAAAAAAH!!!

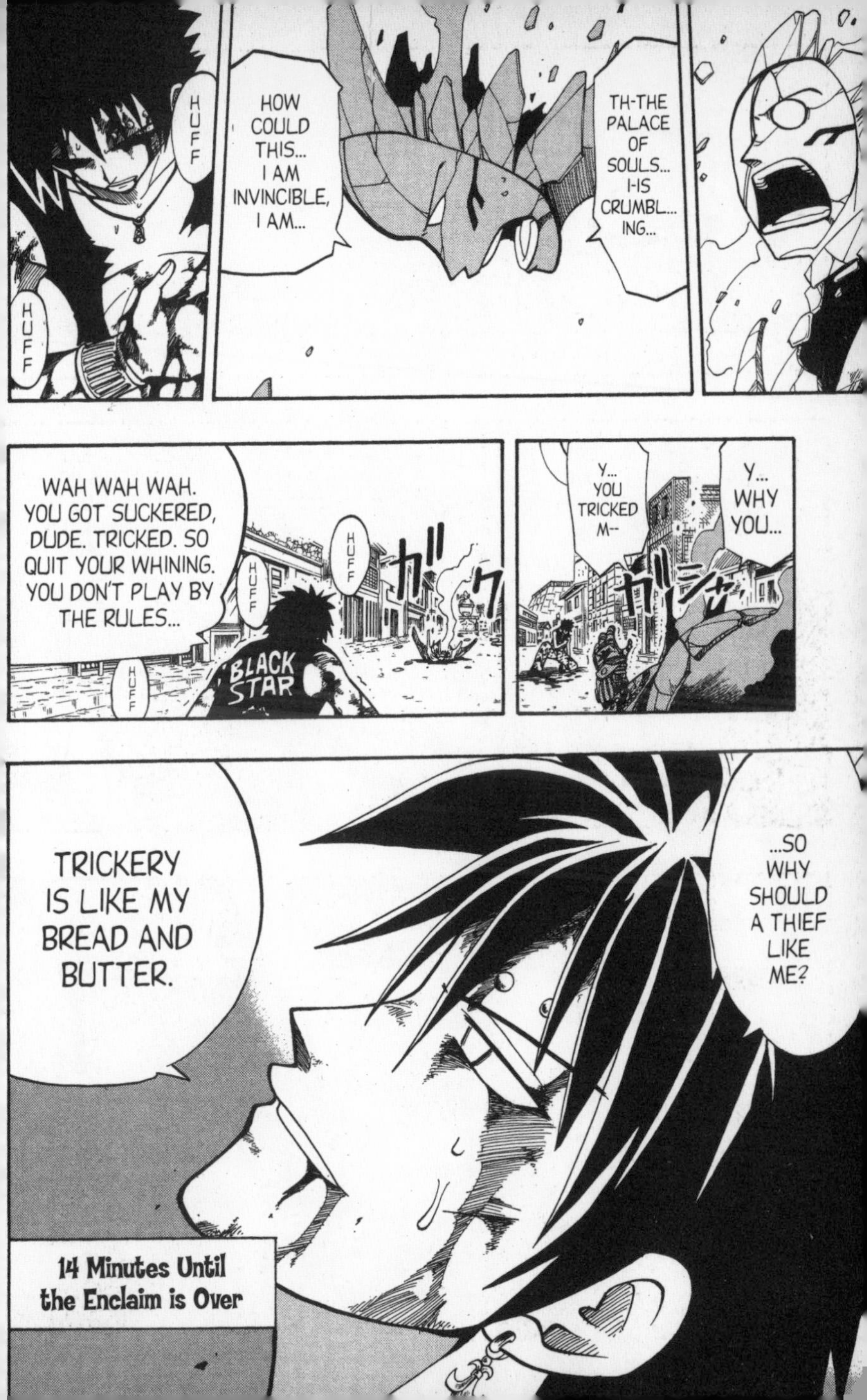
TH-THE PALACE OF SOULS... I-IS CRUMBL... ING...
HOW COULD THIS... I AM INVINCIBLE, I AM...
HUFF
HUFF
Y... WHY YOU...
Y... YOU TRICKED M--
ガシャ
ガク
HUFF
HUFF
WAH WAH WAH. YOU GOT SUCKERED, DUDE. TRICKED. SO QUIT YOUR WHINING. YOU DON'T PLAY BY THE RULES...
HUFF
BLACK STAR
...SO WHY SHOULD A THIEF LIKE ME?
TRICKERY IS LIKE MY BREAD AND BUTTER.
14 Minutes Until the Enclaim is Over

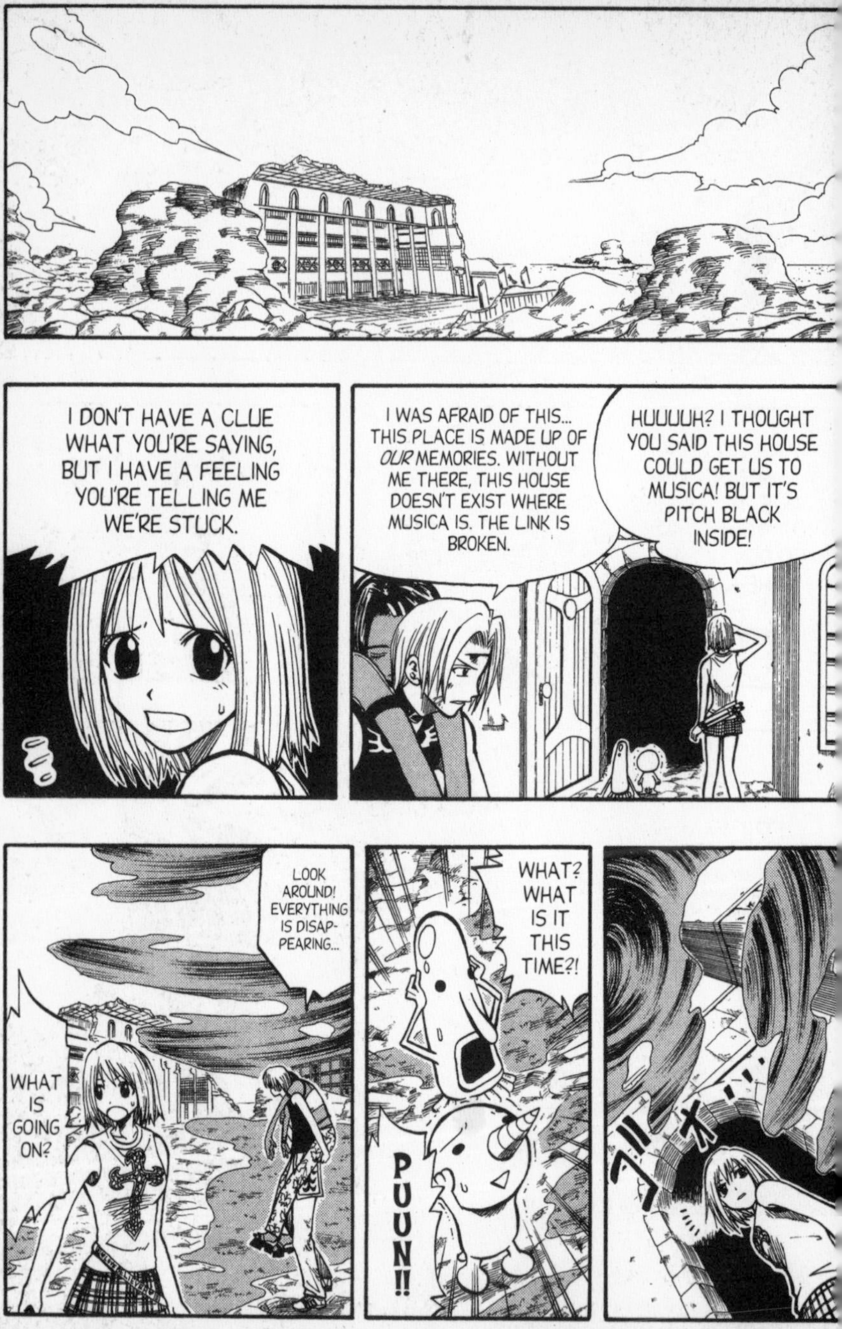
HUUUUH? I THOUGHT YOU SAID THIS HOUSE COULD GET US TO MUSICA! BUT IT'S PITCH BLACK INSIDE!
I WAS AFRAID OF THIS... THIS PLACE IS MADE UP OF *OUR* MEMORIES. WITHOUT ME THERE, THIS HOUSE DOESN'T EXIST WHERE MUSICA IS. THE LINK IS BROKEN.
I DON'T HAVE A CLUE WHAT YOU'RE SAYING, BUT I HAVE A FEELING YOU'RE TELLING ME WE'RE STUCK.
WHAT? WHAT IS IT THIS TIME?!
PUUN!!
LOOK AROUND! EVERYTHING IS DISAP-PEARING...
WHAT IS GOING ON?

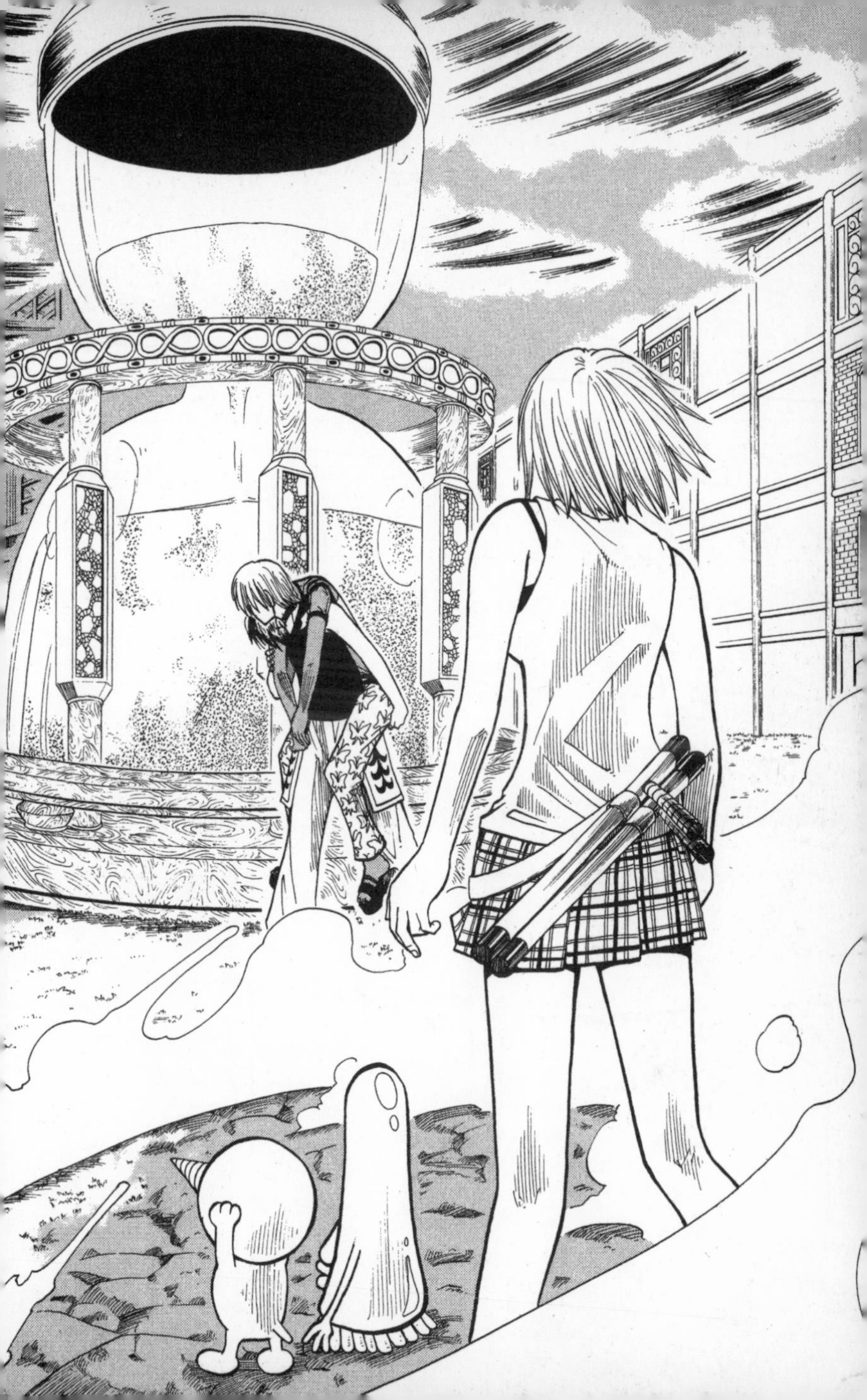

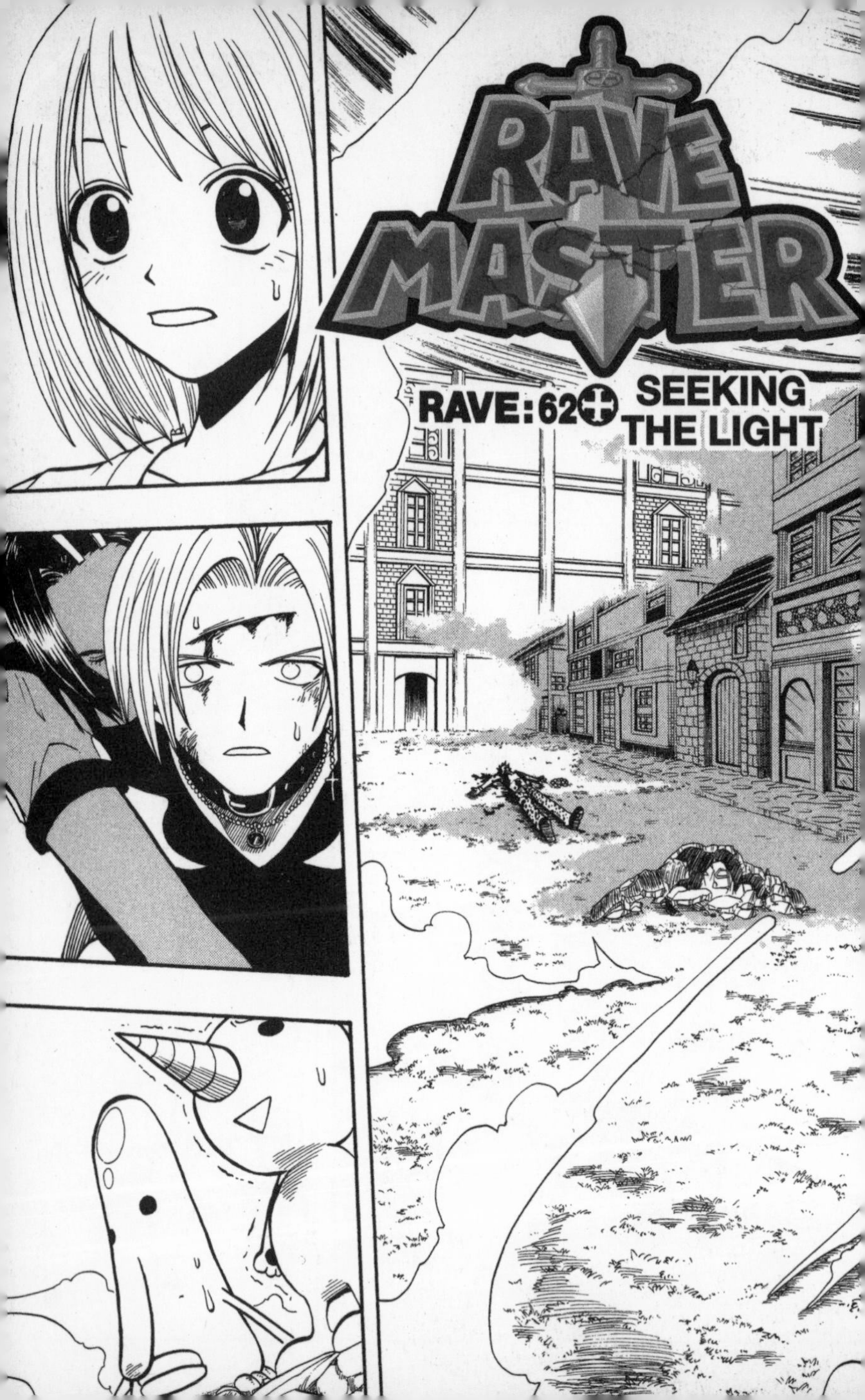

RAVE MASTER
RAVE: 62 SEEKING THE LIGHT

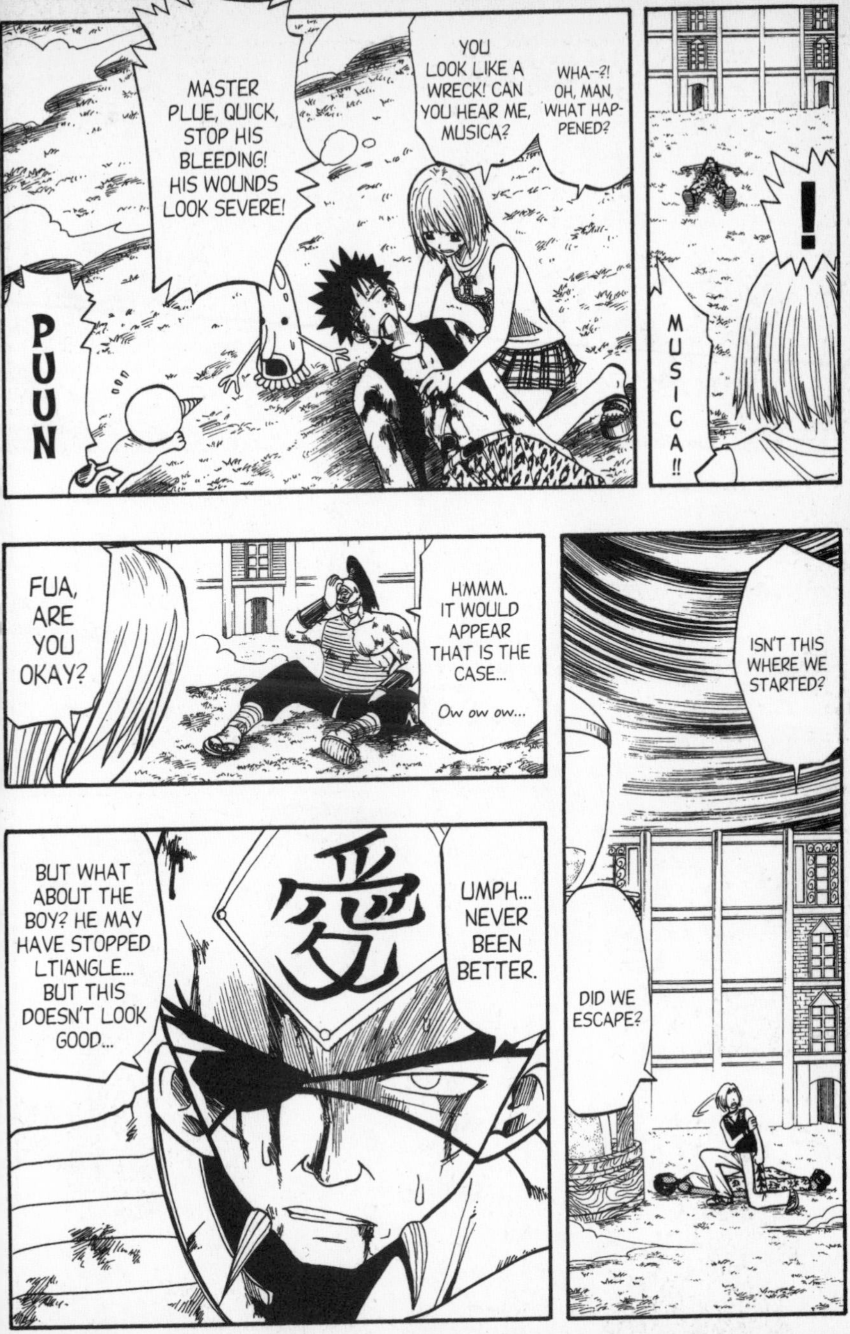
MUSICA!!
!
WHA--?! OH, MAN, WHAT HAP-PENED?
YOU LOOK LIKE A WRECK! CAN YOU HEAR ME, MUSICA?
MASTER PLUE, QUICK, STOP HIS BLEEDING! HIS WOUNDS LOOK SEVERE!
PUUN
ISN'T THIS WHERE WE STARTED?
DID WE ESCAPE?
HMMM. IT WOULD APPEAR THAT IS THE CASE...
Ow ow ow...
FUA, ARE YOU OKAY?
UMPH... NEVER BEEN BETTER.
BUT WHAT ABOUT THE BOY? HE MAY HAVE STOPPED LTIANGLE... BUT THIS DOESN'T LOOK GOOD...

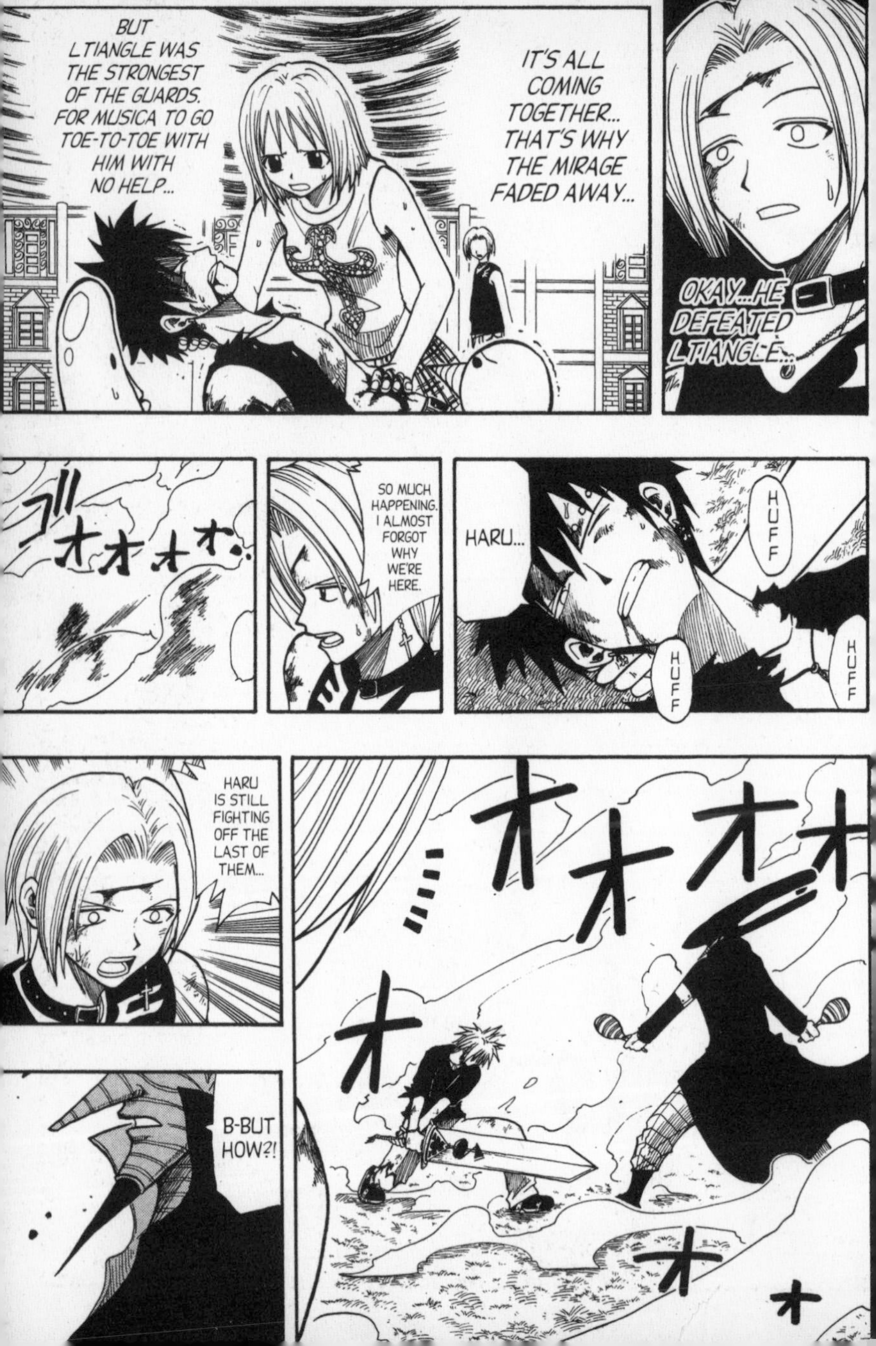
OKAY...HE DEFEATED LTIANGLE...
IT'S ALL COMING TOGETHER... THAT'S WHY THE MIRAGE FADED AWAY...
BUT LTIANGLE WAS THE STRONGEST OF THE GUARDS. FOR MUSICA TO GO TOE-TO-TOE WITH HIM WITH NO HELP...
HUFF
HUFF
HUFF
HARU...
SO MUCH HAPPENING. I ALMOST FORGOT WHY WE'RE HERE.
ゴオオオオ
オオオオ
オ
オ
オ
HARU IS STILL FIGHTING OFF THE LAST OF THEM...
B-BUT HOW?!

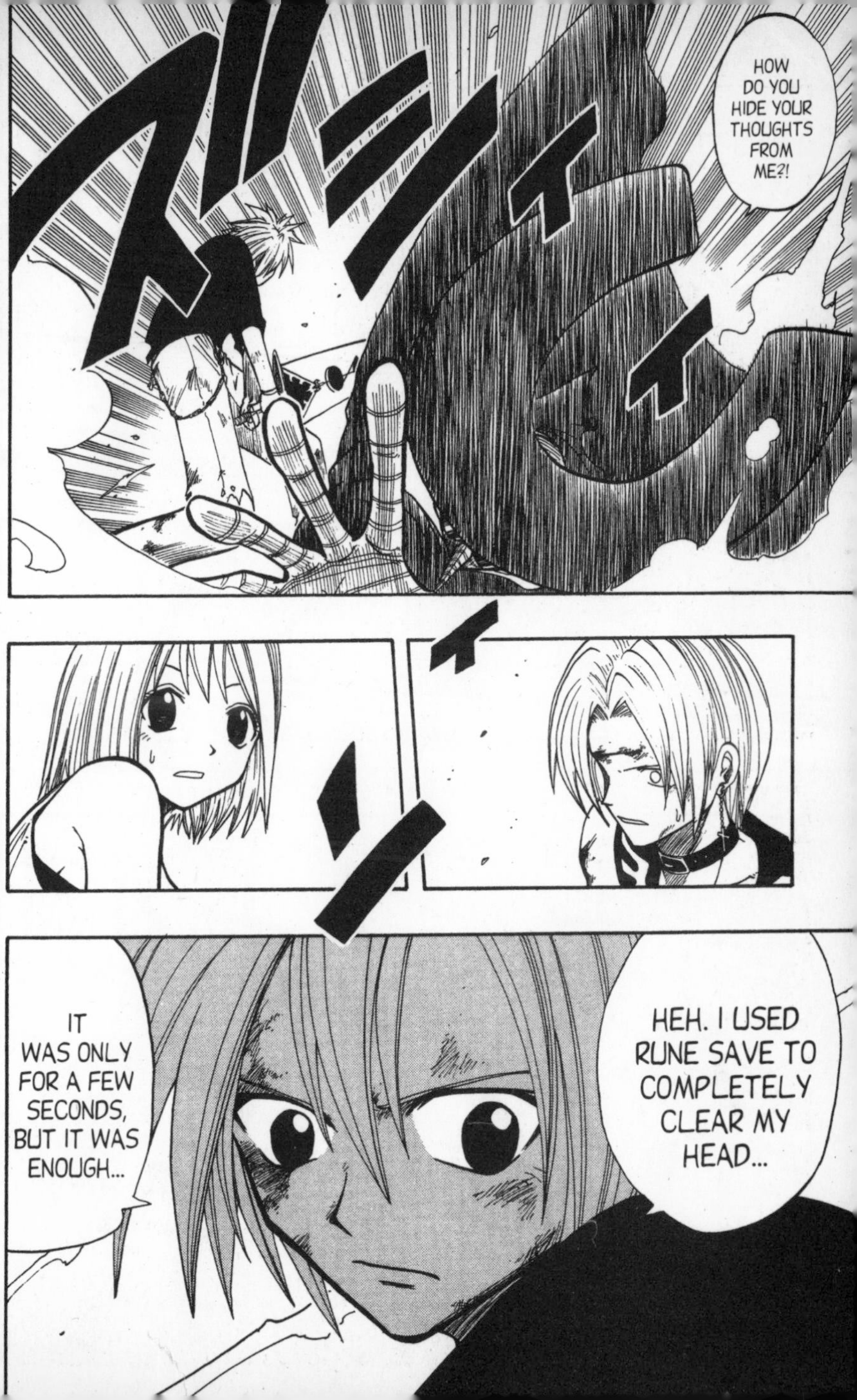
HOW DO YOU HIDE YOUR THOUGHTS FROM ME?!
HEH. I USED RUNE SAVE TO COMPLETELY CLEAR MY HEAD...
IT WAS ONLY FOR A FEW SECONDS, BUT IT WAS ENOUGH...

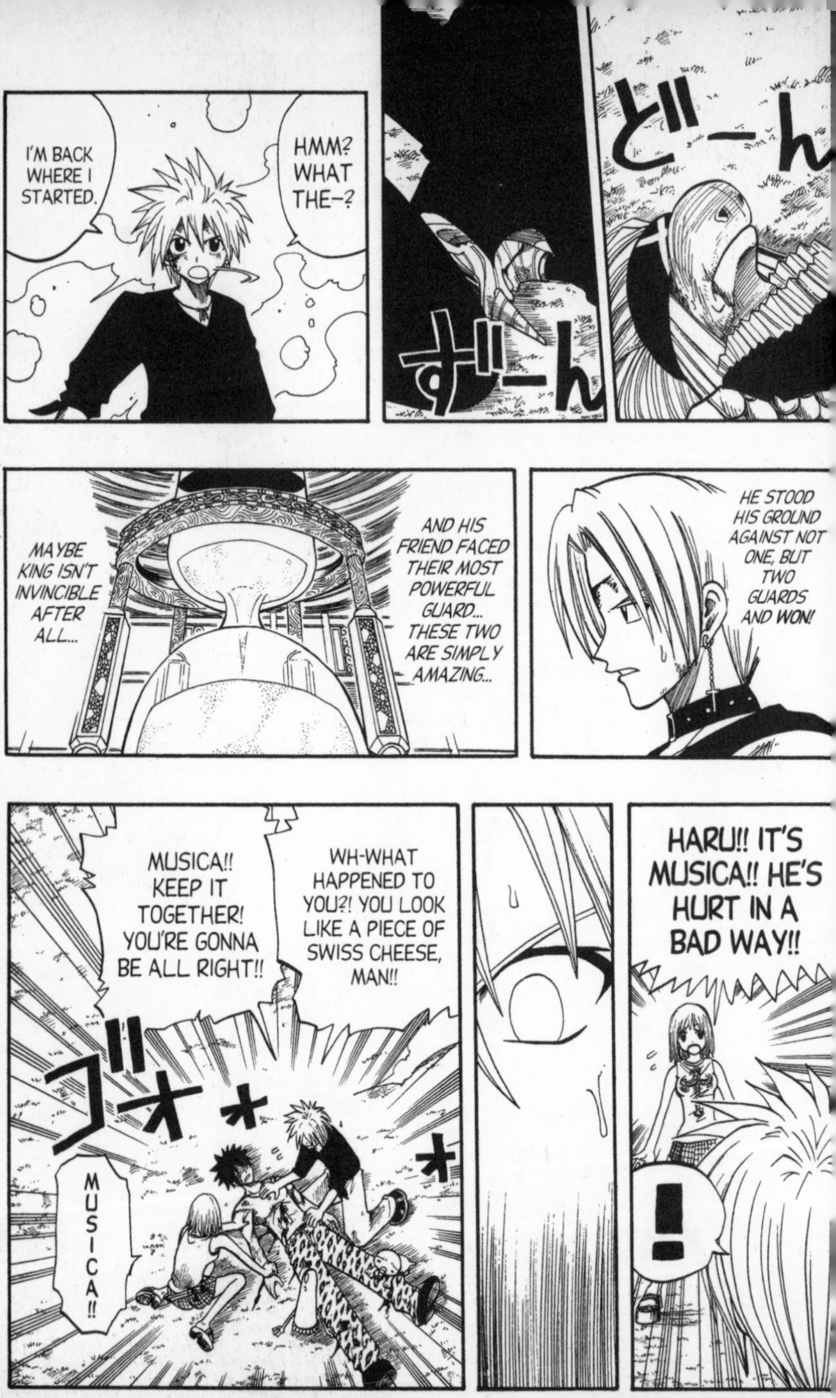
どーん
ずーん
HMM? WHAT THE–?
I'M BACK WHERE I STARTED.
HE STOOD HIS GROUND AGAINST NOT ONE, BUT TWO GUARDS AND WON!
AND HIS FRIEND FACED THEIR MOST POWERFUL GUARD... THESE TWO ARE SIMPLY AMAZING...
MAYBE KING ISN'T INVINCIBLE AFTER ALL...
HARU!! IT'S MUSICA!! HE'S HURT IN A BAD WAY!!
!
WH-WHAT HAPPENED TO YOU?! YOU LOOK LIKE A PIECE OF SWISS CHEESE, MAN!!
MUSICA!! KEEP IT TOGETHER! YOU'RE GONNA BE ALL RIGHT!!
ゴオ
MUSICA!!

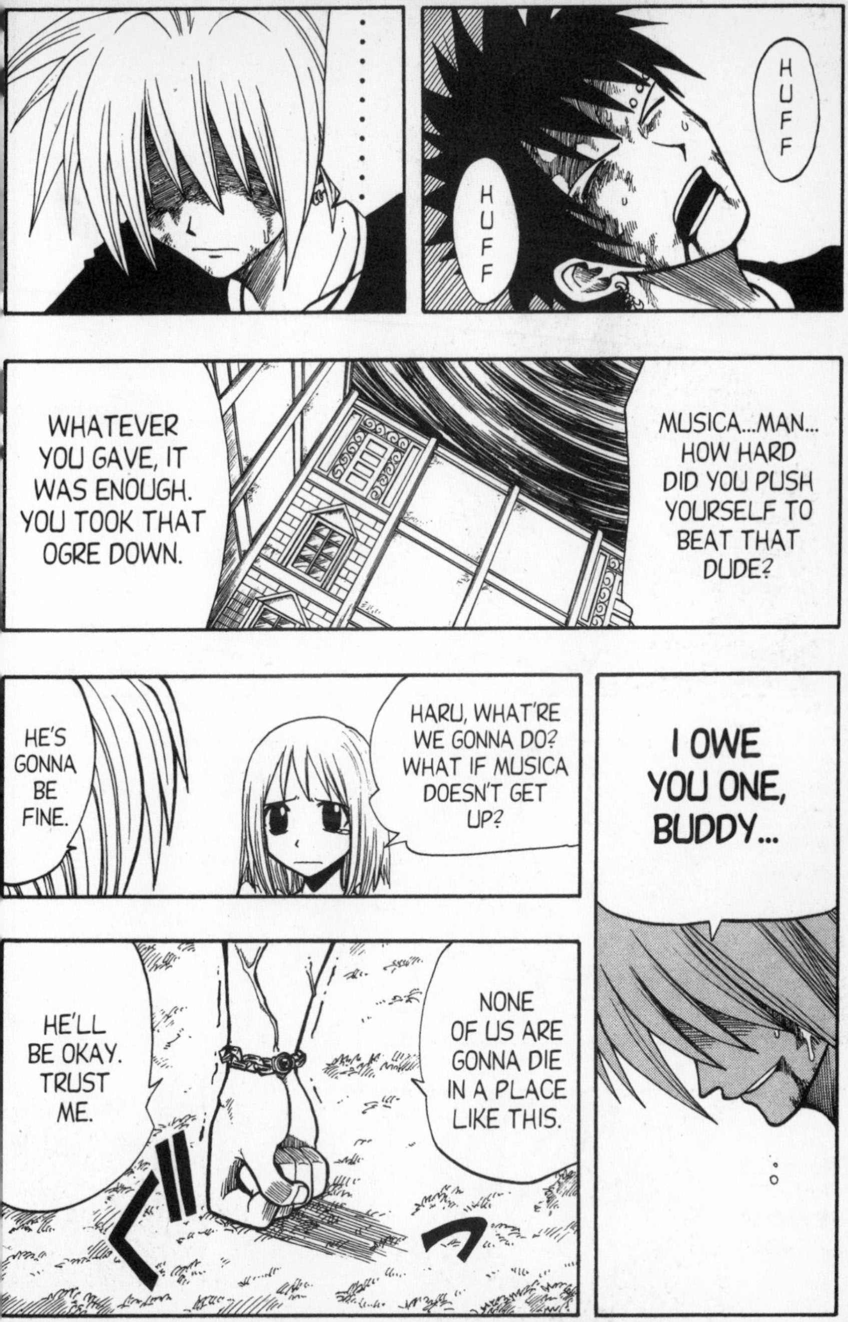
HUFF
HUFF
......
MUSICA...MAN... HOW HARD DID YOU PUSH YOURSELF TO BEAT THAT DUDE?
WHATEVER YOU GAVE, IT WAS ENOUGH. YOU TOOK THAT OGRE DOWN.
I OWE YOU ONE, BUDDY...
HARU, WHAT'RE WE GONNA DO? WHAT IF MUSICA DOESN'T GET UP?
HE'S GONNA BE FINE.
NONE OF US ARE GONNA DIE IN A PLACE LIKE THIS.
HE'LL BE OKAY. TRUST ME.

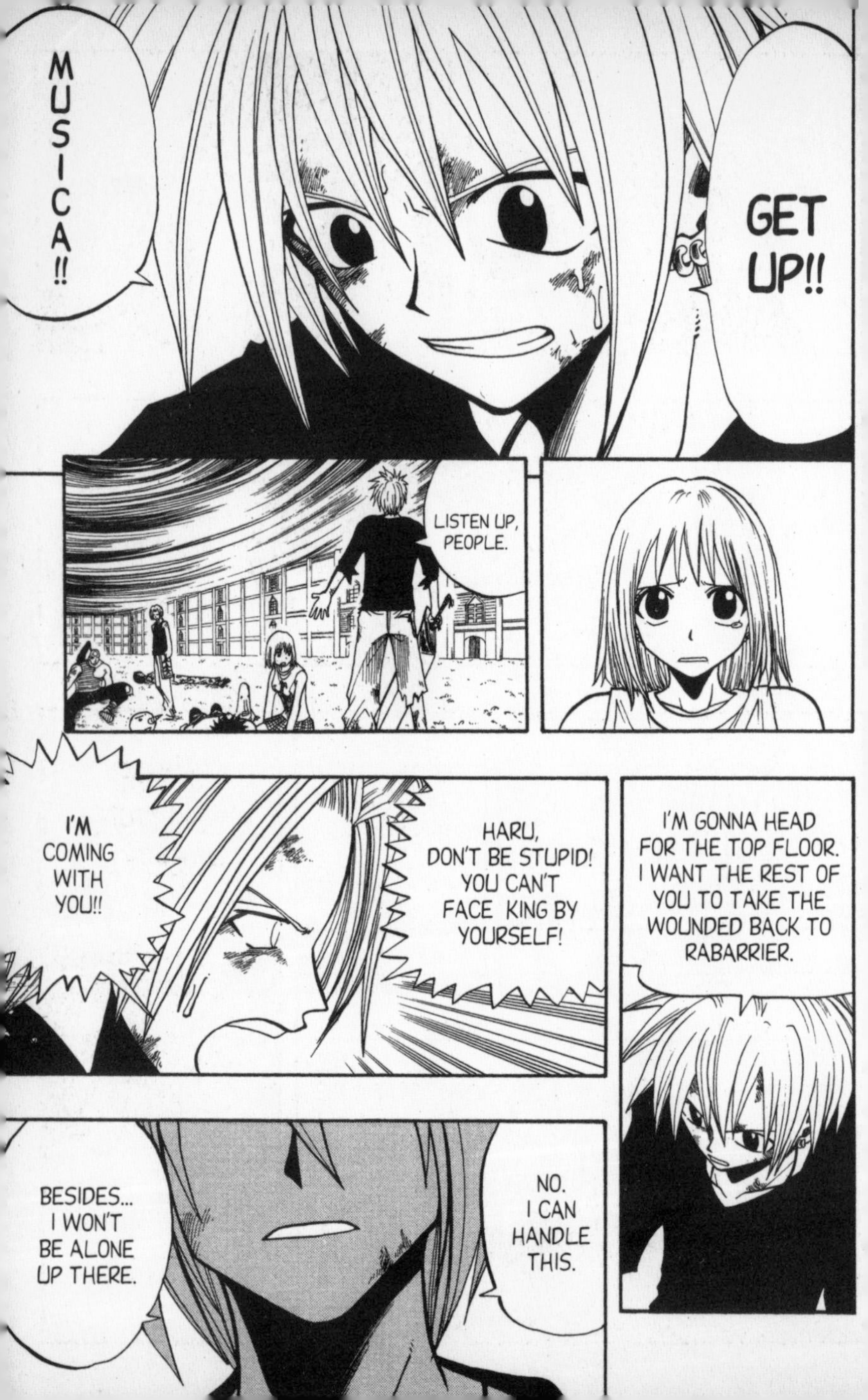
GET UP!!
MUSICA!!
LISTEN UP, PEOPLE.
I'M GONNA HEAD FOR THE TOP FLOOR. I WANT THE REST OF YOU TO TAKE THE WOUNDED BACK TO RABARRIER.
HARU, DON'T BE STUPID! YOU CAN'T FACE KING BY YOURSELF!
I'M COMING WITH YOU!!
NO. I CAN HANDLE THIS.
BESIDES... I WON'T BE ALONE UP THERE.

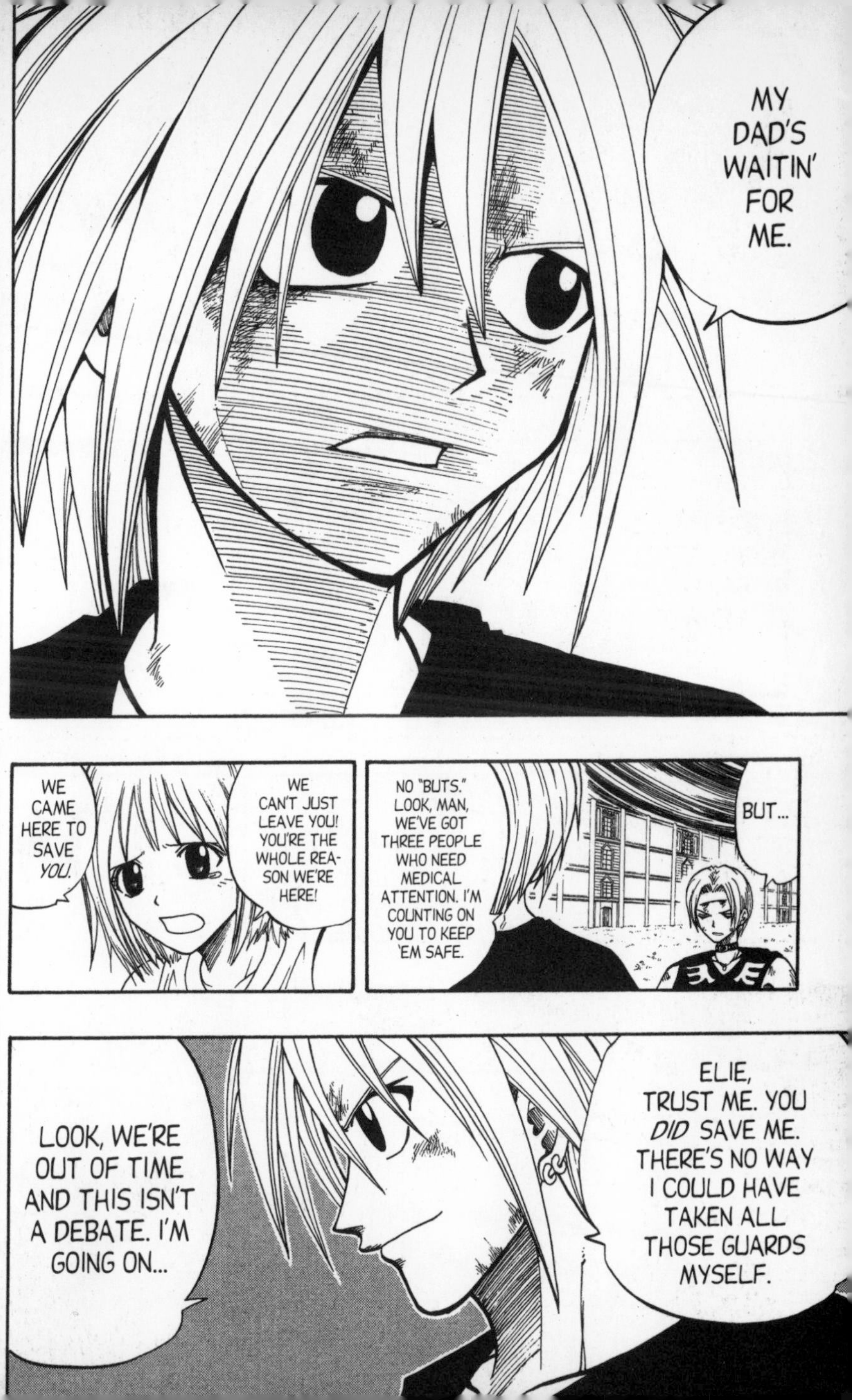
MY DAD'S WAITIN' FOR ME.
BUT...
NO "BUTS." LOOK, MAN, WE'VE GOT THREE PEOPLE WHO NEED MEDICAL ATTENTION. I'M COUNTING ON YOU TO KEEP 'EM SAFE.
WE CAN'T JUST LEAVE YOU! YOU'RE THE WHOLE REA-SON WE'RE HERE!
WE CAME HERE TO SAVE *YOU*.
ELIE, TRUST ME. YOU *DID* SAVE ME. THERE'S NO WAY I COULD HAVE TAKEN ALL THOSE GUARDS MYSELF.
LOOK, WE'RE OUT OF TIME AND THIS ISN'T A DEBATE. I'M GOING ON...

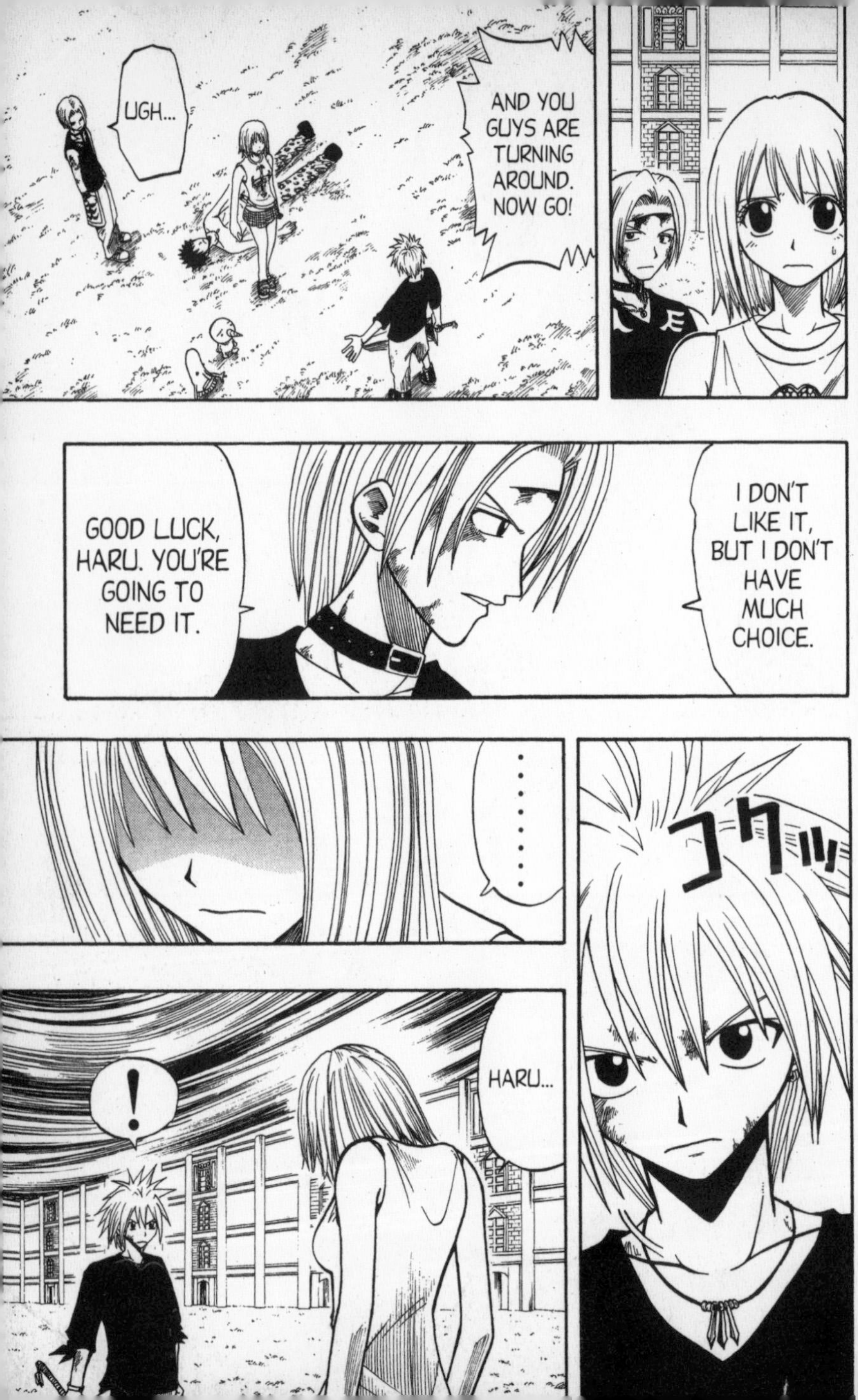
AND YOU GUYS ARE TURNING AROUND. NOW GO!
UGH...
I DON'T LIKE IT, BUT I DON'T HAVE MUCH CHOICE.
GOOD LUCK, HARU. YOU'RE GOING TO NEED IT.
コクッ
......
HARU...
!

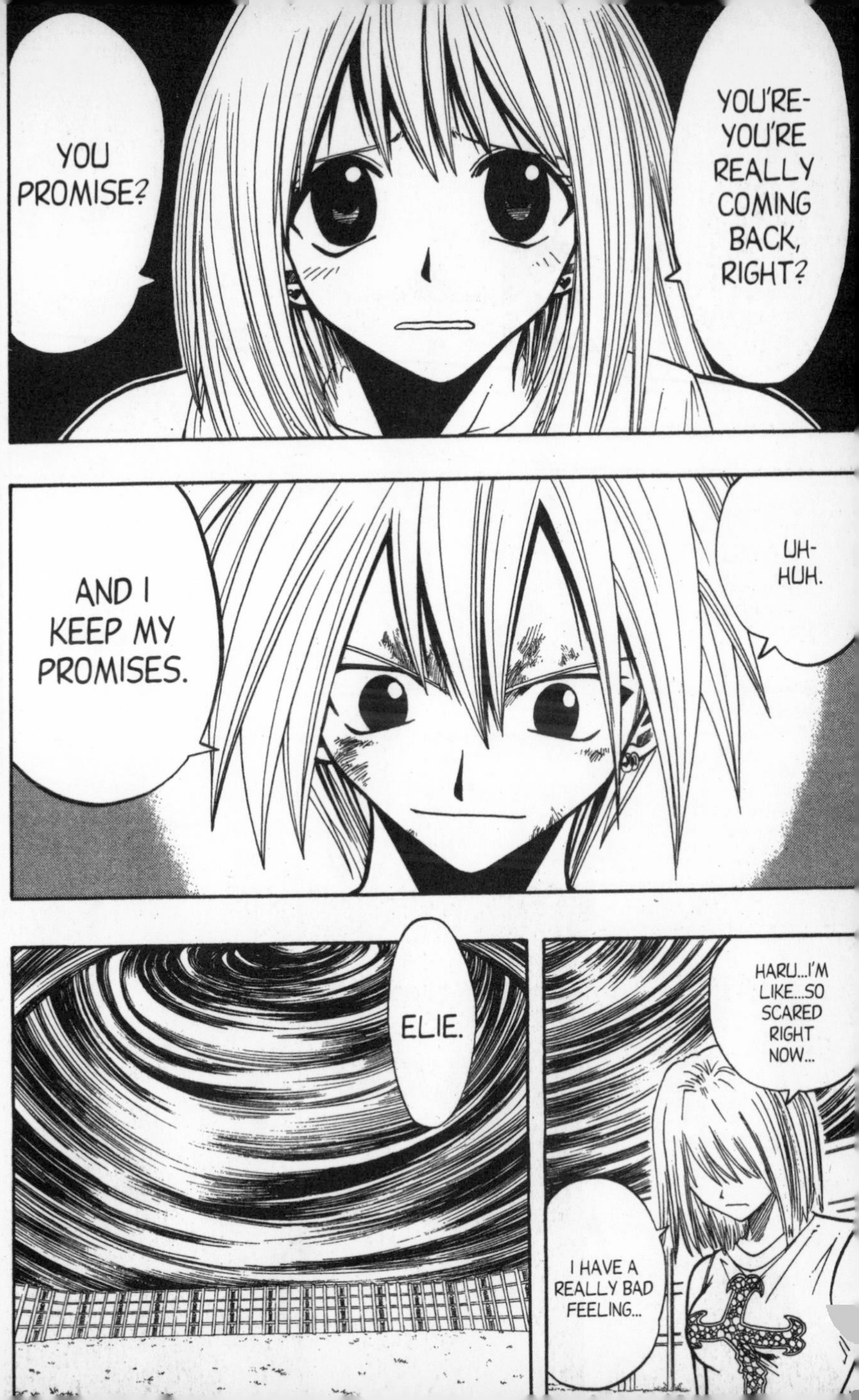
YOU'RE-YOU'RE REALLY COMING BACK, RIGHT?
YOU PROMISE?
UH-HUH.
AND I KEEP MY PROMISES.
HARU...I'M LIKE...SO SCARED RIGHT NOW...
I HAVE A REALLY BAD FEELING...
ELIE.

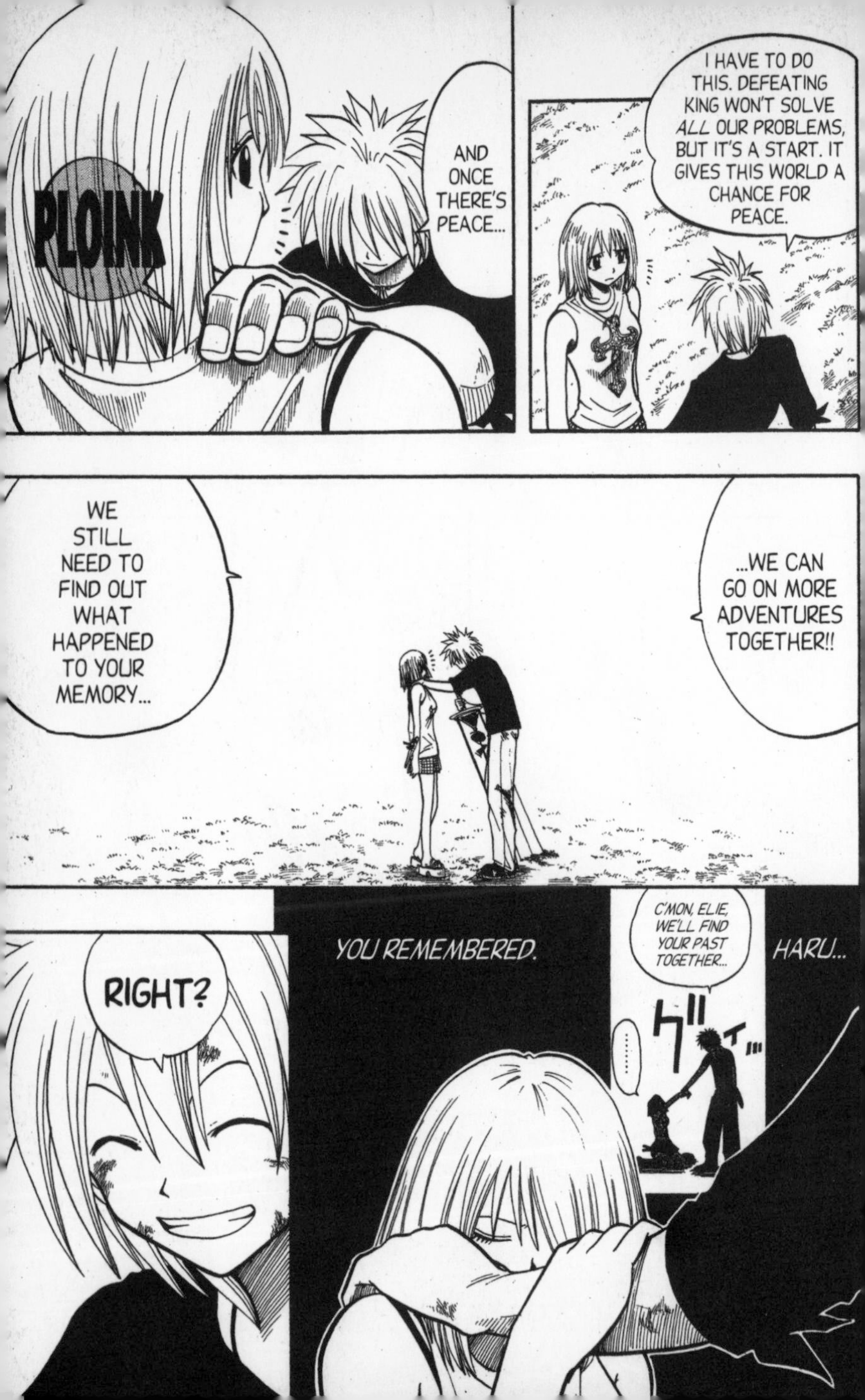
I HAVE TO DO THIS. DEFEATING KING WON'T SOLVE ALL OUR PROBLEMS, BUT IT'S A START. IT GIVES THIS WORLD A CHANCE FOR PEACE.
AND ONCE THERE'S PEACE...
PLOINK
...WE CAN GO ON MORE ADVENTURES TOGETHER!!
WE STILL NEED TO FIND OUT WHAT HAPPENED TO YOUR MEMORY...
HARU...
C'MON, ELIE, WE'LL FIND YOUR PAST TOGETHER...
YOU REMEMBERED.
......
RIGHT?

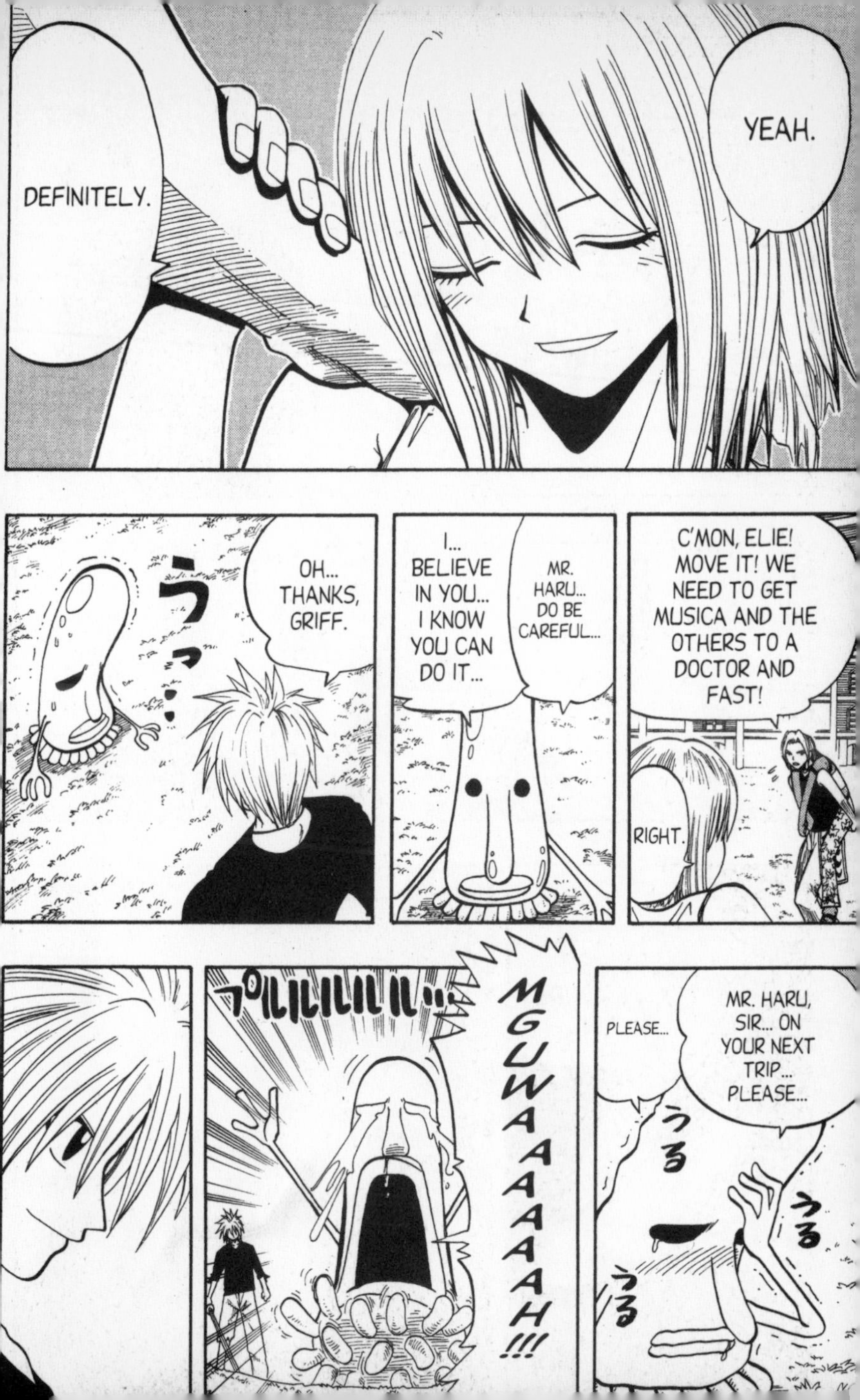
YEAH.
DEFINITELY.
C'MON, ELIE! MOVE IT! WE NEED TO GET MUSICA AND THE OTHERS TO A DOCTOR AND FAST!
RIGHT.
MR. HARU... DO BE CAREFUL...
I... BELIEVE IN YOU... I KNOW YOU CAN DO IT...
OH... THANKS, GRIFF.
うっ
MR. HARU, SIR... ON YOUR NEXT TRIP... PLEASE...
PLEASE...
うる
うる
うる
MGUWAAAAAAAH!!!

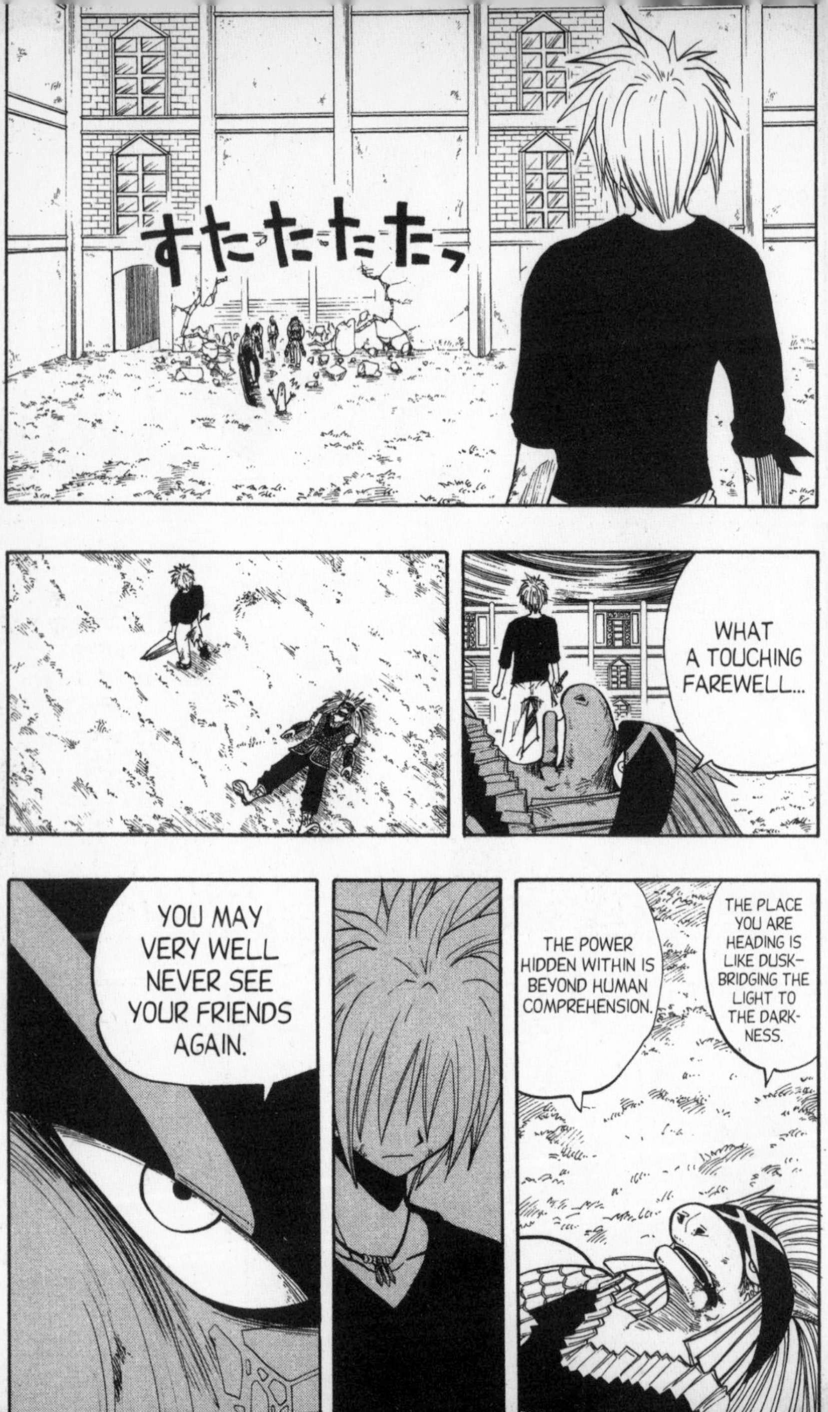
すたたたたっ
WHAT A TOUCHING FAREWELL...
THE PLACE YOU ARE HEADING IS LIKE DUSK—BRIDGING THE LIGHT TO THE DARK-NESS.
THE POWER HIDDEN WITHIN IS BEYOND HUMAN COMPREHENSION.
YOU MAY VERY WELL NEVER SEE YOUR FRIENDS AGAIN.

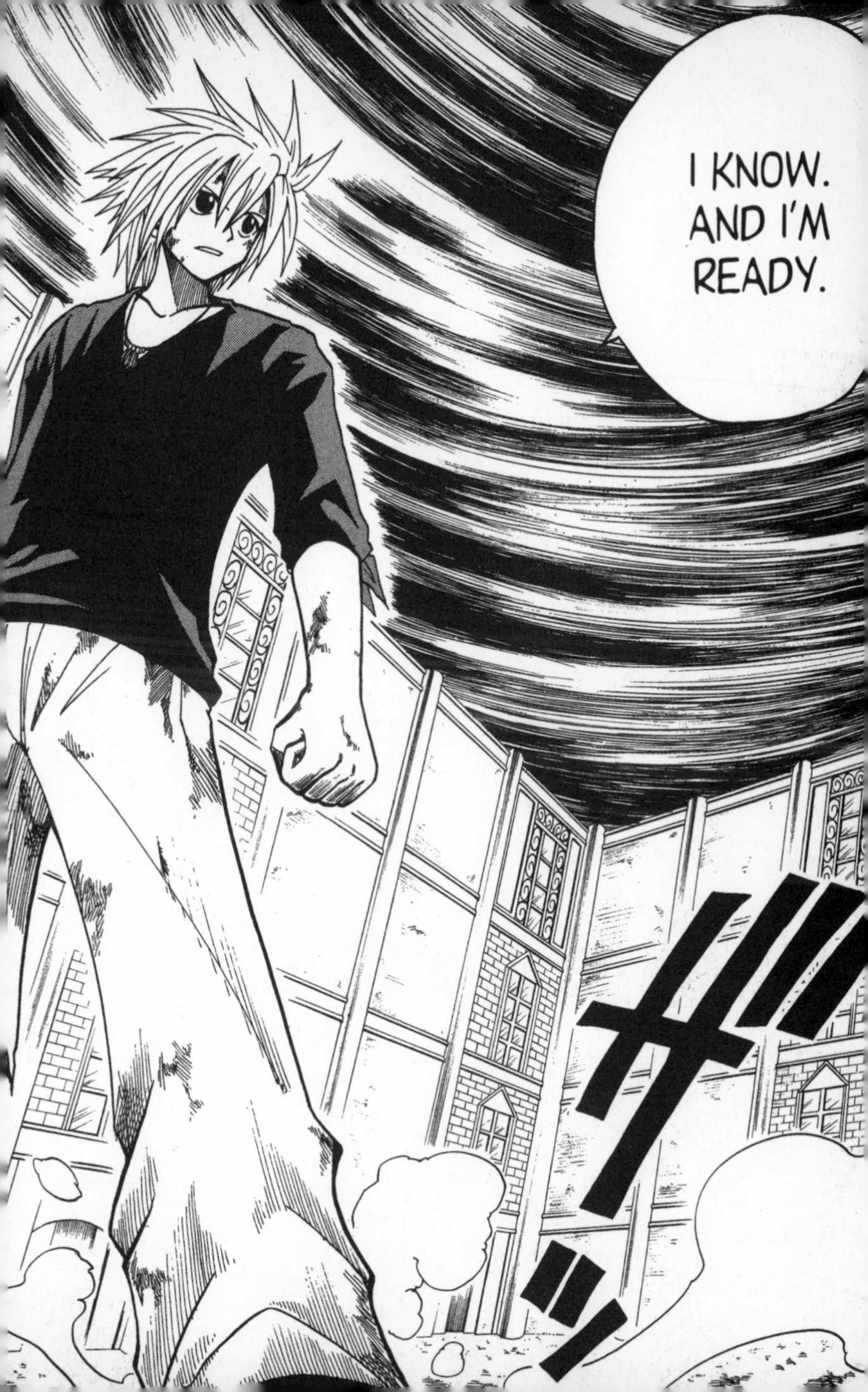
I KNOW. AND I'M READY.

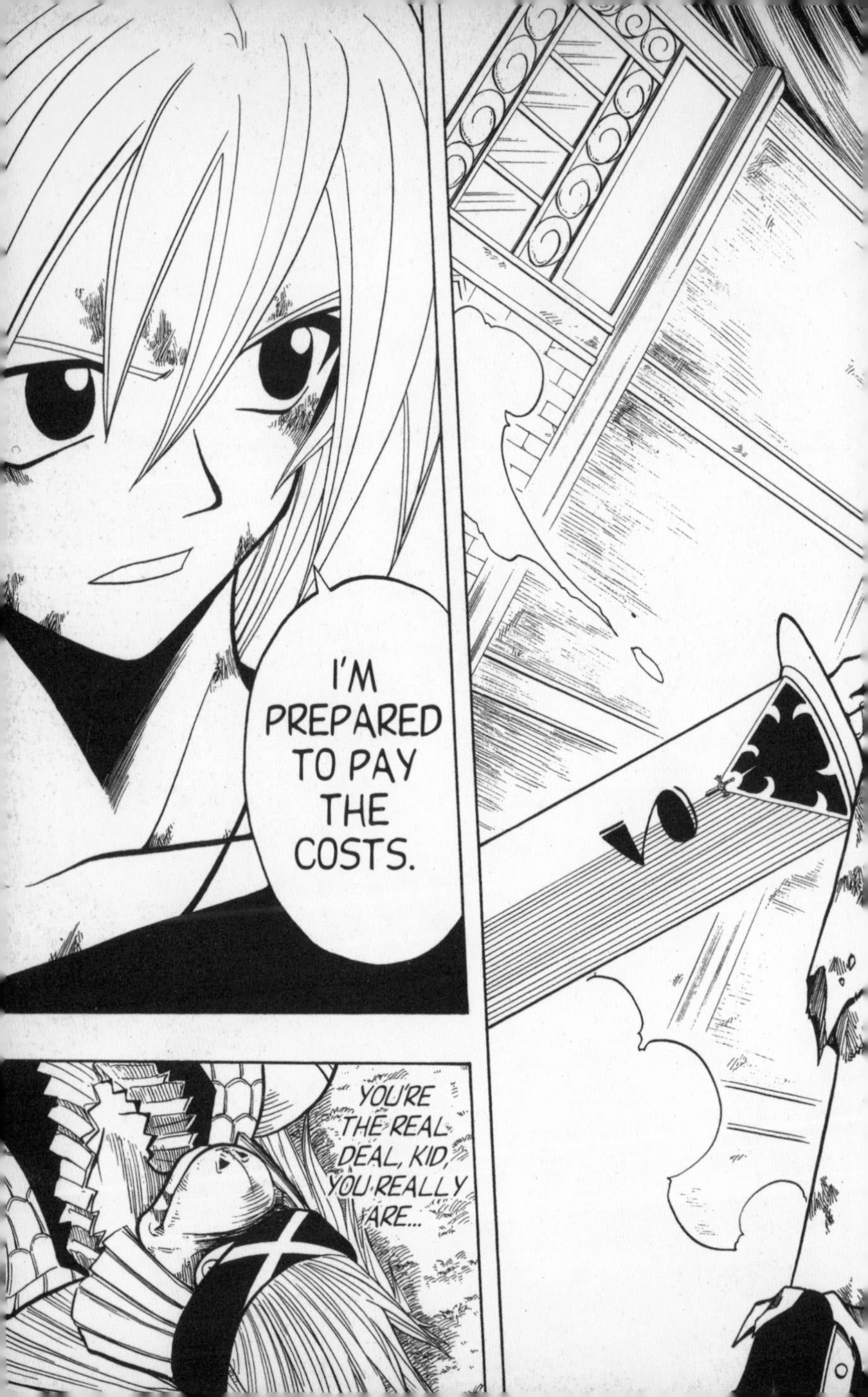
I'M PREPARED TO PAY THE COSTS.
YOU'RE THE REAL DEAL, KID, YOU REALLY ARE...

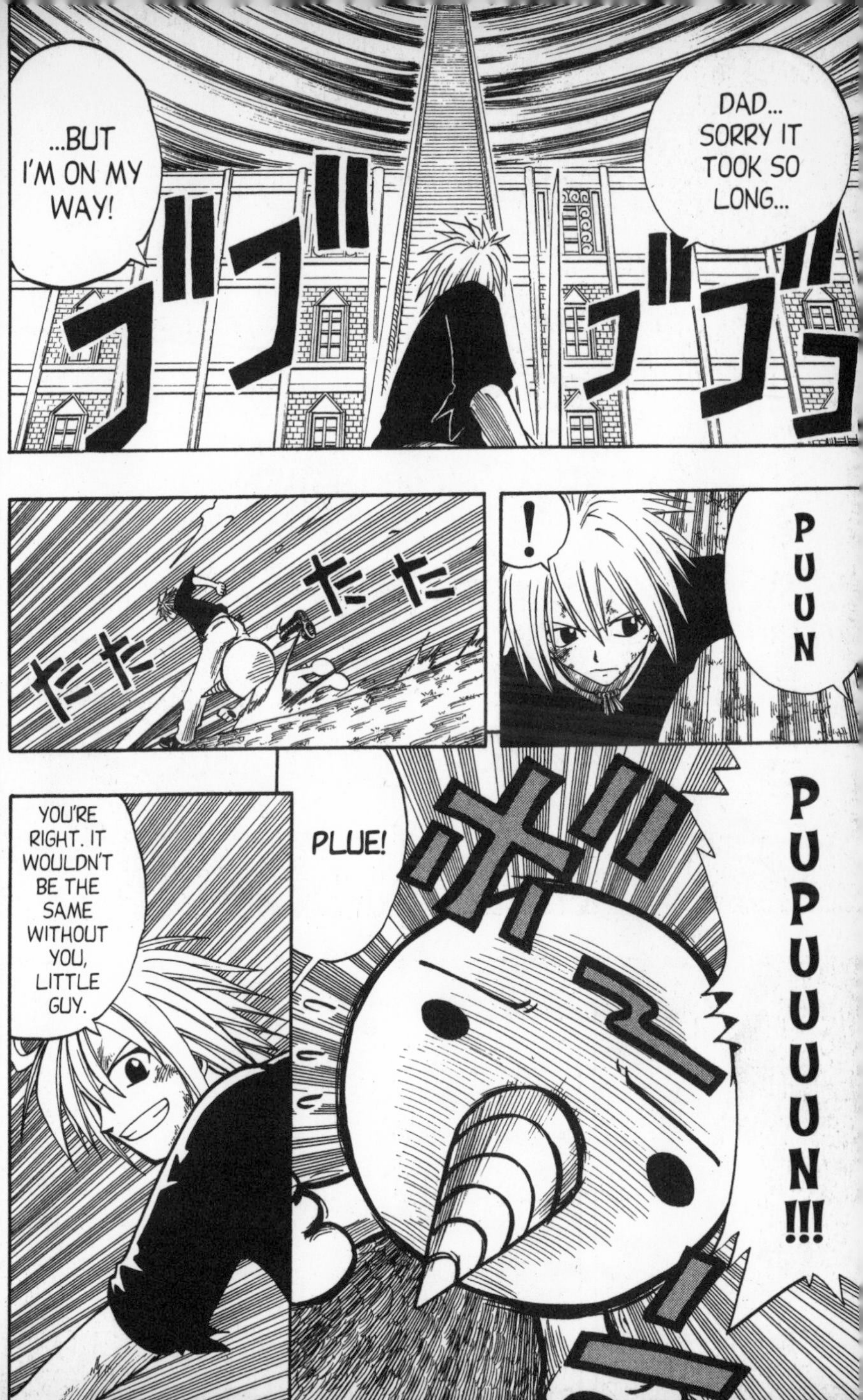
DAD... SORRY IT TOOK SO LONG...
ゴゴゴ
ゴゴ
...BUT I'M ON MY WAY!
!
PUUN
たた
たた
PUPUPUUUUN!!!
PLUE!
YOU'RE RIGHT. IT WOULDN'T BE THE SAME WITHOUT YOU, LITTLE GUY.

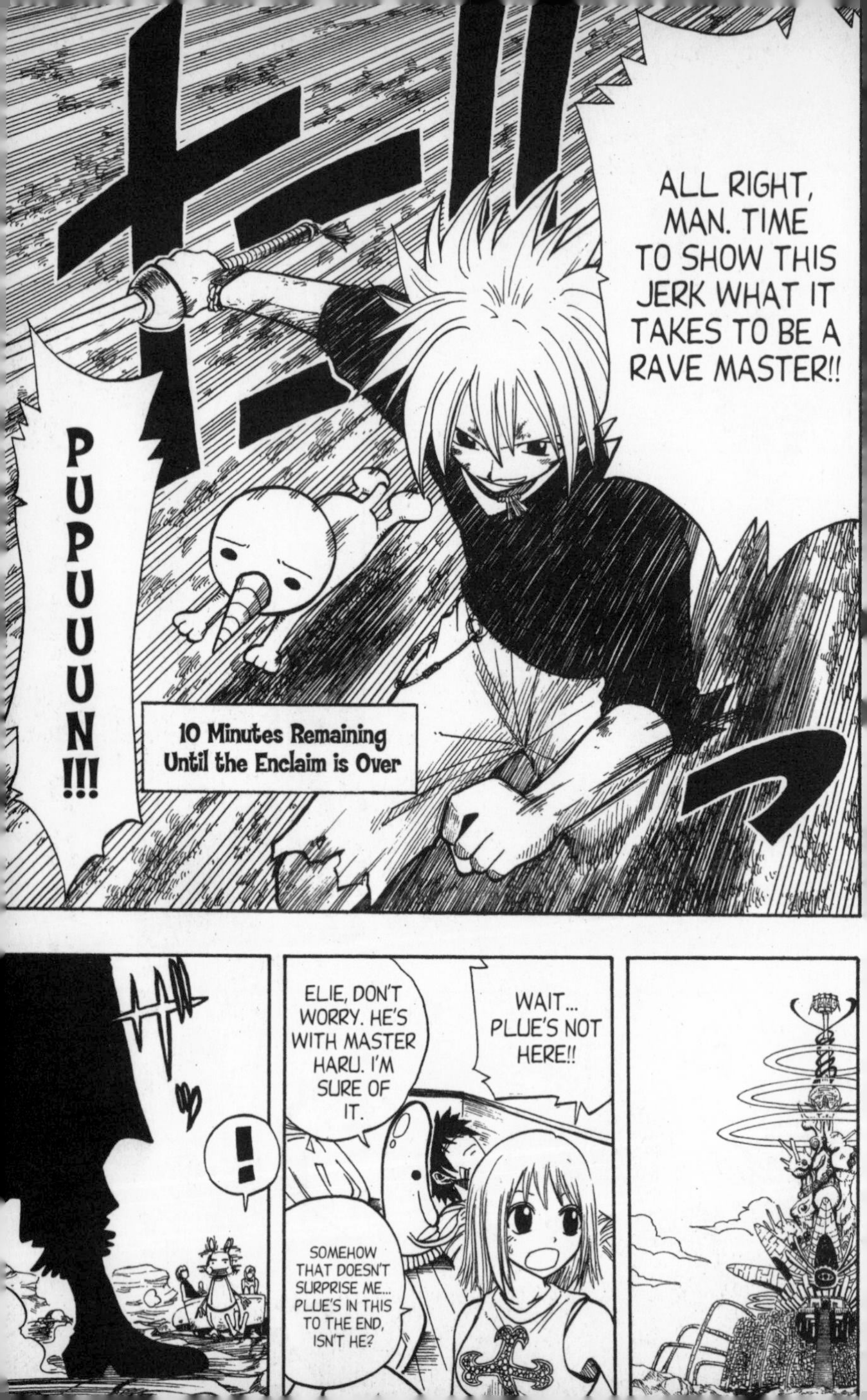
ALL RIGHT, MAN. TIME TO SHOW THIS JERK WHAT IT TAKES TO BE A RAVE MASTER!!
10 Minutes Remaining Until the Enclaim is Over
PUPUUUN!!!
WAIT... PLUE'S NOT HERE!!
ELIE, DON'T WORRY. HE'S WITH MASTER HARU. I'M SURE OF IT.
SOMEHOW THAT DOESN'T SURPRISE ME... PLUE'S IN THIS TO THE END, ISN'T HE?
!

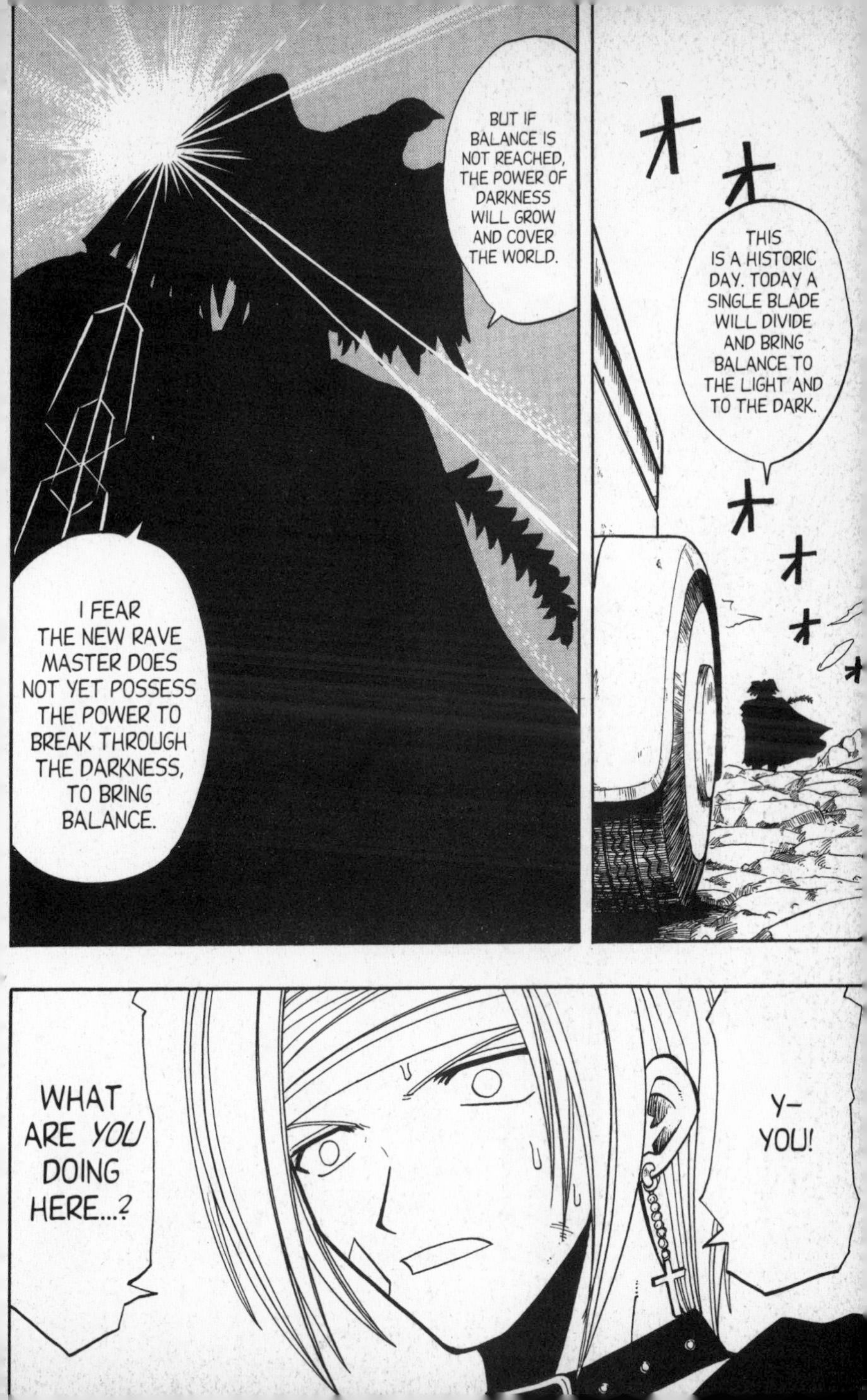
THIS IS A HISTORIC DAY. TODAY A SINGLE BLADE WILL DIVIDE AND BRING BALANCE TO THE LIGHT AND TO THE DARK.
BUT IF BALANCE IS NOT REACHED, THE POWER OF DARKNESS WILL GROW AND COVER THE WORLD.
I FEAR THE NEW RAVE MASTER DOES NOT YET POSSESS THE POWER TO BREAK THROUGH THE DARKNESS, TO BRING BALANCE.
Y— YOU!
WHAT ARE *YOU* DOING HERE...?

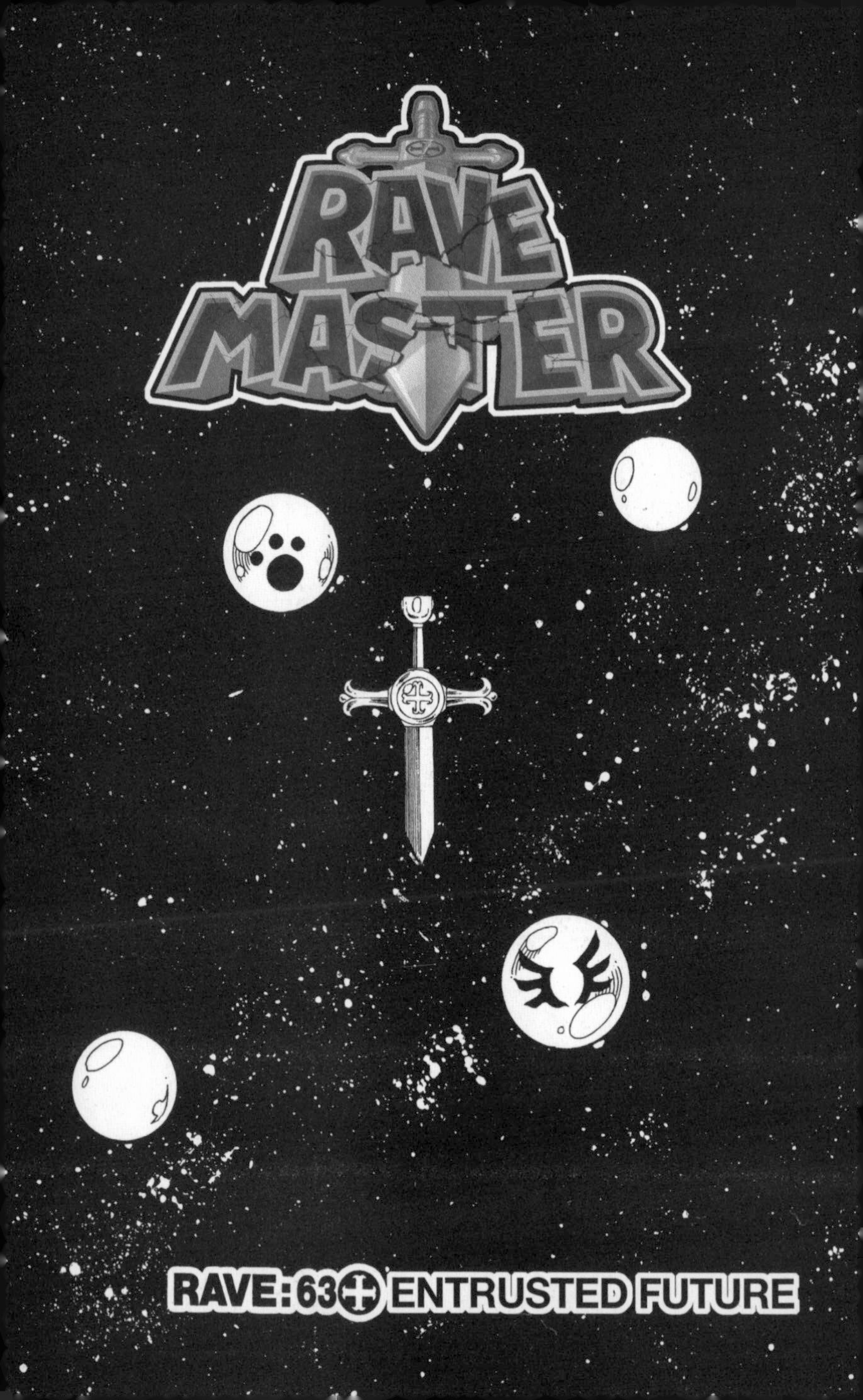
RAVE MASTER
RAVE:63 ENTRUSTED FUTURE

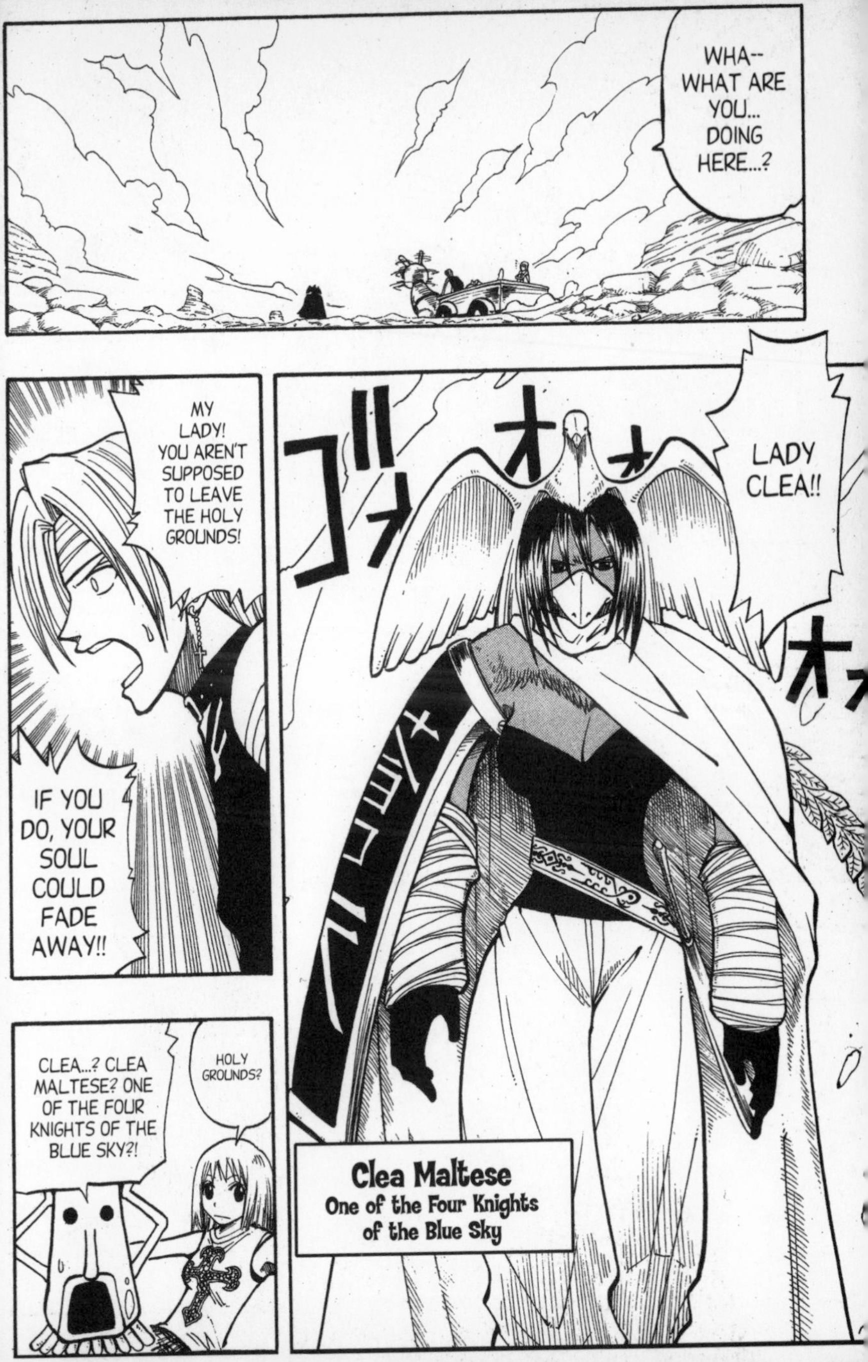
WHA-- WHAT ARE YOU... DOING HERE...?
LADY CLEA!!
Clea Maltese
One of the Four Knights of the Blue Sky
MY LADY! YOU AREN'T SUPPOSED TO LEAVE THE HOLY GROUNDS!
IF YOU DO, YOUR SOUL COULD FADE AWAY!!
HOLY GROUNDS?
CLEA...? CLEA MALTESE? ONE OF THE FOUR KNIGHTS OF THE BLUE SKY?!

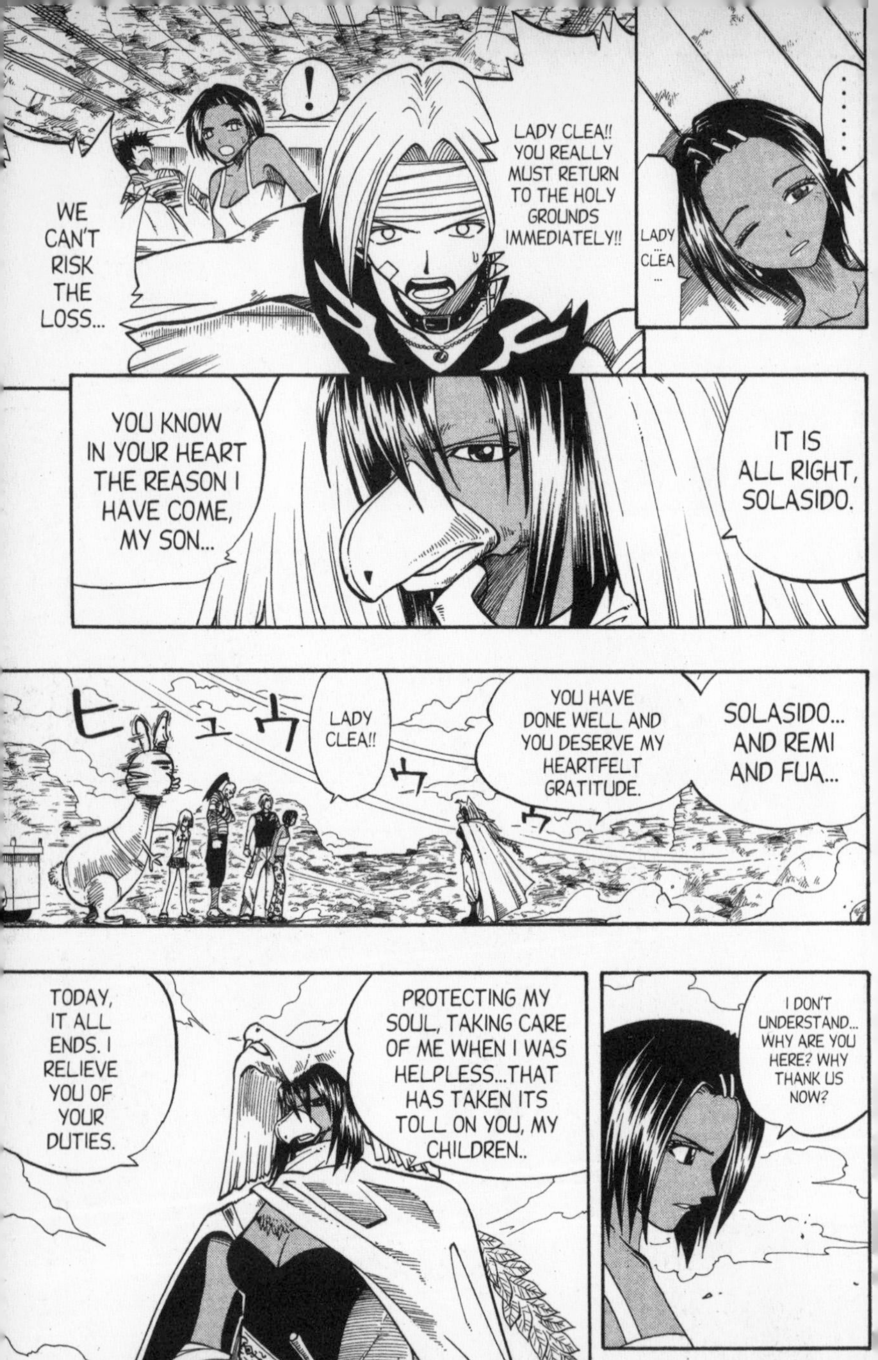
…
LADY … CLEA …
!
LADY CLEA!! YOU REALLY MUST RETURN TO THE HOLY GROUNDS IMMEDIATELY!!
WE CAN'T RISK THE LOSS...
IT IS ALL RIGHT, SOLASIDO.
YOU KNOW IN YOUR HEART THE REASON I HAVE COME, MY SON...
SOLASIDO... AND REMI AND FUA...
YOU HAVE DONE WELL AND YOU DESERVE MY HEARTFELT GRATITUDE.
LADY CLEA!!
ヒュウ
ウ
ウ
I DON'T UNDERSTAND... WHY ARE YOU HERE? WHY THANK US NOW?
PROTECTING MY SOUL, TAKING CARE OF ME WHEN I WAS HELPLESS...THAT HAS TAKEN ITS TOLL ON YOU, MY CHILDREN..
TODAY, IT ALL ENDS. I RELIEVE YOU OF YOUR DUTIES.

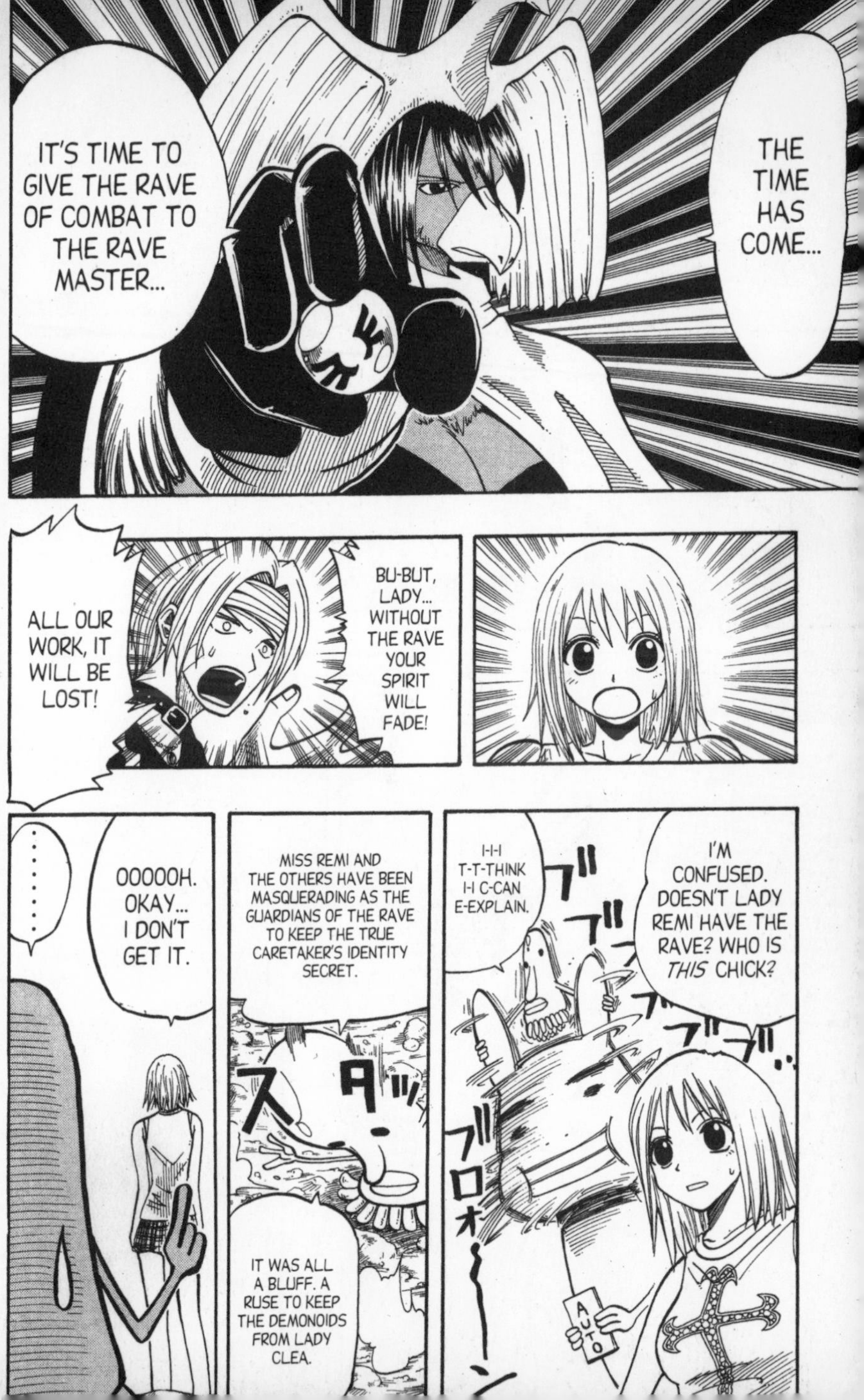
THE TIME HAS COME...
IT'S TIME TO GIVE THE RAVE OF COMBAT TO THE RAVE MASTER...
BU-BUT, LADY... WITHOUT THE RAVE YOUR SPIRIT WILL FADE!
ALL OUR WORK, IT WILL BE LOST!
I'M CONFUSED. DOESN'T LADY REMI HAVE THE RAVE? WHO IS *THIS* CHICK?
I-I-I T-T-THINK I-I C-CAN E-EXPLAIN.
ブロォ～
AUTO
MISS REMI AND THE OTHERS HAVE BEEN MASQUERADING AS THE GUARDIANS OF THE RAVE TO KEEP THE TRUE CARETAKER'S IDENTITY SECRET.
スタッ
IT WAS ALL A BLUFF. A RUSE TO KEEP THE DEMONOIDS FROM LADY CLEA.
OOOOOH. OKAY... I DON'T GET IT.
......

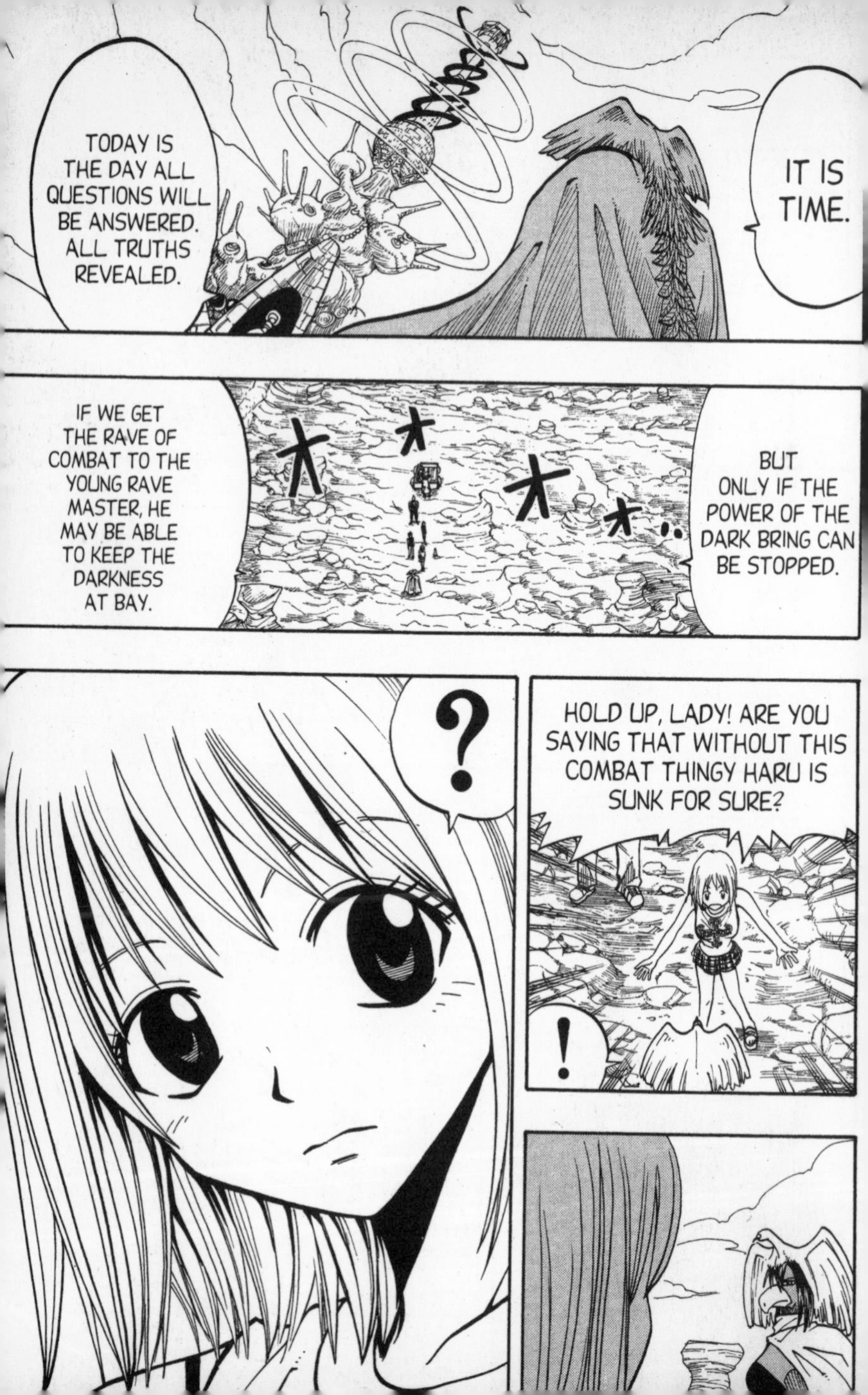
IT IS TIME.
TODAY IS THE DAY ALL QUESTIONS WILL BE ANSWERED. ALL TRUTHS REVEALED.
BUT ONLY IF THE POWER OF THE DARK BRING CAN BE STOPPED.
IF WE GET THE RAVE OF COMBAT TO THE YOUNG RAVE MASTER, HE MAY BE ABLE TO KEEP THE DARKNESS AT BAY.
HOLD UP, LADY! ARE YOU SAYING THAT WITHOUT THIS COMBAT THINGY HARU IS SUNK FOR SURE?
!
?

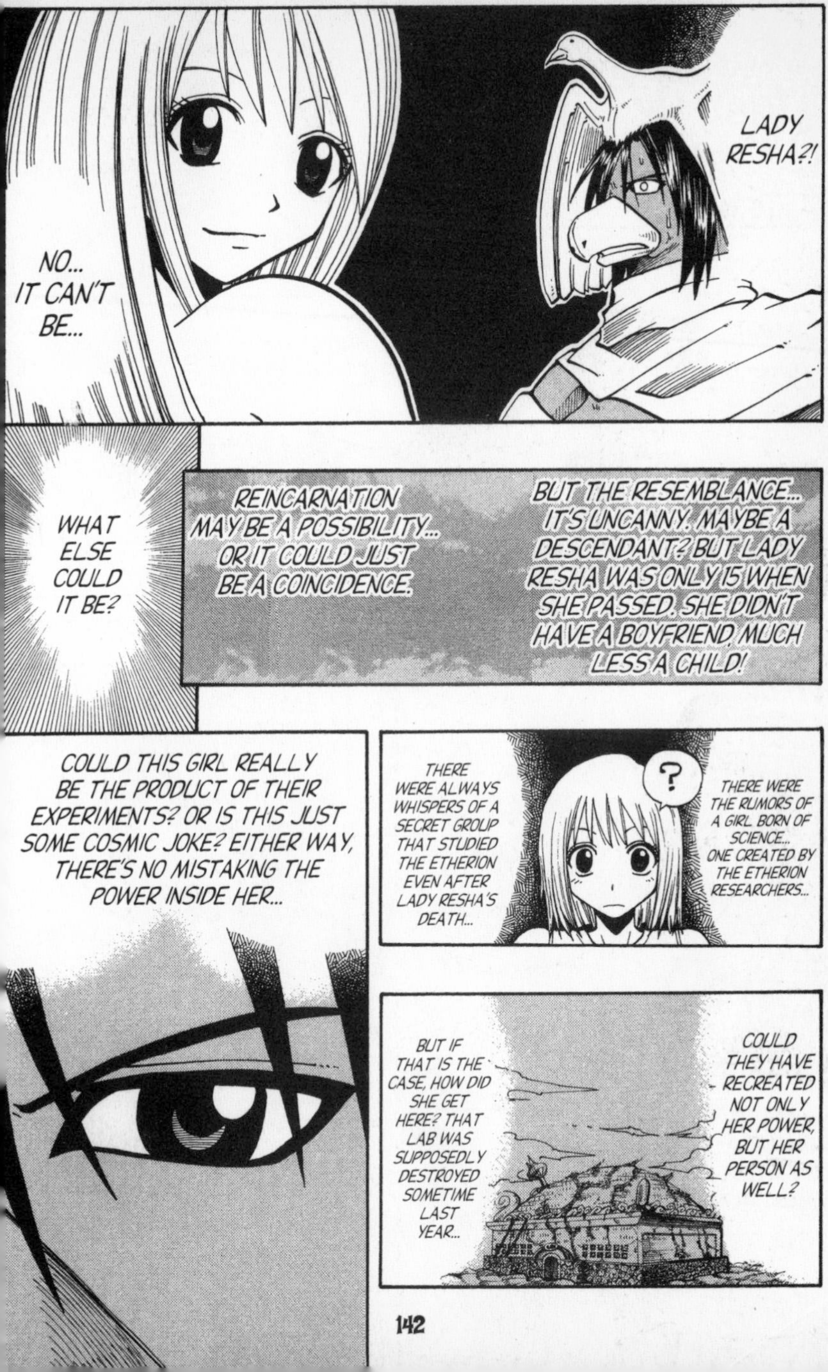
LADY RESHA?!
NO... IT CAN'T BE...
REINCARNATION MAY BE A POSSIBILITY... OR IT COULD JUST BE A COINCIDENCE.
BUT THE RESEMBLANCE... IT'S UNCANNY. MAYBE A DESCENDANT? BUT LADY RESHA WAS ONLY 15 WHEN SHE PASSED. SHE DIDN'T HAVE A BOYFRIEND, MUCH LESS A CHILD!
WHAT ELSE COULD IT BE?
THERE WERE THE RUMORS OF A GIRL BORN OF SCIENCE... ONE CREATED BY THE ETHERION RESEARCHERS...
?
THERE WERE ALWAYS WHISPERS OF A SECRET GROUP THAT STUDIED THE ETHERION EVEN AFTER LADY RESHA'S DEATH...
COULD THEY HAVE RECREATED NOT ONLY HER POWER, BUT HER PERSON AS WELL?
BUT IF THAT IS THE CASE, HOW DID SHE GET HERE? THAT LAB WAS SUPPOSEDLY DESTROYED SOMETIME LAST YEAR...
COULD THIS GIRL REALLY BE THE PRODUCT OF THEIR EXPERIMENTS? OR IS THIS JUST SOME COSMIC JOKE? EITHER WAY, THERE'S NO MISTAKING THE POWER INSIDE HER...

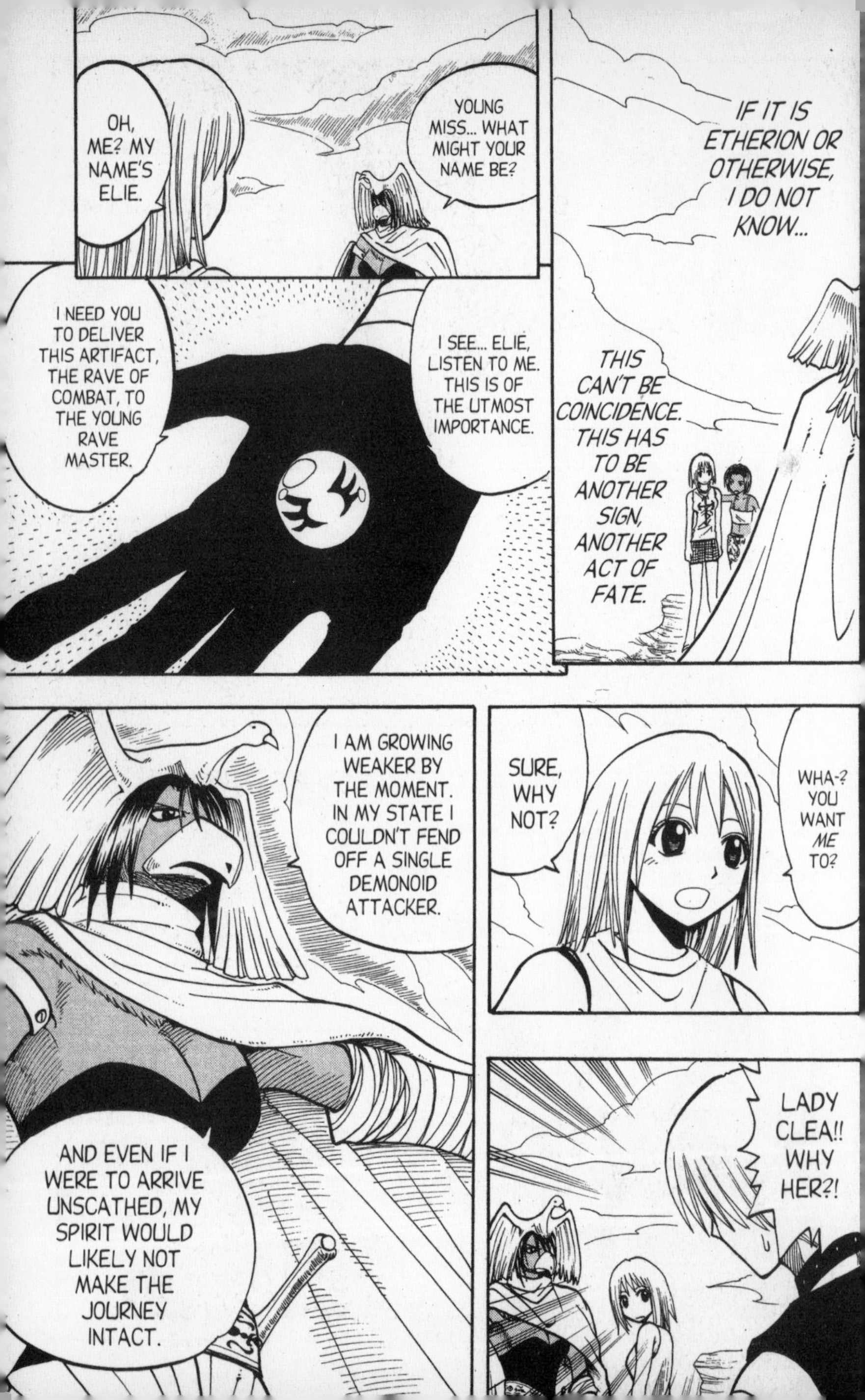
IF IT IS ETHERION OR OTHERWISE, I DO NOT KNOW...
THIS CAN'T BE COINCIDENCE. THIS HAS TO BE ANOTHER SIGN, ANOTHER ACT OF FATE.
YOUNG MISS... WHAT MIGHT YOUR NAME BE?
OH, ME? MY NAME'S ELIE.
I SEE... ELIE, LISTEN TO ME. THIS IS OF THE UTMOST IMPORTANCE.
I NEED YOU TO DELIVER THIS ARTIFACT, THE RAVE OF COMBAT, TO THE YOUNG RAVE MASTER.
WHA-? YOU WANT *ME* TO?
SURE, WHY NOT?
LADY CLEA!! WHY HER?!
I AM GROWING WEAKER BY THE MOMENT. IN MY STATE I COULDN'T FEND OFF A SINGLE DEMONOID ATTACKER.
AND EVEN IF I WERE TO ARRIVE UNSCATHED, MY SPIRIT WOULD LIKELY NOT MAKE THE JOURNEY INTACT.

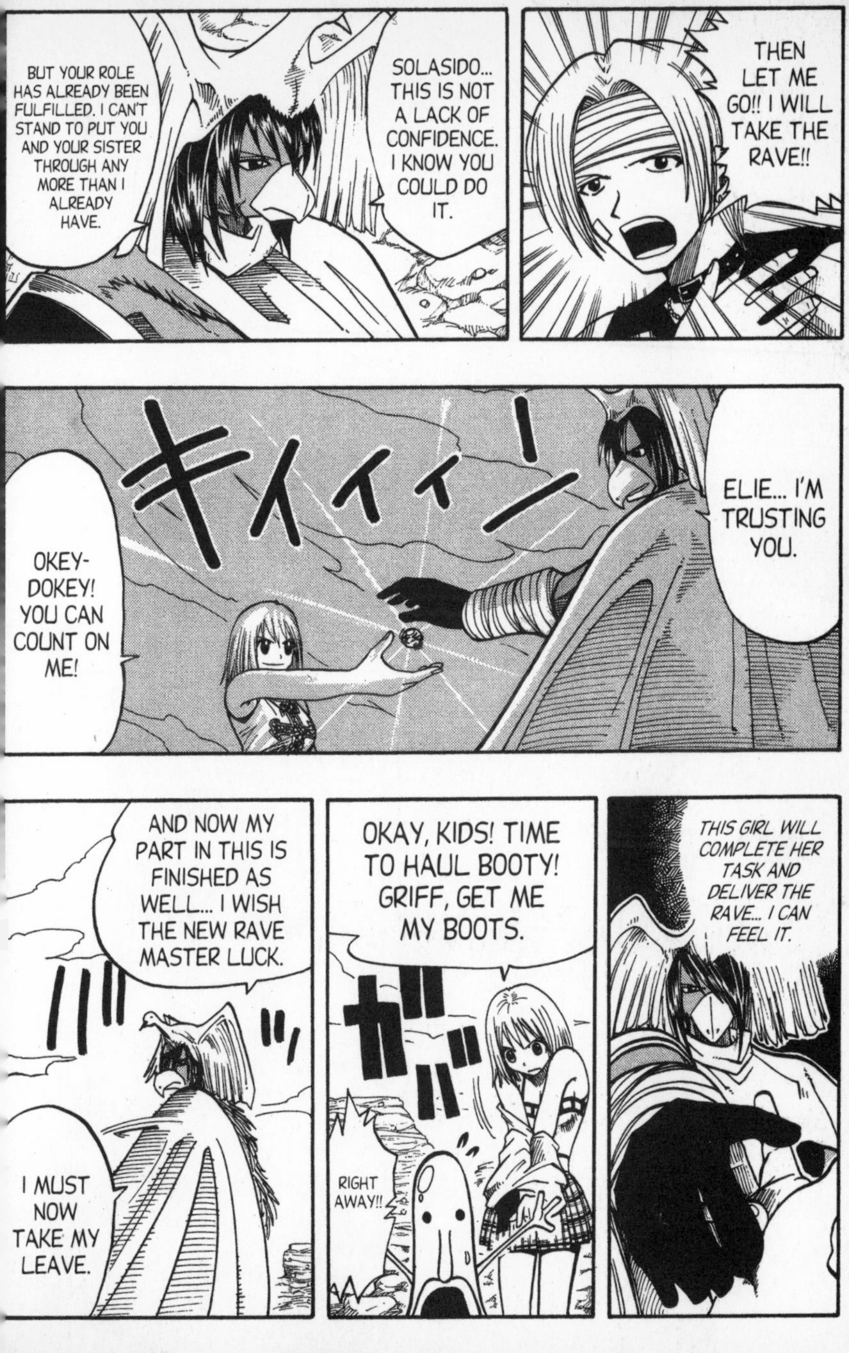
THEN LET ME GO!! I WILL TAKE THE RAVE!!
SOLASIDO... THIS IS NOT A LACK OF CONFIDENCE. I KNOW YOU COULD DO IT.
BUT YOUR ROLE HAS ALREADY BEEN FULFILLED. I CAN'T STAND TO PUT YOU AND YOUR SISTER THROUGH ANY MORE THAN I ALREADY HAVE.
ELIE... I'M TRUSTING YOU.
キイイィーン
OKEY-DOKEY! YOU CAN COUNT ON ME!
THIS GIRL WILL COMPLETE HER TASK AND DELIVER THE RAVE... I CAN FEEL IT.
OKAY, KIDS! TIME TO HAUL BOOTY! GRIFF, GET ME MY BOOTS.
ガバ
RIGHT AWAY!!
AND NOW MY PART IN THIS IS FINISHED AS WELL... I WISH THE NEW RAVE MASTER LUCK.
バッ
I MUST NOW TAKE MY LEAVE.

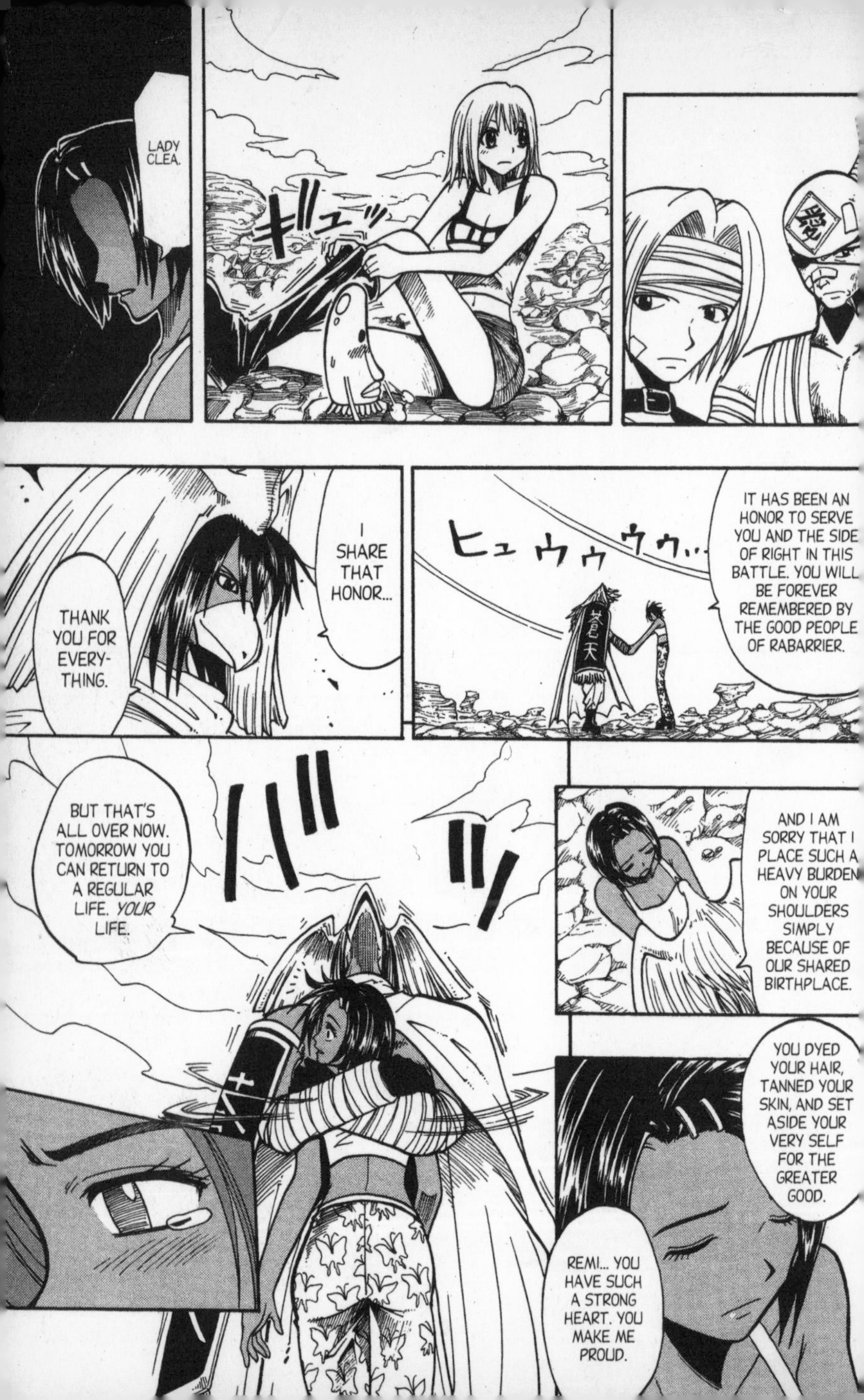
ギュッ
LADY CLEA.
IT HAS BEEN AN HONOR TO SERVE YOU AND THE SIDE OF RIGHT IN THIS BATTLE. YOU WILL BE FOREVER REMEMBERED BY THE GOOD PEOPLE OF RABARRIER.
ヒュウウウウ…
I SHARE THAT HONOR...
THANK YOU FOR EVERY-THING.
AND I AM SORRY THAT I PLACE SUCH A HEAVY BURDEN ON YOUR SHOULDERS SIMPLY BECAUSE OF OUR SHARED BIRTHPLACE.
YOU DYED YOUR HAIR, TANNED YOUR SKIN, AND SET ASIDE YOUR VERY SELF FOR THE GREATER GOOD.
REMI... YOU HAVE SUCH A STRONG HEART. YOU MAKE ME PROUD.
バッ
BUT THAT'S ALL OVER NOW. TOMORROW YOU CAN RETURN TO A REGULAR LIFE. *YOUR* LIFE.

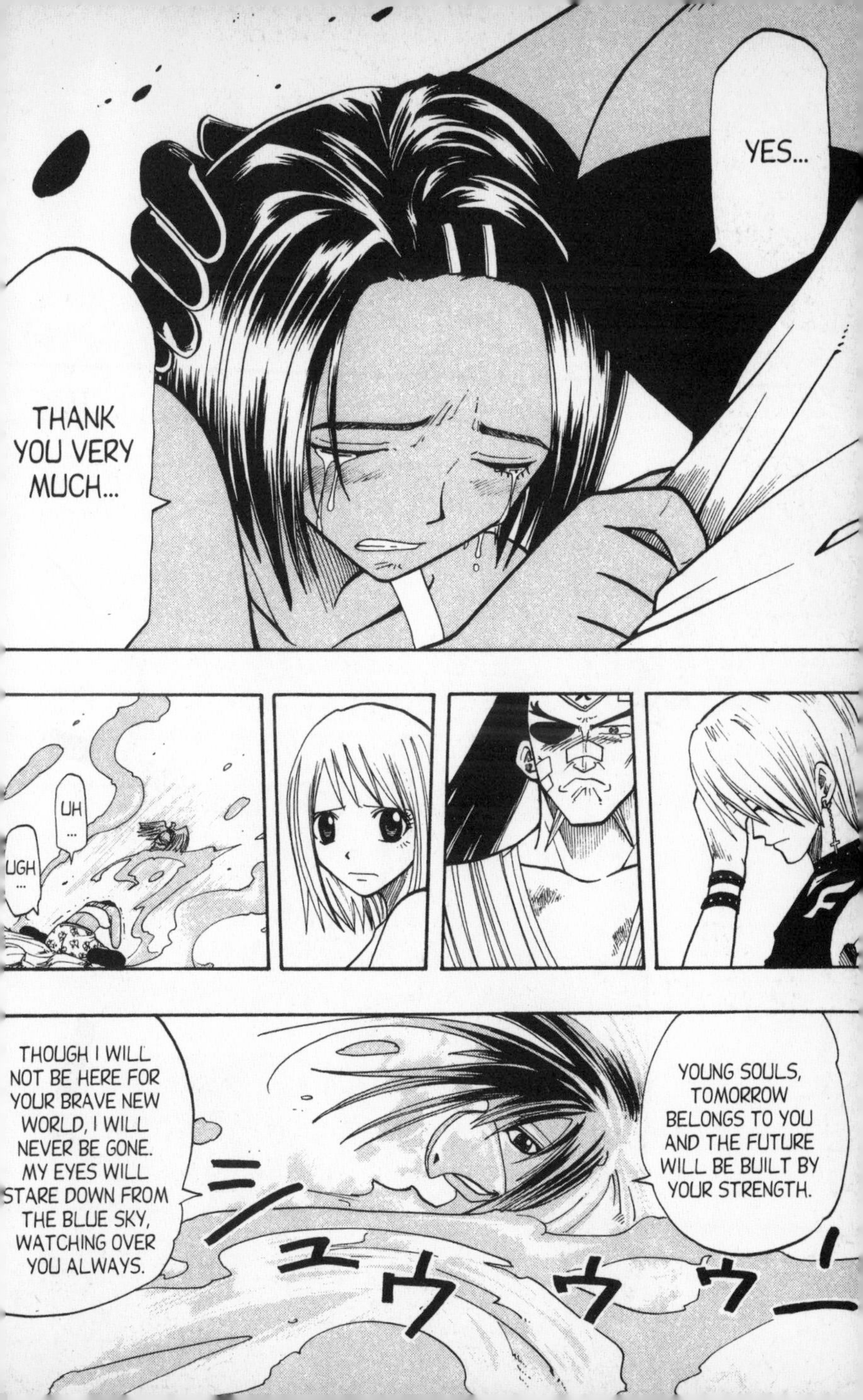
YES...
THANK YOU VERY MUCH...
UH...
UGH...
YOUNG SOULS, TOMORROW BELONGS TO YOU AND THE FUTURE WILL BE BUILT BY YOUR STRENGTH.
THOUGH I WILL NOT BE HERE FOR YOUR BRAVE NEW WORLD, I WILL NEVER BE GONE. MY EYES WILL STARE DOWN FROM THE BLUE SKY, WATCHING OVER YOU ALWAYS.
ニュウウウー

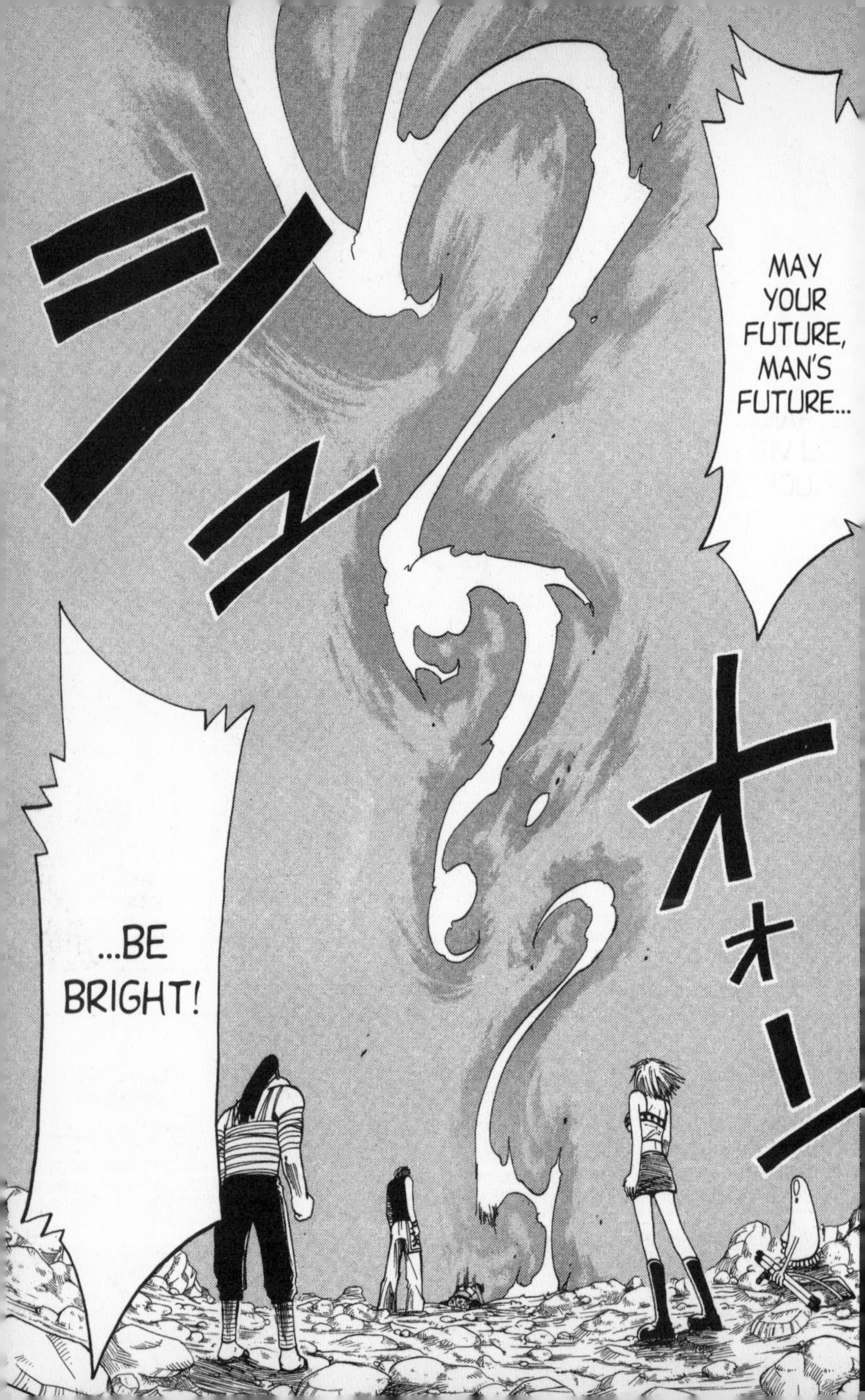
MAY YOUR FUTURE, MAN'S FUTURE...
...BE BRIGHT!

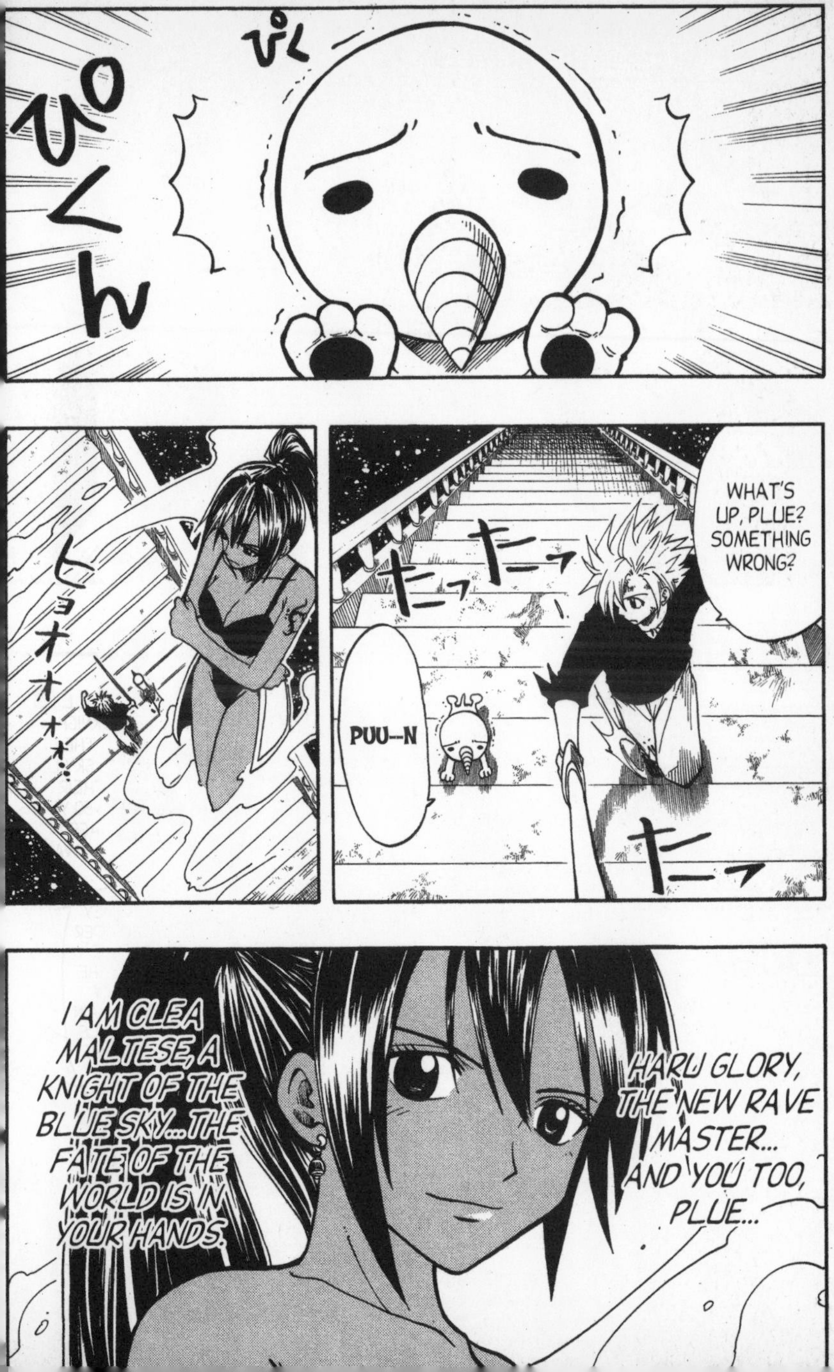

ぴく
ぴくん
WHAT'S UP, PLUE? SOMETHING WRONG?
PUU--N
ヒョオオオ
HARU GLORY, THE NEW RAVE MASTER... AND YOU TOO, PLUE...
I AM CLEA MALTESE, A KNIGHT OF THE BLUE SKY... THE FATE OF THE WORLD IS IN YOUR HANDS.

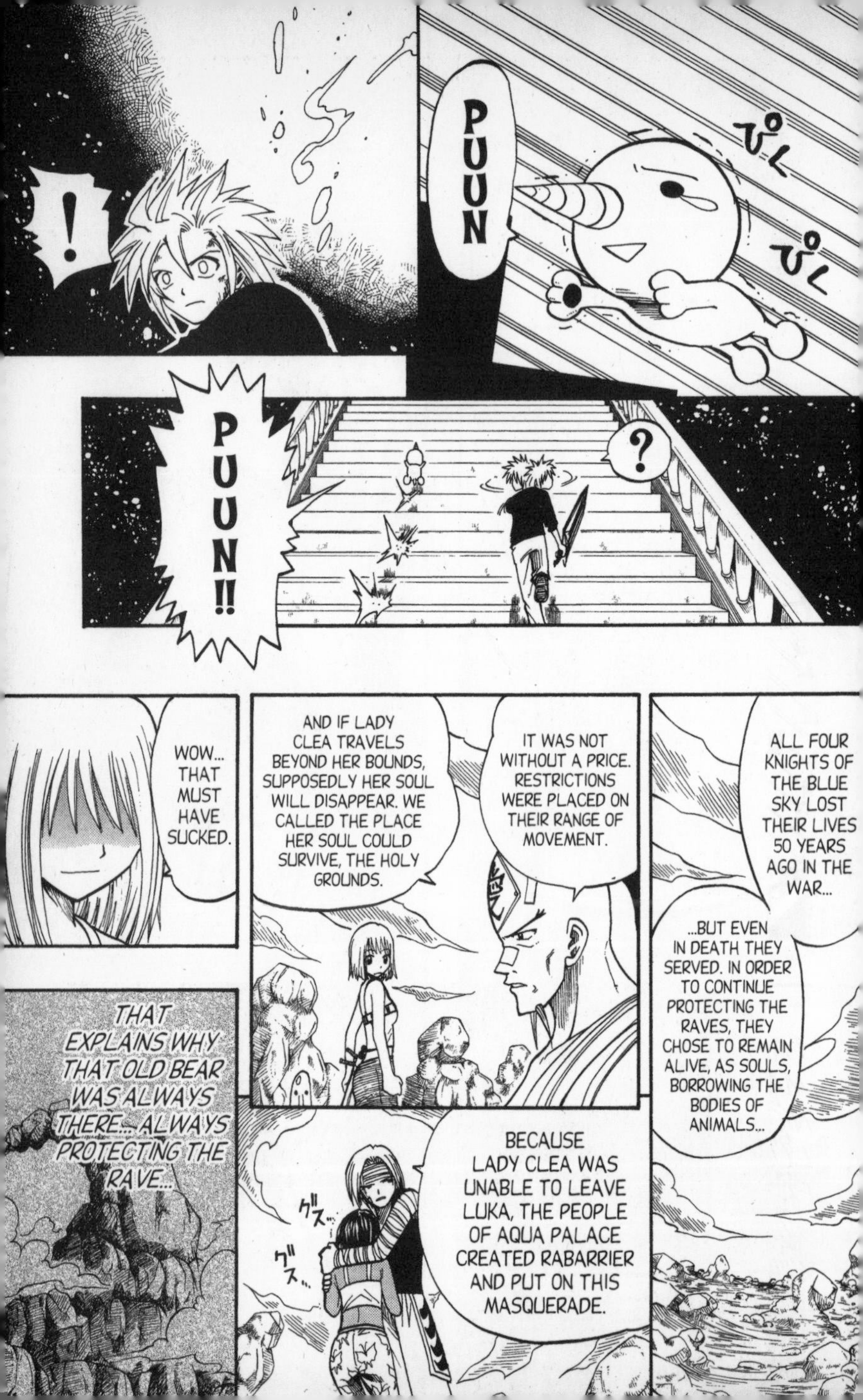
PUUN
!
PUUN!!
?
ALL FOUR KNIGHTS OF THE BLUE SKY LOST THEIR LIVES 50 YEARS AGO IN THE WAR...
...BUT EVEN IN DEATH THEY SERVED. IN ORDER TO CONTINUE PROTECTING THE RAVES, THEY CHOSE TO REMAIN ALIVE, AS SOULS, BORROWING THE BODIES OF ANIMALS...
IT WAS NOT WITHOUT A PRICE. RESTRICTIONS WERE PLACED ON THEIR RANGE OF MOVEMENT.
AND IF LADY CLEA TRAVELS BEYOND HER BOUNDS, SUPPOSEDLY HER SOUL WILL DISAPPEAR. WE CALLED THE PLACE HER SOUL COULD SURVIVE, THE HOLY GROUNDS.
WOW... THAT MUST HAVE SUCKED.
BECAUSE LADY CLEA WAS UNABLE TO LEAVE LUKA, THE PEOPLE OF AQUA PALACE CREATED RABARRIER AND PUT ON THIS MASQUERADE.
グス...
グス...
THAT EXPLAINS WHY THAT OLD BEAR WAS ALWAYS THERE... ALWAYS PROTECTING THE RAVE...

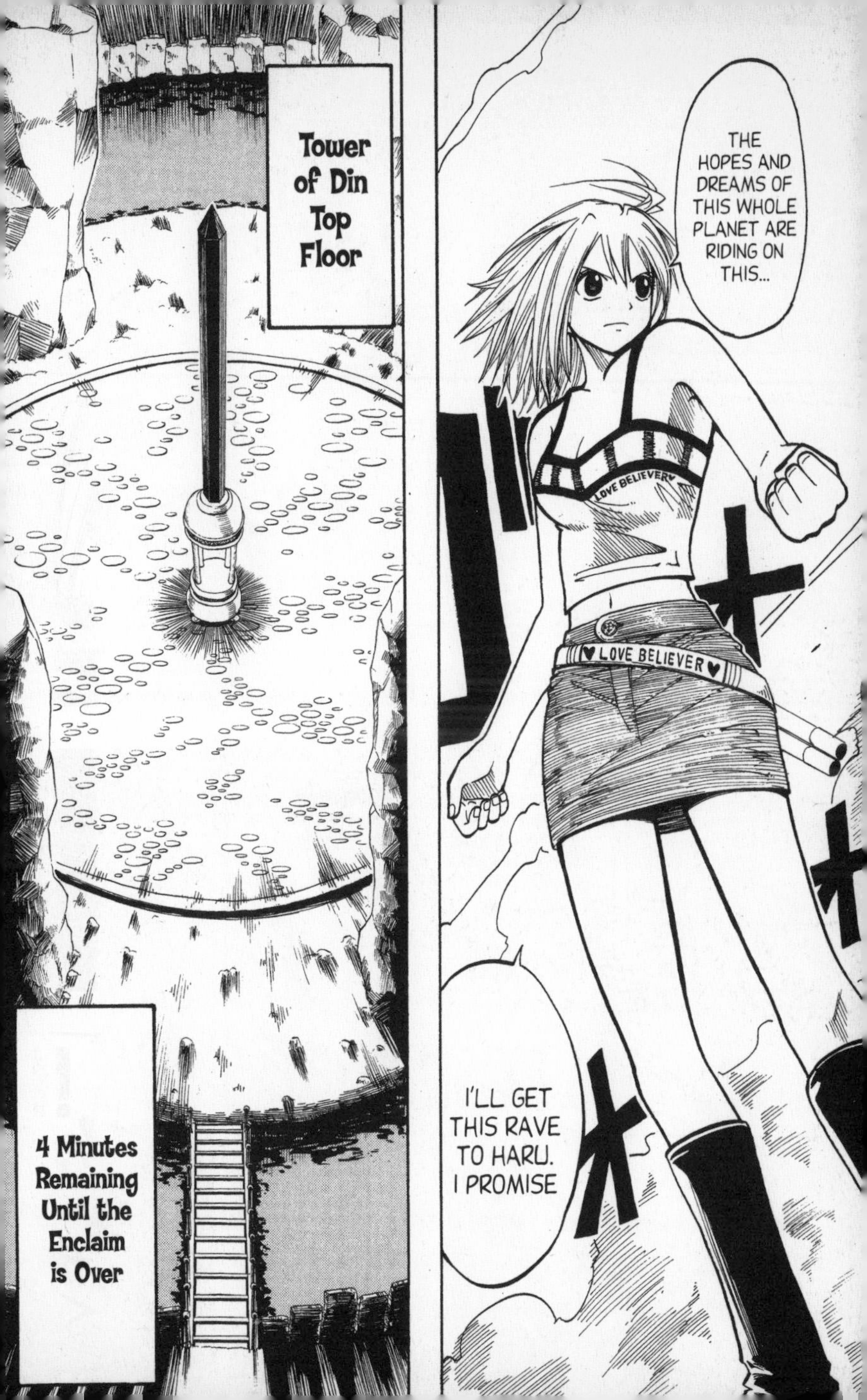
THE HOPES AND DREAMS OF THIS WHOLE PLANET ARE RIDING ON THIS...
LOVE BELIEVER
♥ LOVE BELIEVER ♥
I'LL GET THIS RAVE TO HARU. I PROMISE
Tower of Din Top Floor
4 Minutes Remaining Until the Enclaim is Over

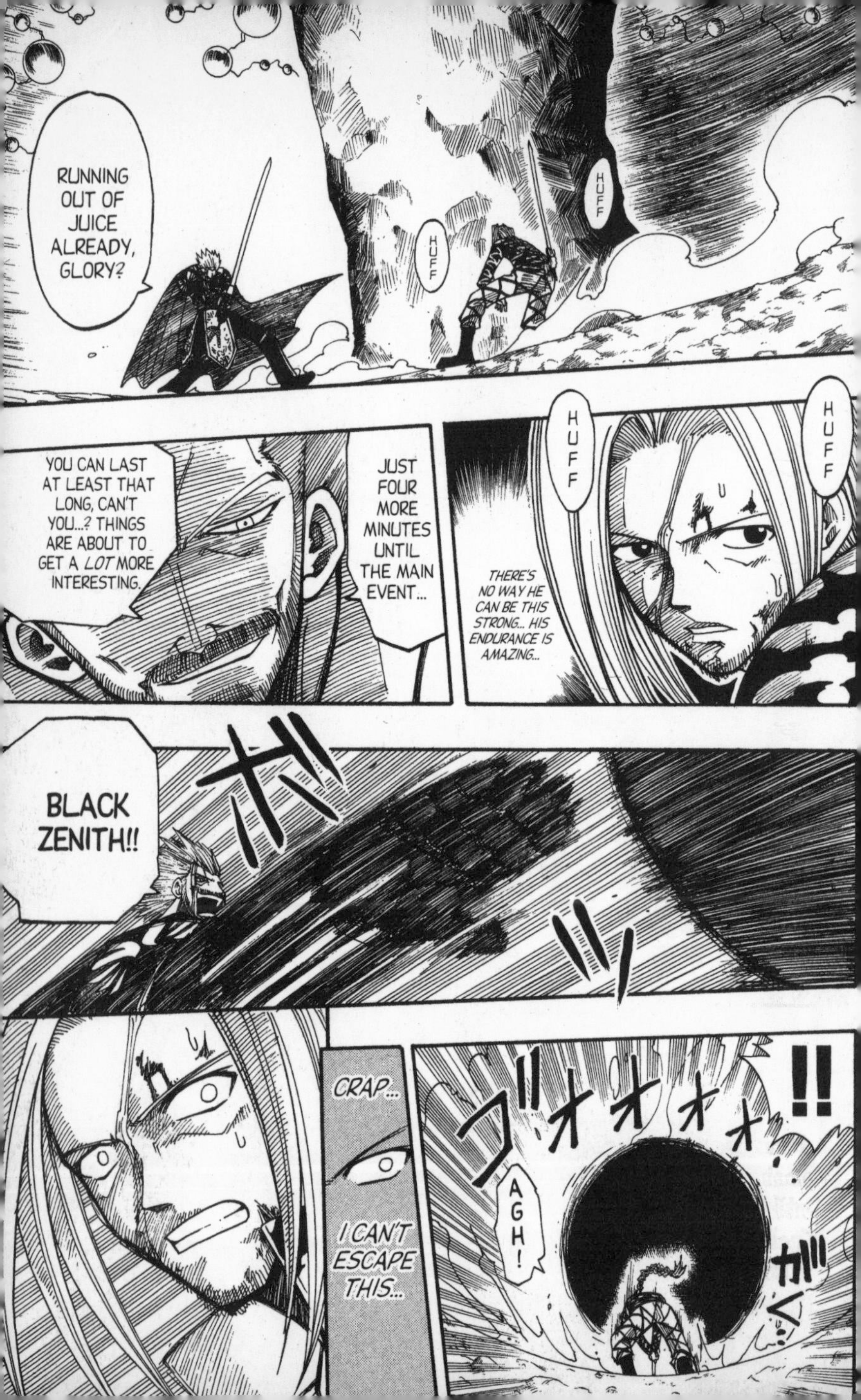
HUFF
HUFF
RUNNING OUT OF JUICE ALREADY, GLORY?
HUFF
HUFF
THERE'S NO WAY HE CAN BE THIS STRONG... HIS ENDURANCE IS AMAZING...
JUST FOUR MORE MINUTES UNTIL THE MAIN EVENT...
YOU CAN LAST AT LEAST THAT LONG, CAN'T YOU...? THINGS ARE ABOUT TO GET A *LOT* MORE INTERESTING.
BLACK ZENITH!!
ゴオオオオ!!
AGH!
CRAP...
I CAN'T ESCAPE THIS...

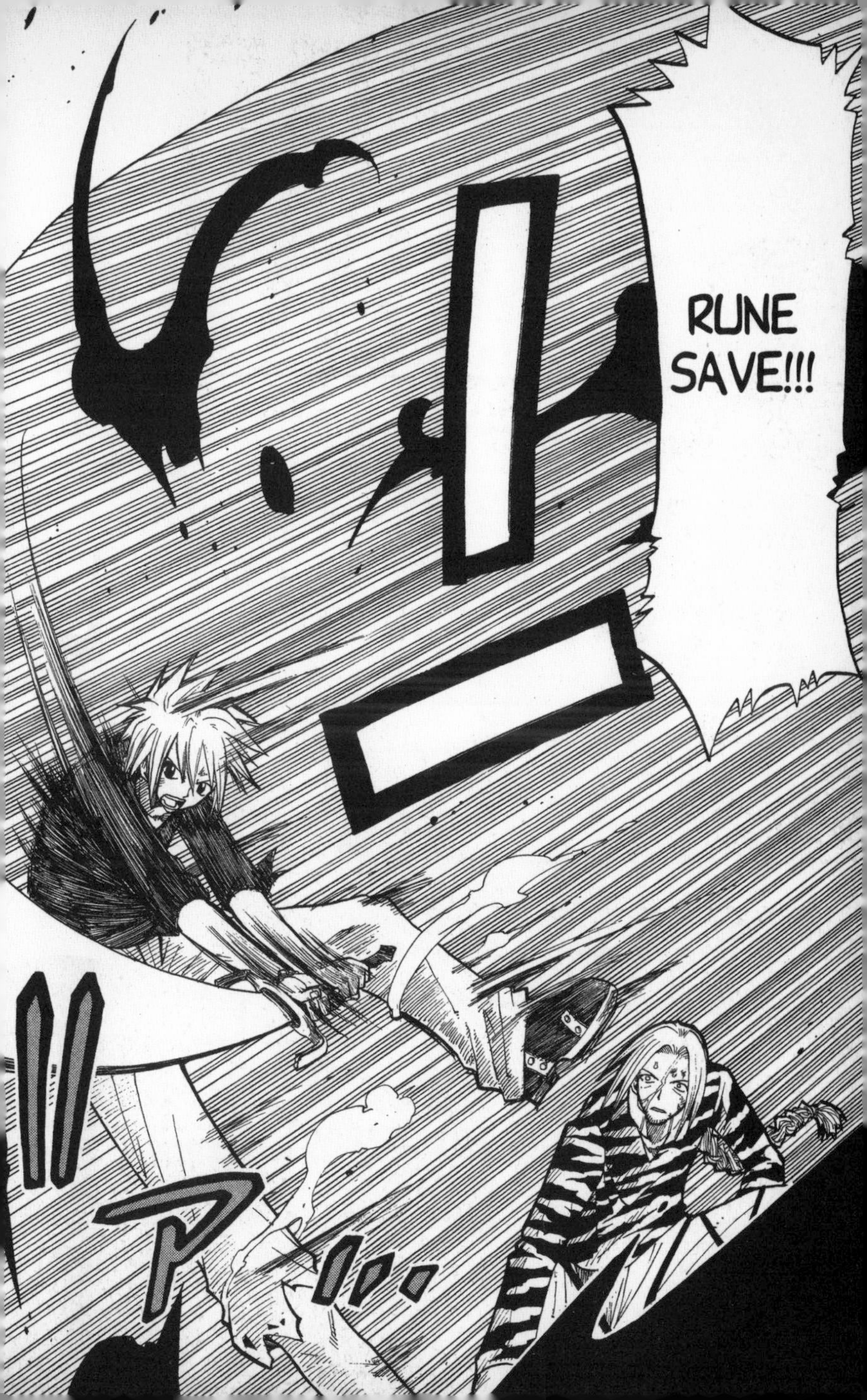
RUNE SAVE!!!

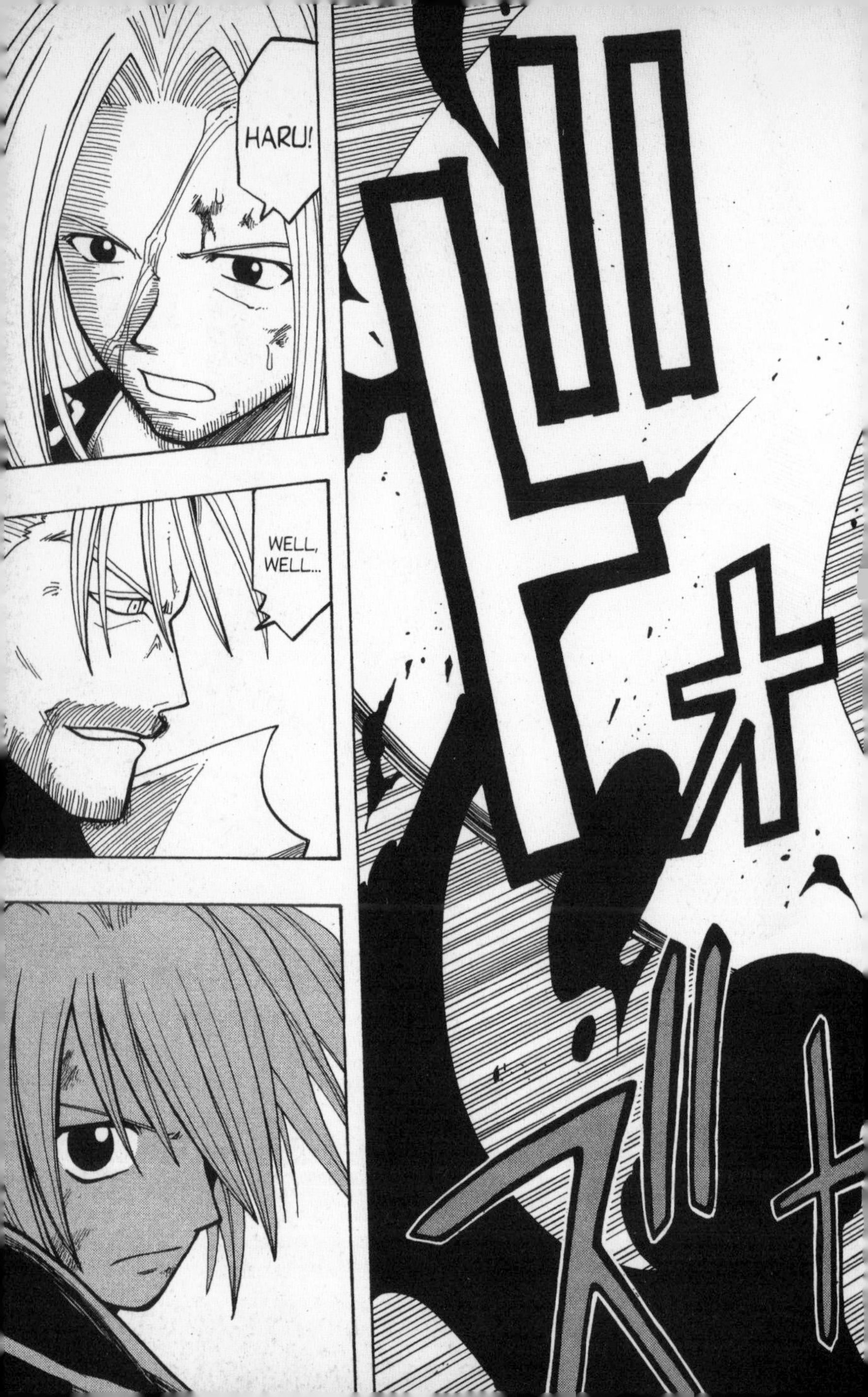
HARU!
WELL, WELL...

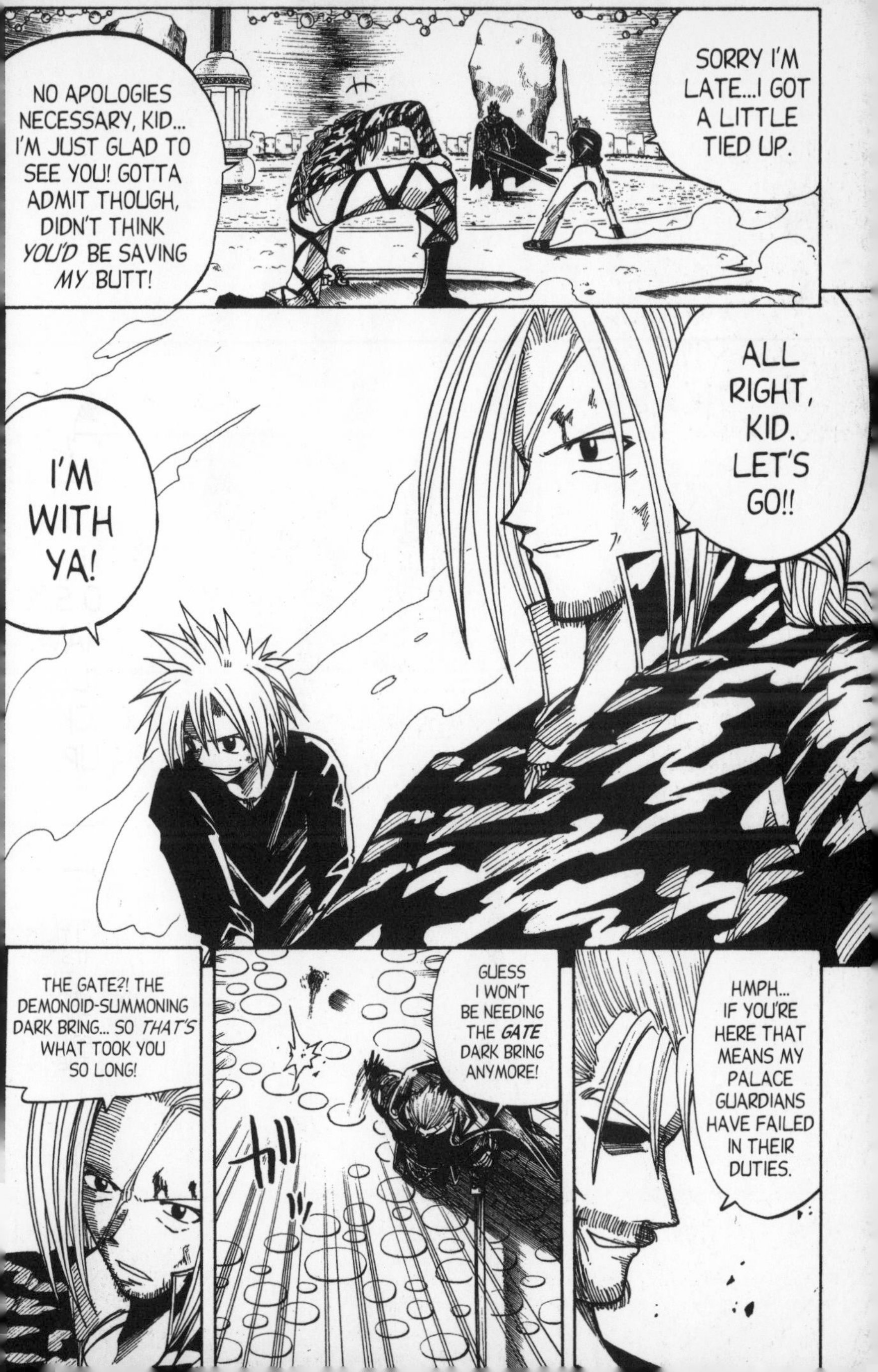
SORRY I'M LATE...I GOT A LITTLE TIED UP.
NO APOLOGIES NECESSARY, KID... I'M JUST GLAD TO SEE YOU! GOTTA ADMIT THOUGH, DIDN'T THINK *YOU'D* BE SAVING *MY* BUTT!
ALL RIGHT, KID. LET'S GO!!
I'M WITH YA!
HMPH... IF YOU'RE HERE THAT MEANS MY PALACE GUARDIANS HAVE FAILED IN THEIR DUTIES.
GUESS I WON'T BE NEEDING THE *GATE* DARK BRING ANYMORE!
THE GATE?! THE DEMONOID-SUMMONING DARK BRING... SO *THAT'S* WHAT TOOK YOU SO LONG!

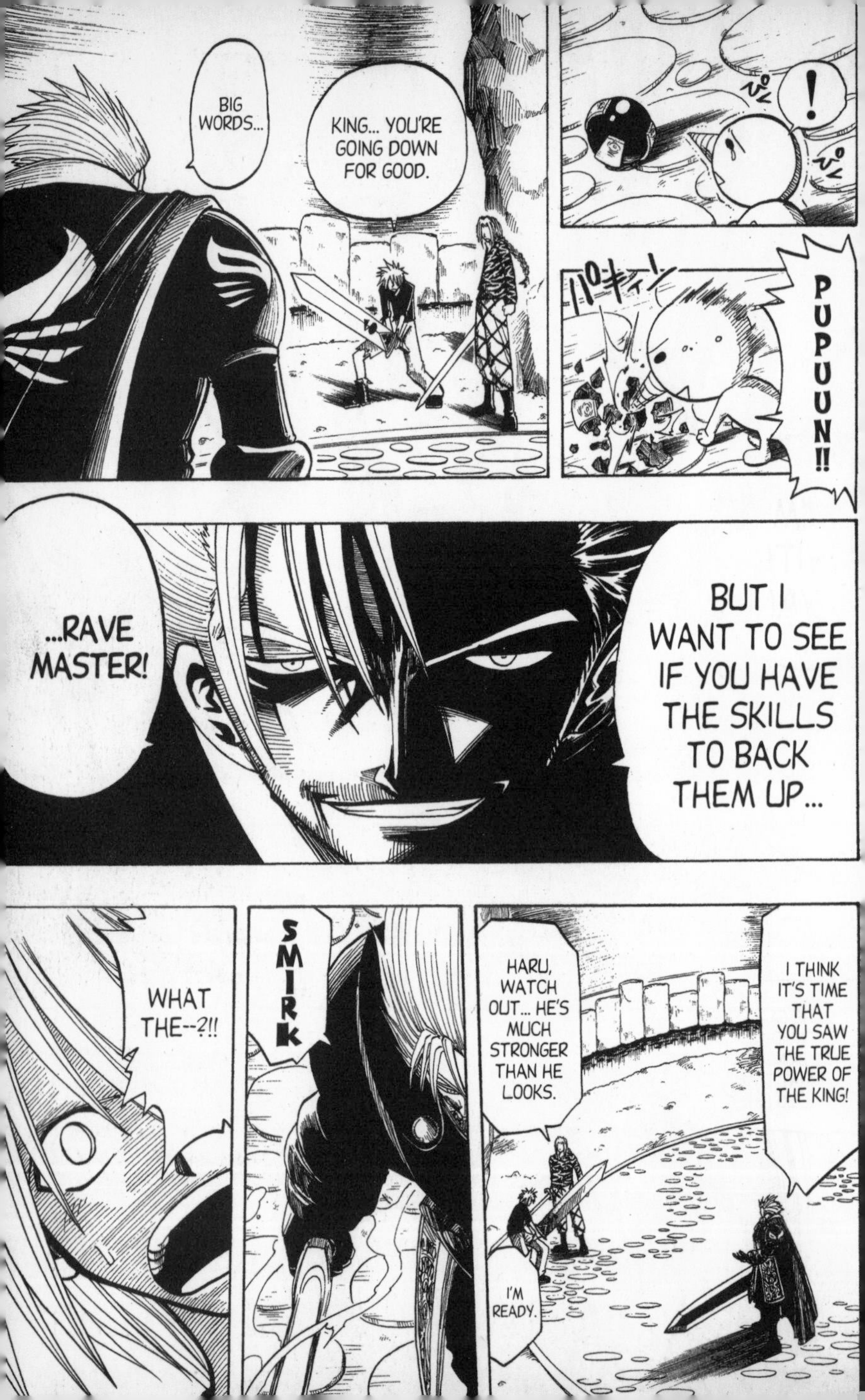
!
パキィーン
PUPUUN!!
KING... YOU'RE GOING DOWN FOR GOOD.
BIG WORDS...
BUT I WANT TO SEE IF YOU HAVE THE SKILLS TO BACK THEM UP...
...RAVE MASTER!
I THINK IT'S TIME THAT YOU SAW THE TRUE POWER OF THE KING!
HARU, WATCH OUT... HE'S MUCH STRONGER THAN HE LOOKS.
I'M READY.
SMIRK
WHAT THE--?!!

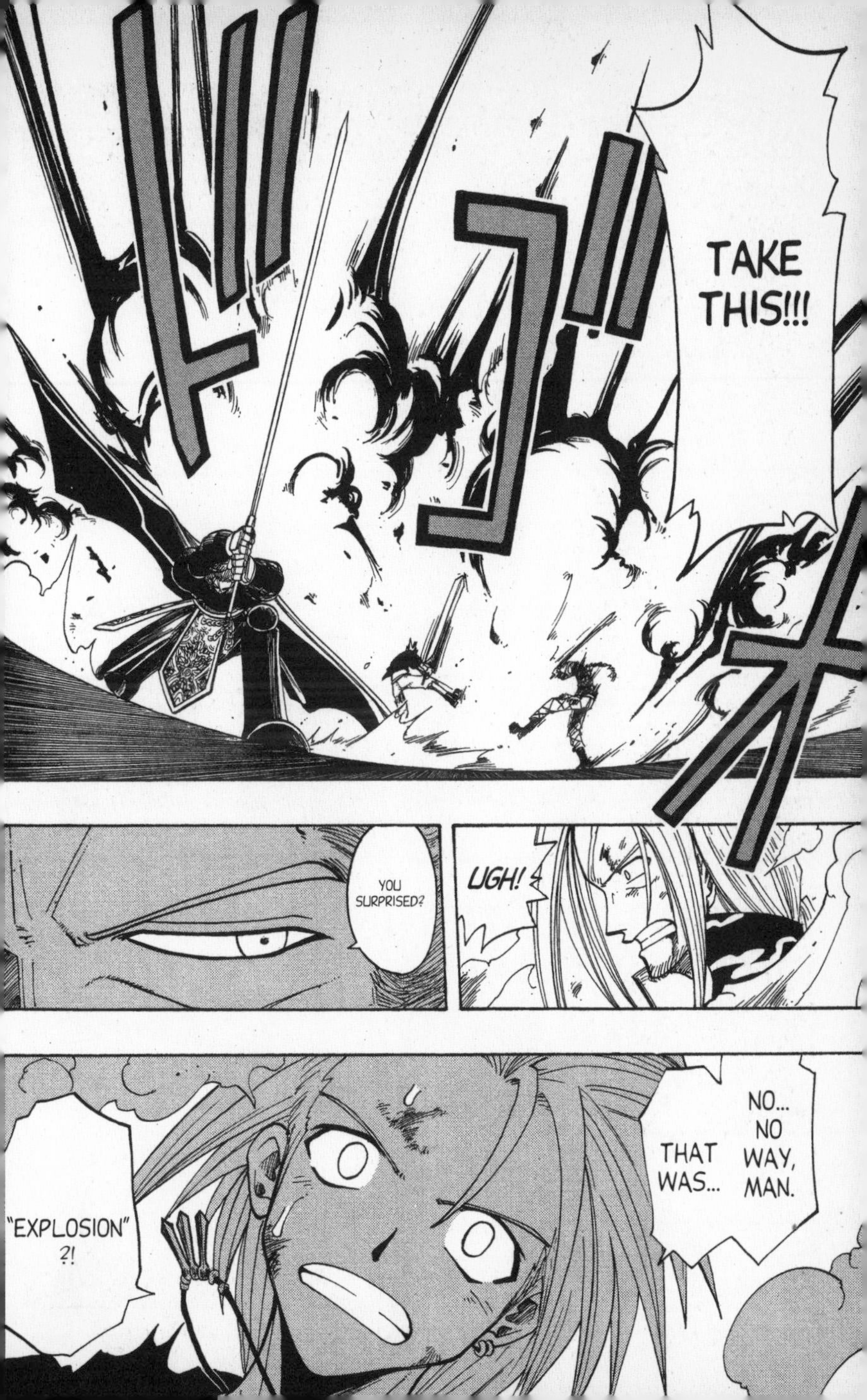
TAKE THIS!!!
UGH!
YOU SURPRISED?
NO... NO WAY, MAN.
THAT WAS...
"EXPLOSION" ?!

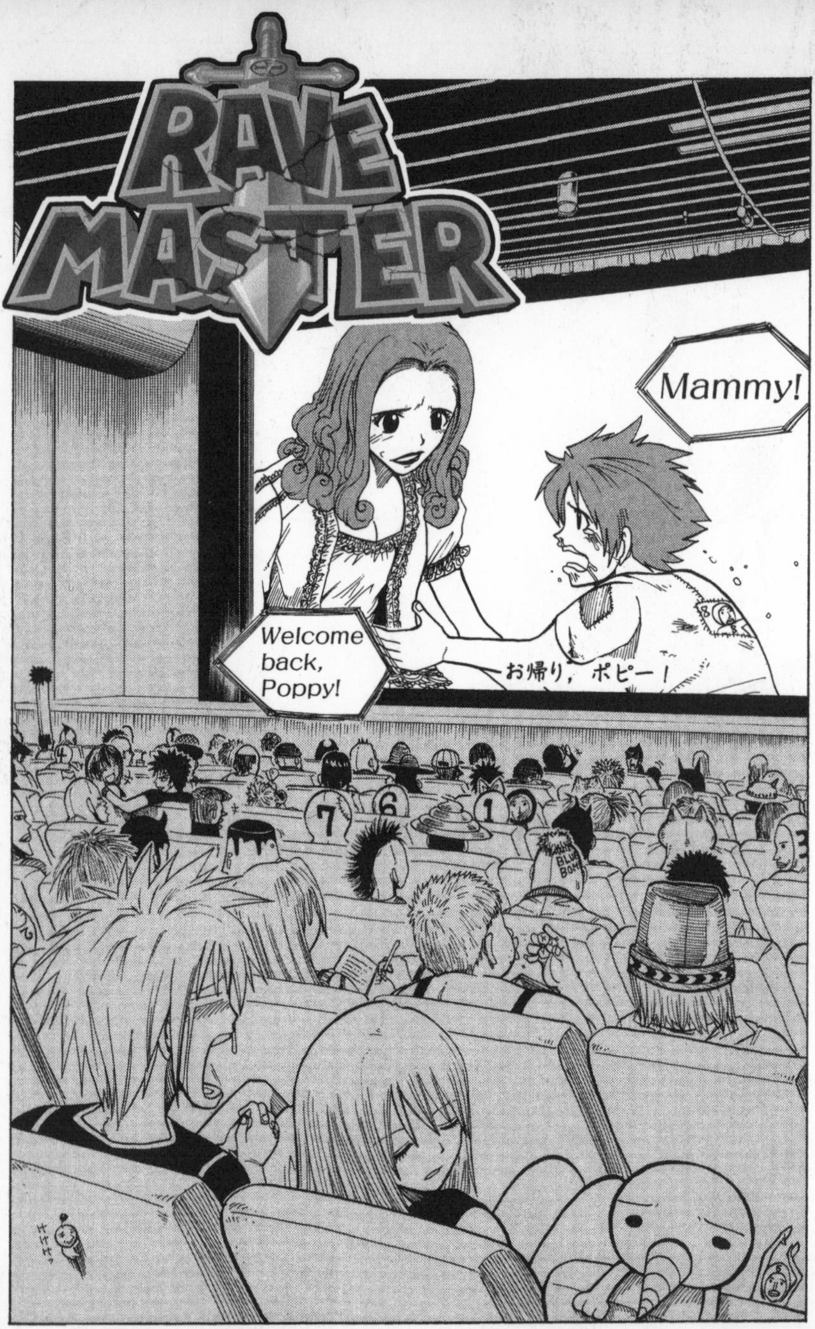
RAVE MASTER
Mammy!
Welcome back, Poppy!
お帰り，ポピー！

RAVE: 64 KING'S ULTIMATE GOAL!

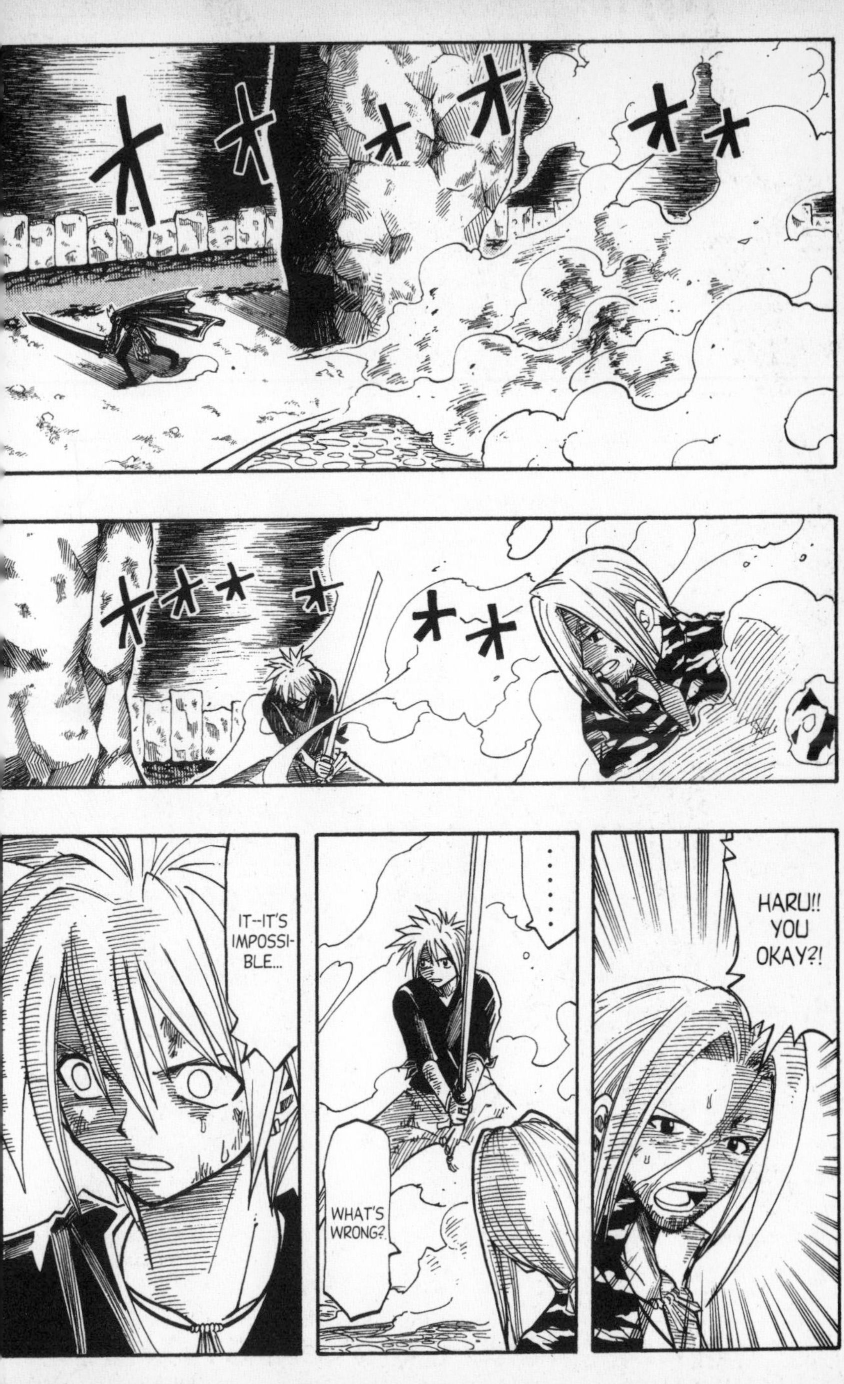
HARU!! YOU OKAY?!
......
WHAT'S WRONG?
IT--IT'S IMPOSSI-BLE...

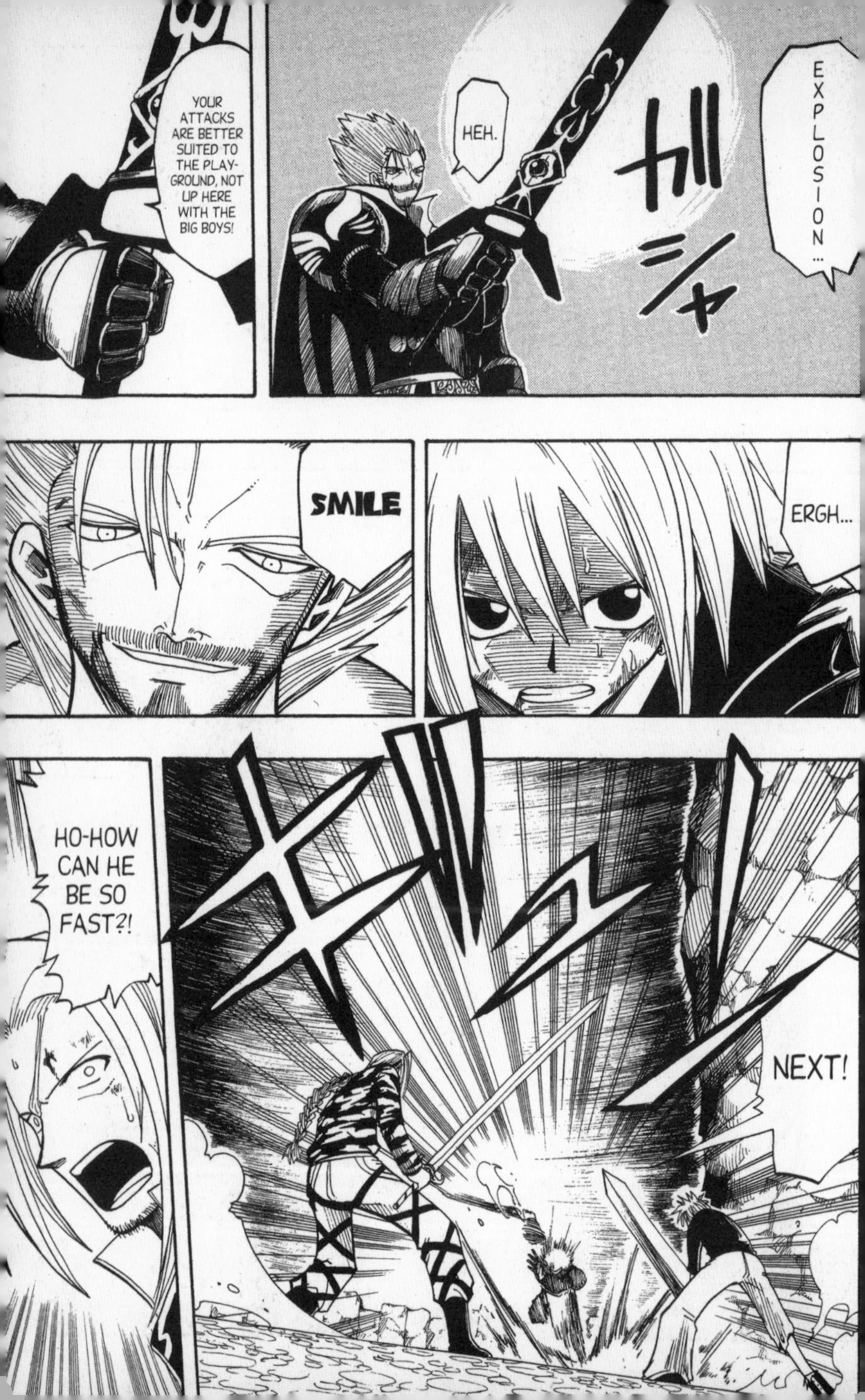
EXPLOSION...
HEH.
YOUR ATTACKS ARE BETTER SUITED TO THE PLAY-GROUND, NOT UP HERE WITH THE BIG BOYS!
ERGH...
SMILE
NEXT!
HO-HOW CAN HE BE SO FAST?!

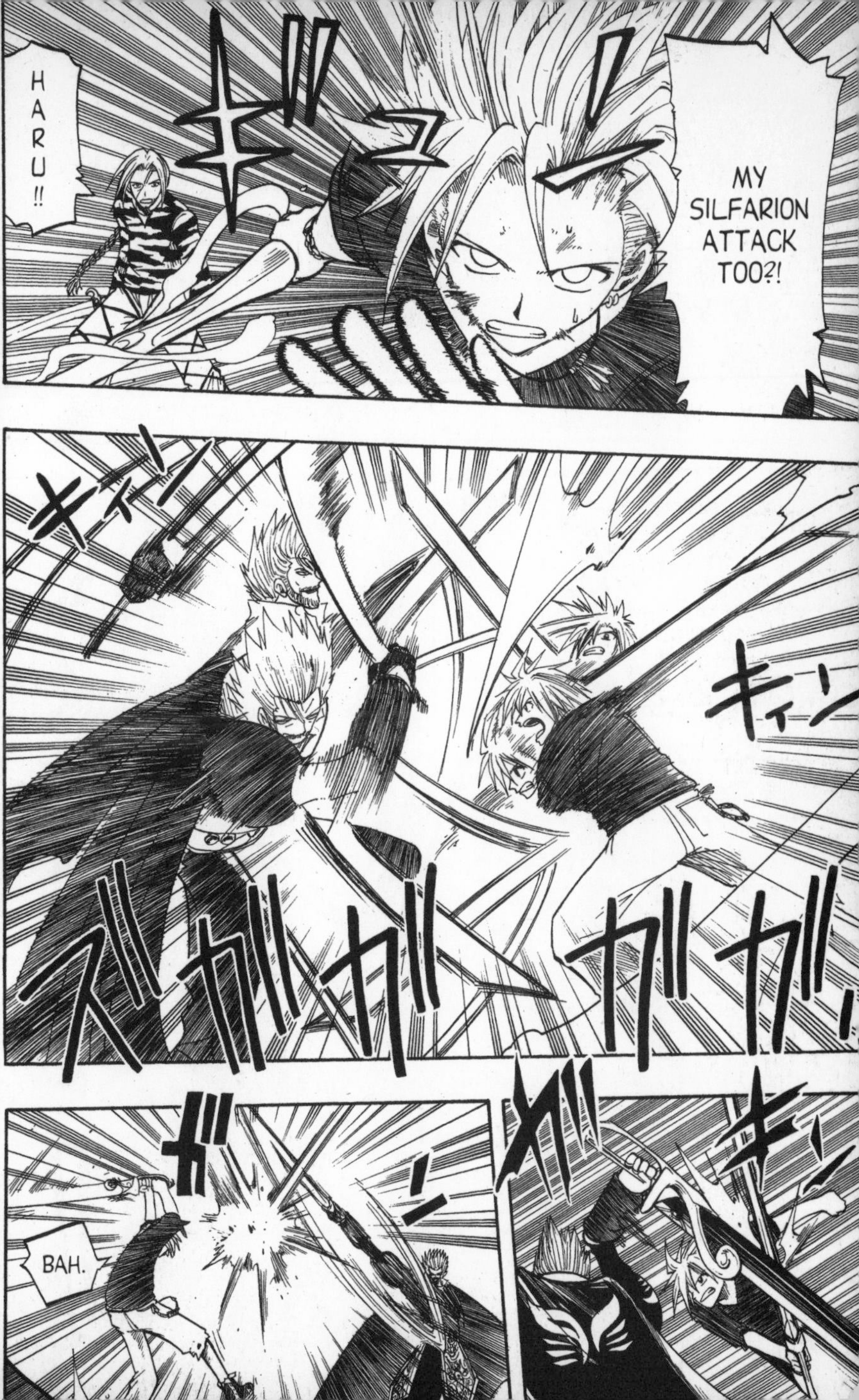
MY SILFARION ATTACK TOO?!
HARU!!
BAH.

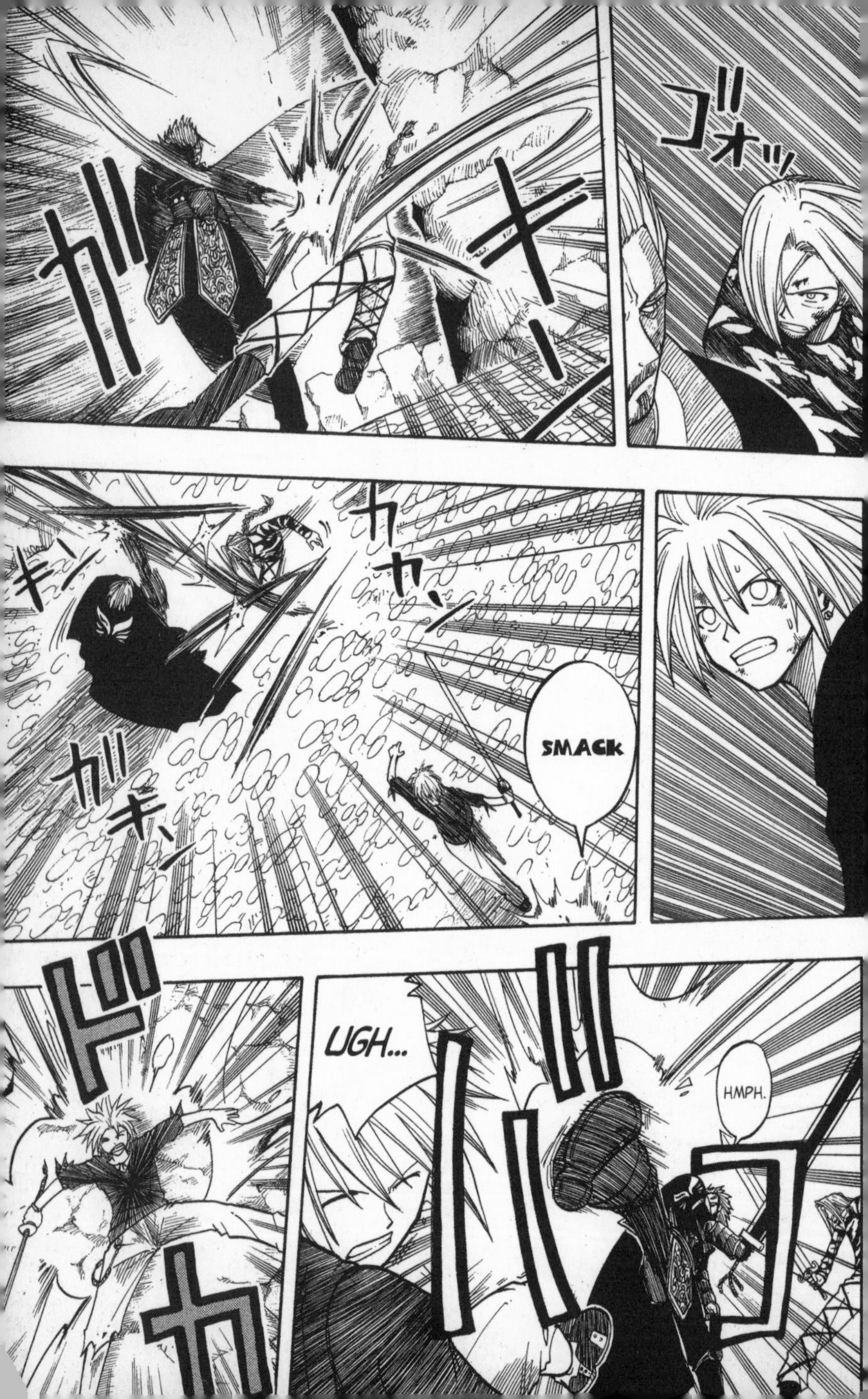
ゴオッ
SMACK
HMPH.
UGH...

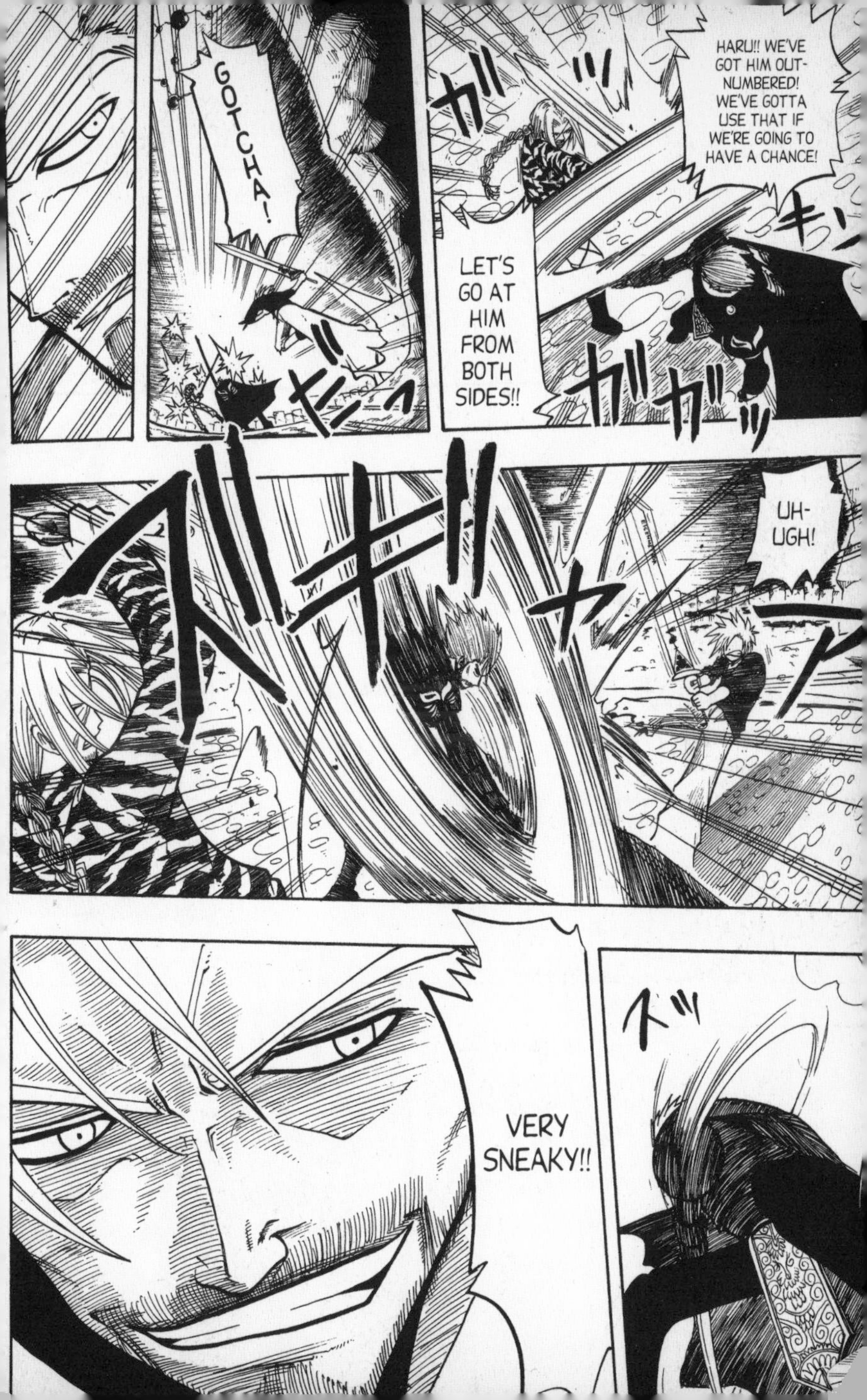
HARU!! WE'VE GOT HIM OUT-NUMBERED! WE'VE GOTTA USE THAT IF WE'RE GOING TO HAVE A CHANCE!
LET'S GO AT HIM FROM BOTH SIDES!!
GOTCHA!
UH-UGH!
VERY SNEAKY!!

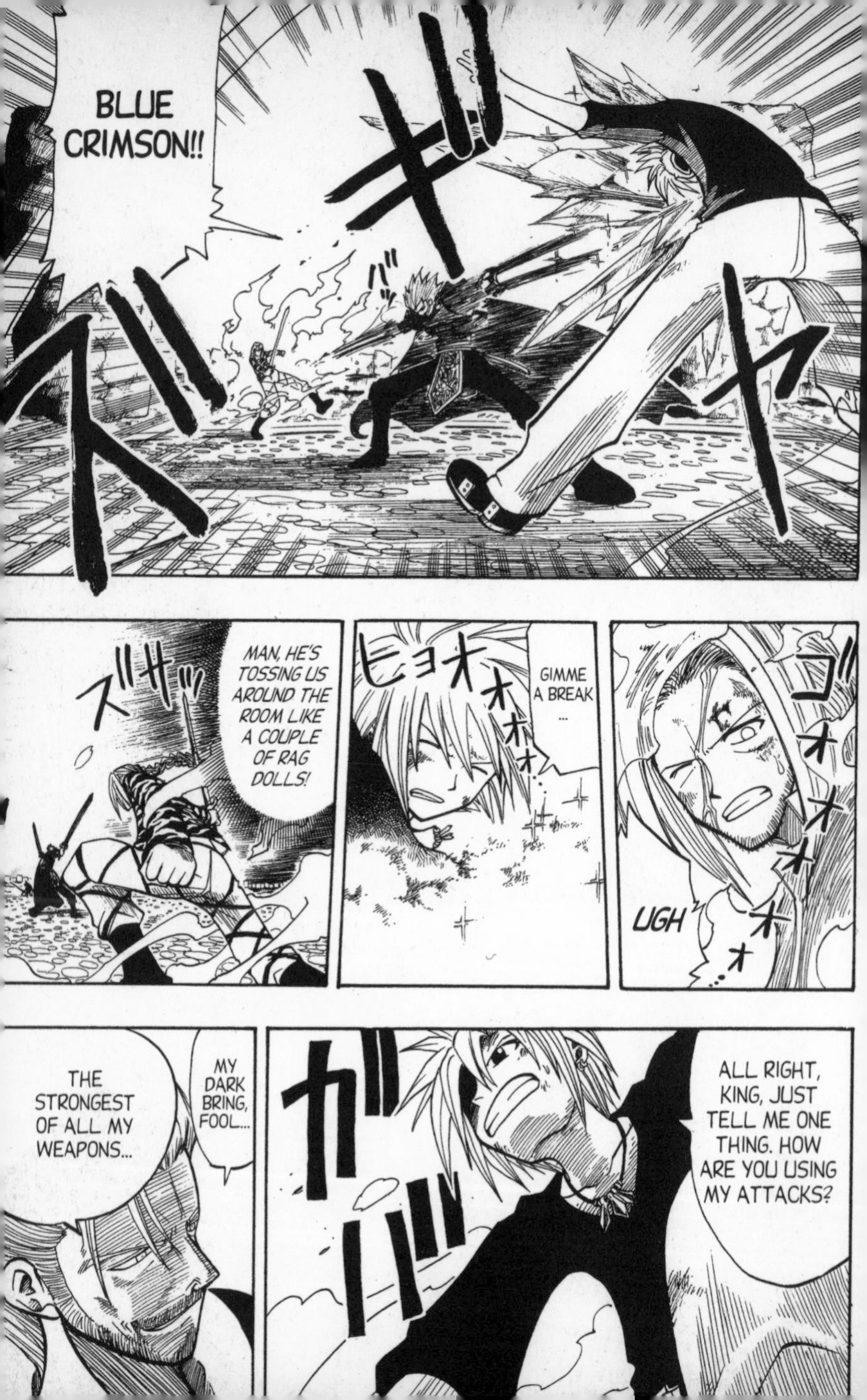
BLUE CRIMSON!!
UGH
GIMME A BREAK ...
MAN, HE'S TOSSING US AROUND THE ROOM LIKE A COUPLE OF RAG DOLLS!
ALL RIGHT, KING, JUST TELL ME ONE THING. HOW ARE YOU USING MY ATTACKS?
MY DARK BRING, FOOL...
THE STRONGEST OF ALL MY WEAPONS...

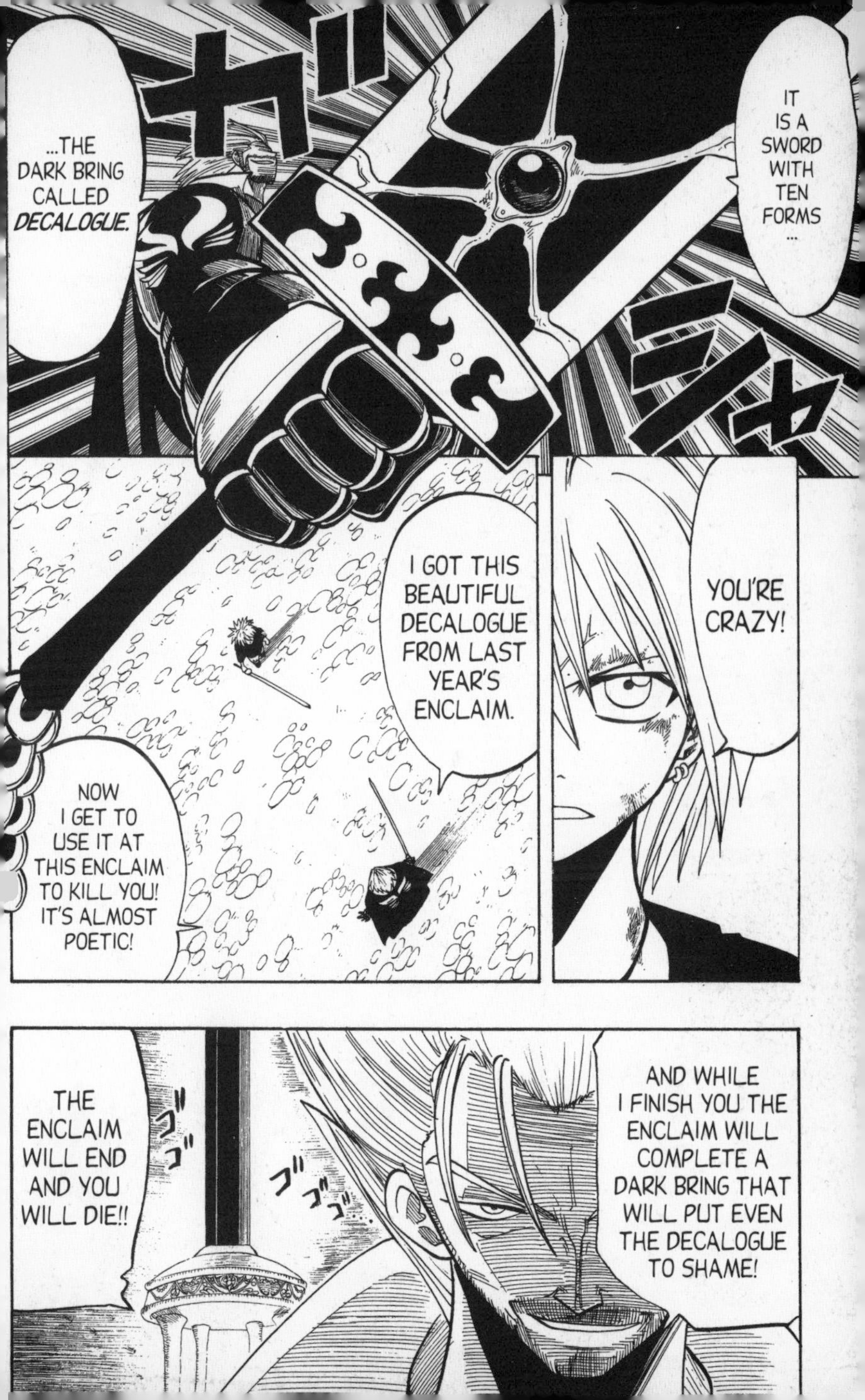
IT IS A SWORD WITH TEN FORMS...
シャ
ガッ
...THE DARK BRING CALLED *DECALOGUE*.
YOU'RE CRAZY!
I GOT THIS BEAUTIFUL DECALOGUE FROM LAST YEAR'S ENCLAIM.
NOW I GET TO USE IT AT THIS ENCLAIM TO KILL YOU! IT'S ALMOST POETIC!
AND WHILE I FINISH YOU THE ENCLAIM WILL COMPLETE A DARK BRING THAT WILL PUT EVEN THE DECALOGUE TO SHAME!
ゴゴゴ...
ゴゴ
THE ENCLAIM WILL END AND YOU WILL DIE!!

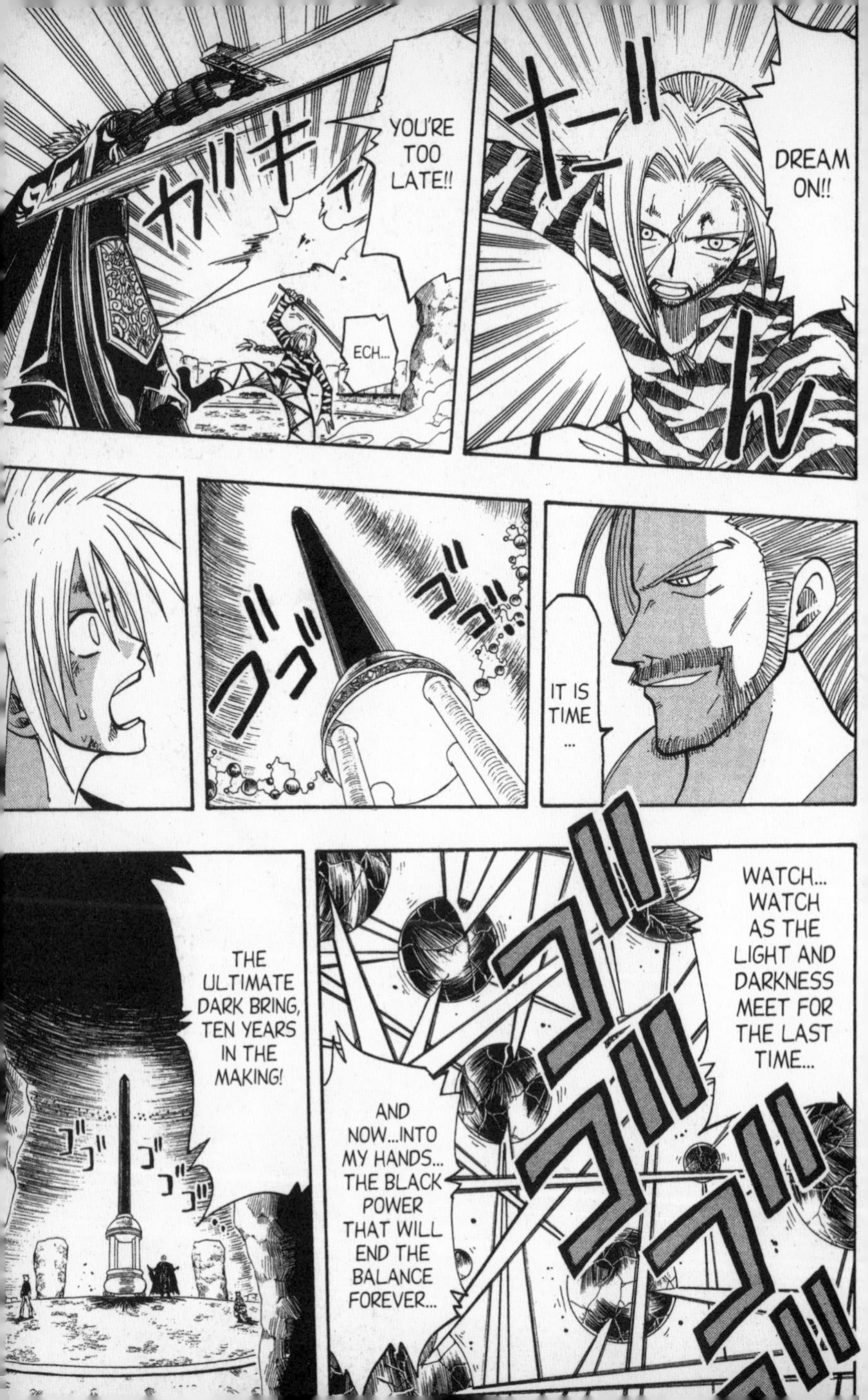
DREAM ON!!
YOU'RE TOO LATE!!
ECH...
IT IS TIME ...
WATCH... WATCH AS THE LIGHT AND DARKNESS MEET FOR THE LAST TIME...
AND NOW...INTO MY HANDS... THE BLACK POWER THAT WILL END THE BALANCE FOREVER...
THE ULTIMATE DARK BRING, TEN YEARS IN THE MAKING!

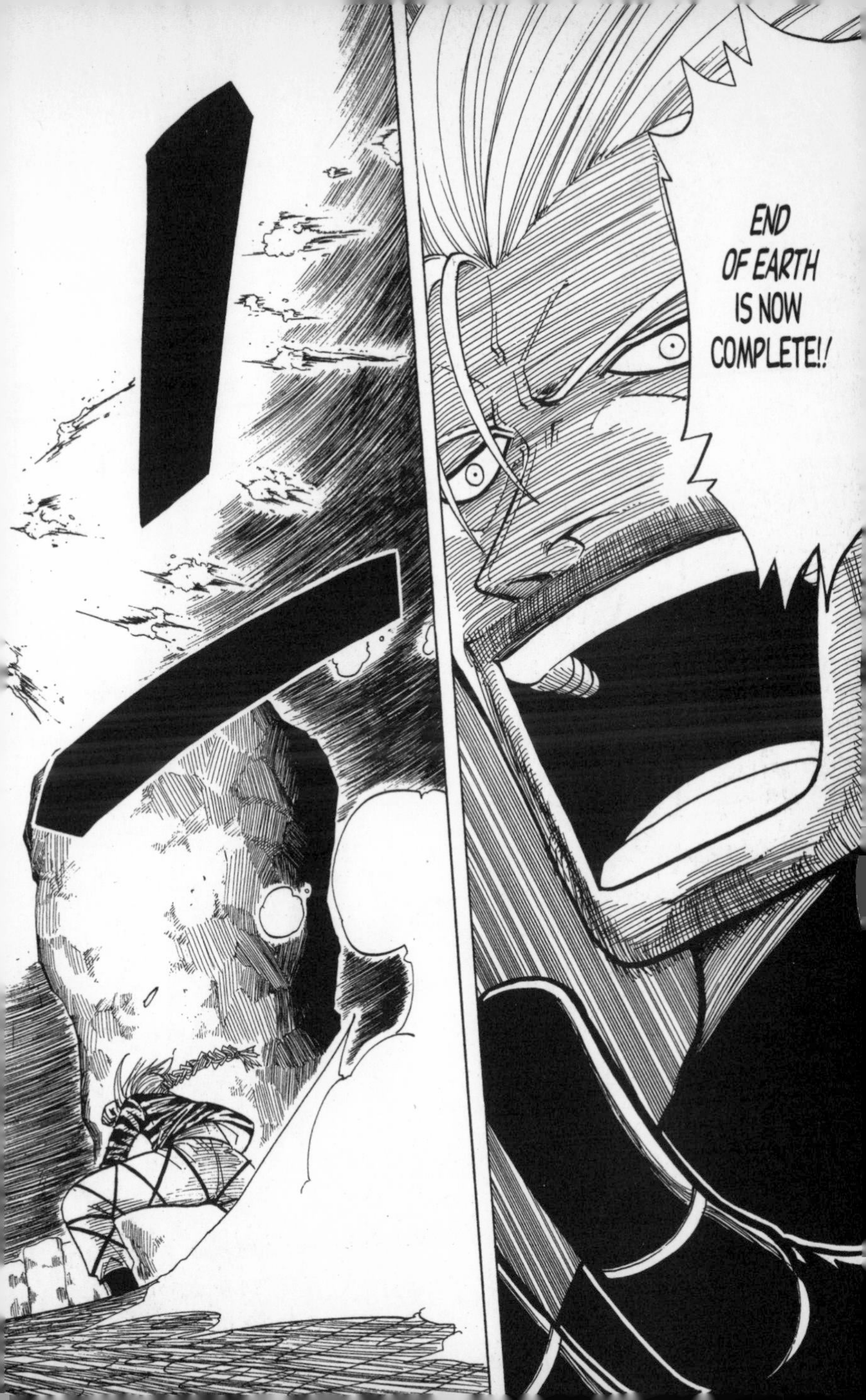
END OF EARTH IS NOW COMPLETE!!

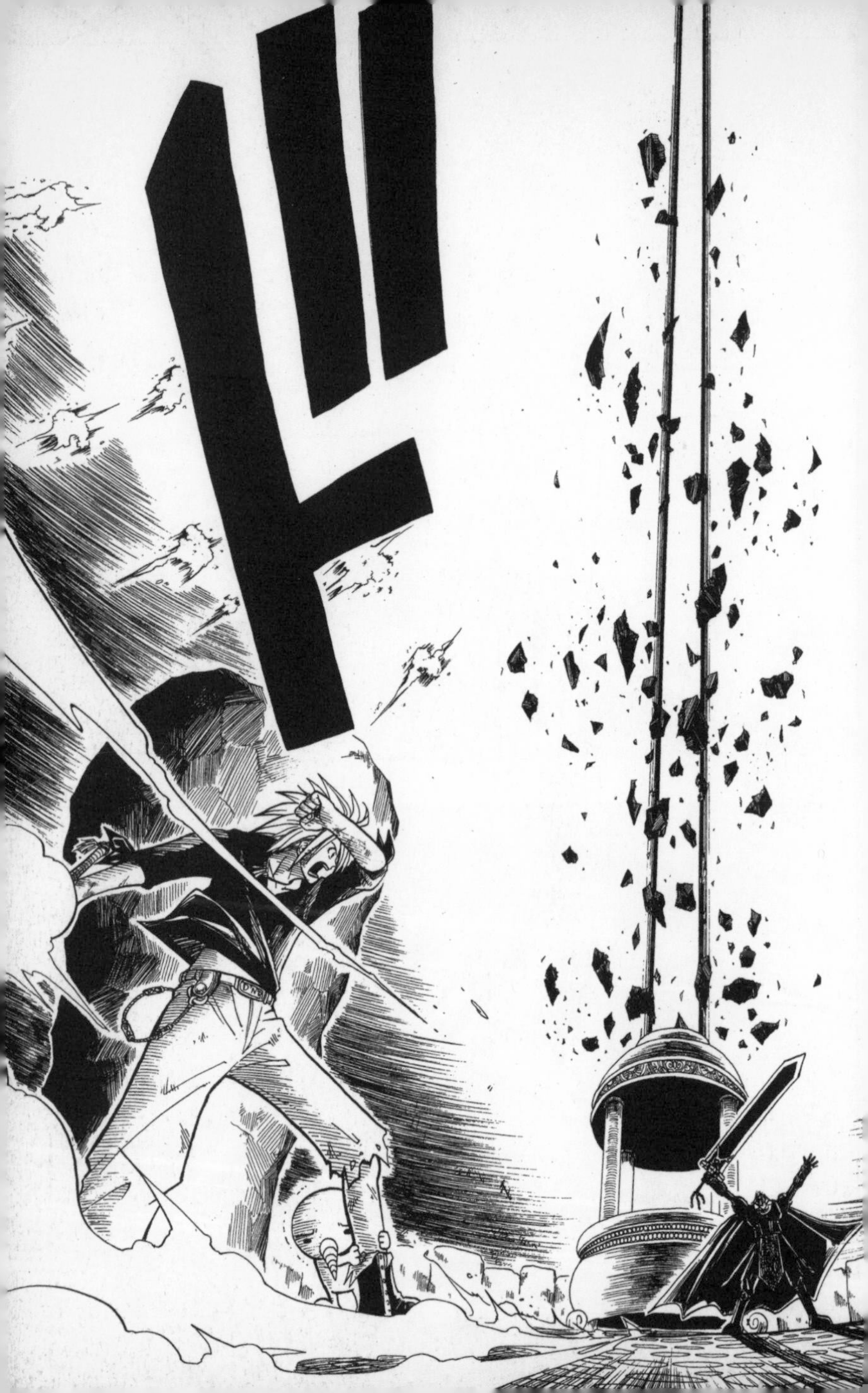
ド

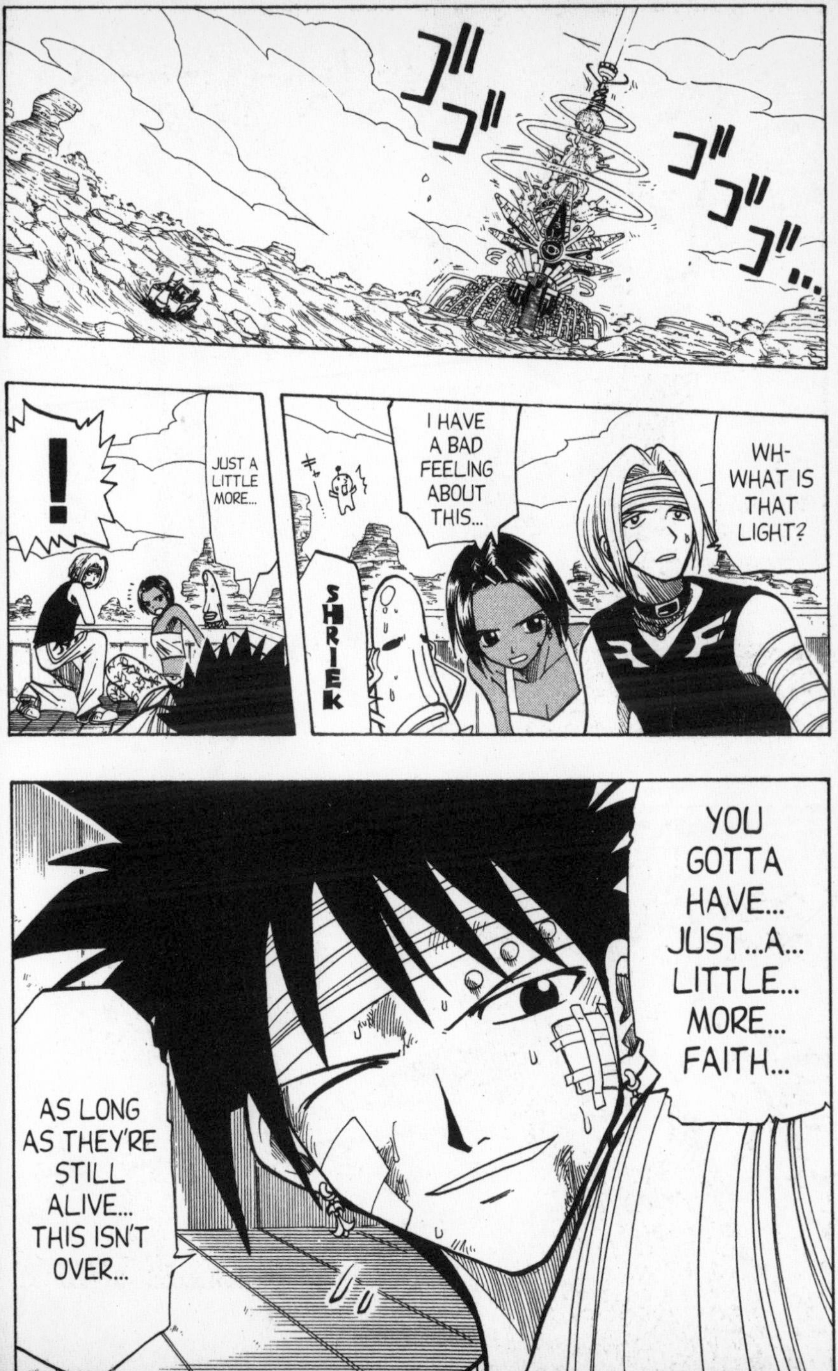

ゴゴゴ…
ゴゴ
WH- WHAT IS THAT LIGHT?
I HAVE A BAD FEELING ABOUT THIS...
SHRIEK
JUST A LITTLE MORE...
!
YOU GOTTA HAVE... JUST...A... LITTLE... MORE... FAITH...
AS LONG AS THEY'RE STILL ALIVE... THIS ISN'T OVER...

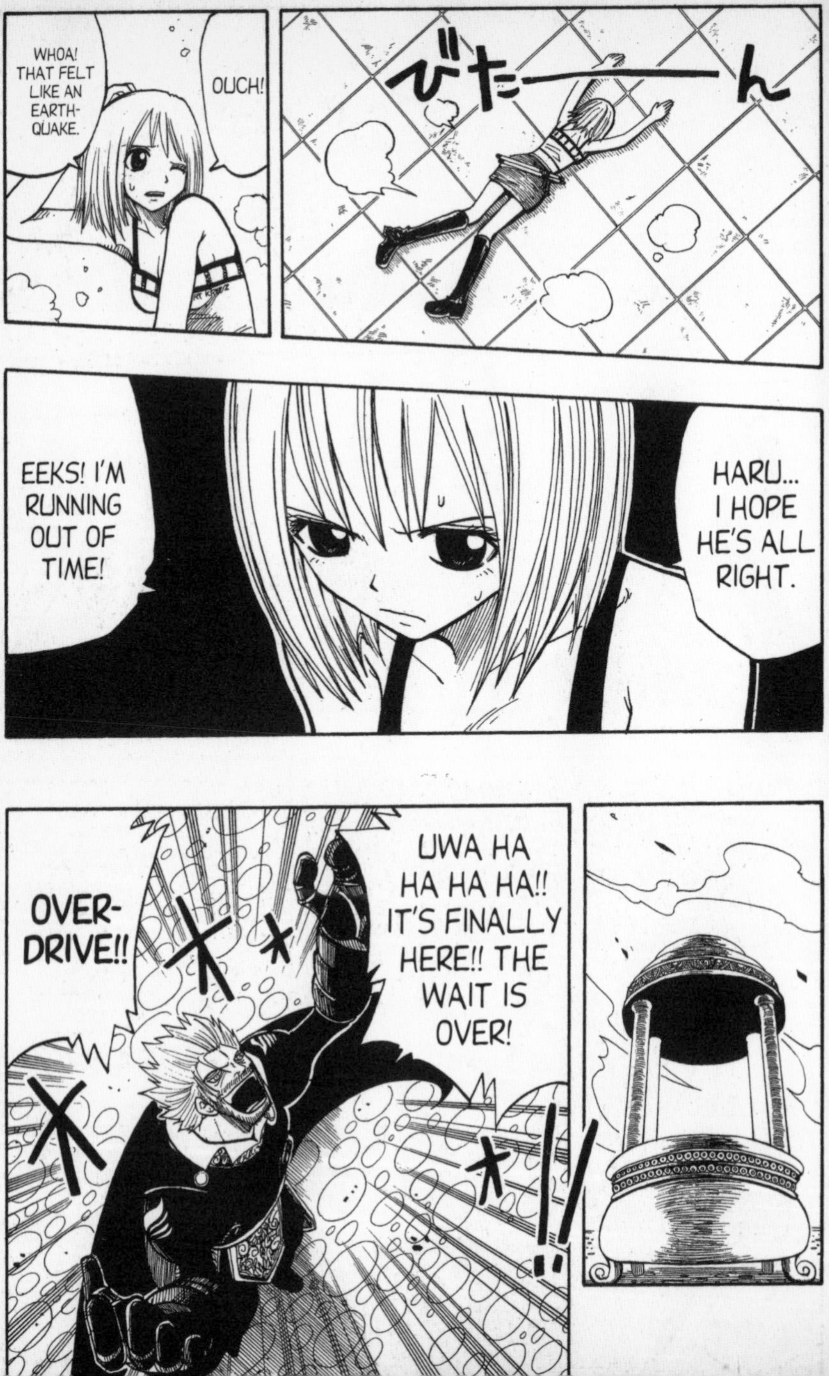
びたーーーん
OUCH!
WHOA! THAT FELT LIKE AN EARTH-QUAKE.
HARU... I HOPE HE'S ALL RIGHT.
EEKS! I'M RUNNING OUT OF TIME!
UWA HA HA HA HA!! IT'S FINALLY HERE!! THE WAIT IS OVER!
OVER-DRIVE!!

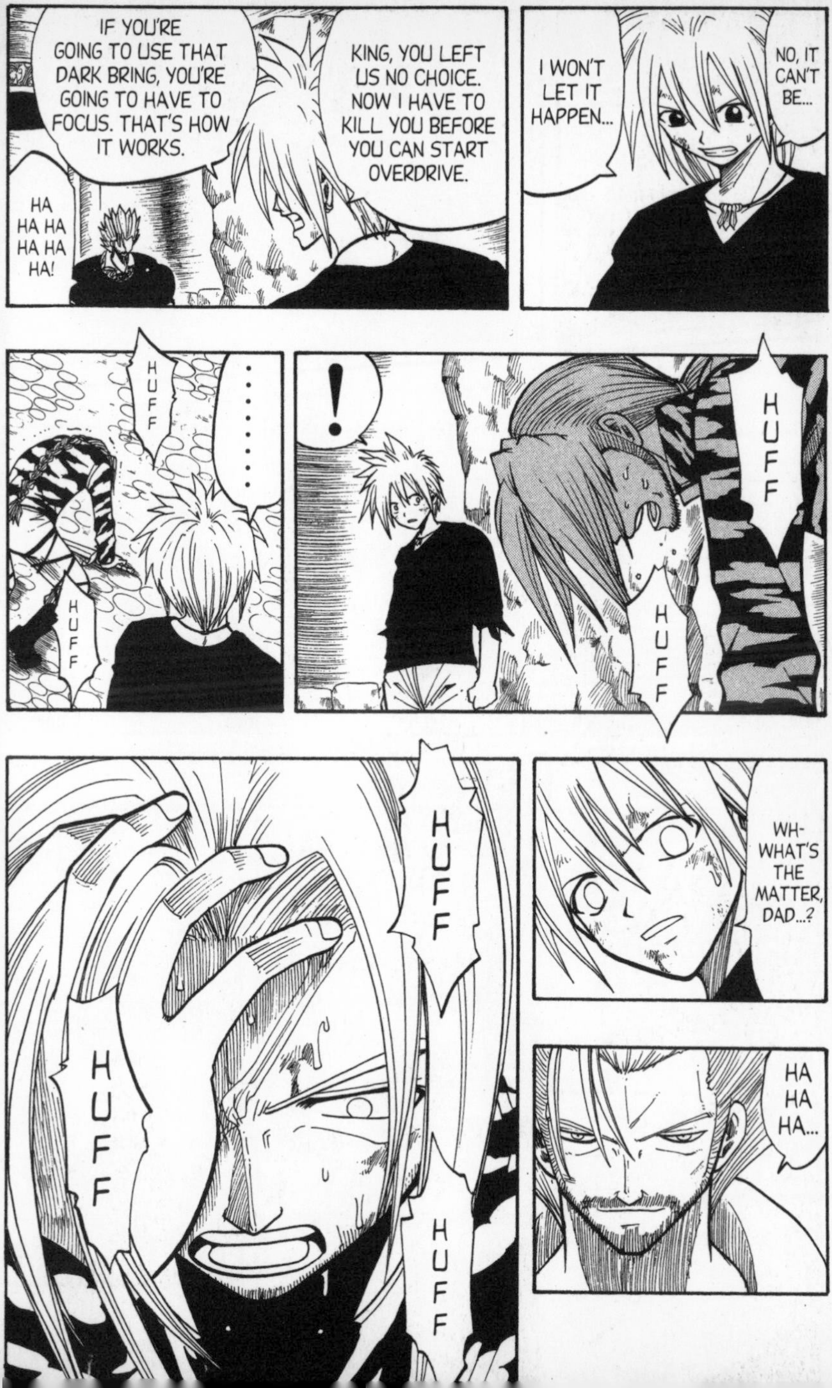
NO, IT CAN'T BE...
I WON'T LET IT HAPPEN...
KING, YOU LEFT US NO CHOICE. NOW I HAVE TO KILL YOU BEFORE YOU CAN START OVERDRIVE.
IF YOU'RE GOING TO USE THAT DARK BRING, YOU'RE GOING TO HAVE TO FOCUS. THAT'S HOW IT WORKS.
HA HA HA HA HA HA!
HUFF
!
HUFF
......
HUFF
HUFF
WH- WHAT'S THE MATTER, DAD...?
HA HA HA...
HUFF
HUFF
HUFF

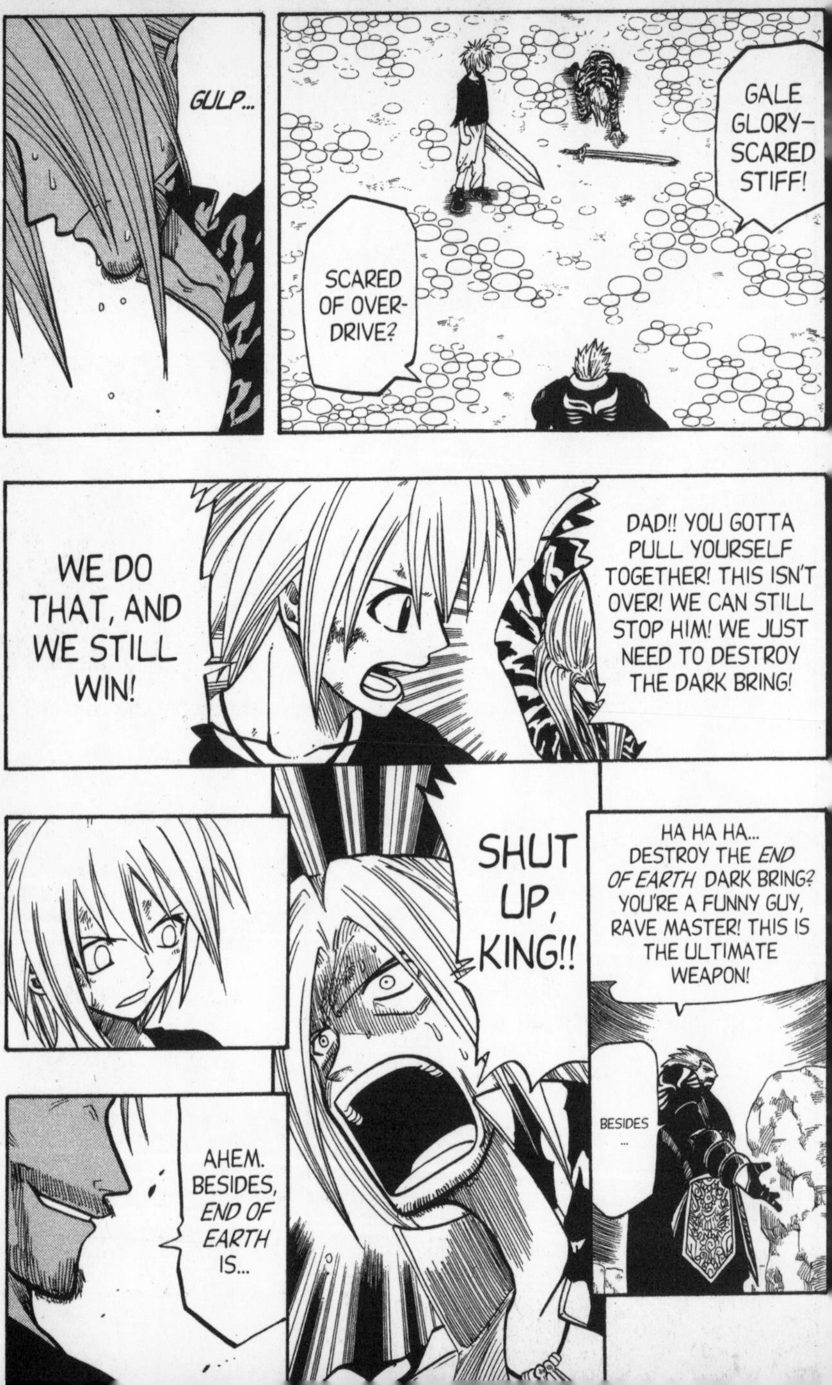
GALE GLORY— SCARED STIFF!
SCARED OF OVER-DRIVE?
GULP...
DAD!! YOU GOTTA PULL YOURSELF TOGETHER! THIS ISN'T OVER! WE CAN STILL STOP HIM! WE JUST NEED TO DESTROY THE DARK BRING!
WE DO THAT, AND WE STILL WIN!
HA HA HA... DESTROY THE *END OF EARTH* DARK BRING? YOU'RE A FUNNY GUY, RAVE MASTER! THIS IS THE ULTIMATE WEAPON!
BESIDES...
SHUT UP, KING!!
AHEM. BESIDES, *END OF EARTH* IS...

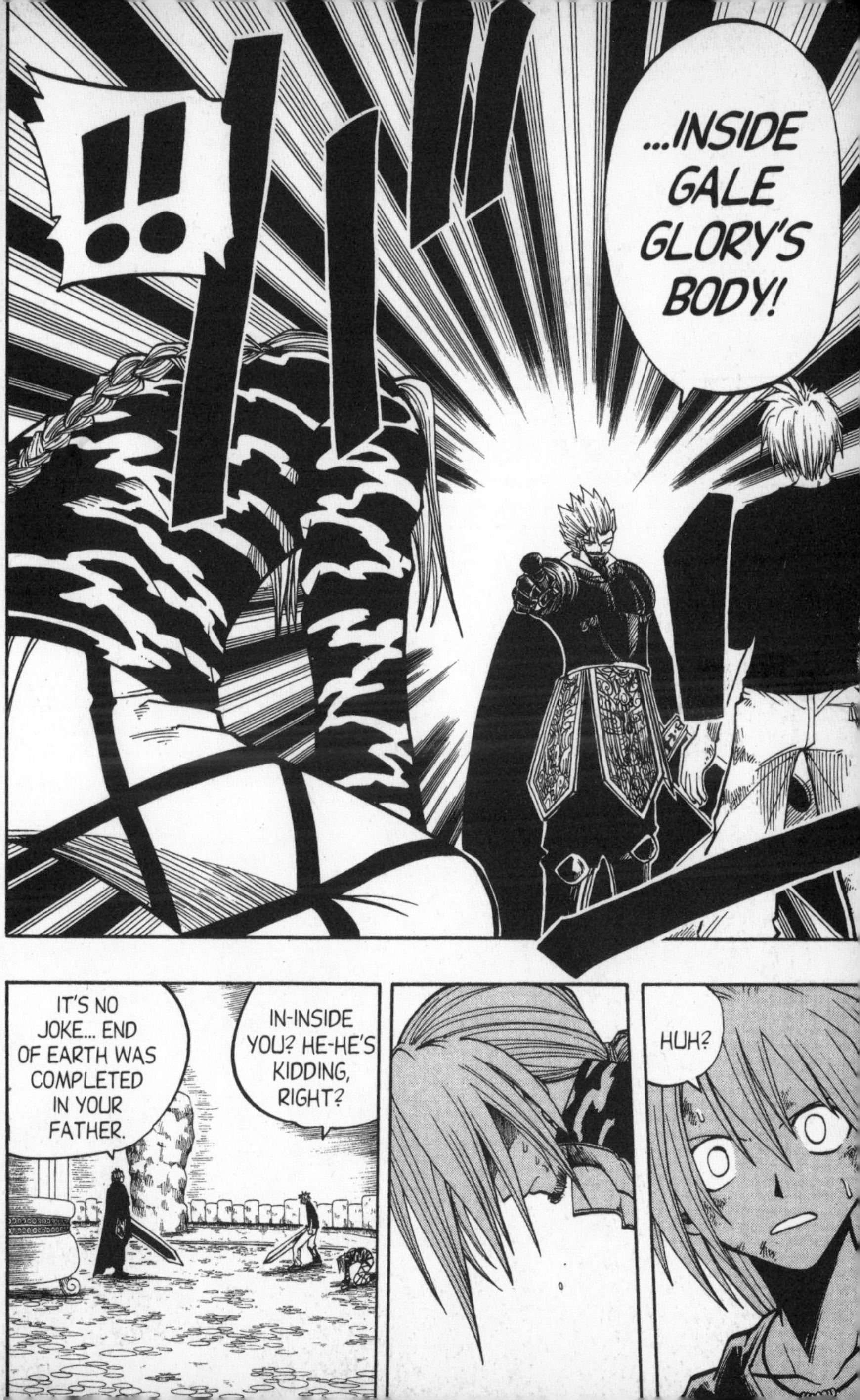
...INSIDE GALE GLORY'S BODY!
!!
HUH?
IN-INSIDE YOU? HE-HE'S KIDDING, RIGHT?
IT'S NO JOKE... END OF EARTH WAS COMPLETED IN YOUR FATHER.

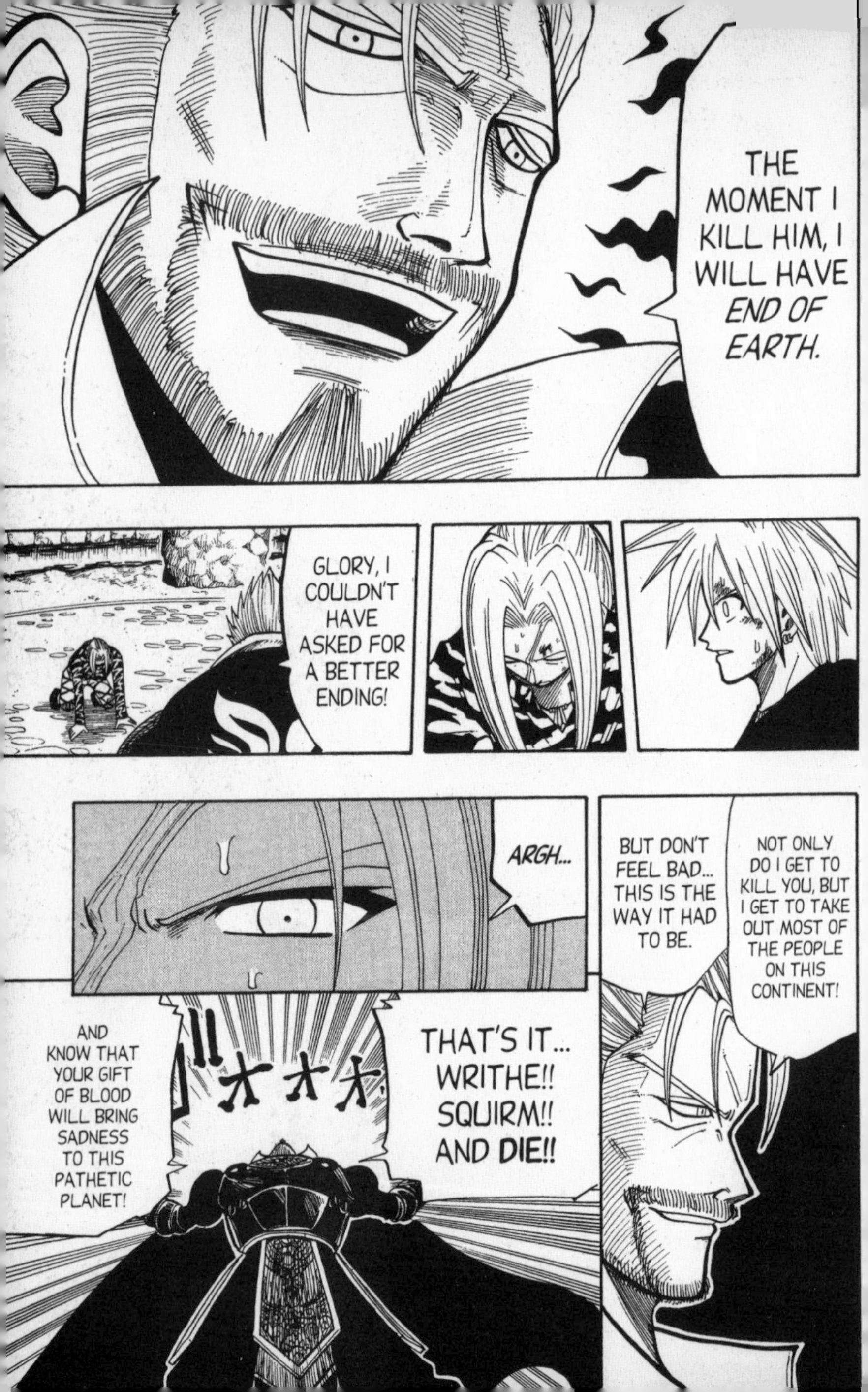
THE MOMENT I KILL HIM, I WILL HAVE *END OF EARTH.*
GLORY, I COULDN'T HAVE ASKED FOR A BETTER ENDING!
NOT ONLY DO I GET TO KILL YOU, BUT I GET TO TAKE OUT MOST OF THE PEOPLE ON THIS CONTINENT!
BUT DON'T FEEL BAD... THIS IS THE WAY IT HAD TO BE.
ARGH...
THAT'S IT... WRITHE!! SQUIRM!! AND **DIE!!**
AND KNOW THAT YOUR GIFT OF BLOOD WILL BRING SADNESS TO THIS PATHETIC PLANET!

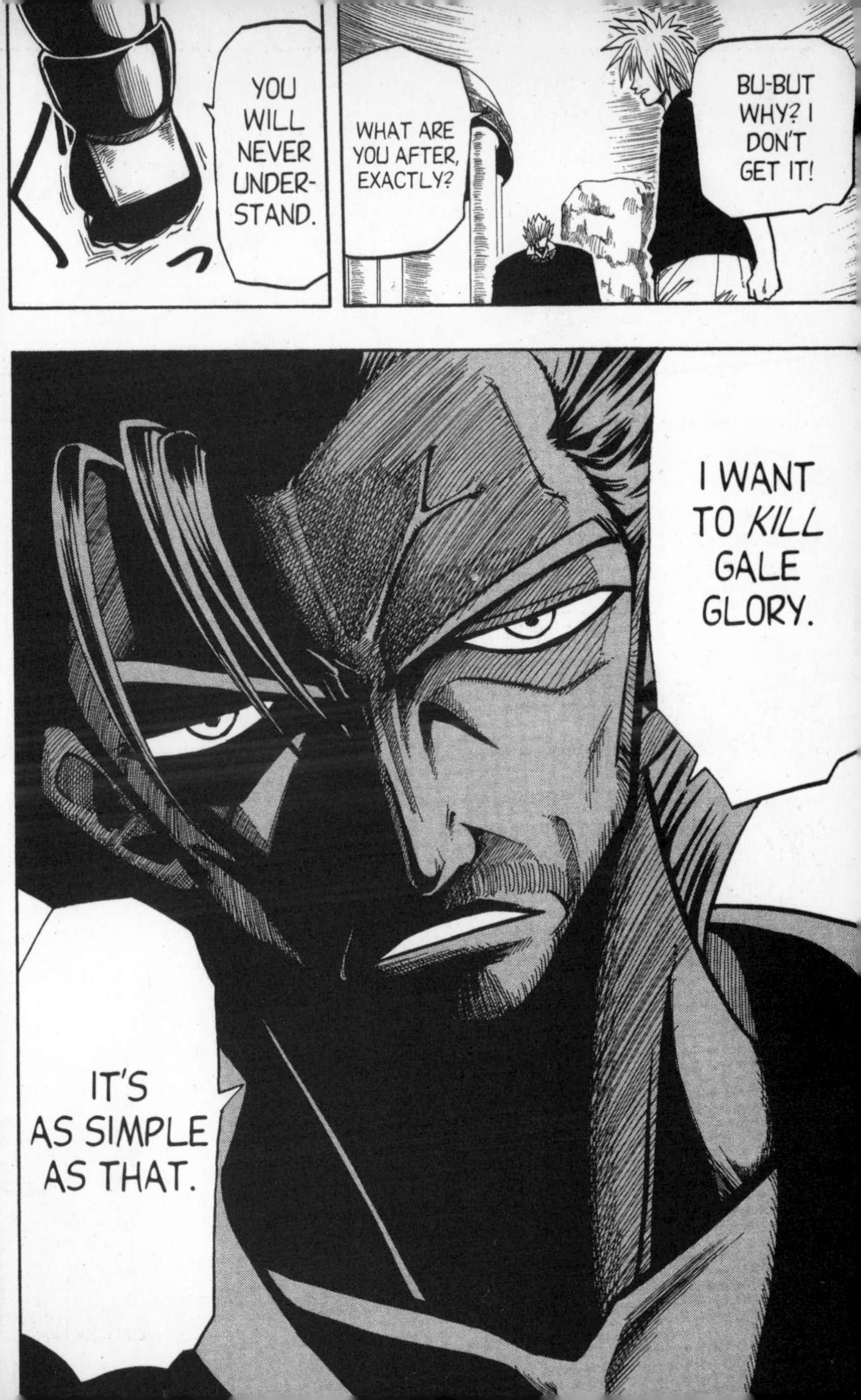
BU-BUT WHY? I DON'T GET IT!
WHAT ARE YOU AFTER, EXACTLY?
YOU WILL NEVER UNDERSTAND.
I WANT TO *KILL* GALE GLORY.
IT'S AS SIMPLE AS THAT.

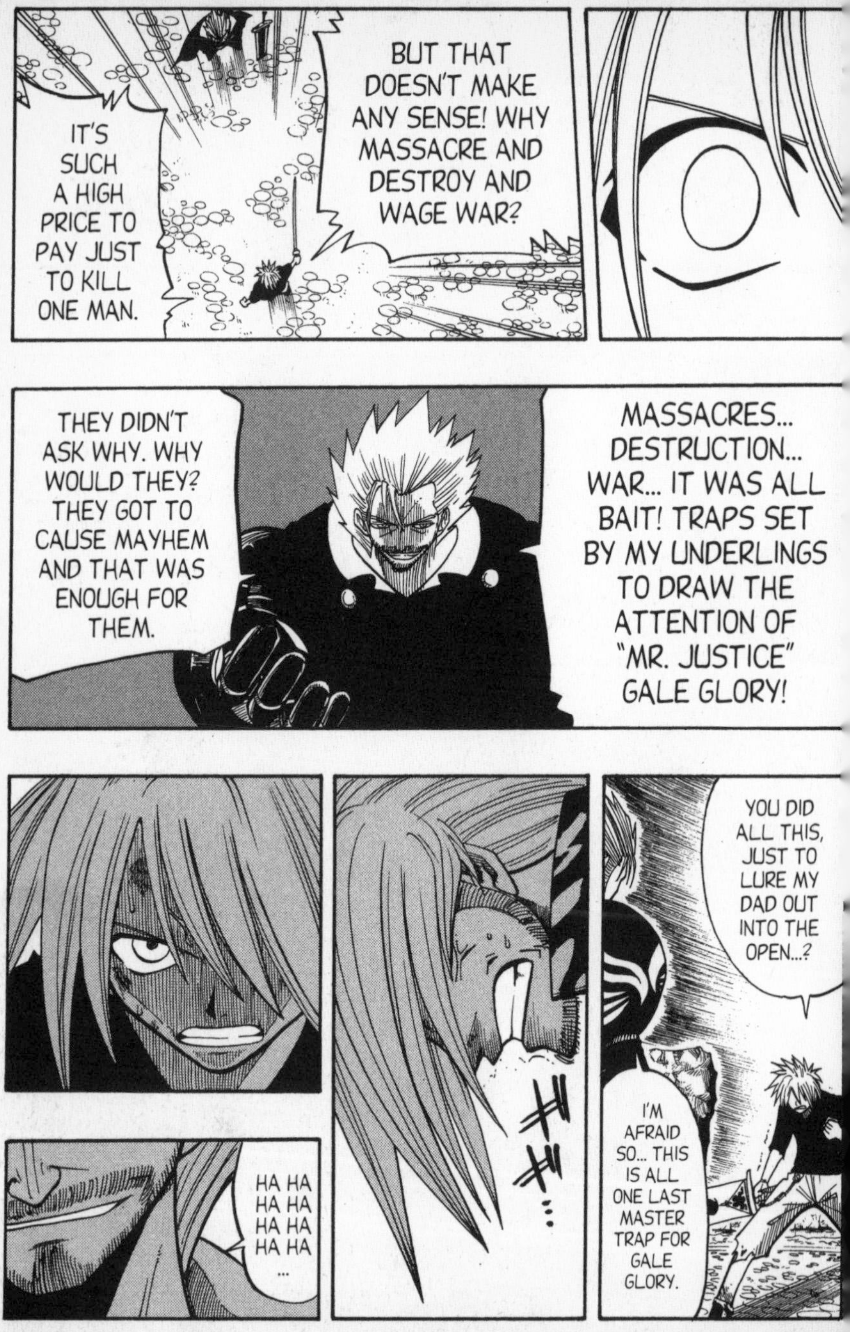
BUT THAT DOESN'T MAKE ANY SENSE! WHY MASSACRE AND DESTROY AND WAGE WAR?
IT'S SUCH A HIGH PRICE TO PAY JUST TO KILL ONE MAN.
MASSACRES... DESTRUCTION... WAR... IT WAS ALL BAIT! TRAPS SET BY MY UNDERLINGS TO DRAW THE ATTENTION OF "MR. JUSTICE" GALE GLORY!
THEY DIDN'T ASK WHY. WHY WOULD THEY? THEY GOT TO CAUSE MAYHEM AND THAT WAS ENOUGH FOR THEM.
YOU DID ALL THIS, JUST TO LURE MY DAD OUT INTO THE OPEN...?
I'M AFRAID SO... THIS IS ALL ONE LAST MASTER TRAP FOR GALE GLORY.
HA HA HA HA HA HA HA HA ...

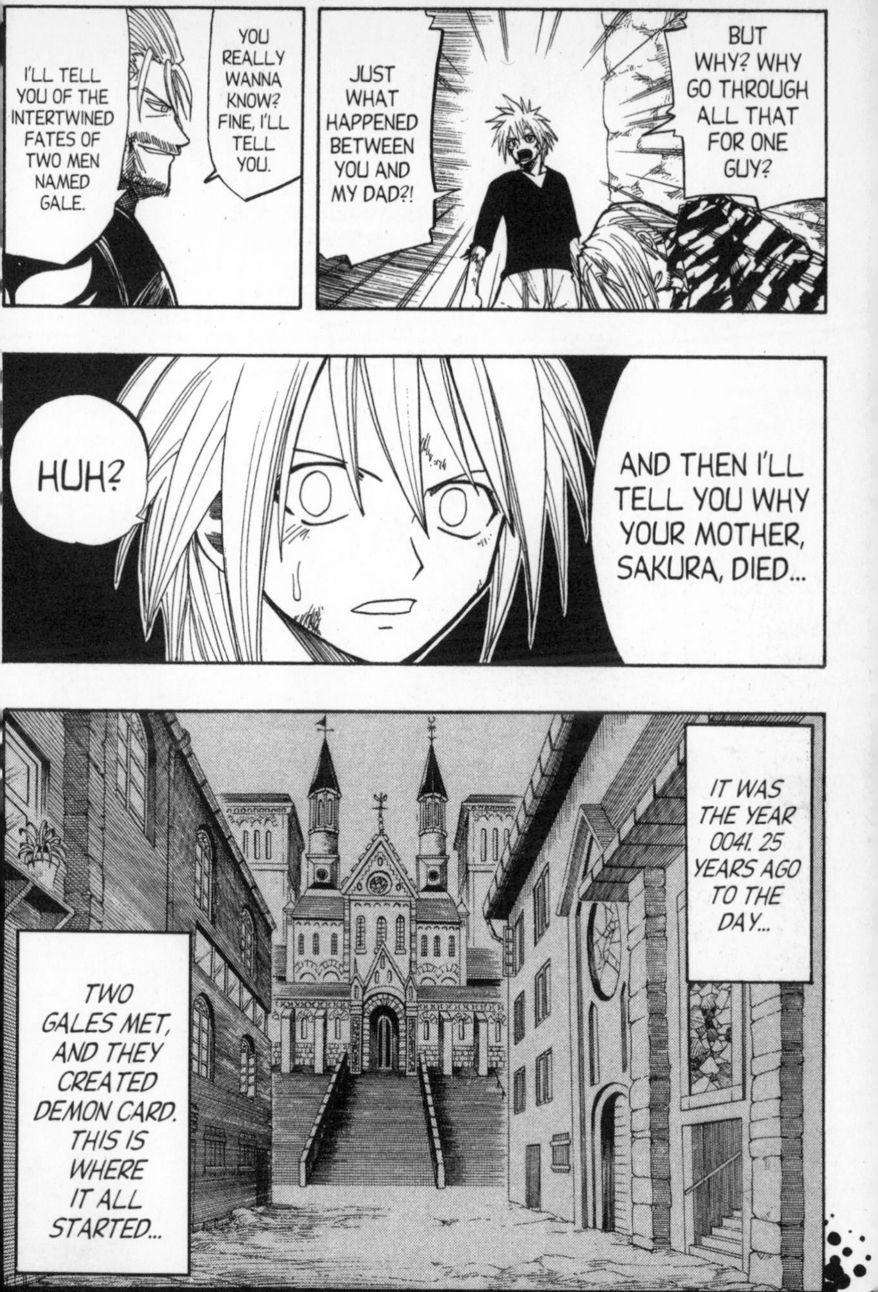
BUT WHY? WHY GO THROUGH ALL THAT FOR ONE GUY?
JUST WHAT HAPPENED BETWEEN YOU AND MY DAD?!
YOU REALLY WANNA KNOW? FINE, I'LL TELL YOU.
I'LL TELL YOU OF THE INTERTWINED FATES OF TWO MEN NAMED GALE.
AND THEN I'LL TELL YOU WHY YOUR MOTHER, SAKURA, DIED...
HUH?
IT WAS THE YEAR 0041. 25 YEARS AGO TO THE DAY...
TWO GALES MET, AND THEY CREATED DEMON CARD. THIS IS WHERE IT ALL STARTED...
TO BE CONTINUED

FIVE PALACE GUARDIANS, CAPTAIN: LTIANGLE, THE DEAD ANGLE

WEAPON: DB (TRANSPARENT)
BIRTHDAY / AGE: MARCH 3, 9951 / 115YO
HEIGHT / WEIGHT / BLOOD TYPE:
    230CM / 196KG / UNKNOWN
BIRTHPLACE: UNDERWORLD - NORWAN TOWN
INTERESTS / HOBBIES: OBSERVING
SPECIAL TALENT: DRAFTING
LIKES: HIS OWN ARMOR
HATES: RON GLACE

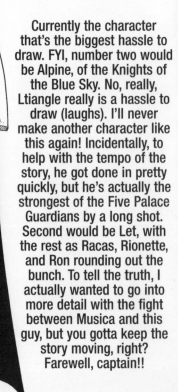

Currently the character that's the biggest hassle to draw. FYI, number two would be Alpine, of the Knights of the Blue Sky. No, really, Ltiangle really is a hassle to draw (laughs). I'll never make another character like this again! Incidentally, to help with the tempo of the story, he got done in pretty quickly, but he's actually the strongest of the Five Palace Guardians by a long shot. Second would be Let, with the rest as Racas, Rionette, and Ron rounding out the bunch. To tell the truth, I actually wanted to go into more detail with the fight between Musica and this guy, but you gotta keep the story moving, right? Farewell, captain!!

PALACE GUARDIAN:
LET, OF THE DRAGON PEOPLE

WEAPON: NONE (BAREHANDED)
BIRTHDAY / AGE: DECEMBER 4, 0044 / 22YO
HEIGHT / WEIGHT / BLOOD TYPE:
   177CM / 80KG / UNKNOWN
BIRTHPLACE: UNKNOWN
INTERESTS / HOBBIES: TRAINING
SPECIAL TALENT: ZOOLOGY
LIKES: BATTLE, STRONG OPPONENTS
HATES: PEACE

Boy, do I love this character.
By the way, out of all the Palace
Guardians, this guy is the only one
that's not a demonoid. The Dragon
race is separate from the demonoids,
see. And in wanting to make his
personality different from the others,
I also chose to have him not possess
any DB. It's not like I was just being
lazy, all right? Well, to be honest,
around the time these guys first came
out, there had been so many different
DB all over the place, I was having a
bit of writer's block with that.
Seriously...I'm not too smart.
I often get sharp commentary from
the readers about the DB, too. "That's
just way too convenient!" Haha.
Seriously. I do get a lot of these... I'll
be sure to plan things out better for
the next (??) series.

PALACE GUARDIAN:
RACAS, THE COUNTERATTACKER

WEAPON: DB (RHYTHM COUNTER)
BIRTHDAY / AGE: FEBRUARY 28, 0041 / 25YO
HEIGHT / WEIGHT / BLOOD TYPE:
   185CM / 78KG / UNKNOWN
BIRTHPLACE: UNDERWORLD - NORWAN TOWN
INTERESTS / HOBBIES: COLLECTING MUSIC
SPECIAL TALENT: MARACAS, DANCING
LIKES: THE CAPTAIN
HATES: GARBAGE

I made this guy up to help break the way-too-serious tone that has plagued the story since we got to Din Tower. Honestly, this guy's a moron. Of course, his name comes from "maracas." In other words, no thought involved in this one. Speaking of, I've gotten letters from people who have stumbled upon a pattern. If you add "ma" to the beginning of all the names of the demonoids, their names turn into words that are connected to them:

Gnet -> Magnet

Zahrshippe ->
Mazahrshippe (Mothership -> submarine)

Sihngan -> Masihngan (Machinegun)

Ltiangle -> Ma(u)ltiangle

Rionette -> Marionette

Let -> Malet (Mallet)

Ron Glace ->
Maron Glace (chestnut (maron) sweets...)

PALACE GUARDIAN: RIONETTE, THE SHADOW MASTER

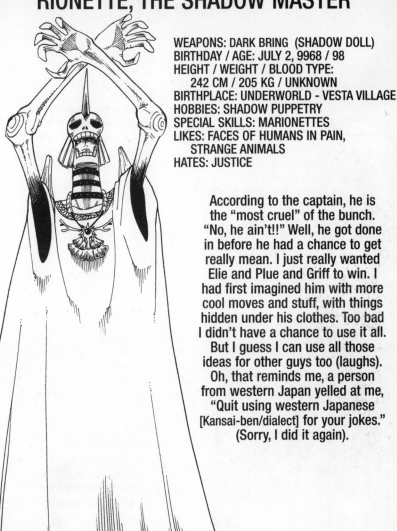

WEAPONS: DARK BRING (SHADOW DOLL)
BIRTHDAY / AGE: JULY 2, 9968 / 98
HEIGHT / WEIGHT / BLOOD TYPE:
    242 CM / 205 KG / UNKNOWN
BIRTHPLACE: UNDERWORLD - VESTA VILLAGE
HOBBIES: SHADOW PUPPETRY
SPECIAL SKILLS: MARIONETTES
LIKES: FACES OF HUMANS IN PAIN,
    STRANGE ANIMALS
HATES: JUSTICE

According to the captain, he is the "most cruel" of the bunch. "No, he ain't!!" Well, he got done in before he had a chance to get really mean. I just really wanted Elie and Plue and Griff to win. I had first imagined him with more cool moves and stuff, with things hidden under his clothes. Too bad I didn't have a chance to use it all.

But I guess I can use all those ideas for other guys too (laughs).

Oh, that reminds me, a person from western Japan yelled at me, "Quit using western Japanese [Kansai-ben/dialect] for your jokes." (Sorry, I did it again).

PALACE GUARDIAN: RON GLACE

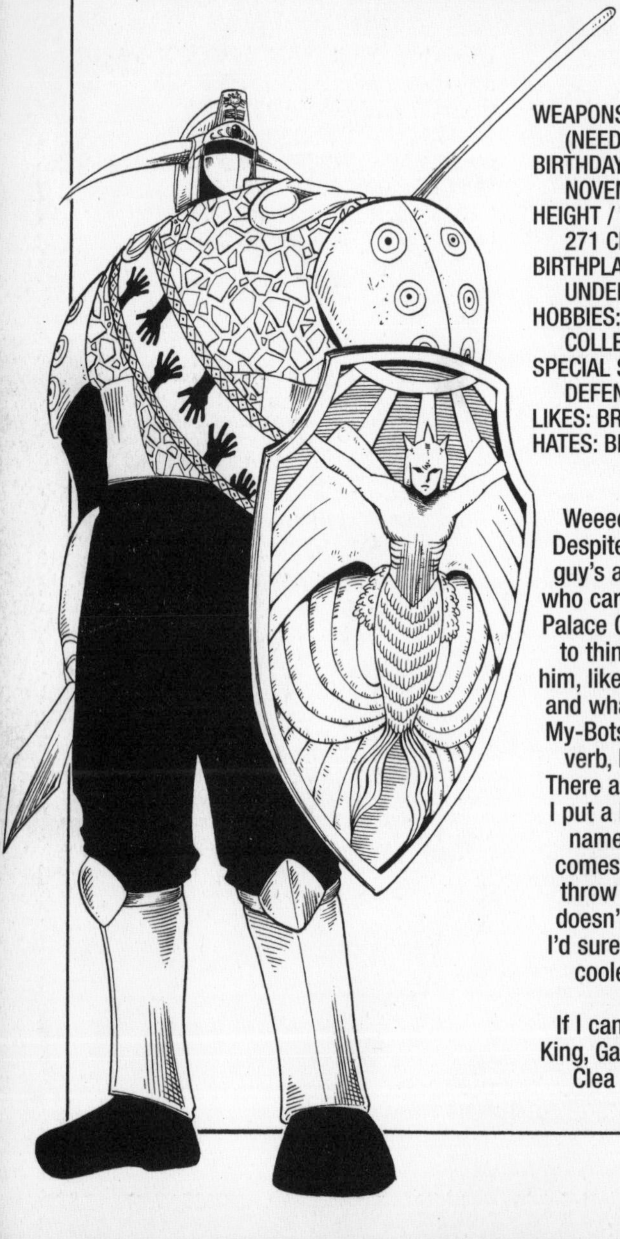

WEAPONS: DARK BRING
(NEEDLE PAIN)
BIRTHDAY / AGE:
NOVEMBER 9, 0064 / 2
HEIGHT / WEIGHT / BLOOD TYPE:
271 CM / 270 KG / UNKNOWN
BIRTHPLACE:
UNDERWORLD - BROSSA TOWN
HOBBIES:
COLLECTING STICKERS
SPECIAL SKILLS:
DEFENSIVE ABILITY
LIKES: BREAKING THINGS
HATES: BEING PATIENT

Weeeeeeeeaaaaaaakkkk!! Despite his appearance, this guy's a real wimp!! Oh well, who cares? Just like the other Palace Guardians, I was trying to think of a back story for him, like "he is really this xxx," and what I came up with was My-Botsu (I made up the new verb, botsuru). Mmhmm... There are a lot of times when I put a lot of thought into the names, and then when it comes time to decide, I just throw out some name that doesn't mean anything. But I'd sure love to think of some cooler stories and stuff.

If I can, I'll have profiles for King, Gale, Solasido, Remi, and Clea in the next volume.

Artist's Tools Page

I'VE HAD LOTS OF PEOPLE ASKING ME WHAT KINDS OF TOOLS I USE WHEN I DRAW COMICS, SO HERE'S MY ANSWER.

Pen

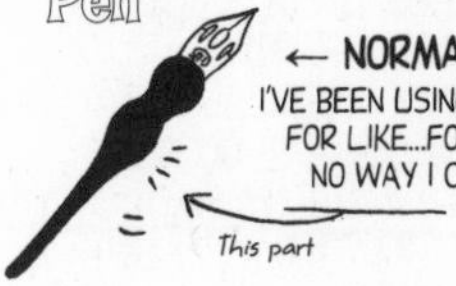
This part

← **NORMAL G PEN**

I'VE BEEN USING THE SAME HANDLE FOR LIKE...FOREVER, SO THERE'S NO WAY I CAN CHANGE NOW.

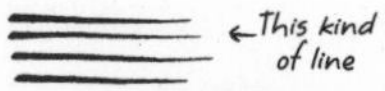
← This kind of line

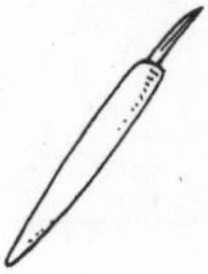

← **SOMETHING CALLED A ROUND PEN**

I USE THIS FOR DRAWING BACKGROUNDS AND STUFF. IT GIVES ME A NICE, THIN LINE.

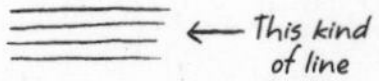
← This kind of line

Ink

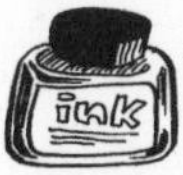
ink

← **PILOT INK (FOR DRAFTING)**

I LIKE IT BECAUSE IT DRIES FAST AND IS EASY TO USE.

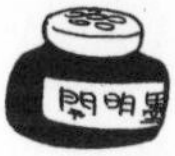
開明墨

← **KAIMEI INDIA INK**

I LIKE THE WAY THE INK SPREEEEEAAAADS OUT.
THESE ARE THE TWO INKS I USE.

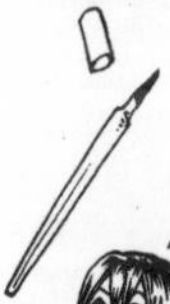

←**BRUSH PEN (PILOT)**

I USE THIS WHEN I'M FILLING IN BLACKS, AND DRAWING SHINE ON HAIR AND STUFF. THE TIP IS A SPONGE. OH YEAH, I ALSO USE THIS FOR WRITING LETTERS/CHARACTERS, TOO.

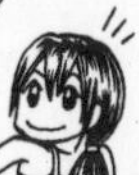

ぐもーん ← These types of letters

Eraser

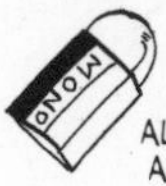
MONO

← **MONO ERASER**

I USE THESE BECAUSE I'VE ALWAYS HEARD EVERYONE ELSE AROUND USES THEM. YUP! VERY EASY TO USE!

Whiteout

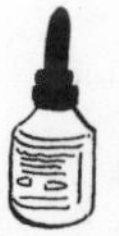

←**DOCTOR MARTIN'S**

I HAVE A LOT OF WHITEOUT, AND SOMETIMES I USE DIFFERENT ONES FOR DIFFERENT SITUATIONS, BUT THIS IS THE ONE I LIKE THE BEST. JUST WISH IT WAS A LITTLE CHEAPER.

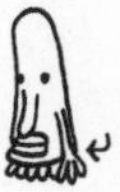

Fiber-tipped pens

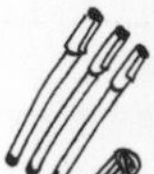

← **SIGMA PENS**

NICE AND CONVENIENT WITH ALL THE DIFFERENT THICKNESSES. BTW, MY BORDER LINES ARE DRAWN WITH A #8.

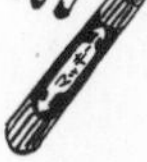

← **ZEBRA MARKERS**

USEFUL FOR WRITING LETTERS AND COLORING IN BIG SPOTS OF BLACK.

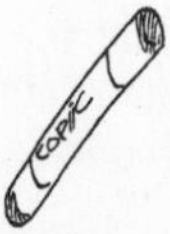
COPIC

← **COPIC MARKERS**

I DO MY COLOR SPREADS WITH THESE ALMOST EXCLUSIVELY. LATELY I'VE BEEN USING A COMPUTER TO FIX THEM UP AFTERWARDS TOO.

Screen Tone

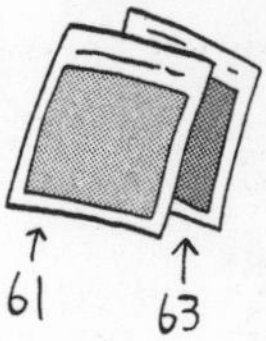
↑
61
↑
63

← **IC SCREEN TONE**

THE ONLY ONES I USE ARE #61 AND #63, GRADATION TONES. ON RARE OCCASIONS I'LL USE OTHERS, BUT I REALLY SUCK AT DOING TONES, SO I TRY NOT TO USE 'EM TOO MUCH.

RAVE 0077 Levin Sits Watch

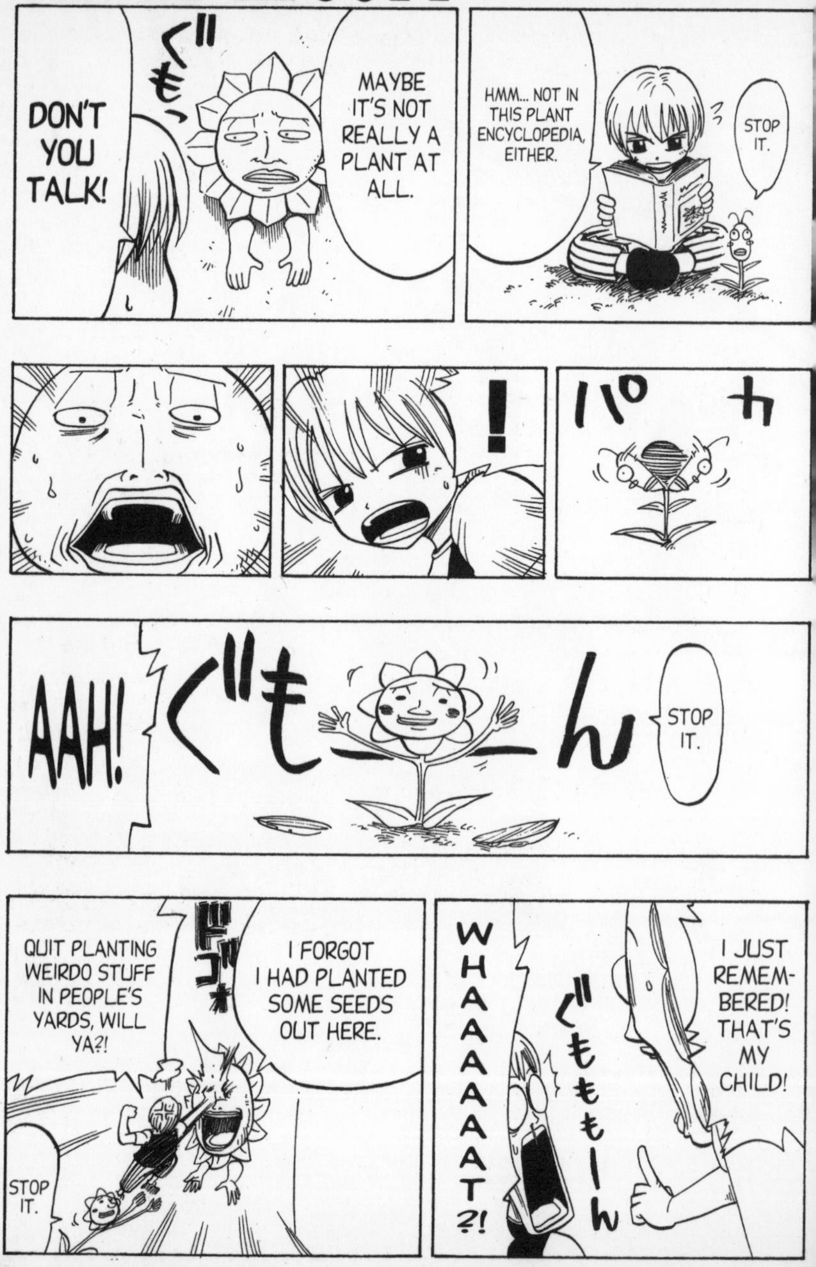
HMM... NOT IN THIS PLANT ENCYCLOPEDIA, EITHER.
STOP IT.
MAYBE IT'S NOT REALLY A PLANT AT ALL.
ぐもっ
DON'T YOU TALK!
パカ
!
STOP IT.
ぐも―ん
AAH!
I JUST REMEMBERED! THAT'S MY CHILD!
ぐもも―ん
WHAAAAAAT?!
I FORGOT I HAD PLANTED SOME SEEDS OUT HERE.
ドゴォ
QUIT PLANTING WEIRDO STUFF IN PEOPLE'S YARDS, WILL YA?!
STOP IT.

Art a la Rave

SPECIAL 2

Rave

HARU&PLUE

STORY INTRO

"OUR MOTTO IS "IF SOMEONE TAKES IT, TAKE IT BACK." WE'RE AN INVINCIBLE DUO, BAN MIDO AND GINJI AMANO. WE'RE THE GETBACKERS, WITH ALMOST A 100% SUCCESS RATE!" NOW AVAILABLE IN AMERICA TOO!

Haru & Plue celebrity fan art, courtesy of Rando Ayamine, artist of

GetBackers

THANK YOU VERY MUCH FOR TAKING TIME OUT OF YOUR BUSY SCHEDULE TO DRAW THIS PICTURE FOR ME. I ACTUALLY MET AYAMINE-SENSEI AT A CERTAIN PARTY RIGHT ABOUT THE TIME MY SERIES STARTED GETTING PUBLISHED. BOY, AYAMINE-SENSEI, YOU ARE AN AMAZING ARTIST! I SAID THIS IN VOLUME 4 TOO, BUT THIS SURE IS GOOD INSPIRATION FOR ME. EVERY TIME I GET THESE AMAZING ILLUSTRATIONS, SO I FEEL A BIT BAD ABOUT MAKING THE ARTISTS WORK SO HARD FOR THIS. SPEAKING OF WHICH, RECENTLY, AS PART OF SOMETHING PUT ON BY MY PUBLISHER, I HAD A ROUNDTABLE DISCUSSION WITH AYAMINE-SENSEI, AS WELL AS KAMIJYO-SENSEI, WHO CONTRIBUTED AN ILLUSTRATION TO THE LAST VOLUME. IT WAS AT A GET-TOGETHER FOR A COLLABORATIVE WORK OF GB+KYO+RAVE (NOT THAT THEY NEED RAVE OR ANYTHING TO MAKE IT GO). I COULD TELL BOTH OF THESE GREAT ARTISTS ARE REALLY PASSIONATE ABOUT THEIR WORK. WELL, I'M THAT WAY TOO, BUT YOU KNOW, I WAS JUST REAL HAPPY, THINKING HOW MUCH I LOVE COMICS. AYAMINE-SENSEI, KAMIJO-SENSEI, LET'S HANG OUT TOGETHER SOMETIME!!

Afterwords

BOY, WAS THAT OPENING ILLUSTRATION FOR CHAPTER 57 (THE BALL WHERE EVERYONE'S DANCING) A TOUGHIE!!

YIPPEE!! ...YES, MASHIMA HERE. HELLO. SO, EVERYONE, WHAT DID YOU THINK? DID YOU LIKE THE DRAWING? IT HAS NOTHING TO DO WITH THE STORY, BUT SOMETIMES I JUST GET IN THE MOOD TO DO SOMETHING REALLY HARD. PRETTY WEIRD, HUH? EVEN THOUGH I KNOW IT'LL BE REALLY HARD, I JUST FEEL LIKE DOING IT ANYWAY, WITH LOTS OF LITTLE DETAILS AND STUFF. AND THANKS TO THAT, I ENDED UP FINISHING MY STORY COMPLETION A DAY LATER THAN NORMAL. AND SOMETIMES I JUST GET AN ITCH TO DRAW BIG CROWD SCENES TOO, WITH LOTS OF PEOPLE WALKING EVERYWHERE. AND WHEN I'M CLOSE TO MISSING A DEADLINE, I JUST GET MY ASSISTANT(S) TO FINISH FOR ME. HMM. YOU MAY BE THINKING THAT IF I HAVE ENOUGH FREE TIME FOR THESE COMPLICATED ILLUSTRATIONS, I SHOULD SPEND MORE TIME ON THE COMIC ITSELF. BUT BELIEVE ME, I SPEND PLENTY OF TIME MAKING THIS THE BEST COMIC I CAN MAKE IT (LAUGHS). I GUESS IT'S MY OWN WAY OF RELAXING (LAUGHS). SURE, IT'S TOUGH, BUT IT'S MY OWN WEIRD RELAXATION TECHNIQUE.

THAT REMINDS ME, RECENTLY MY CONTACT TOLD ME, "YOUR ART'S BEEN GETTING BETTER LATELY, COMPARED TO BEFORE," SO I WENT BACK AND LOOKED AT SOME OF MY EARLIER WORK. YES, BACK IN VOLUME 1, I HAD SOME PRETTY HORRIBLE ART. LOOKING BACK ON IT NOW, I JUST SLAMMED IT SHUT. NOW I'M THINKING I'M STARTING TO IMPROVE AND ALL, BUT I KNOW I STILL HAVE A LONG WAY TO GO. GOTTA WORK HARDER. I'M AIMING FOR A 100 IN MY ART, BUT I'D ONLY GIVE MY VOLUME 1 A SCORE OF 1. I THINK I'M AT ABOUT A TWO RIGHT NOW. IMPROVING ONE POINT A YEAR, MAKES ME A LITTLE FAINTHEART-ED TO THINK ABOUT THAT. BUT WITH THAT FORMULA, I'LL ONLY NEED ANOTHER 98 YEARS TO MAX OUT MY PICTURE-POWER (MY NEW WORD). SO THAT MEANS, I'LL BE ABOUT 121 YEARS OLD. IN OTHER WORDS, I PLAN ON SPENDING MY WHOLE LIFE IMPROVING MY CRAFT. YUP! NOT BAD! MY NEXT GOAL IS A PICTURE-POWER RANKING OF THREE! JUST SO YOU KNOW, THIS IS A PERSONAL STANDARD, SO I DON'T JUDGE OTHERS' WORK WITH THIS SCALE. SO ALL YOU ASPIRING ARTISTS OUT THERE! DECIDE YOUR OWN IDEAL PICTURE-POWER GOAL, DRAW OUT YOUR PICTURE-POWER POTENTIAL, AND DEVOTE YOUR LIFE TO IT!!

-

HIRO MASHIMA, AT 121 YEARS OLD

Next time in Rave Master:

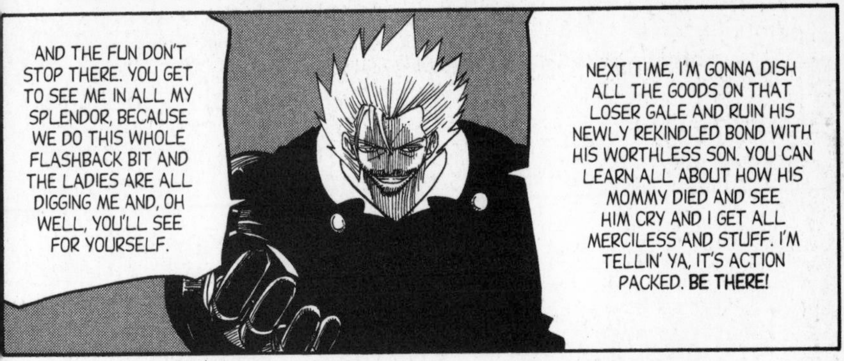
NEXT TIME, I'M GONNA DISH ALL THE GOODS ON THAT LOSER GALE AND RUIN HIS NEWLY REKINDLED BOND WITH HIS WORTHLESS SON. YOU CAN LEARN ALL ABOUT HOW HIS MOMMY DIED AND SEE HIM CRY AND I GET ALL MERCILESS AND STUFF. I'M TELLIN' YA, IT'S ACTION PACKED. **BE THERE!**
AND THE FUN DON'T STOP THERE. YOU GET TO SEE ME IN ALL MY SPLENDOR, BECAUSE WE DO THIS WHOLE FLASHBACK BIT AND THE LADIES ARE ALL DIGGING ME AND, OH WELL, YOU'LL SEE FOR YOURSELF.

Call for Fan Art and Stuff!

HEY ASPIRING MANGA ARTISTS! WANT TO SEE YOUR PICTURES IN PRINT? WELL, IF YOU THINK YOU CAN DRAW A COOL LOOKING HARU, A SEXY ELIE OR A FUNNY PLUE, SEND 'EM THIS WAY! WE'LL PICK ONE LUCKY WINNER FROM EACH ROUND AND SEND THEM A SPECIAL PRIZE! WHAT DO HAVE TO LOSE? NOTHING!

HOW TO SUBMIT:

1) SEND YOUR WORK VIA REGULAR MAIL (NOT E-MAIL) TO:

RAVE MASTER FAN ART
C/O TOKYOPOP
5900 WILSHIRE BLVD.
SUITE 2000
LOS ANGELES, CA 90036

2) ALL WORK SUBMITTED SHOULD BE IN BLACK AND WHITE AND NO LARGER THAN 8.5" X 11". (AND TRY NOT TO FOLD IT TOO MANY TIMES!)

3) ANYTHING YOU SEND WILL NOT BE RETURNED. IF YOU WANT TO KEEP YOUR ORIGINAL, IT'S FINE TO SEND US A COPY.

4) PLEASE INCLUDE YOUR FULL NAME, AGE, CITY AND STATE FOR US TO PRINT WITH YOUR WORK. IF YOU'D RATHER US USE A PEN NAME, PLEASE INCLUDE THAT TOO.

5) IMPORTANT: IF YOU'RE UNDER THE AGE OF 18, YOU MUST HAVE YOUR PARENT'S PERMISSION IN ORDER FOR US TO PRINT YOUR WORK. ANY SUBMISSIONS WITHOUT A SIGNED NOTE OF PARENTAL CONSENT CANNOT BE USED.

6) FOR FULL DETAILS, PLEASE CHECK OUT
HTTP://WWW.TOKYOPOP.COM/ABOUTUS/FANART.PHP

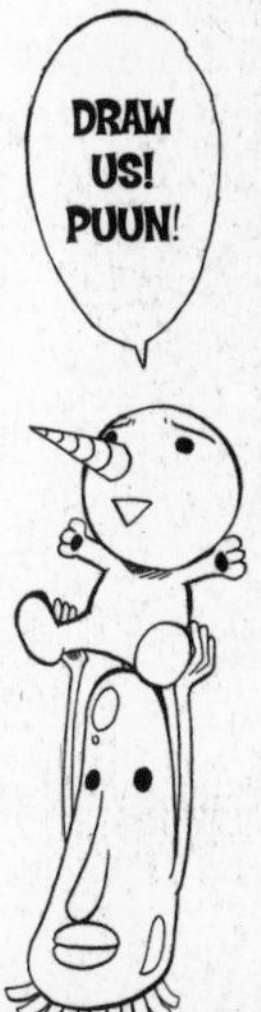
DRAW US! PUUN!

DISCLAIMER: ANYTHING YOU SEND TO US BECOMES THE PROPERTY OF TOKYOPOP INC. AND, AS WE SAID BEFORE, WILL NOT BE RETURNED TO YOU. WE WILL HAVE THE RIGHT TO PRINT, REPRODUCE, DISTRIBUTE, OR MODIFY THE ARTWORK FOR USE IN FUTURE VOLUMES OF RAVE MASTER OR ON THE WEB WITHOUT PAYMENT TO YOU.

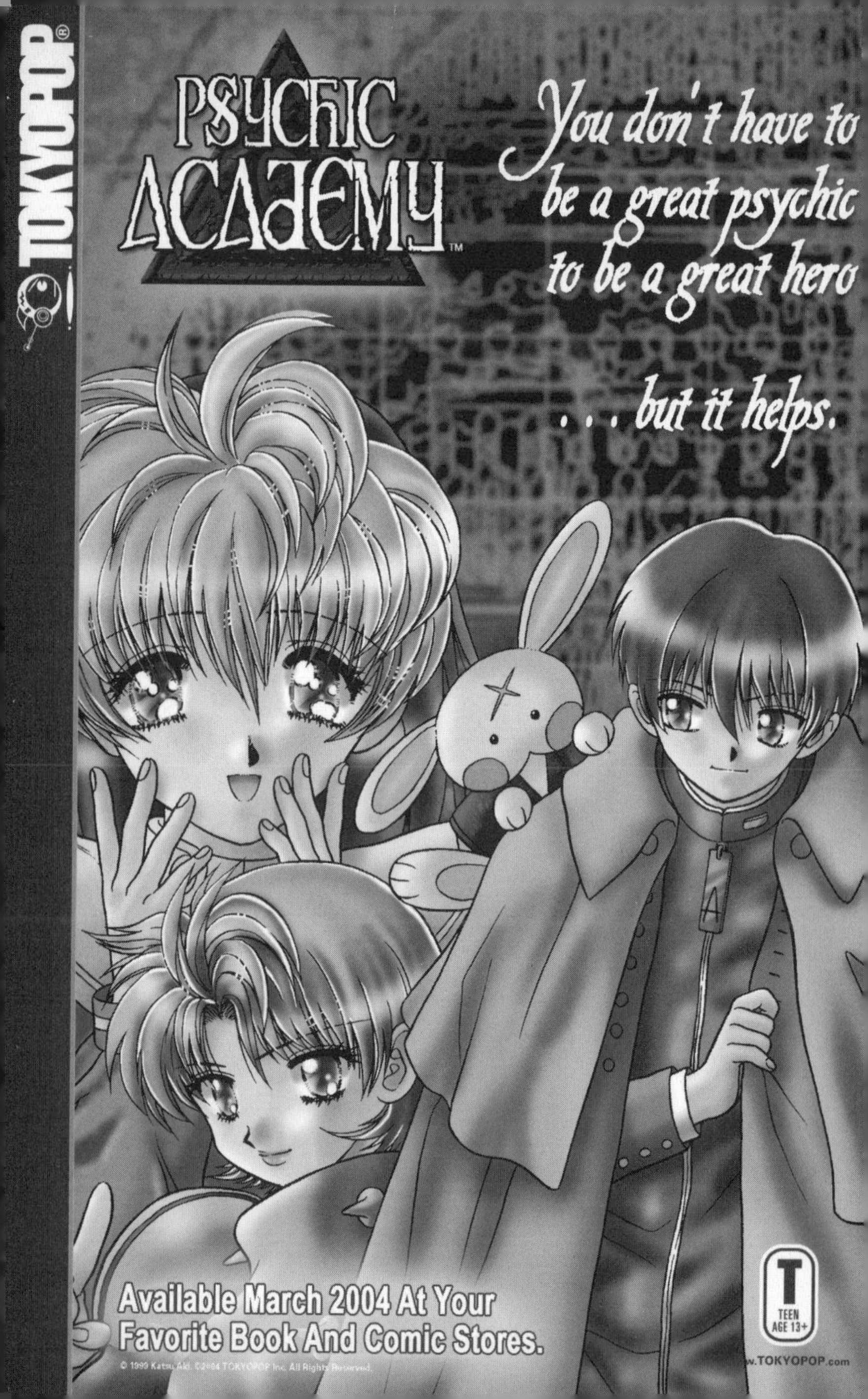
TOKYOPOP®
PSYCHIC ACADEMY™
You don't have to be a great psychic to be a great hero
. . . but it helps.
T TEEN AGE 13+
Available March 2004 At Your Favorite Book And Comic Stores.
© 1999 Katsu Aki. ©2004 TOKYOPOP Inc. All Rights Reserved.
w.TOKYOPOP.com

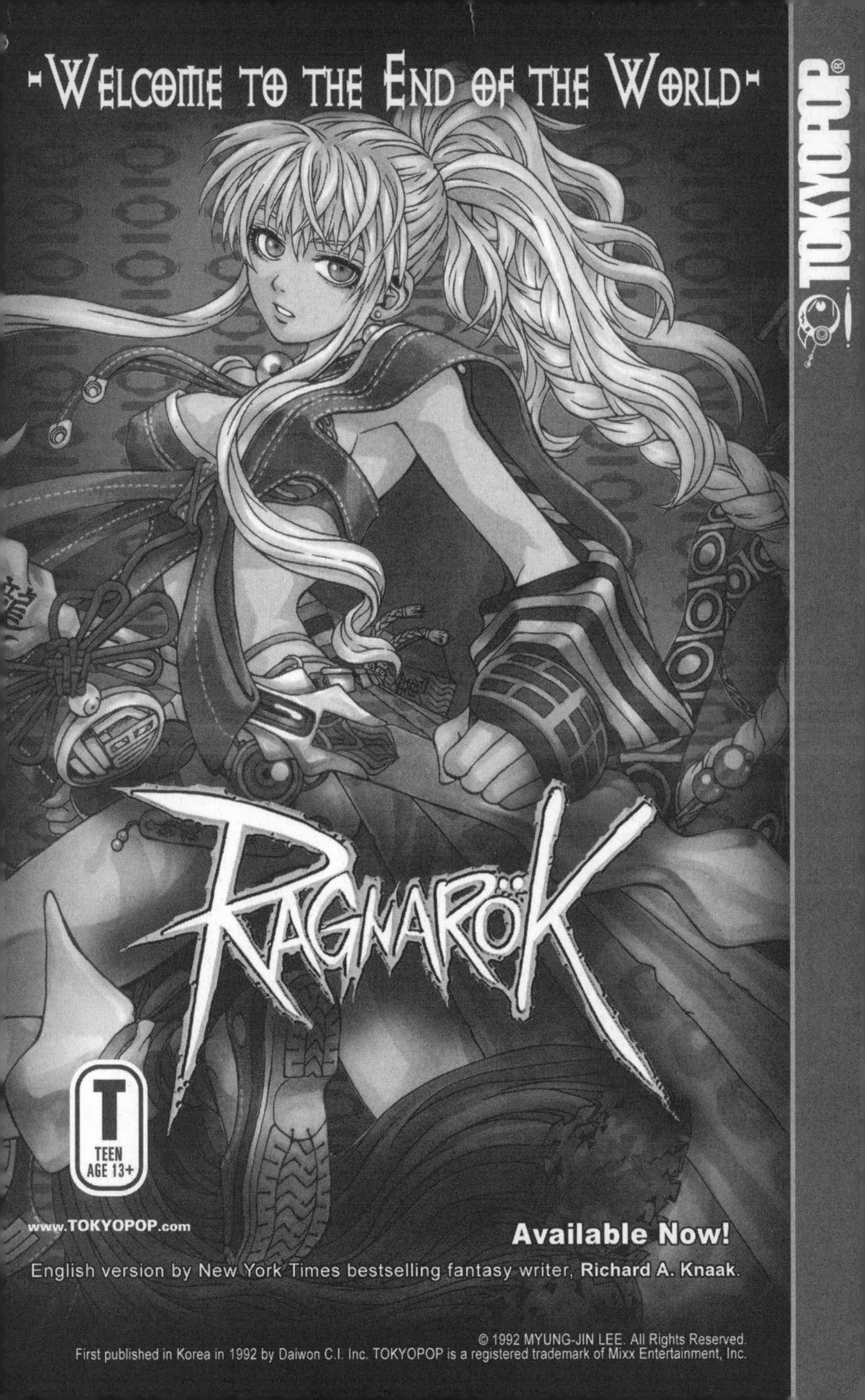

-Welcome to the End of the World-
TOKYOPOP®
Ragnarök
T
TEEN
AGE 13+
www.TOKYOPOP.com
Available Now!
English version by New York Times bestselling fantasy writer, Richard A. Knaak.
© 1992 MYUNG-JIN LEE. All Rights Reserved.
First published in Korea in 1992 by Daiwon C.I. Inc. TOKYOPOP is a registered trademark of Mixx Entertainment, Inc.

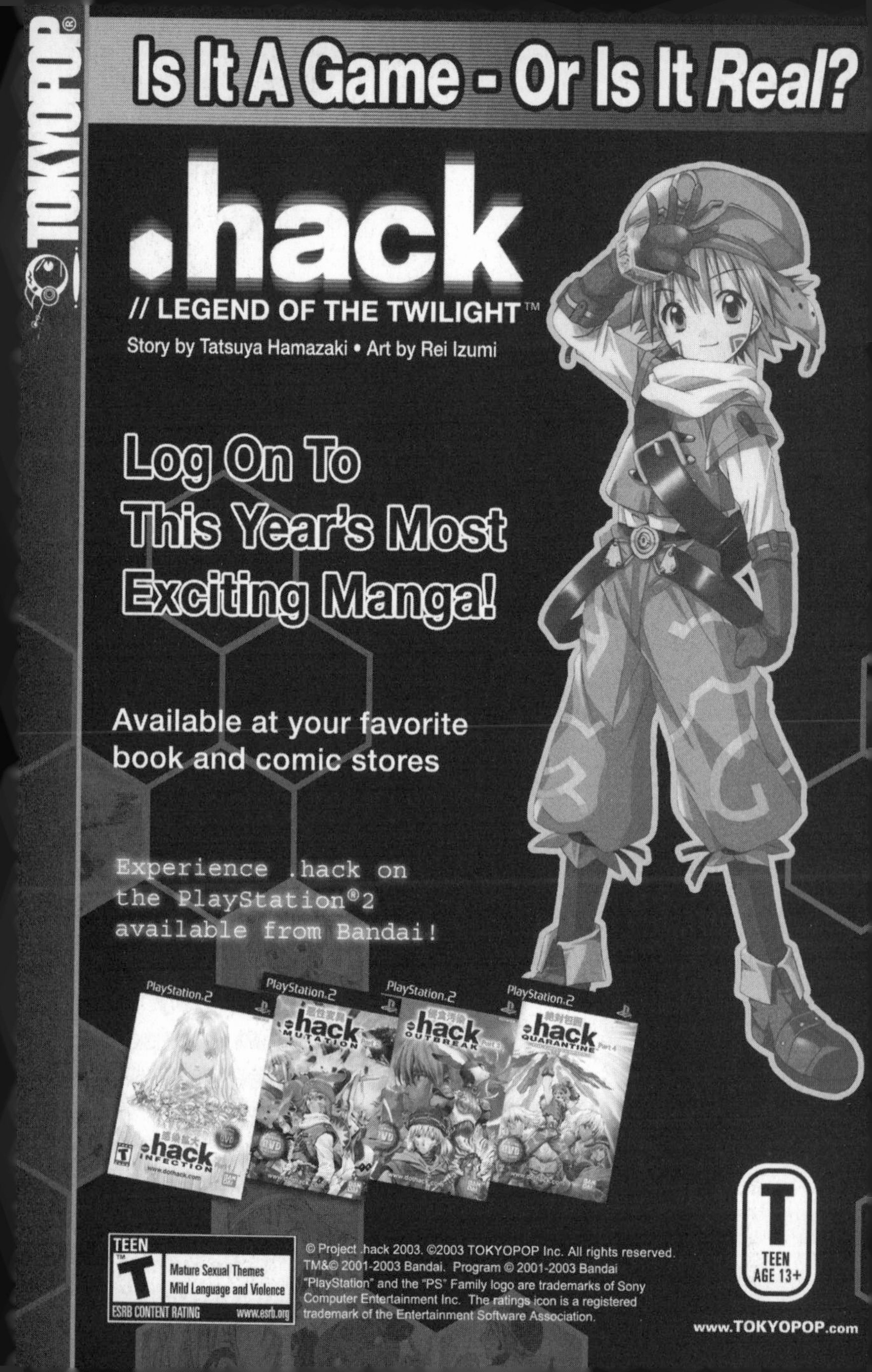
TOKYOPOP®
Is It A Game - Or Is It Real?
.hack
// LEGEND OF THE TWILIGHT™
Story by Tatsuya Hamazaki • Art by Rei Izumi
Log On To
This Year's Most
Exciting Manga!
Available at your favorite
book and comic stores
Experience .hack on
the PlayStation®2
available from Bandai!
PlayStation.2
.hack INFECTION
PlayStation.2
.hack MUTATION
PlayStation.2
.hack OUTBREAK
PlayStation.2
.hack QUARANTINE Part 4
TEEN
T
Mature Sexual Themes
Mild Language and Violence
ESRB CONTENT RATING www.esrb.org
© Project .hack 2003. ©2003 TOKYOPOP Inc. All rights reserved.
TM&© 2001-2003 Bandai. Program © 2001-2003 Bandai
"PlayStation" and the "PS" Family logo are trademarks of Sony
Computer Entertainment Inc. The ratings icon is a registered
trademark of the Entertainment Software Association.
T
TEEN
AGE 13+
www.TOKYOPOP.com

ALSO AVAILABLE FROM TOKYOPOP®

PRINCESS AI
PSYCHIC ACADEMY
RAGNAROK
RAVE MASTER
REALITY CHECK
REBIRTH
REBOUND
REMOTE
RISING STARS OF MANGA
SABER MARIONETTE J
SAILOR MOON
SAINT TAIL
SAIYUKI
SAMURAI DEEPER KYO
SAMURAI GIRL REAL BOUT HIGH SCHOOL
SCRYED
SEIKAI TRILOGY, THE
SGT. FROG
SHAOLIN SISTERS
SHIRAHIME-SYO: SNOW GODDESS TALES
SHUTTERBOX
SKULL MAN, THE
SMUGGLER
SNOW DROP
SORCERER HUNTERS
STONE
SUIKODEN III
SUKI
THREADS OF TIME
TOKYO BABYLON
TOKYO MEW MEW
TRAMPS LIKE US
TREASURE CHESS
UNDER THE GLASS MOON
VAMPIRE GAME
VISION OF ESCAFLOWNE, THE
WARRIORS OF TAO
WILD ACT
WISH
WORLD OF HARTZ
X-DAY
ZODIAC P.I.

NOVELS

CLAMP SCHOOL PARANORMAL INVESTIGATORS
KARMA CLUB
SAILOR MOON
SLAYERS

ART BOOKS

ART OF CARDCAPTOR SAKURA
ART OF MAGIC KNIGHT RAYEARTH, THE
PEACH: MIWA UEDA ILLUSTRATIONS

ANIME GUIDES

COWBOY BEBOP
GUNDAM TECHNICAL MANUALS
SAILOR MOON SCOUT GUIDES

TOKYOPOP KIDS

STRAY SHEEP

CINE-MANGA™

ALADDIN
ASTRO BOY
CARDCAPTORS
CONFESSIONS OF A TEENAGE DRAMA QUEEN
DUEL MASTERS
FAIRLY ODDPARENTS, THE
FAMILY GUY
FINDING NEMO
G.I. JOE SPY TROOPS
JACKIE CHAN ADVENTURES
JIMMY NEUTRON: BOY GENIUS, THE ADVENTURES OF
KIM POSSIBLE
LILO & STITCH
LIZZIE MCGUIRE
LIZZIE MCGUIRE MOVIE, THE
MALCOLM IN THE MIDDLE
POWER RANGERS: NINJA STORM
SHREK 2
SPONGEBOB SQUAREPANTS
SPY KIDS 2
SPY KIDS 3-D: GAME OVER
TEENAGE MUTANT NINJA TURTLES
THAT'S SO RAVEN
TRANSFORMERS: ARMADA
TRANSFORMERS: ENERGON

For more
information visit
www.TOKYOPOP.com

02.03.04T

ALSO AVAILABLE FROM 😎TOKYOPOP®

MANGA

02.03.04T

STOP!

This is the back of the book.
You wouldn't want to spoil a great ending!

This book is printed "manga-style," in the authentic Japanese right-to-left format. Since none of the artwork has been flipped or altered, readers get to experience the story just as the creator intended. You've been asking for it, so TOKYOPOP® delivered: authentic, hot-off-the-press, and far more fun!

DIRECTIONS

If this is your first time reading manga-style, here's a quick guide to help you understand how it works.

It's easy... just start in the top right panel and follow the numbers. Have fun, and look for more 100% authentic manga from TOKYOPOP®!

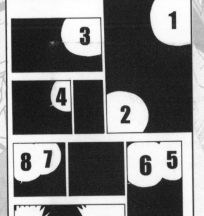